KAWARI

変

KAWARI

How Japan's Economic
and Cultural Transformation
Will Alter the Balance of Power
Among Nations

MILTON EZRATI

PERSEUS BOOKS
Reading, Massachusetts

Many of the designations used by manufacturers and sellers to distinguish their products are claimed as trademarks. Where those designations appear in this book and Perseus Books was aware of a trademark claim, the designations have been printed in initial capital letters.

ISBN 0-7382-0107-3

Library of Congress Catalog Card Number: 99-60683

Copyright © 1999 by Milton Ezrati

All rights reserved. No part of this publication may be reproduced or transmitted in any form or by any means, electronic or mechanical, including photocopy, recording, or any information storage and retrieval system, without permission in writing from the publisher. Printed in the United States of America.

Perseus Books is a member of the Perseus Books Group

Jacket design by Bruce W. Bond
Text design by Faith Hague
Set in 10.75-point Simonici Garamond by Faith Hague

123456789—040302010099
First printing, May 1999

Perseus Books are available at special discounts for bulk purchases in the U.S. by corporations, institutions, and other organizations. For more information, please contact the Special Markets Department at HarperCollins Publishers, 10 East 53rd Street, New York, NY 10022, or call 1-212-207-7528.

Find us on the World Wide Web at
http://www.aw.com/gb

*To Irene, who loved ideas, and
to her great-granddaughter Isabel,
who seems to as well.*

CONTENTS

PREFACE

THIS BOOK IS ABOUT CHANGE IN JAPAN. The Japanese word in the title, *kawari,* literally means "change" or "alternative." I had wanted to use another Japanese word, *dappi,* which means "metamorphosis," the change that occurs when a caterpillar turns into a butterfly, and also when a people suddenly shift their way of thinking or proceeding. But *dappi* sounded too strange to Western ears to use as a title. Nonetheless, this is what is happening in Japan. She is transforming herself into something that is totally different from the country we know today. Her transformation will affect people well beyond her borders, in Asia more than other parts of the world, but given the reach of Japan's economy and her potential diplomatic and military power, everyone on the planet will feel Japan's metamorphosis in some way.

I have tried to keep a practical tone throughout. The book identifies powerful, impersonal forces that will alter the cultural and economic face of Japan. It describes the directions of this change and the huge risks attached to the transition. The book takes a Japanese perspective, and describes the new Japan that will emerge as her government, businesses, and people wrestle with the practical imperatives facing them. Most of my references are to newspaper items and Japanese sources. There are enough references to Western sources, however, to let the reader know where Japan-watchers stand in the debate.

Unlike much Western writing on Asia, this book resists the temptation to create a false contest between Japan and the West, or to use Japan as a foil for America, or as an object lesson. There are no heroes, no villains. The book refuses to declare Japan a winner or a loser. Nothing outside a sports arena is that clear cut, and relations between nations are not football matches. Nor are they a "zero sum game." One nation does not necessarily succeed at the expense of others. Indeed, prosperity in one place frequently brings prosperity elsewhere.

While I am fully aware of the hazards of predicting the direction of change over long periods—especially in a complex, sophisticated, and potentially volatile nation like Japan—the pressures nonetheless are clear. My premise is that, with all the undeniable risks, Japan will emerge from this chrysalis of change a more complete power on the world stage than she is today, and will become a major force for development and security in Asia.

New York City
Spring 1999

ONE

METAMORPHOSIS

To think seriously about the global future is to think seriously about Asia. Vast, populous, rich, and growing richer, despite its recent financial setbacks, Asia is increasingly the focus of international planners in business, finance, and government. China naturally dominates their attention. It is undergoing dramatic change, has powerful economic and military potential, and, consequently, introduces great uncertainty into all plans and prospects. Japan, though also powerful, receives less attention. Because she has remained so steady and predictable for so long—since the end of the Second World War, in fact—she tempts the planners to simplify their task by assuming constancy in her future. Such an assumption is wrong. Despite her past stability, in coming years Japan will change radically, become more volatile, less predictable, and possibly even dangerous.

   Few who know Japan can doubt her ability to surprise. More than any other people on earth, the Japanese will make themselves over whenever they sense failure in their existing practices or priorities. Witness, for example, Japan's dramatic self-transformation in the middle of the nineteenth century. Until 1853, when Commodore Matthew Perry anchored a small American war fleet in Edo Bay, she had lived, isolated and unchanged, in a feudal state for 250 years. But the Japanese saw in that fleet's superior power and technology the inadequacy of their nation's political, economic, and social structures. They responded almost immediately by rethinking their priorities, revising their attitudes, and reversing long-revered Japanese practices. Within fifteen years of Perry's visit, Japan had overthrown her feudal government and had begun to remake herself along Western lines. Within twenty-five years of this visit, Japan had completely thrown off her medieval, isolationist patterns and was on her way to becoming a modern military and industrial power. And, after just fifty years, the island nation defeated the Czar's navy and emerged victorious in the Russo-Japanese War. Within fifty years of that remarkable victory, and less than one hundred years after Perry's visit, Japan in 1945 amazed the world again with an equally startling metamorphosis. Her utter defeat in the Second World War made it clear that the imperial-militaristic experiment into which she had flung herself had failed. Once again the Japanese responded with a radical shift. Suddenly, as if with one mind, they abandoned their ferocious devotion to militarism and began the single-minded peaceful pursuit of manufacturing, exporting, and commerce for which they are now well known.

Today, Japan stands once more on the verge of another radical transformation. Again, the change will result from her doubt about her present political and economic practices and their capacity to meet future challenges. Unlike past transformations, which came in response to security threats, this one will come from the more impersonal forces of her maturing economy, the globalization of economic and financial arrangements, and the rapid and relentless aging of her population. Though lacking the high drama of a military confrontation, these influences are no less powerful. Fundamental and inexorable, they will force Japan to adjust or face economic decline. Japan will not choose decline.

If history is any guide, Japan's transformation, once it gains momentum, will break completely with the past. Her economic and demographic imperatives will make it increasingly difficult for her to carry on as the world's workshop. Her huge trade surplus will shrink into deficit, and her high rate of savings will fall. But these changes will not necessarily weaken her. Japan will push out into the rest of Asia, using its ample human and economic resources to preserve her wealth and position. She will adjust her national focus from domestic manufacturing and exports to remaking herself as a regional and global center for management, finance, and design—a kind of "headquarters nation" for a regional division of labor. The change will not stop with economics. This new national emphasis will breed new politics and new policies. Japan's global diplomatic presence will rise and follow her economic march into Asia, and, because this historically unstable area lies outside her direct political control, she will, against her own instincts, rebuild her military power. Although this metamorphosis will impel Japan to shed many of the hallmarks of her former success, other elements of the transformation will offer her means for retaining her wealth and dominance. Indeed, she will gain stature on the world stage, more, in fact, than at any time since the outset of the

Second World War. Japan will go from the nation that owned much but influenced little, to a nation that owns even more and influences a great deal, a full-fledged power in every sense of the word.

The risks involved in such a tremendous change are profound. There is much room for mistakes and misunderstandings. Certainly, the rise of Japan's diplomatic and military profile will unnerve other nations, as well as the Japanese. Many still remember well Japan's last great push into Asia during the 1930s and 1940s, and the ostensibly economic "Greater East Asia Co-Prosperity Sphere" that served as the pretext for her imperial conquests. But it is easy to exaggerate the similarities to the past and its security concerns. Japan has no desire to repeat her old mistakes, even as she increasingly vies for dominance in the region with a powerful and aggressive China. Rather than resort to force first, as she did sixty years ago, this time she will rely on superior technology, organization, education, and business connections. If handled correctly by the rest of Asia—and also by the United States—Japan's change might even *enhance* security in the region.

The Japanese system, which is about to change so radically, has its origins in the devastation of World War II. This system, *Nihon ryu*—as the Japanese would say, or Japan's "way"—emphasizes economic growth above all else. Aiming, as it did, at rebuilding the nation and eventually catching up with the West, this "way" developed around a highly regulated, closed, planned, and centralized structure. Run largely through the cooperation between big business and the nation's civil service bureaucracy, it focused almost exclusively on manufacturing and exports, even at the expense of its citizens' well-being. And until recently, the Japanese public supported this approach with a national spirit seldom seen in the West, except perhaps, in time of war. This system has been enormously successful too. It brought Japan from ruin in 1945 to the prestigious position as the world's second largest economy today.

But the pressure for change has been building steadily. The fundamental forces of globalization and the economy's maturation were straining Japan's "way" even in the boom years of the 1980s, and have become impossible to ignore in the face of Japan's current financial and economic difficulties. Stagnant growth rates, the frailty of Japan's financial institutions, and the failures of policy correctives, which once worked so well, have highlighted the system's vulnerability. After nearly two generations of unwavering economic success, these unmistakable signs of fundamental problems have shocked the Japanese people as well as her policy makers, and seriously undermined the once strong consensus behind the system. Many of the practices that both natives and foreigners thought were part of Japan's ancient culture have begun to come unraveled. The complex and exclusive web of Japan's retail distribution system, about which American trade negotiators have complained for years, has torn. Firms have begun to abandon the much lauded system of "lifetime" employment, and given up their former eagerness to cooperate with the government and with one another. The misfortunes of the 1990s have made it clear that rather than being expressions of traditional culture, such practices were only the temporary products of a period of extraordinary economic growth that is now coming to a close.

The lack of government success in dealing with these difficulties has intensified people's doubts about the efficacy of Japan's "way." Many Japanese, believing that their government and bureaucratic controls would prevent such problems, feel deeply betrayed by their leaders, especially the bureaucrats in whom they once put so much trust and to whom they gave so much power. The civil service bureaucracy, which once commanded great respect—particularly the Ministry of Finance—has become an object of contempt in Japan. A reform movement has sprung up among prominent business people, academics, journalists, and even some government officials. Arguing that the old way has failed, these reformers want to break the power of the bureaucrats and loosen their close, centralized control over Japan's economy and society. The movement aims to deregulate industries, liberalize markets, and open the country to foreign firms and imports. Naturally, the reform effort has faced resistance from entrenched interests, leading many Western observers to express skepticism about the prospect for any substantive change in Japan. But the fundamental pressures facing the country have stiffened the reform effort. It has begun to have an effect. The country, in fact, is well along the path of reordering its priorities and dismantling its once cherished but no longer sustainable practices and structures.

In coming years, Japan's transformation will accelerate as her economy and social institutions begin to cope with an especially powerful agent of change: the rapid aging of her population. Every industrialized nation expects its population of elderly and retired to increase, but Japan will face the phenomenon at its most extreme. By early in the twenty-first century, one Japanese in four will be older than sixty-five years. Such a huge retired population is unprecedented in history. It will force change mostly by creating a severe labor shortage. Japan has had such a low birthrate for so long that she lacks the young people to step into the shoes of the newly retired. By the second decade of the new century, for every dependent retiree Japan will have fewer than two people working. That is almost double the present weight of retired, and a far higher proportion than is expected for the United States. Unlike the

United States, or even Europe, Japan has virtually no prospect of youthful immigration to relieve the strain on her labor force. These demographic pressures, together with the influences of economic maturation and globalization, will force Japan to make a series of adjustments that will alter the face of the nation and the rest of Asia as well.

It is primarily this burden of pensioners on her workforce that will sap Japan's ability to maintain her position as a great center of production and exportation. No nation can remain a manufacturing powerhouse, exporting a large portion of her products, when a substantial proportion of her population is retiring from active production. Her export growth will slow, and imports will have to increase in order to supplement the production of her overburdened workers as they strive to meet the legitimate economic demands of a large elderly population. Her mighty trade surplus will dwindle. At the same time, Japan's labor shortage will impel her industry to expand into the rest of Asia, where it can find cheap, abundant labor and fast-growing domestic markets. With this, she will lose more manufacturing and export capacity, and so face an even greater dependence on imports. Eventually Japan will need to liberalize her old, exclusive trade policies and her other economic controls just to facilitate the necessary flow of overseas products from her own transplanted industry and other sources. That change will, in turn, further encourage importing, eventually causing her envied trade surplus to slide into deficit.

Under such pressure, Japan's entire domestic economy will have to reorient itself. Japanese business will shift focus from manufacturing to an un-Japanese emphasis on service industries, such as management, research, communications, design, and finance. She will need these capabilities to manage her increasingly important overseas production interests and ensure that her people enjoy the profits derived from them. The pattern is reminiscent of what happened to American industry in the 1970s and 1980s. This broad shift in Japan will, in its turn, increase the pressure to open, deregulate, and generally liberalize commerce, industry, employment, and especially finance. Japan will require extensive financial flexibility to support the "headquarters" role that she will take on for her extensive overseas interests. She will also need to attract foreign financial capital to compensate for the loss of savings as her huge elderly population ceases putting money aside and begins to live off past savings. The government will look to financial markets for help in financing the budget deficits that will rise as it attempts to keep up with ever-expanding pension obligations, which are even more poorly funded than Social Security is in the United States.

Faced with increasing economic vulnerability to foreign sources, Japan will have to deviate even more from her past patterns. Eventually, she will have to increase her diplomatic and military profiles to serve and protect her important foreign sources of wealth. She will hesitate at first. Since World War II, Japan has followed a very reserved line with regard to diplomatic and military matters. But no nation can expose its production facilities to foreign governments (as Japan will have to in coming years) without developing enough power—both diplomatic and military—to protect those vital interests. In time, Japan's needs will force her to assert herself internationally and behave in Asia with increased independence from the "security" relationships with the United States. Diplomatic strains will inevitably develop between Japan and the United States as well as other Asian nations. Since diplomacy, by its nature, has a military component, the strains will become much more dangerous than recent trade disputes have been, especially given Japan's newness to the game. But she will develop all these capabilities quickly. Japan already has a powerful military but has downplayed this significant force because of the legacy of World War II. In time, to bolster her diplomacy, she will want the world to know of her military power. She will also want to enlarge it and, significantly, change its character from a purely defensive force to a strike force. The nature of Japan's alliance with the United States will change in this environment, as will all power relationships in Asia.

Such transformations in any nation are fraught with risk. Japan is especially vulnerable. Her weakness, ironically, lies in one of the sources of her post-war success: her culture's powerful response to a common purpose. When, as in most of the past fifty years, national objectives are clear, Japan's group-oriented culture can produce a remarkable national spirit, great drive, industry, and discipline. But with the kind of uncertainty that the future holds, this cultural craving for great national purpose can work to the nation's—and possibly the world's—distinct disadvantage. As the Japanese lose faith in their established priorities and practices, their quest for a meaningful and successful national endeavor could prompt them to grab at almost any alternative approach that presents itself, even if it is not entirely rational—or possibly is destructive. It was, after all, this cultural trait during a previous period of uncertainty that lead Tokyo to militarism in the 1930s, and to national disaster in the 1940s. While it seems unlikely at the moment, such extremism is by no means out of the question.

Along with all these risks (or perhaps because of them) Japan will offer great business and investment opportunities as she opens her markets, shifts the orientation of her domestic economy, and invites management and financial expertise to assist in her transition. Foreign producers will find a welcoming market in Japan, where they once met only opacity and official resistance. Financial firms and especially firms with experience in management and communications will find a much wider field of interest in Japan and a much more fluid environment than at any time since the country began rebuilding after World War II.

These business opportunities, as well as the overall national transformation, will develop best in an environment in which leadership, inside and outside Japan, facilitates the change. By signaling future directions to business and others, huge risks may be ameliorated. Reform in Japan can help contain the dangers implicit in Japanese culture. The United States can head off friction with Japan's new diplomatic needs by loosening the structure of its alliance, allowing her the increased maneuvering room that she will need. To avoid unnecessary tension, all the nations involved in the region will need to explore alternative means to maintain Asia's power balance as these changes remove the constants of the past. This last effort will depend heavily on the United States and probably will be best served by a new or strengthened multilateral structure. Although Asian nations have always shown a reluctance to cooperate in such arrangements, the stakes certainly are high enough to warrant the effort. Left unattended, Japan's response to her economic and demographic pressures could become very dangerous indeed. When well managed, Japan will find a means to meet her challenges that will benefit both herself and Asia.

TWO

DESCENT
FROM HEAVEN

THE GREAT HANSHIN EARTHQUAKE, THE most severe to hit the country since before World War II, struck Kobe city in the early morning hours of January 17, 1995. Thousands died, tens of thousands were injured, and hundreds of thousands more were left homeless. While the carnage shocked the world, it had a disproportionate impact on Japanese confidence. The country's scientific community and civil service authorities had labeled Kobe an unlikely spot for a quake, and the Japanese, including the people of Kobe, believed them. So when the earth moved in Kobe, people felt betrayed by the officials in whom they had placed so much trust. The psychic damage was so great that much of the Japanese commentary following the event gave the impression that the country had deserved the Hanshin quake, or at least the horrible surprise of it. The disaster somehow gave expression to growing feelings of inadequacy, inability to cope with present challenges, malaise, and doubt. The link between Kobe's catastrophe and Japan's "way" may have had more basis in metaphor than in reason, but to many Japanese it was real enough. It was as if some deity or, at least a force much stronger than Japan, Inc., was telling the country that something was fundamentally wrong.

COMPLACENCY DESTROYED

Kobe's quake began ten miles beneath the earth's surface, under the Akashi Strait that links the city's lovely semicircular bay to the sea. For decades, the Philippine Sea Continental Plate pushed hard against the Eurasian Plate on which Kobe City, its port, its picturesque hills, and all of its many export shipping cranes sit.[1] The earth ruptured just a few miles south of town. The gash it created was not really impressive. It ran for a few kilometers across the northern part of Awaji Island, which separates the city's bay from the sea, and resembled a miniature canyon only a few feet wide. But the tremendous force destroyed downtown, severely damaging 150 square kilometers (58 square miles) of the metropolitan area that was home to one and a half million people.[2] The older houses, dating from the initial postwar rebuilding, fared the worst. Their light walls buckled and their heavy tiled roofs fell in, killing many, particularly the city's frail and elderly. Newer, more sophisticated and complex buildings fared better, despite their greater height. The quake damaged walls and beams, but the flexibility of the new structures kept them from collapsing, and their inhabitants remained relatively safe.[3] Gas mains broke, fires started, ruptured water mains hampered firefighting, and the lack of effective emergency management left roadways choked with refugees.[4] In some areas relief efforts came so slowly that most of the rescue work was done by the survivors in each neighborhood, without official help or direction.[5] When it was over, the quake and the fires had caused some ¥10 trillion ($91 billion at the exchange rate of the day) of damage and destroyed 100 hectares (247 acres) of the city (an area equal to about one-third of New York's Central Park), of which 66 hectares (163 acres) were entirely burned out.[6] Fifty-five hundred people died; 26,000 more were injured; 190,000 structures were destroyed; and over 235,000 people were left homeless.[7] The destruction severed the trunk line of the famous bullet train of which Japan is so proud, and denied water, gas, and electricity to over one million people.[8]

In addition to the losses brought by the quake, the Japanese were stunned by official mismanagement and the extent to which it exacerbated the suffering. Many "earthquake proof" structures, about which Japan's Construction Ministry once bragged, had failed utterly, humiliating Japan in the eyes of the world, or so many Japanese felt. The picture of 200 meters of the Hanshin elevated expressway plopped on its side, cars and trucks spilled onto the ground, was, in Japanese eyes, tantamount to seeing the imperial army led off to POW camps.[9] Rescue efforts were poorly managed and the restoration of public services took weeks, and in some cases, months. Railway service in the area took six months to resume fully. Certain sections of the Hanshin expressway did not reopen until fourteen months after the quake. For most inhabitants, electricity and telephone service were restored relatively quickly, but a full restoration of power and communications took weeks. The repair of gas lines did not start until four days after the main shock, and then it took months to secure all the leaks that had caused the fires. Three months after the quake, Kobe still had 100,000 households without gas for cooking and heat. Two months after the quake, 100,000 homes still had no water.[10] When then Prime Minister Murayama visited the disaster sight, the usually respectful public chided him, saying that they needed water more than a look at the Prime Minister.[11] For a nation that had held its government bureaucracy in particularly high esteem and touted its efficiency, foresight, and responsiveness, this failure went beyond embarrassment. Japanese boasts of the superiority of their civil servants quickly changed to indictments of bureaucratic ineptitude.

Critics took grim delight in the irony that, on the day of the quake, officials had scheduled a workshop on "urban earthquake hazard reduction" in nearby Osaka. Cruelly, several commentators suggested that the *experts* might have gained insight by simply moving the workshop to Kobe.[12] Many Japanese commentators noted that Japan's Coordinating Committee for Earthquake Prediction (*Yochiren*) had rejected several warnings by seismologists at Ryuko University about Kobe's vulnerability. According to one Ryuko seismologist, Masaki Kimura, *Yochiren* actually forbade the publishing of his findings, referring to him as a "common researcher" who should keep his "nose out of earthquake prediction."[13] Perhaps the experts at *Yochiren* had sound reasons for rejecting Kimura's work, but in light of the Kobe quake, their high-handed manner rankled many.

Japanese bitterness toward bureaucrats and government officials reached a heightened level of intensity when people compared Kobe with California's Northridge quake, which had occurred in January 1994, exactly a year before Kobe's disaster. When that trembler hit Southern California, many Japanese smugly declared Japan to be much better prepared. Toshio Mochizuki, the head of Tokyo University's Center for Urban Disaster Prevention, reviewed the news from California and voiced Japan's official universal reaction: "In Japan, highways will never collapse." After seeing the pictures of Kobe's Hanshin expressway lying on its side, he conceded tersely, "I now realize how näive I was."[14] Not everyone in Japan was so restrained. For weeks after the quake, Japanese newspapers were full of self-mocking recollections of such official claims of the invulnerability of Japanese highways, railroads, and buildings.[15]

But the greatest disillusionment stemmed from how slowly the Japanese government responded to the disaster, and also from the downright stupidity of the civil service. In contrast to California's administrators, whom Japanese officials had denigrated, Japan lacked an effective disaster plan or chain of command in Kobe. The local government in Southern California responded within an hour of the main shock, police took control of passable roads for emergency use, and undamaged municipalities sent help. California's governor requested and received Washington's assistance within nine hours of the main Northridge shock. In Kobe, it took the local government five hours after the main shock even to begin to respond. The Hyogo prefectural governor, who had local jurisdiction, waited for over twenty-four hours to request help from Japan's self-defense forces, a failure that needlessly delayed the deployment of 16,000 rescuers. The governor's office claimed not to know the procedure by which it could call in these forces.[16] To many Japanese, it was doubly embarrassing that the governor's office used ignorance as an excuse. Even when the rescuers arrived, the civil authorities failed to provide effective direction. It took days before the local police restricted the use of Highway Route 43, the only usable road linking Kobe and Osaka. So the city burned and people died from neglect while fire trucks, ambulances, and other emergency vehicles inched through twenty-mile-long traffic jams.[17]

The response of the central government provided no comfort to those still searching under the rubble for Japan's administrative superiorities. When the nation's meteorological agency first reported the quake some twenty-one minutes after it hit, there was no one to receive the fax at the National Land Agency, which is in charge of disaster contingencies. Neither Prime Minister Murayama nor any cabinet official was informed through government channels. Murayama knew of some trouble from a television report that he happened to catch that morning, but he was not aware of the extent of the disaster when he attended a regularly scheduled cabinet meeting at ten o'clock that morning, almost five full hours after the main shock. He was not briefed until noon. Indeed, the National Land Agency waited until almost noon that day to begin coordinating relief efforts.[18]

Reports piled up of civil servants who valued their own prerogatives above people's lives. One popular story described officials of the Ministry of Agriculture, Forestry, and Fisheries insisting that the search dogs of a Swiss rescue team go through the usual quarantine before entering the country.[19] After arriving in Japan, members of another Swiss rescue team languished for three days because of red tape before officials permitted them to enter Kobe. A British team was held up for six days, and then its search experts were sent to buildings that the Swiss team had already searched.[20, 21] A French rescue team was held up by the bureaucracy for three days after arriving, then was never given a guide or interpreter. Its doctors were forbidden to help because they lacked Japanese medical licenses.[22] The same civil servants were accused of turning away offers from the United States military to send in personnel and

supplies to help with the relief efforts.[23] Particularly galling to Japanese commentators was the Ministry of Construction's resistance to a visit by American
seismologists because the Ministry did not want them to see the evidence that
made a lie of their boast about the durability of Japanese highways.[24]

The man on the street in Tokyo or Osaka, as well as many prominent
Japanese, point to all these delays, stupidities, and failures as reasons why
Kobe suffered so much more than Northridge, which had 61 deaths (only 1.1
percent of Kobe's toll), 9,000 injured (34.6 percent of Kobe's), and 14,000
houses destroyed (7.4 percent of Kobe's).[25] To some extent, the comparisons
are unfair. California's quake registered 6.7 on the Richter scale, compared
with Kobe's 6.9.[26] Given the logarithmic nature of the Richter measure, this
difference is much greater than it would appear. But fairness means less to the
Japanese public than its perception of the failure of the civil service bureaucracy to perform adequately, let alone with the foresight, intelligence, and efficiency that it claimed for itself and that Japan expected.

Some comments took on an apocalyptic tone that went far beyond the
facts of the earthquake. These linked Kobe's pain and disaster generally to
Japan's lust for economic growth, particularly the desire for advanced industrial development. Koji Taki, a prominent Japanese social and literary critic,
spoke of the quake as a warning of "the danger of death which seems to be rising from the expansion of human civilization." The editor-in-chief of the
respected *Insider* magazine asserted that Japan "shaved sacred mountains" for
land reclamation in Kobe Bay, and that this was justification for the quake if
not its cause. This editor even went on to refer to the "wrath of heaven" and
"signs of the end" appearing in Japan, because there are more "intricate and
complicated city functions...than anywhere else in the world."[27] In only
slightly more restrained tones, the conservative *Yomiuri Shimbun,* Japan's
largest circulation newspaper, wrote editorials about the public's "sense of
'doomsday'," while former prime minister Morhiro Hosokawa warned that
"Japan is like a ship on the verge of sinking."[28] Another *Yomiuri Shimbun* editorial picked up the tone and referred to the postwar advance of the economy
as "threatening to ruin our very existence."[29]

The overblown, mystical language, though not entirely logical, is understandable in light of Kobe's devastation and the public disillusionment that
went along with it. It certainly is easy to sympathize with, especially given the
other shocks to the Japanese self-image that followed Kobe. On March 20,
1995, only two months after the Kobe quake, the Aum Shinrikyo religious cult
released sarin nerve gas in a Tokyo subway, killing 12 and injuring 5,000. A
subsequent investigation revealed the full extent of the cult's murderous

behavior over a long period, shattering Japanese assumptions of greater security, rationality, and modernity over other nations. Ten days after the nerve gas
attack, while absorbing the revelations about the cult, the Japanese public
received news of a gunman who shot down Takaji Kunimatsu, the head of
Japan's national police agency, in front of his Tokyo home. A month later,
investigators raided a large credit cooperative to obtain evidence of illegal
lending. Such police actions have become almost commonplace since then, but
it was all shockingly new at the time. Then in June, a disgruntled bank
employee hijacked a domestic All Nippon Airlines flight. Separately, a number of bank officials, formerly pillars of the financial community, were arrested
for lending improprieties. In fall 1995, Daiwa Bank deflated Japanese managerial pretensions, when it revealed that poor management controls had
enabled an employee stationed in New York to hide trading losses amounting
to ¥110 trillion ($1.2 billion at the exchange rate of the day), for years.[30]

As the evidence of governmental, bureaucratic, and managerial inadequacy grew, it became difficult for the Japanese to remain complacent about
themselves and their system for running their economy and society. By the end
of 1995, reports of long-lived official and corporate corruption accumulated
rapidly. High-ranking Ministry of Finance officials admitted to speculating in
the financial markets that they were charged with policing and regulating. Even
worse, they admitted to using what they called "donations" from associates,
who were described as "shady" in their market dealings, and then confessed to
forgetting to report their gains to the tax authorities, an agency that they also
oversee. In a separate and equally shocking revelation, local government officials admitted to using taxpayer funds to entertain central government officials
at "swank" restaurants and other "watering holes."[31] As the year closed, Toshio
Yamaguchi, former labor minister and member of the Diet, Japan's Parliament,
was arrested for accepting illegal loans. It was only the second arrest of a sitting
Diet member in twenty-eight years, but to the man on the street, it spoke volumes about what might have been concealed during all that time.[32]

Nineteen ninety-five was a particularly bad year, but in the years since
then revelations of scandal, corruption, and official incompetence have continued to fill the pages of Japanese newspapers and magazines. The initial
arrests of bankers and financiers in 1995 were followed by a string of raids and
indictments, most of which centered on lending improprieties, and the bribery
of civil servants.[33] After the Daiwa losses were revealed, subsequent reports
exposed management failures in four other major Japanese financial companies that allowed employees to cover up huge losses. One of the most spectacular was a ¥171 trillion ($1.5 billion at the exchange rate of the day) loss

sustained by a single trader at Sumitomo Corporation.[34] In the area of public failure, as opposed to corporate, early 1997 brought news of the arrest of Nobuharu Okamitsu, former vice minister at the Ministry of Health and Welfare, for taking bribes connected with the construction of specially subsidized nursing homes.[35] By 1998, raids on the once sacrosanct Ministry of Finance were exposing a number of improprieties that led to arrests and suicides.[36] As far as public confidence was concerned, one of the most harmful revelations was the news that officials at Donen, the government-run Nuclear Power Reactor and Nuclear Fuel Development Corporation, lied to the Diet and to the public about a fire in one of its reactors north of Tokyo. Investigators discovered that during the blaze, Donen officials continued their regular agency golf tournament.[37] While the incident caused no loss of life, this example of official arrogance was so similar to the failures of the bureaucrats during the Kobe disaster that people wondered if such attitudes and irresponsibility were systemic.

All these revelations have made it difficult for the Japanese to support even a remnant of the old image of their civil servants and business leaders as more earnest, diligent, hard-working, and prescient than their Western counterparts. That fact has raised even more fundamental doubts about everything Japan is and does. Keigo Okanagi, professor of psychiatry at the University of Tokyo, spoke of the severe "psychological blow to the Japanese people" that resulted from the Kobe disaster and the subsequent realization of the inadequacies of their officials and the system that gave them so much respect and power. A *New York Times* reporter who interviewed Okanagi wrote that the nation's humbling added to "the tangle of feelings the Japanese have about precisely who they have become and just where they fit in the modern world."[38] Painfully, people have begun to doubt the basic elements of Japan's "way": its willingness to cede tremendous power to its civil service bureaucracy, its single-minded emphasis on economic growth and exports, and its insistence on a centralized industrial policy based on a government-business partnership. A few years ago Japan was touting her approach as a superior alternative to Western capitalism, though such talk has now quieted, even within East Asian circles. The doubts that emerged during this time raised questions about national priorities and practices that had remained unquestioned in Japan since her rebuilding after the Second World War.

Seemingly intractable economic and financial problems have added to the sense of national despair. Japan's economy fell into recession in the early 1990s. Her stock and real estate prices, after peaking at astronomical levels in 1989, plunged with the recession, losing more than half their value in a matter of months. These reverses put tremendous strain on the financial system, burdening banks with huge losses and an overhang of bad loans. Since Japan was wholly unaccustomed to economic or financial setbacks, these reverses upset her people more than they might have elsewhere. Public anxiety increased as the decade wore on, and Japan could not get her economy going, revive her stock and real estate markets, or relieve the strain on her banking system. The old management and control techniques, which Japanese bureaucrats had bragged about for decades, were failing. So by the mid-1990s, just as scandal and official ineptitude began to weigh most heavily on the Japanese consciousness, her citizens had to grapple as well with a spreading sense of economic and financial failure. In some respects, the economic problems were the hardest to bear, because Japan's "way" focused on the economy. As these economic problems dragged on into the closing years of the decade, anxieties rose still higher in response to a parallel financial and economic crisis that erupted in Korea and the emerging economies of Southeast Asia. These troubles elsewhere in Asia have complicated Japan's own domestic economic and financial difficulties, and hindered the prospects for their resolution. But Asia's pain had a far more telling effect on the Japanese psyche. These nations were imitators of the Japanese "way," at least with regard to economics. They, along with Japan, touted the effectiveness of a centralized approach with guidance and planning from the civil service bureaucracy and an emphasis on export. Their failures compounded Japanese despair and added disproportionately to the sense that this "way," however useful it once was, had lost its efficacy for the future.

Japan's loss of spirit and enthusiasm for her old approach has become obvious to even a casual visitor. Not long ago, the Japanese commonly described themselves and their country as *tomaranai,* a word that literally translates as "unstoppable" but effectively means unbeatable. As always with the Japanese, they used the word politely and with the appearance of personal humility. Nonetheless, the expression exuded a seemingly unshakable confidence in themselves, their race, and their "way." By the mid-1990s, the word had dropped from usage. Once the Japanese used the word *endaka,* which refers to a rapid rise in the value of the yen, to evoke feelings of national strength. At a 1992 conference, the Japanese economist and investment consultant Nobumitsu Kagami could hardly suppress a smile of pride when he translated the word to a gathering of prominent Australian bankers, academics, and financiers. Now when the word *endaka* is spoken, it issues from a fear that the United States will use it to hurt the economy further by pricing Japanese exports out of world markets.[39]

This self-doubt in some ways resembles the feeling that overwhelmed

Americans in the 1970s, when failure in Vietnam, the ascent of OPEC, and Watergate shook the country's confidence and complacency. For the Japanese now, as for Americans then, it carries the sense of a lost future, the feeling that the population and leadership have collectively deceived themselves about who they are, what they are capable of, how they fit into the world, and, more importantly, about the character of their society. But for the Japanese, the implications of such feelings have greater significance than they did for Americans. More than any other nation on earth, the Japanese value a sense of common purpose. When it exists, they can exhibit a kind of national "team spirit" seldom seen in the West. But when that sense dissipates, the Japanese can sink more deeply into despair than other peoples. That certainly seems the direction these days. Recent police data show a 50 percent jump in suicides since the mid-1990s.[40] Newspapers have begun to report which Tokyo commuter trains encounter the most suicides. Therapists, previously rare in Japan, are experiencing a boom.[41]

All the years of striving and sacrifice suddenly seem pointless. To many Japanese, almost fifty years of astonishing national effort yielded only a brief period of power and prestige in the 1980s before the ground slid out from under them. A recent survey by the *Nihon Keizai Shimbun* revealed that over half the people of Japan now expect the country to lose its status as the major economic power in Asia in less than ten years.[42] Another poll taken by the Japanese advertising agency Hakuhodo found that only 23 percent of the respondents thought of Japan as stable. That figure is down from 40 percent in a similar survey taken in 1990. Half of those recently surveyed described Japan's economy as fundamentally in decline.[43] Guests at private Japanese clubs once commonly heard members speculate on their next major move in Europe, America, or Southeast Asia. A lot of it was just bragging, but nonetheless it spoke to great energy and an expectation of continuous expansion and success. These days, an eavesdropper is more likely to hear executives muse sentimentally about old classmates who found greater happiness by going into the family business than did the fast-track types who studied abroad, climbed the corporate ladder, and led Japan in its fight to beat the West at its own game of global business and finance.[44]

The young especially seem to have fallen prey to this new, depressed spirit. A relatively recent survey of high school students revealed that 60 percent saw Japan's future as "dark." These young people were described as lacking the team spirit and confidence so prominent in previous years. They seemed to be "groping for [new] concrete guidelines and principles."[45] According to corporate executives who deal with the new recruits right out of university, these new graduates are very unlike the ambitious, hard-working crop of earlier years. Those earlier rookies had all the characteristics typically associated with Japanese workers. They saw careers in working extraordinarily hard to advance their firms' and their country's interests in the global economy. Today's rookies seem only intent on protecting their positions. As one Japanese journalist put it, the "kids" are ready to "dig in" and hide under "stress reduction manuals." Less kind, Sakio Sakagawa, the president of a major Tokyo training firm, described the new attitude as simply "small-minded."[46]

Takeo Nakamura, the senior managing director of a major Japanese financial institution, put this new, sad attitude—for both the mature and the young—into an especially sharp focus. When he was president of his firm's American subsidiary, he enjoyed telling Americans how the Second World War taught Japan the uselessness of the military approach. In defeat, he claimed, Japan learned better than the victors that the answer to national success lay in an unswerving concentration on business and economics. These days, he puts on a brave face for Western clients, but in private conversation will occasionally let slip his concern that Japan has somehow got it wrong again.

THE SYSTEM—BUREAUCRATIC CONTROL

The approach or "way" in which the Japanese have begun to lose confidence has never yielded easily to definition or description. It is a subtle and elusive arrangement that observers, pro and con, have characterized as a unique brand of capitalism. It has absorbed the complete attention of a large number of book-length studies.[47] Many of these descriptions differ on details, but almost all agree that Japan has built her system around highly regulated arrangements in which business and government have cooperated for years in a manner almost unprecedented in the West, except perhaps in times of great national emergency. The civil service bureaucracy has wielded tremendous power in this cooperative effort to order society and direct the economy, not, as in Western nations, for the increased prosperity of individuals, but rather as an instrument of national power. While this bureaucracy is far from a monolith and, indeed, has often shown signs of becoming balkanized around narrow interests, the structure generally has had a more centralized, top-down character than that of most Western nations. Japan's system certainly has lacked the tension created by competing governmental, business, and individual interests that typifies the United States.

Although Japan's system has begun to change, especially in recent years, its basic structure still has its roots in the nation's response to the chaos left by the Second World War. At that time, clear direction by government agencies seemed to be the best way to marshal meager physical and financial resources for the urgent task of redevelopment. Actually, Japan's top-down approach to social and economic organization can trace a longer and more august lineage, going back well before 1945. After all, Japan, like so many other Asian powers, especially China, comes from a Confucian heritage that expressly advocates a paternalistic social order managed by an elite class of civil servants. Indeed, just using the English term "civil servant" obscures this Eastern attitude. Confucian thought sees career administrators not as servants of the public, the way Westerners like to characterize them, but rather as philosopher kings, a priestly class with special insight and a mandate to order society from above. The Japanese never use the word "servant" when referring to public officials. Instead they use the word *okami,* which literally means "those who are above or superior." When a senior ministry man leaves his post to enter private industry, they call it *amakudari,* the "descent from heaven." Even in everyday language, the Japanese refer to what Westerners call a civil servant as *jokyo kota komu-in,* literally, "senior national duty person." Duty is closer than service to the Confucian notion of the role of civil servant; he or she works less to help people than to follow some higher external obligation, as a soldier follows his cause, or a priest his religion. Even the Japanese pejorative for bureaucrat, *kankyou,* refers to someone who exercises arbitrary power. It shares nothing with the common sense of the Western pejorative, which typically implies stuffiness and hierarchical inflexibility.

Aside from the influence of Confucius, a lack of space and resources has long impelled Japan to accept a restrictive social order that stresses cooperation with the central authority. Even in medieval times the islands were overpopulated, especially relative to their meager amounts of arable land and natural resources. With such conditions fostering the internecine wars of her early history, Japan embraced the shoguns' imposition of order through highly regulated arrangements. Without it, the Japanese feared, the country would tear herself apart.[48] In the mid-nineteenth century, when Japan first opened to the rest of the world and suffered a civil war, she again relied on a small group of elite to direct her industrialization and modernization in what historians refer to as the Meiji Restoration, or the Meiji period.[49] It worked. Drawing on her traditions, she marshaled her resources and galvanized her people to needed action. In the span of thirty years, the Meiji leadership, with the people's enthusiastic support, turned Japan from a medieval state into a modern military-industrial power.

Throughout the centuries of a top-down directed society and economy—

whether Confucian, shogonate, or Meiji—Japan could never have been described as having a socialist or command economy. There was always private property and some freedom to dispose of it as the owner saw fit. But at the same time, Japan, unlike Britain or America, never quite trusted the market to direct economic action. Even as Japanese economic development gained momentum early in this century, the powerful controlling impulse resisted Western liberal market traditions. In the mid-1930s, the senior civil servant Shinji Yoshino made the anti-market attitude explicit by describing free markets as sources of "confusion."[50] Japan's civil servants always preferred harmony (*wa*) and symbiosis (*kyosei*) over the turbulence of the free market, a concept which they have invariably referred to as *kato kyoso,* "excessive competition." Their perspective blames competition for the wasteful accumulation of industrial capacity in the wrong places, and the subsequent, undesirable, boom-bust pattern of Western business cycles.

This long-standing desire to control the economy and its financial market seemed completely applicable in the late 1940s, when Japan established the institutions, practices, and priorities that have guided her redevelopment and growth to the present day. After the devastation of the war, she lacked the industrial plant, equipment, roads, rail transport, and communication facilities essential to a modern industrialized state. To exacerbate the situation further, in the late 1940s, some six million Japanese nationals from her former empire returned to the home islands, as did what remained of her armies—millions of potential working hands with no tools.[51] Japan desperately needed to rebuild in order to employ her people and provide for them. The patterns of the Meiji period's development presented themselves as a fine model, as did many of the centrally directed practices from the extensive wartime organization. The army, of course, disbanded, but the centralized direction remained.

The impetus for a directed and concerted development effort was powerfully reinforced by the early postwar prime minister, Shigeru Yoshida. When he spoke of economic growth, he spoke not in terms of the people's well-being but in terms of national power. To him, individual wealth would be the byproduct, not the goal of Japan's new "way." The real goal was for Japan to catch up with, and ultimately overtake, the American economy. In a 1951 speech on the Japan-United States security treaty, he made his objective crystal clear: "Just as the United States was once a colony of Great Britain but now is the stronger of the two…if Japan eventually becomes a colony of the United States, [it] will eventually become the stronger."[52] Yoshida's challenge to Japan echoed the commitment in the Meiji period: build up economic power to free Japan from dependence on any nation. And from the late 1940s through the 1950s, when the whole country was desperately poor and dependent on the United States, Yoshida's goal received the overwhelming support of the Japanese people. The Tokyo-based historian Ivan Whitney Hall described Prime Minister Yoshida's speech and the country's embrace of its message as nothing less than a commitment to "deliberate, humorless, and relentless economic war."[53]

Accordingly, Japan drew on her well-established traditions of giving her civil service bureaucrats an array of power levers to achieve this single, clear objective. Initially, central direction was so powerful that the bureaucracy developed five-year plans like the communist command economies of the time. In 1947, Japan's cabinet established the Soviet-sounding Secretariat for Long-Range Planning, though it was quickly disbanded.[54] Despite the death of formal planning in the late 1950s, the civil service bureaucracy continued nonetheless to direct the economy to achieve Yoshida's straightforward objective. And though the ultimate array of rules, laws, restrictions, and moral suasions placed at the bureaucracy's disposal boggle the mind in their complexity and detail, the fundamental structure has remained straightforward enough.

The power to direct the economy was lodged in two ministries in particular: the Ministry of Finance (MOF) and the Ministry of International Trade and Industry (MITI). The MOF became premier by gathering under its control all financial regulation, the Bank of Japan, budgeting, and taxing authority. If the United States were to create an equivalent, it would have to combine in a single agency the Federal Reserve System, with both its monetary policy and its bank regulatory functions; the Securities and Exchange Commission; the Office of the Comptroller of the Currency; the Office of Management and the Budget; the Congressional Budget Office; and the Treasury Department, including the Internal Revenue Service. As the MOF gained power in Japan, it went beyond even this. Referred to as "the ministry of ministries," the MOF enlarged its powers by taking over the job of drafting tax legislation, thereby also bringing under its control the equivalent of the staffs of the tax writing committees in both houses of Congress.[55] The MOF eventually came to orchestrate what the Japanese refer to as *okurashigen-an*, the process by which the senior civil servants from all the ministries prepare the initial draft of each year's national budget for the Diet's approval. With this tremendous power at its disposal, the MOF worked with its sister agency, MITI, to shape Japanese trade, financial, tax, and government spending policies in order to pursue former Prime Minister Yoshida's goal of economic independence and power.

What is often called the "Iron Triangle" formed around MITI and indirectly the MOF. Though this term commonly refers to a close cooperation among the civil service bureaucracy, government, and business, it has always been a rather close-knit group, not nearly as broadly based as the general description implies. Elected officials have played a minor role, lobbying the bureaucrats on behalf of their constituents and giving a political patina to the bureaucracy's directives, but otherwise working toward the basic economic objectives and the means chosen by the ministries to reach them. The MOF and MITI, of course, took the lead from the start, with secondary roles for the other ministries, particularly the Ministries of Construction, Transportation, and Labor. The business side of the triangle has always included only the biggest firms. The powerful trade associations, like the well-known Keidanren Federation, became the real players and gained enormous power among their member firms precisely because they had access to the critical ministries in the Iron Triangle. Power on the business side of the triangle also devolved to the *keiretsu,* families of firms, usually led by a bank or trading company, in which the member firms hold shares in one another, do business among themselves, and generally support each other. Organized labor never gained a place in this power nexus. Because Japan's unions formed around companies and not, as in the West, around industries, the corporations have represented them in the Triangle. Labor's subordinate position goes back to the Second World War, when in 1941, to secure steady production for the war effort, Prime Minister Tojo disbanded the old industrywide unions and replaced them with industrial patriotic associations, called *sangyo hokoku-kai,* that worked hand-in-glove with management to heighten production and improve efficiency.[56] In the great drive to rebuild following the war, a continuation of this arrangement suited Japanese leadership. While patriotism played a less dominant role in the relationship than during the war, the substance remained.

In a practical sense, the Iron Triangle quickly became a communications and intelligence-gathering network. Through its Triangle contacts business learned what the civil service bureaucracy and, to a lesser extent, the elected government wanted of it. The civil service relied on the business part of the group to provide critical market signals beyond those that emerged from its immense data-gathering operations. Relying on these sources, the bureaucrats set the tactics and strategies of economic policy. The interaction of these parties and subsequent direction of the economy ran smoothly and looked to the world like an easy consensus, because each player in the small group that made up the Triangle understood the others' agendas, and, at least until recently, all subscribed to former Prime Minister Yoshida's objectives and the practices established to achieve them. An early Brookings Institution report on Japan's approach captured the feeling of this arrangement: "The Japanese tradition of private acceptance of government leadership and widespread recognition that government officials [civil service, not elected officials] have knowledge, experience, and information superior to that available to the ordinary firm, as well as the sharing of values, beliefs, and political preference by government [and civil service] officials and business leaders, all contributed to the success of the method."[57] For as long as the bureaucrats trusted the input they received from the business side of the Triangle and the businesspeople believed in the superior wisdom and insight of the civil service officials, the economic direction occurred smoothly through an informal "administrative guidance" the Japanese call *gyosei shido.* There was no hint of the coercion that Western authorities surely would require to mount such a coordinated approach.

Japan's rapid growth in the early postwar period earned this system the confidence of all involved. The strong consensus supporting it strengthened further, and consequently so did the level of responsiveness to its guidance and suggestions. But for all the genuine enthusiasm and real cooperation sustained throughout this long period of development, bureaucratic direction has also commanded obedience, because everyone has been well aware that bureaucrats have the power, should they need it, to punish those who refuse to cooperate and reward those who do. Of course, civil servants never have had the authority to command private industry, but they have controlled government spending and have reserved lucrative government contracts for only dutiful firms. Compliance with ministry direction has always carried an implicit promise of help should something go wrong. Japanese civil servants have never tried to hide this special official support. Referring to it as *yamagoya,* after the shelters installed at intervals on mountain hiking trails, officials have frequently pointed out how the implicit promise of official help to compliant firms, like the climbers' knowledge of these shelters, has emboldened industry to push harder and reach beyond where they otherwise might.[58] More than such straightforward rewards, however, the bureaucracy has exercised its power and threatened its use through its extensive taxing, licensing, and other authorities. By use of these, the bureaucrats have determined which firms would get credit as well as access to the most profitable business opportunities, making these powerful persuaders indeed.

The labyrinthine complexity of the Japanese tax code has helped to maintain bureaucratic power and keep the control system running smoothly. The Japanese system has always kept statutory tax rates high, making businesses especially interested in finding relief through loopholes. To receive that tax relief, businesses have had to pursue those activities favored by the tax writers, who, of course, are the bureaucrats. In this way, the civil service has enticed business to focus its resources on an array of officially preferred endeavors, such as investing in energy efficiency, setting up pension funds, buying particular kinds of capital equipment, and engaging in exporting.[59] As it developed, the list of potential tax incentives became so long, so diverse, and frequently so ambiguous that a firm's tax liability became almost a negotiated item between itself and the MOF. This has left the civil servants at the Finance Ministry with even more leverage over Japanese corporations. In some respects, the approach is reminiscent of the New York State Liquor Authority. Set up after the repeal of prohibition in the early 1930s, the Authority imposed so many rules on what it saw as dangerous activities that no liquor seller could possibly comply with them all. This left the authority's agents with the power to close any establishment at any time.[60] It invited corruption, and still does, but also left civil servants with tremendous power to control not only business activity but social behavior as well. In just this way, Japan's civil service has used the tax code to affect the entire country by influencing how all Japanese businesses, and to a lesser extent individuals, spend their time and money.

Licensing, too, has served as a bureaucratic control, especially since Japan requires a license for virtually all business enterprises, even second-hand furniture shops (under the Antiques Trading Law).[61] The ability to hold up or expedite a critical license has always bent even huge business establishments to a ministry's will. The ability to grant a lucrative license as a subsidy has always elicited enthusiastic corporate cooperation with a ministry. In the early postwar years, this kind of manipulation was much starker than now. In the early 1950s, for example, MITI granted the lucrative sugar import license to the export shipbuilding industry. This hardly seems to offer what securities analysts call a "natural synergy." But MITI wanted the shipbuilders to succeed in the export market, and sugar imports gave them enough surplus income to compete ferociously by cutting the export prices on their ships by 20–30 percent.[62] The ministries and industries have moved toward subtler interactions more recently. But the licensing power, with all its implication for control, has remained.

The Finance Ministry's ability to use these taxing, licensing, and regulatory powers to direct credit flows has provided an especially effective tool for advancing top-down control of the economy. The leverage has diminished of late because Japanese financial markets have responded to international influence and have experienced some deregulation, but still (and certainly for much of the postwar period), Japan's system gave the MOF tremendous power in this regard. The primary means of control developed because the Finance Ministry and the Bank of Japan gained the authority to regulate all Japanese financial institutions, and, recognizing the Ministry's power to promote their business or shut it down altogether, they became eager to curry favor with the civil servants. Japanese banks and other financial institutions have spared little over the years in contributing to the achievement of Ministry aims, and have responded quickly and thoroughly to the Bank of Japan when it gave them its informal "window guidance" (*mado guchi kisei*), the financial equivalent of "administrative guidance." Through these means, the civil service bureaucracy has for much of this time simply directed credit to firms and industries whose development would best suit Japan's national goals. If that were not enough, the MOF has enhanced its power through its control of the Treasury Investments and Loan Authority, which directs, among other funds, the huge assets in Japan's postal savings scheme. Usually, these moneys were invested in Japanese government bills and bonds, but the MOF has enticed banks and other financial institutions to do its bidding by making portions of these desirable assets available. Furthermore, the Finance Ministry has gotten its way from time to time through its control over Japan's extensive system of semipublic development and export finance banks. Without having to persuade private lenders, senior civil servants at the Ministry simply have directed the lending by these bodies to wherever they wanted and at whatever rate suited them.[63] Taken together, these controls have effectively directed credit and have enabled the MOF to exercise a critical influence on the shape of capital investment, plant construction, and consequently, the overall path of economic development and growth in Japan.

The list of power levers could go on for pages. Through Japan's Fair Trade Commission, the Ministry of Finance has long had the discretion to approve all mergers and acquisitions, giving itself yet another means to reward compliant companies and punish recalcitrant ones. Control over industry and local government has also devolved to the civil service through its power to determine land allocation and rights-of-way. The bureaucracy has enhanced its power over the years by placing its own retirees into senior and consulting positions at major manufacturers, banks, and trading companies. This extensive network of old boys, who, as they say, "descended from heaven," has acted as a bureaucratic fifth column to persuade reluctant managements to comply with the official ministry programs and objectives. Not all control has been aimed at business either. The civil service bureaucracy has exercised influence over politicians through the selective enforcement of electoral rules as well. A large group of expressly loyal retired civil servants has also found seats in the Diet, working earnestly to see that legislation complied with the wishes of their former colleagues. Indeed, this group has grown to sufficient prominence that it acquired the name, *kanryoha,* "the bureaucrats' faction."[64] Bureaucratic power also has extended to the media through the civil services' authority to accredit news organizations. Nonaccredited organizations have been barred from taking notes at briefings or participating in "pool reports." Having approval, therefore, has become a valued asset to a reporter and a publication. It would take a brave editor or publisher to risk losing such an asset by crossing senior civil servants. Thus, the press has frequently proven itself a willing conspirator in ministry efforts to protect or embarrass politicians or companies according to their levels of cooperation.[65] David Benjamin, a veteran Japan-watcher, went so far as to describe Japanese reporters as "puppets of government propaganda and bureaucratic blackmail."[66]

In addition to controlling business, finance, the Diet, and the press, bureaucratic power in Japan has gained strength through the nearly complete lack of accountability enjoyed by civil servants.[67] Having the ability to pressure elected officials, the civil service has avoided review by the Diet. Japan never really developed the institutional means to review civil service policy or actions. Because the Ministry of Finance gained control of Japan's Board of Audit, it has held power over other ministries, but no independent body has ever called this "ministry of ministries" to account, and consequently the bureaucracy as a whole has not been held accountable. The civil servants have written the legislation that the Diet has ratified and only rarely repudiated. When, from time to time, the civil services' plans have failed, the politicians have taken the public heat, not the bureaucrats. This well-established old pattern is why the antibureaucratic reaction to the Kobe disaster was so new and so upsetting to the Japanese. For all that happened, no authority called or could call for an investigation into the failures surrounding Kobe. Japan has seen none of the testimony or committee hearings that typify the United States in similar circumstances. Some thirty years ago, mercury poisoning caused by industrial wastes in the village of Minamata-byo was so widespread that its symptoms acquired the name Minamata-byo Disease. Yet no bureaucrat or associated business faced a fine or other penalty. More recently, the remarkable public praise for Naoto Kan's insistence (when Minister of Health and Welfare) that his ministry take responsibility for the transmission of AIDS-tainted blood, speaks volumes to how rare such accountability was and still is.

With both politicians and businesses aware of the tremendous power of the civil servants and their virtual invulnerability, cooperation has flowed smoothly without officials having to pull many of these levers, especially in an open way. There never was a point to fighting city hall, especially when it has been so invulnerable, and could generously reward cooperation and thoroughly punish resistance. This has suited the bureaucrats down to the ground.

As lovers of order and harmony, *wa,* they have always preferred an environment in which they could influence matters through the simple threat of power, or better yet, a thorough understanding of that threat, a device the Japanese call *nukanai katana,* the "undrawn sword." To create this easy environment, the civil servants have consistently promoted a small, "old boys" network in the Iron Triangle. They have resisted outsiders—foreign owners and domestic entrepreneurs—who might misunderstand and challenge bureaucratic suggestions, thus forcing the actual use of power instead of just the understood threat. This worked well for most of the postwar period. It inculcated a strong habit of obedience in Japanese business and the public. At the same time, the unquestioned position of the civil servants in the bureaucracy tempted them to develop a habit of command and a willingness to take control. This environment has enabled them to shape the economy and society according to their own lights, without having to consider any of the opposing interests and constituencies that bedevil official decision makers in the West.

THE SYSTEM—SUPPRESSING CONSUMPTION

Having this effective control structure at its disposal, Japan's civil service bureaucracy and its Iron Triangle consistently sought to meet Prime Minister Yoshida's challenge to make Japan economically independent, second to none. Starting in the late 1940s and early 1950s the system set out to channel as much of the nation's economic might as possible into industrial development. The emphasis lay on building up manufacturing so that domestically made goods would replace imported ones and Japan could become a net exporter. It was a tremendous effort. Foreign aid was limited—the United States was less generous to Japan than it was to Germany during the Marshall Plan. Before the Cold War shifted American attitudes toward its former enemies, there was even talk of exacting war reparations from Japan. To rebuild in this environment, Japan knew she had to channel her limited economic and financial resources away from households and make them available for capital investment in manufacturing, the industrial infrastructure, and, after the initial buildup, quality improvement, productivity enhancement, and modernization. This basic purpose has directed the tremendous power and control of the civil service bureaucracy and the Iron Triangle since.

Japan's powerful preference for industry over the individual has shown up directly and indirectly in just about every economic law, regulation, or bureaucratic power lever used in the past or in use today. Mandated rates for electricity have always been lower for preferred industries, and there has been a powerful bias against the consumer in favor of business. For years, households have paid about twice the rate per kilowatt that industry has. A similar preference has also been seen in water costs, with households paying about twice the unit rate. One particular study from the early 1990s discovered that while Japanese households used on average about 18.7 percent of Japan's water, they paid 35.9 percent of the total cost.[68] The implicit subsidy went to industry. Tax laws, too, reflected Japan's clear preference. Both individuals and businesses have faced high statutory rates and the same complexity in the tax code, but the authorities have seen to it that most of the loopholes for relieving the tax burden accrued to business and industry, not to households. Though statutory corporate tax rates have remained high by world standards, the loopholes afforded Japanese firms have resulted in their paying less tax than companies in most other advanced countries. According to studies by the Organization of Economic Cooperation and Development (OECD), the Paris-based think tank of the world's developed nations, Japan's effective corporate taxes have run much lower than those of other nations: 40 percent lower than Germany or the U.K., and 25 percent below those in the United States.[69] The official bias has always run in favor of *big* business in particular. The household sector and smaller firms have had to pick up the burden for the public purse that the system has spared major industry. Japanese government figures show that bigger corporations on average have received a 42.1 percent break from the statutory tax rate, small corporations only a 4.5 percent break, and individual households hardly any at all.[70]

But Japan's system has done more than provide subsidies and tax incentives to support business. To ensure that industry has all the economic and financial resources it needs for investment in efficiency, expansion, and modernization, as well as to protect itself from imports, the Iron Triangle has consistently discouraged consumption and actively promoted or forced saving by households and individuals. This approach might seem counterproductive to those accustomed to the economic policies of the United States. In the States, high levels of consumption are thought to help business by giving it an active domestic market for its products. But Japan's orientation has always been the export market. Japanese officials have never looked to the Japanese consumer to support business. They have viewed the Japanese domestic consumer not as a customer of Japanese business but as a competitor for the capital and other economic resources that industry has needed to grow and compete in the export market. This conflict was especially acute during the early postwar scarcities, and provided roots for the present system. With an economy suffering from limited production capacity, allowing any consumer gratification beyond certain minimums threatened to attract imports, and to limit the system's ability to direct production to those activities urgently needed for industrial development and competition in export markets. So, quite logically, given the circumstances of the time, the bureaucrats managing the economy set out to suppress consumption. They have continued that pattern, with only minor retractions, up to the present, even though the economy's productive capacity has expanded beyond the wildest dreams of the postwar years.

The foreign visitor sees evidence of this anticonsumer policy as soon as he exits customs and immigration at Tokyo's Narita airport. Travel is expensive and inconvenient in order to prevent individuals' spending at all, but especially on foreign goods and services. Unless this visitor arrives at a very odd hour, he steps into an exceedingly crowded, wholly inadequate terminal building that is remarkably small for a facility serving a major world capital. Because Narita, like other Japanese airports, is far from the city, the visitor will not dare to take a taxi that could cost over ¥24,000 (about $200 depending on the exchange rate of the day) for the trip. So if friends or his company contact have not sent a car for him, he must fight his way through a milling crowd to a counter at the back of the terminal where he can buy a ticket for ¥2,700 (about $21) on the "limousine bus" bound for various hotels or the Tokyo City Air Terminal. Depending on traffic and the location of the hotel, the journey may take 1½ to 2 hours. If the traveler has to go on to a provincial city, he must change terminals to catch a domestic flight. Connections are poorly timed, because most regional airports, by bureaucratic design, support few international flights or none at all.

While making international travel inconvenient and unpleasant, the Ministry of Transportation has worked steadfastly in other, more telling ways to keep the Japanese from traveling to or spending in foreign lands. Until 1963, the law actually forbade foreign vacations to Japanese citizens. Since then, official pricing guidelines have discouraged travel by frequently forcing the Japanese to pay twice the fare they would be charged if they could buy tickets outside of Japan. Ministry rules also have long restricted the seat capacity in tourist sections on international flights, limited landing rights, restricted the number of international airports allowed in the provinces, and the number of flights overall.[71] At the height of Japan's boom in the late 1980s, for example, the bureaucrats still limited Osaka's new international airport to one runway because, they said, Japan could not "afford more than one."[72] The world's ample supply of intrepid Japanese tourists raises the question of how many more there might have been, and how much more they might have spent abroad, if Japanese regulations, prices, and facilities were as accommodating as in Western nations. While the Japanese tourist is burdened with such hurdles, commerce, as always, has received assistance from the regulators. The civil servants have seen to it that flights have ample business class seats to accommodate the Tokyo financiers and industrialists, and, in contrast to Western airports, cargo planes have never had trouble getting runway slots, even at the busiest times. For years Tokyo's Narita Airport has been rated as the world's biggest cargo airport.[73]

Along with air travel, Japan's complex real estate laws and regulations have contributed to the campaign restricting individual consumption while freeing up financial and economic resources for industry. The regulators set out to make real estate transactions irksome and expensive. Even after ten years of declining real estate prices from the boom days of the late 1980s, the rules have managed to keep the cost of housing in Japan higher relative to people's means than almost anywhere else in the world. Recent studies have pegged Japanese housing prices at over seven times the average worker's annual pay, which is more than twice the ratio in the United States.[74] Such an expense has required tremendous savings on the part of any would-be Japanese homeowner. The system has increased the amount of savings needed even more, by denying would-be Japanese homeowners the flexible mortgage vehicles commonly available in other countries. After purchasing a home, the huge initial outlay leaves people with little to spend on consumer items, both inexpensive domestically produced items and luxury imports. If an individual gives up on purchasing and chooses to rent instead, the regulations conspire to keep the cost of even small spaces high enough so that the renter has little income left for other consumption, at least when compared with Western counterparts. Official economic statistics may count spending for rent as consumption, but it is a kind that the bureaucracy has happily permitted, because it does not compete for the economic resources that go into industrial development, growth, and exportation.

Official efforts to keep the price of housing high have centered around a series of laws and regulations that deliberately limit the supply of residential property in this already space-deprived nation. The effort has gone so far as to zone land for agriculture within city limits that in any other nation would be used to support suburban development or high-rise apartment blocks. A tourist can easily spot small farmer plots right in Tokyo neighborhoods and some rather large fields among the fast-food stops, gas stations, and hotels that line the route between downtown Tokyo and Narita airport. Beyond zoning, the bureaucracy has ensured that land will remain agricultural by giving farm owners an almost complete tax exemption. Any effort to switch from growing cabbages, cucumbers, and rice to building apartments would impose on the owner a huge tax penalty, the prospect of which has dissuaded many potential developers. The law has also blocked farmers and small homeowners from selling out to developers by levying a tax of up to 96 percent on any capital gains.[75] To reinforce this pattern of intentionally inefficient residential land use further, Japan has continually supported a 1941 law that limits landlords' ability to raise rents and terminate leases.[76] This has worked just as rent control in New York City has, encouraging long-term tenants to stay in low-rent apartments that are larger than they need, forcing up rents on the remaining available space, and discouraging developers from constructing new residential rental units.

Beyond the constraining impact of high rent on consumption, the cost of housing also has cut spending by forcing families into tiny spaces. With less space, they consume less energy and have less room for consumer items, particularly larger import items, such as General Electric refrigerators. But the official drive to discourage consumer spending has gone beyond even this. As with air travel and real estate, Japan's bureaucracy has also structured retail trade to keep the cost of the good life unaffordably high, particularly when imports are involved.

The primary means by which bureaucrats have restrained retail spending is the *Daitenho* or Large-Scale Retail Store Law. The law, when first passed in 1956, required special MITI approval for any store with floor space of over 500 square meters (5,380 square feet)—space that would fail to accommodate a moderate-sized suburban American supermarket or even the standard Gap store in a typical American mall.[77] *Daitenho* has undergone some amendment over the years and has eased a lot more recently, but generally it has kept per capita retail shelf space in Japan down to half of America's, a difference not explained by the relative sizes of the countries.[78] Of course, Tokyo's lavish department stores are the exceptions. But any visit to a suburban or working-class neighborhood shows the law's effect. Shopping there can only be described as inconvenient, unpleasant, and, because many goods frequently are not available, frustrating. That in itself has discouraged spending, but the law has suppressed consumption still further by effectively keeping out the sort of large, efficient retailers who have encouraged consumer spending in America and Europe by offering low prices and wide selections. Although the situation is beginning to change, the law still impedes the growth of retail establishments that sell in volume sufficient to make sourcing with imports feasible, at least on a scale comparable with the West.

The constriction of retail trade seems like a small thing, but it has had a major impact. Whereas Japanese wholesalers and manufacturers have bought and sold at prices competitive with those in the rest of the world for years,

Japanese retail prices have remained higher than in other nations, even considering Japanese manufacturing costs or the fluctuations of currency values.[79]
Personal computers, for example, including Japanese-made ones, retail for 50
to 100 percent more in Tokyo and Osaka stores than in New York or Chicago.
Clothing, shirts, ties, skirts, blouses, men's suits, and inexpensive off-the-rack
items, cost two-to-three times as much in Tokyo as in New York. The difference in the cost of groceries, in particular, stands out. Many travelers to Japan
mention $40 melons. It is not quite that bad—these prices prevail at specialty
shops in wealthy Tokyo districts only. But even in working-class neighborhoods, the prices are onerous. Rice, still the staple of the Japanese diet, costs
¥5,000 (about $40 at the average exchange rate of the last few years) for a ten-
kilo bag. Compare that with an average U.S. price of about $.79 per pound or
about $17.38 for that same ten-kilo bag. Apples in a working-class neighbor-
hood in Tokyo sell for ¥300 ($2.40) a kilo, while they cost closer to $.80 a
pound in Los Angeles, or about $1.76 a kilo. Milk in Tokyo suburbs sells for
¥170 ($1.36) a liter. In a typical U.S. suburb, it goes for $1.49 for a half gallon
or about $.70 a liter. Lettuce costs ¥300 ($2.40) a kilo in suburban Japan, compared with $.95 a pound in suburban America, or about $2.00 a kilo.[80]

In addition to keeping the cost of living high, Japan's official effort to
suppress consumption has included denying individuals options for borrowing. The lack of financing products has made it difficult to buy such big-ticket
items as cars, appliances, and furniture. Not only has this situation eliminated
the competition with industry for economic resources, it has also kept households from competing with business for credit. In fact, until the 1980s, the
average individual's ability to borrow or charge a purchase was extremely limited—credit cards, installment payments, even mortgages were rare. Indeed,
efforts in the late 1980s to introduce catalog sales into Japan were stymied
because so few consumers had credit cards or even checking accounts. Even
now, facilities for mortgage lending in Japan are restricted, extremely so by
American standards.[81] By limiting financial products, the Ministry of Finance
has circumscribed the options available to Japanese savers. Until the late
1980s, the best way for the Japanese to grow their savings, short of stock market speculation, was to rely on postal savings deposits. These paid little interest and effectively provided Japanese industries with ample amounts of inexpensive capital to finance their expansion and modernization plans. The
individual savers were compensated partly by tax breaks for small savings
accounts under what was called the *maruyu* system. In order to compensate
for the difference in the government budget, these individuals faced higher
general income tax rates or higher excise levies. Like so much else in Japan,

the net effect transferred wealth from households to industry. Business got cheap financial capital from individual savers who lent at low rates because they got a tax break, which they unknowingly financed themselves by paying higher taxes elsewhere. Even today, after some liberalization in Japanese financial markets, the system gives the individual saver or borrower few financial options when compared with his American or European counterpart.

Not content with the effective suppression of consumption as a means to keep out imports, the civil service bureaucracy sought directly to limit imports and promote exports. Leading that effort was the long-standing policy of holding down the foreign exchange value of the yen. Keeping the yen cheap made Japanese goods less expensive to foreigners and foreign goods more dear to Japanese. As a result, Japanese consumers have lost the wide assortment of goods at attractive prices that their Western counterparts have enjoyed for a long time. To the planners at the MOF and MITI, that sacrifice is a small price to pay for the promotion of Japan's exports and industrial development, and thus Japanese economic power and independence. Beyond the cheap-yen policy, the civil service bureaucrats have set rules at all levels to achieve their goal of directly limiting imports, though (in typical Japanese fashion) they have avoided anything as obvious as erecting tariff walls to keep out imports. Such an act may have invited a direct attack from Japan's trading partners and the World Trade Organization. In fact, Japan can claim, with at least superficial justification, that when it comes to tariffs and such obvious trade restrictions, she is one of the most open economies on earth. Japan has never needed tariffs. She learned long ago how to keep out imports without such blunt instruments. In the nineteenth century, when Japan was forbidden by the Western powers to establish tariffs, one of her first finance ministers, Shigenobu Okuma, began to develop oblique means to block imports that have since become an art form. In that early phase, Japan experimented with subsidies for domestic import competitors, import licensing, and the imposition of high excise taxes that ostensibly did not discriminate between domestic and imported goods, but actually were aimed at areas where foreign products dominated.[82] Many of these practices have prevailed for much of the post-World War II period.

Sometimes actions to keep out imports seem almost petty. For example, with bureaucratic help, Japan Tobacco won regulations to have American cigarette brands placed out of consumers' line of vision in vending machines or on retail shelves.[83] With the organizing power of the bureaucrats, the entire anti-import effort can sometimes get pretty vicious. In 1993, American glass producers alleged that MITI organized Japanese glass producers to boycott any Japanese distributors who handled American glass.[84] While this allegation was never proven, it is nonetheless indicative of tactics available to Japan's civil servants. Even the seemingly bumbling chaos among bureaucrats, when foreign firms seek to gain access to the Japanese consumer, has served the purpose of keeping out imports, or at least delaying them and making the effort expensive for the foreign firm. Eamonn Fingleton, long-time Japan-watcher, has told the story of an American healthcare company that checked with twenty-six different Japanese agencies on labeling for one of its products. All approved of what they saw or at least did not object. But as soon as sales started, the Ministry of Health and Welfare stopped them, pointing out that it was against Japanese regulations to have the American parent company's name on the label. The ploy made the whole sales effort much more expensive for the American firm than if the Ministry had made the rule known earlier. It was a more effective way of discouraging the whole venture than straightforward resistance.

Although each of these bureaucratic rules and maneuvers alone seems like a matter of minor concern, taken together, they have shaped Japan's economy. In this system, the civil service bureaucracy has achieved the goals that it set for itself in response to former Prime Minister Yoshida's challenge. The economy has grown rapidly around manufacturing and export. This success, combined with the tremendous focus of Japan's central direction, has unnerved many Western observers. Not too long ago it created in some a sense of awe mingled with fear for Western economies with their seemingly less effective and unfocused free market biases. The title of Eamonn Fingleton's book, *Blindside: Why Japan Is Still on Track to Overtake the U.S. by the Year 2000,* speaks to this fear, as do countless articles, broadcasts, and focus groups. While recent setbacks in Asia have quieted Western anxieties, the Japanese began to suffer increasing doubt about the efficacy of their system and its priorities, even when Western fears were most acute. There is good reason for these doubts. As Japan's economy has matured and markets have become more global, notions of national economic power and independence have become ambiguous. The long-term focus on exports might have succeeded in securing Japan's independence from foreign suppliers, but it has just as surely made her dependent on foreign consumers and the economic policies of the nations where those customers reside. Perhaps the disproportionate pessimism and almost apocalyptic response to the Kobe earthquake speak to a subliminal recognition of these ambiguities, and to doubts about the nation's prospects if Japan continues into the future wedded to the practices and priorities of the last fifty-plus years.

THREE

THE BREAKDOWN OF OLD WAYS

For all the generalized sense of loss associated with the Kobe quake and other events of 1995, the problems with Japan's established system have definite roots in two longer-term, fundamental trends: the maturation of her economy and the globalization of markets. The former has slowed the underlying pace of economic advancement, a major problem for Japan's growth-based system. The latter has rendered Japan vulnerable to uncontrollable and unpredictable influences from the rest of the world. These trends have made economic and financial planning more complex and far less certain than they once were, both for business and for the country's directing bureaucrats. Priorities, once clear, have become confused and control mechanisms bedeviled. All are significant problems for Japan's centrally directed system. Though the pressure from these trends has built gradually over time, they seem to have reached a critical mass in the seemingly intractable economic and financial difficulties that have beset Japan throughout the 1990s, and more recently, hit other Asian nations that had consciously imitated Japan's "way." These setbacks have rocked Japanese confidence as powerfully as the Great Hanshin Earthquake rocked Kobe, slapping down a former complacency and forcefully bringing home the message of deep-seated problems with the old system. As the Japanese have awakened to the adverse underlying trends, they have begun to change their ways of thinking and to deconstruct the old system that once seemed so secure and so durable.

FINANCIAL CRISIS, RECESSION, AND LONG-TERM PRESSURES REVEALED

Japan's financial crisis has all the hallmarks of a major turning point for the country. Its closest Western parallel is the 1929 stock market crash in the United States and the banking failures of the early 1930s at the beginning of the Great Depression. Japanese stocks fell by almost half in only nine months following their peak late in 1989. They then declined another 40 percent into mid-1998.[1] These losses combined are equivalent to a drop of over 6,500 points on the New York Stock Exchange's Dow Jones Index. By late 1993, the price of commercial property in Tokyo had dropped more than 50 percent from its highest peak of the cycle in 1989, and in the succeeding five years fell another 30-plus percent.[2] According to the Organization for Economic Cooperation and Development (OECD), the Paris-based think tank of the world's developed nations, the loss of wealth from these stock and real estate crashes was huge, estimated at over ¥900 trillion (about $7 trillion at the average exchange rate during the time). That equals two times Japan's overall annual GDP of 1998.[3] To date, neither market, stock or real estate, has begun to recover the lost ground in earnest.

Most threatening to Japan's economic and financial health is what these losses did to her banks' balance sheets. Because Japanese bankers had invested freely in equities and real estate, their capital base and that of the whole financial system shrank as these markets fell. (This would be impossible in the West, because regulators prohibit banks from investing their own capital in stocks.) And because the banks and other financial institutions had lent freely to others who secured their debts with inflated stock and land values, the market crashes destroyed the collateral, which backed much of their lending as well. Both events just about bankrupted the entire system. Even the official announcements reveal a banking disaster far beyond the scale of the savings and loan crisis in the United States during the late 1980s. In 1998, Japanese regulators estimated the value of "nonperforming" loans (those significantly delinquent) at around ¥75 trillion (about $600 billion at the average exchange rates of the late 1990s) or about 12 percent of all bank lending.[4] But official estimates in such situations are always conservative. These figures fail to include the bad debt held by financial institutions other than banks, or other questionable bank loans. Private analysts have calculated all such shaky loans at more than two or three times the government figure. If these private estimates are accurate, then the adverse environment places more than 30 percent of Japanese bank lending in jeopardy.[5]

As if to underscore the significance of Japan's economic and financial setbacks, the economies of Korea and the Southeast Asian nations—all imitators of Japan's system—followed Japan with financial crises and economic troubles of their own. In the late 1990s, stock markets plummeted in Indonesia, Thailand, Malaysia, Korea, the Philippines, and other once unbeatable economies. Just as in Japan, inflated real estate values fell along with the price of stocks. Currencies of these Asian states plunged against the U.S. dollar, European units, and, of course, the yen. Firms saw their profits shrink, in many cases into the red. Companies closed their doors. People were laid off. Some nations saw rioting and a change of government. Economies that had experienced tremendous growth rates slowed and fell into recession. The Japanese, especially the banks, had huge interests in these countries, and so saw their burdens of bad loans compounded. The whole effect greatly complicated Japan's efforts to refurbish and strengthen her financial sector, and it has heightened concerns that immediate problems have links to more fundamental inadequacies in Japan's system.

The link between these immediate economic and financial setbacks and more fundamental influences is most evident in the role played by economic illusions in creating today's problems. People simply and incorrectly believed in the power of the Japanese system to protect the economy from all adversity. Effectively, those involved felt that the system made them immune to economic cycles and to the natural tendency for economies to slow as they develop into maturity. They also felt sheltered from the fluctuations that typically affect economies as they become prominent in global trade and financial dealings. Under the influence of these illusions, the Japanese and their Asian imitators felt no need to implement the safeguards in lending and investing that are common elsewhere in the world. Typically, in the mature economies of the West, businesspeople and bankers make contingency plans for the economic slowdowns, recessions, or shocks from the global market that are an integral part of mature, globalized economies. But believing that the Japanese system could continue to deliver rapid growth indefinitely and that the Iron Triangle could support economically unjustifiable structures, Japan and her Asian imitators developed plans and lent money without either seeking safeguards or asking questions about economic viability. Official assurances of support inadvertently encouraged irresponsible behavior among lenders and borrowers, a circumstance that the financial community refers to as a "moral hazard."

Having exposed themselves in this way, the Japanese faced a cascade of problems when the effects of economic maturation and globalization began to show that their assumptions were wrong.

It is easy to see how such dangerous attitudes developed. For years Japan's system had created rapid, steady economic growth and increasing levels of wealth. During the thirty years prior to the start of Japan's economic downturn in the early 1990s, the country had enjoyed remarkable economic success, unrivaled in the industrialized world and without interruption. Her real gross domestic product (GDP) grew at the stunningly rapid rate of 4.5 percent a year.[6] The country suffered only five quarters in which the economy failed to grow, and only one instance when a period of contraction extended beyond three months. Although the yen increased in value during this time against all major currencies, including a whopping 60 percent against the U.S. dollar, Japanese exporters adjusted to keep exports leading the economy's advance. By comparison, during this time the United States, despite its faster rate of population growth, increased its real GDP by only 3.1 percent a year and suffered sixteen quarters of contraction off and on, with the longest stretch of decline extending for almost a year.[7] During the glory days of Japan's seemingly endless economic surge, investors, both domestic and foreign, bought Japanese real estate and equity shares in order to participate in what they believed was the country's unmatched growth potential and promising financial returns. In the 1980s, that buying drove up prices on the Tokyo Stock Exchange at the fantastic rate of 20 percent a year, much more than the rate at which the economy itself grew. In just the two-year stretch from December 1987 to December 1989, the value of Japanese shares soared by more than 90 percent.[8] Real estate, particularly in Tokyo, followed the same pattern, rising rapidly and selling at astronomical levels.

While it lasted, investors got rich fast. They exuded the confidence and arrogance that typically accompanies the acquisition of such wealth. This was a time when Setsuya Tabuchi, former Chairman of Nomura Securities, pointed out, without exaggeration, that in the fashionable Akasaka ward of Tokyo, a piece of land no bigger than a newspaper page sold for the equivalent of $30,000. He boasted that the value of the Imperial Palace in Tokyo exceeded the value of all the real estate in California combined, and that the value of all the land in Japan equaled two times the value of all real estate in the United States plus the market value of all the stocks on the New York Stock Exchange.[9] He spoke the truth, but in hindsight it is obvious how ridiculous and unsustainable this pricing situation was. In the late 1980s, stocks on the Nikkei Index (Japan's equivalent of the Dow Jones Industrial Average) reached such high prices that it would have taken Japanese industry more than seventy years to buy them back, even if all the peak year's earnings of these companies were devoted to that purpose every year.[10] Clearly, nobody expected to wait this long for returns. They counted on rapid growth to boost earnings sufficiently to produce the payback a lot sooner. (It is worth noting for the sake of comparison that stocks in the United States, at the market's most euphoric, reached prices that would have taken corporate America twenty-eight years to purchase.)[11]

But in the early 1990s, when the first signs of an economic slowdown belied the assumptions on which all these valuations were based, the pricing, lending, and wealth patterns quickly unraveled. Japan found herself in a financial crisis. Actually, the recessionary news that broke these delusions was rather mild by Western standards. The economy began to slow after 1989, peaked again in 1992, and then began an erratic decline that by 1995 had brought the country's real GDP down by only 1.5 percent, which is less than the average American recession of the last thirty years and the mild dip in the U.S. economy in the early 1990s.[12, 13] To be sure, Japan remained mired in a stagnant economic situation through the late 1990s, but it took years for the unemployment rate to rise to above 4 percent of the existing labor force. Admittedly, that figure was well up from the start of the recession, but it was still below unemployment rates in America and especially Europe, even after years of economic growth.[14] The economic setbacks were hardly pleasant, but they were far less severe than what the United States, Great Britain, and Continental Europe were accustomed to suffering from time to time. Still, having previously deluded themselves, the Japanese were shocked by their initial recession and then by their economy's failure to respond, as it once did, to efforts by the government to promote a recovery through public works spending and to the Bank of Japan's decision to cut short-term interest rates to less than 1 percent.[15]

It is this strange combination of financial havoc and a mild, if elongated, recession that points so clearly to the illusions behind the system and its deeper underlying problems. If Japan had suffered her financial crisis because of another oil embargo or perhaps a crash in foreign markets, these problems would be easily explained. Her people could have borne the hardship without doubts, as an unfortunate but unavoidable outgrowth of other people's problems. If some extraordinary disaster had set the economy back, the Japanese simply would have steeled themselves to the task of rebuilding as they have so many times in the past. But this simple recession has no such origin. It appears to have emerged organically as a natural evolution of Japan's domestic economy. It is not a disaster; it is just difficult. Yet her financial arrangements have all but fallen apart. A nation's financial structure should stand up better to the normal ups and downs of its own economy's cycles. Even the "PKO," or price-keeping operations of the Ministry of Finance and the Bank of Japan, failed to help. In the past, these official programs to pressure institutions into buying financial instruments—stocks, bonds, currencies—have stabilized prices in decline. One such operation even stopped the global slide in stock prices in October 1987, an event about which the MOF boasted with some volume. Now, the extreme financial strain and inability to rectify this straightforward economic situation indicate that things have changed fundamentally. They point to a basic fragility in Japan's "way" and to the fallacy of its assumptions. The setbacks have revealed that Japan, like any other nation, will see a slower pace of economic growth as her economy matures. It is also clear that Japan is as vulnerable as any to the increased competition from a more globalized economic environment. It is now quite obvious that the system is poorly suited to the future.

Even though the forces of economic maturation and globalization have developed over years, an awareness of them has come only now, because previously the Japanese and their civil service bureaucrats could always excuse them away. The 1970s, for instance, offered the major distraction of the energy crisis. When the globalization and maturation trends began to slow the pace of economic growth and baffle the old practices of the Iron Triangle, the 1973 embargo by the Organization of Petroleum Exporting Countries (OPEC) and the oil price increases during the rest of the decade offered a plausible alternative explanation as to why the economy was behaving less robustly than it had in earlier years. Of course, the oil price pressures were real. They required considerable adjustment by Japan, which she made.[16] Actually, responding to the energy crisis was a cinch for Japan's system. Central direction coped well with the single focus of the trouble, while the atmosphere of emergency galvanized the people to the required extra effort. So the crisis excused both policy makers and the Japanese people from the need to question their "way." When the oil distractions disappeared in the 1980s, the great stock price and real estate boom served as another ready distraction from the underlying forces. Everyone seemed to be getting rich so fast that Japan appeared immune to normal economic laws. Few bothered to look at the signs of economic slowdown or the growing impact of international capital flows and global competition, especially from elsewhere in Asia. But with the recession and financial crisis in the 1990s, it became impossible to hide from the fact that these well-established trends were bringing fundamental change to Japan, just as they have elsewhere.

UNDERMINING OLD CONTROLS AND BIASES

Each nation's economy matures and reacts to globalization differently, depending on its relative strengths, endowments, geography, and history. While the necessary adjustments are invariably painful, they have proven particularly difficult for Japan because they have completely disrupted the conditions on which she built her postwar economic miracle. To be sure, much of what created Japan's tremendous growth remains. The Japanese are still hard working, diligent, thrifty, intelligent, dutiful, and possessed of what some describe as a "will to win."[17] These qualities have contributed to her great economic and national success and promise to continue to do so. But Japan's fabulous past success owes much to a unique set of circumstances: the particular nature of her underdevelopment in the decades following the war, a clear model for fruitful investment, and a cheap currency that sheltered the domestic economy from the vicissitudes of world markets. She set up an ingenious system to exploit these conditions. The system still exists, but the conditions do not.

In the late 1940s, when Japanese leadership decided to focus single-mindedly on economic growth, they saw a clear means to that end. The country had a well-educated and disciplined workforce but a dearth of factory space, machinery, roads, rail links, ports, and telecommunications—in short, no industrial infrastructure. By suppressing consumption and emphasizing private and public investment in these needed facilities, Japan's system marshaled its resources to supply her impressive workforce with the infrastructure it needed. During that same early period, Japan had the added benefit of a tested model for growth: the Western economies, especially the United States. She used these more developed economies as a guide for: how to invest, what technologies were most effective, what products provided the best returns, and where world markets were taking product development. The centralized nature of the system enabled it to exploit this information through the close cooperation of business and the bureaucracy of the Iron Triangle. Because at the time her people were desperately poor, they willingly supported the growth-at-all costs approach, despite its anticonsumer bias.

Also in these early, heady days, Japan had shelter from foreign disruptions. There were, of course, the defense guarantees offered by the United States, but more importantly, Japan had the cheap yen. In the late 1940s, the

American occupation set the exchange rate for the yen at ¥360 to the dollar.[18] Because Japan had so much less to offer the world commercially than did America, a share in Japan (which is what a unit of currency basically represents) was, at that time, fairly discounted against the dollar. But as Japan developed and was able to offer so much more, the yen became more valuable. Yet the exchange rate remained constant, as did all exchange rates under the Bretton Woods international monetary agreements, which gave currency stability to the postwar world. In short order, perhaps even by the 1950s, the yen became severely undervalued given the economic realities. The cheap yen provided a great advantage to Japanese trade. It held down the price of Japanese exports, prompting the world to do much of its shopping in Japan. It made imports dear, prompting the Japanese to do little buying outside the domestic market, except for raw materials needed by Japanese industry. The yen became very undervalued, in time making Japanese goods so competitively priced that buying from Japan was where foreigners began and the last place foreigners cut back in hard times. Japanese exports grew steadily, despite the various recessions and booms elsewhere in the world.[19]

Sheltered from global competition and armed with a domestic growth strategy superbly attuned to her circumstances, Japan grew at a legendary pace in the postwar years. By 1970, she had become a first-class industrial power and had just about caught up with the West. Her economy was already the third largest on earth after the United States and the Soviet Union. Her per capita income approached that of Western Europe and her manufacturing might was evident (see Table 3.1). Japan's foreign trade balance had shifted from deficit to surplus by the mid-1960s, and by 1970, she built that surplus up to an impressive 11 percent of GDP. By the late 1980s, there could be no doubt that she had developed into a full-fledged industrial power. Her economy was second only to the United States. By 1990 the value of Japan's manufacturing output had grown to within 17 percent of America's, and her per capita income exceeded America's by almost 10 percent. Her trade surplus had expanded to an impressive ¥3.1 trillion ($22.5 billion at the exchange rate of the day).[20]

Ironically, it is the system's success that has undermined its future effectiveness. Development stole the very means by which Japan's "way" delivered rapid expansion in the first place. Past advances in the economy issued directly from the system's ability to provide the country's eager workers with the much-needed tools of industry. This contributed both to absolute industrial capacity and to each worker's productivity. But economic development erased this once dire need for productive capital. The system had so suppressed consumption and encouraged spending on factories and machinery that in the

TABLE 3.1
A COMPARISON BETWEEN JAPAN
AND OTHER DEVELOPED ECONOMIES

	GDP ($ Billions)				*Per Capita GDP ($)*			
	1960	*1970*	*1980*	*1990*	*1960*	*1970*	*1980*	*1990*
Japan	44.5	203.7	1,059.3	2,932.1	473	1,953	9,069	23,742
United States	514.7	1,011.6	2,708.1	5,489.6	2,848	4,932	11,888	21,967
United Kingdom	72.4	123.9	537.4	975.5	1,382	2,228	9,545	16,995
Germany	72.1	184.5	809.9	1,501.5	992	2,375	10,344	18,911

	Manufacture Output ($ Billions)			
	1960	*1970*	*1980*	*1990*
Japan	15.4	73.3	309.7	852.6
United States	103.5	242.6	593.0	1,032.1
United Kingdom	22.9	35.6	125.8	201.3
Germany	n/a	184.5	n/a	789.3

Sources: International Monetary Fund, *International Financial Statistics*, 1996 and earlier years. World Bank, *World Development Report*, 1996.

1950s and 1960s Japan invested around 30 percent of GDP a year in capital goods.[21] By the early 1990s, the accumulated capital—the stock of factories and machinery—stood at a higher level relative to the nation's labor force or business sales than in any other country in the world.[22] As the scarcity of equipment and infrastructure turned into abundance and then surfeit, the system's strong bias toward spending on equipment and industrial infrastructure lost touch with Japanese reality. Subsequent investments in machinery and infrastructure did less and less each year to increase output and enhance productivity. In response, the underlying pace of economic growth slowed, and returns on investment fell back toward levels available in other nations (see Table 3.2, p. 44). Without acknowledging the underlying trends explicitly, Japanese government statisticians bowed to observed reality and reduced their estimates of the economy's real growth potential from 8 percent in the 1950s and 1960s, to 6 percent in the 1970s, to 4 percent in the mid-1980s, and to 3.5 percent more recently.[23] Some private analysts put the economy's current growth potential at the low figure of only 2 percent.[24] (Potential growth in the United States is generally estimated at between 2 and 2.5 percent.)[25]

TABLE 3.2
SIGNS OF ECONOMIC MATURATION

	1955–64	1965–74	1975–84	1985–94
Japan				
Real GDP growth[a]	9.5	7.7	3.9	3.0
Productivity growth[b]	8.7	9.1	4.3	3.5
Economic return on investment[c]	46.3	23.9	13.7	9.7
United States				
Real GDP growth[a]	4.1	2.8	2.8	2.4
Productivity growth[b]	5.8	3.1	2.8	2.2
Economic return on investment[c]	31.4	18.9	19.7	17.2
Germany				
Real GDP growth[a]	4.8	3.1	2.2	2.5
Productivity growth[b]	6.1	5.3	3.0	2.3
Economic return on investment[c]	n/a	n/a	n/a	n/a
United Kingdom				
Real GDP growth[a]	3.3	2.2	1.9	2.3
Productivity growth[b]	3.4	3.6	3.4	4.1
Economic return on investment[c]	31.6	17.7	17.2	19.0

[a] GDP percent growth after removing the effects of inflation, expressed at an annual rate.
[b] Percent growth in output per man-hour in manufacturing, expressed at an annual rate.
[c] Increment to economic growth per unit of investment, average for the period.

Sources: International Monetary Fund, *International Financial Statistics*, 1996 and earlier years. McGraw-Hill, Data Resources Data Base; Council of Economic Advisors, *Economic Report of the President*, 1996.

The economy's maturation has also diminished the former responsiveness to public spending initiatives by which the system's masters in the Iron Triangle once so effectively guided it. Early on, Japan's aching need for an industrial infrastructure gave the government great leverage over the economy. A little additional money spent on rail links, ports, or power facilities generated a dramatic surge in productivity and economic growth, while a small cutback cooled the economy considerably. But as increased levels of economic development created an abundance of plant, equipment, and infrastructure, a little more or less meant less to the economy's performance either way. The lost effectiveness of the old government spending lever became painfully apparent during efforts to battle the recession and the sluggish economy in the 1990s. Japanese authorities, true to their old patterns, promoted several special spending packages on public works to combat the economic difficulties. These efforts cumulated over time to a huge amount, exceeding 15 percent of the country's annual GDP.[26] The packages added to the annual budget deficit, running it up, by some measures, above 8 percent of GDP.[27] Yet, for all the spending and the strain on government finances, the mature state of development had so reduced the impact of such outlays that the economy hardly responded. Eventually, the Ministry of Finance, frustrated by the failures of the old ways, allowed an income tax cut to help stimulate the economy. The bureaucrats resisted this measure because it further undermined the old system. Income tax cuts benefit individuals and promote consumption, both of which are contrary to the system's long-standing anticonsumer, pro-capital spending bias. Furthermore, tax cuts decrease bureaucratic power by rendering their tax incentives less attractive and by shifting control over income and spending from the government to individuals and businesses. Yet they were forced to yield because the old spending levers were failing.

The surfeit of capital equipment that is part of Japan's economic maturation has torn at other seams in the old system by pitting business against the bureaucracy. Despite the capital surplus, the bureaucracy has stuck to the old approach and continued to pressure firms to spend on plant and equipment. The bureaucrats have pressed the issue especially hard in the 1990s in an effort to move the economy out of recession and stagnation. But the already existing surfeit of capital equipment and structures gave the companies little to invest in improving productivity. They came to see the waste in it and the danger to their income statements. They began to balk at bureaucratic urgings, and began to make dramatic cutbacks. Although investment in plant and equipment has remained higher than in the West, the pace in the 1990s has dropped considerably from the 30 percent or more of GDP in the old days.[28]

The slowdown in capital spending by businesses has undermined the old system still further by removing an important financial prop from the scheme of bureaucratic control. In the early days, businesses spent all their profits, and then some, to support the nation's fantastic rate of capital spending. This left Japanese industry dependent on credit from Japanese banks and highly vulnerable to the agenda of the bureaucracy, which of course, controlled the flow of credit from the banks. But by the 1990s, as economic maturation removed the need for such heavy capital spending, Japanese companies were able to curtail such outlays and generate surplus cash flows. Their profit growth slowed, but their capital spending slowed even more. By 1990 earnings, which during the strong-growth period of the 1960s covered only 60 percent of corporate spending needs, exceeded such needs by some 10 percent.[29] Japanese businesses became net savers. They began to pay off bank loans. Companies used the surplus profits to increase their equity stakes in their own operations. Between 1980 and 1990, for instance, companies' equity holdings as a percentage of overall capital (including long-term debt) rose by 33.6 percent overall, and in manufacturing, it rose by 58.5 percent.[30] Companies grew less and less dependent on bureaucratic allocations of credit. Concurrently, and like so many other democracies of the time, the Japanese government was coming under pressure to increase social spending, and so began to run budget deficits. As a borrower, the government became dependent on corporate capital surpluses. Her businesses began to feel the shift in relative power. Freer than ever from the ministries' control of credit, and determined to protect their new equity stakes, businesses became a lot less anxious to please civil servants than they once were. In the wonderfully understated words of the modern Japanese historian Takafusa Nakamura, business began to "resist administrative guidance."[31] News of overt resistance remains rare. The Iron Triangle has an interest in suppressing it. Yet certain stories, like the dispute between All Nippon Airways (ANA) and the Ministry of Transportation, have begun to emerge. ANA pushed aggressively for faster deregulation and in response the Ministry so severely chided ANA's management that President Seiji Fukatsu resigned in disgust.[32] So far, the bureaucrats have had their way, but Mr. Fukatsu's willingness to fight, and publicly declare his reasons for resigning, speaks to the new, less subservient mood in Japanese business circles.

At the same time, Japan's successful economic development and technological sophistication have thwarted the guidance system of the old approach as well. In the past, Japan could rely on the more advanced West, particularly the United States, to set the course for future development. Success emerged from massive, coordinated efforts along the clearly defined avenues effectively laid out by more developed nations abroad. But now, quite up to speed with the United States in almost every aspect of business, technology, and product design, Japan has less to learn from Western technology. She has lost her old developmental pathfinder. Mere emulation has given way to the need for true innovation, and MITI (as well as the rest of the bureaucracy) has had to grope in the dark, along with the rest of the developed world, to determine the next developmental step. Bureaucratic leaders have lost the easy basis on which they once, with a fair measure of certainty, could marshal the nation's resources behind tried and true developmental plans, thereby delivering a succession of technological fillips to Japanese productivity and overall economic growth. This loss has taken from the bureaucrats the instrument of their earlier prescience, and with it the people's confidence in their authority.

MITI has shown some awareness of the altered situation by increasing industrial and scientific research. In the years since 1985, Japan has raised its public and private spending on pure research and development at a yearly rate of 15 to 16 percent. Though rising fast, the level of R&D spending is still below that of the United States, especially the government's share.[33] A recent survey by Japan's Science and Technology Agency shows the government's share of such spending in Japan at only 21.5 percent compared with 36.1 percent in the United States and 37.2 percent in Germany. Some of this difference has to do with Japan's relative lack of defense spending. But much of it, according to Toshio Ochiai, Director General of the Science and Technology Agency's planning bureau, has to do with the lingering effect of relying on the West to provide the "seeds" of new technology. Identifying this strategy as "obsolete" now that Japan has caught up with her old pathfinders, Mr. Ochiai and his colleagues have urged the bureaucracy to enlarge its research role and have received encouragement.[34] But even if the ministries respond by bringing the figures up to American or German levels or even higher, the fullest research effort may not guarantee the returns that their diligent imitation of the West once did. Independent research risks many more dead ends and failures than does observing a leader's clear path to success.

Meanwhile, this whole technology issue and Japan's overall development have begun to chip away at the old system's rationale for centralization. Under the old approach, the bureaucrats could orchestrate a coordinated effort based on successful models from abroad. But with home-grown research and innovation, Japan will require a diversity of effort, where many people and firms experiment with different technologies, innovations, and product designs. This broad and eclectic effort does not lend itself to the orchestration and coordination of the old centralized system. Instead of top-down bureaucratic direction, Japan will need people and companies who are willing to take business risks without the government support and assurances offered in the past. In effect, Japan will have to reverse her decades-old practice of excluding and discouraging entrepreneurs and risktakers from power in order to foster harmonious cooperation. Instead, she will need their willingness to experiment with new products and uncertain business ventures. Such people and firms are not likely to support a "way" based on centralized bureaucratic direction. Indeed, one is anathema to the other.

Similarly, Japan's developmental and economic maturation has soured the public's attitude toward centralized bureaucratic direction. As the Japanese grew richer, they began to value a wider diversity of objectives than they

did in the past, when poverty and humiliation made catching up with the West
an overriding concern. New and different desires and values have muddled the
old, clear priorities. Loyalty to the system and acquiescence to its direction
have become less palatable to the country's ever more sophisticated and well-
traveled citizenry. People have chafed at centralized direction and become less
supportive of the old single-minded growth agenda. It is not simply a case of
wealth bringing a desire for more leisure and earlier retirement, though Japan
has seen a rise in this as well. As they have seen the nation gain great economic
strength, the Japanese people have begun to advocate spending less on industrial development and more on pollution controls, parks, and the arts. They
also have advocated tax cuts in order to give individuals more control over
their own incomes. As this change gains momentum, it will, of course, further
promote the new diversity.

While these myriad issues and effects of the economy's maturation have
weakened the old system, so too, has the relentless march of globalization. As
useful as it once was to Japan to shield herself from the outside world, it was
a foregone conclusion that she could not carry on with it indefinitely. The first
signs of globalization were evident early on via the currency. In August 1971,
the wall to the world that her cheap yen had provided began to fall when President Nixon abolished the gold convertibility of the dollar. For the first time
in over a quarter-century, since the signing of the postwar Bretton Woods
agreements, international currency values were free to fluctuate. The yen
moved both up and down, but over the long haul gained relative value against
other currencies. With each step up against the dollar, the rising yen removed
more and more of the old cushion between Japan's domestic economy and the
economic actions and policies of other nations. Appreciating from ¥315 to the
dollar in 1970 to ¥135 to the dollar in 1990, the yen's rise continued through
the mid-1990s, not only against the dollar but against other currencies as well.
Over these thirty years, the yen appreciated 65 percent against the U.S. dollar,
73 percent against sterling, and 34 percent against the deutschemark.[35] Even
the short-lived weakness of the yen in the late 1990s did little to reverse these
long-term advances. At least in this one crucial way, the world had intruded
on Japan's economy and its financial markets. Her policy makers could no
longer pursue their pro-growth, pro-export agenda without considering conditions in other economies and other markets.

Attempts to regulate the yen against other currencies have taught both
the Ministry of Finance and the Bank of Japan a tough lesson about the ability of globalization to diminish control over the domestic economy. It hit home
in the wake of the Plaza Accord of 1985. So called because it was made by

world bankers at New York's Plaza Hotel, the agreement decreased the foreign exchange value of the dollar. When news of the Accord reached foreign exchange markets, the yen began to rise fast—too fast, in fact, for Japanese industry and exporters to compensate as they had in the past. True to the old system, the Bank of Japan and the Ministry of Finance worried about the effect of the currency shift on their pro-industry, pro-export agenda. They set out to stem the rise of the yen with an easy monetary policy that pumped money into Japanese financial markets and drove down interest rates from 5 percent in 1985 to 2.5 percent by 1988.[36] These officials hoped that by decreasing returns on yen deposits they could impel currency speculators to shift to other currencies, thus slowing or even reversing the yen's rise on foreign exchange markets. It worked for a while. The yen fell a little against the dollar between 1987 and 1989.[37] But the tremendous flow of liquidity needed to push interest rates down helped to foster the great surge in asset prices that ended in the severe banking crisis of the 1990s. Since no central banker anywhere in the world would allow such an asset bubble to develop if it could be avoided, the only conclusion to draw is that the Bank of Japan and the Ministry of Finance believed that the currency situation imposed on them by the outside world left them no choice. They settled on the evil of a financial bubble over the evil of a rising yen. The financial control they once enjoyed was lost.

More recently, aspects of globalization beyond currency fluctuations have thwarted bureaucratic control in Japan's old system. With the growth of electronic money transfers, the Internet, and global networks of firms, civil servants in Japan—and everywhere for that matter—have had difficulty determining exactly who or what they are regulating. The new technology is making it easier than ever for individuals and companies, inside and outside Japan, to use computer links to avoid the strict regulation on which Japan's system has relied. People and firms even avoid and evade taxes through these means. For a long time, firms of every nationality have used overseas offices to book profits selectively, choosing whatever site has offered the lowest tax rates. But with funds now moving instantaneously around the world, and the identification of where products and services are produced and sold becoming vague, the issues of what is taxed, who taxes it, and what is regulated have become difficult to administer. By cutting out banks and other financial intermediaries, the Internet and other electronic links have compounded problems for regulators, because they and tax collectors use such institutions to collect information on people and firms.

An exemplary story of cross-border transfers and the ability to avoid regulatory control comes from the Middle East, though it could have occurred anywhere. During Iraq's initial attack on Kuwait City, a Kuwaiti bank manager faxed his records to a subsidiary in Bahrain. The next morning the Bahraini institution opened with all the accounts, assets, and records that were in Kuwait on the previous day. The original customers and shareholders not only avoided Iraqi control, they also sidestepped the subsequent freeze by the United States on Kuwaiti assets.[38] While the exigencies of war are not always present, the pressures of business are. Japan has her own story of electronically circumventing official control. In 1994, the Japanese postal service raised first-class rates by 30 percent to ¥80 ($.72 at the exchange rate of the day) per letter. Japanese direct mailers noticed that Hong Kong could send a first-class letter to Japan for the equivalent of ¥30 ($.27), so they sent their sales material in bulk to Hong Kong, where it was sorted and sent back to Japan. Japanese postal authorities tried to regain control by banning bulk mailing to Hong Kong. The direct mailers responded by sending their material electronically to Hong Kong, where it was printed, sorted, and mailed to Japan.[39] Japan lost jobs, revenues, and control.

So far Japanese regulators are losing this fight, which explains their intense attention to the Internet. Richard Humphry of the Australian Stock Exchange described how in the new electronic age, national tax and regulatory schemes have become less a means of controlling business and fund flows and more of an opportunity for business and investment arbitrage by private firms.[40] The pattern clearly will continue to loosen control, and, through the pressures of this business arbitrage, force a convergence of different countries' tax and regulatory regimes. Though Japan's firms have come to this game late, they have reacted swiftly to the chance for escaping from their heavily regulated world. Until such capabilities became apparent, Japanese business had paid scant attention to networking software. Now, according to a recent study by IDC Japan, Japanese firms are increasing spending on personal computers and networking software at a rate of 15 to 30 percent a year, although other spending on information technology is growing more slowly.[41] As this process gains momentum around the world, it will force all economies to make adjustments to avoid losing business to countries with more accommodating tax and regulatory regimes. The greatest adjustment will, of course, fall on the more highly regulated economies, such as Japan's. Her system will suffer disproportionately.

It is ironic that in response to globalization and economic maturation the Japanese government has contributed greatly to weakening Japan's old system, no doubt unwittingly. The government's role in this began in the early 1980s, as huge increases in wealth from Japan's economic development drew public criticism of the single-minded, growth-at-all-costs character of the system. As in all other advanced democracies at the time, politicians responded by increasing social spending, which of course led to chronic budget deficits. These deficits came on top of debts incurred by Japan's extravagant spending to counter the energy crises of the 1970s. Between 1980 and 1990, before the recession even took hold, Japanese government deficits had added some ¥159.2 billion a year ($1.1 billion at the average exchange rate of the period) to the national debt.[42] As mentioned previously, the government became dependent on surplus corporate cash flows to finance the debt, which altered the power balance between government and companies and eroded the once overwhelming government advantage. In addition, because the deficit financing required a vast expansion of government bond issuance, Japan sought a means of selling those bonds more widely by floating issues in Europe. Between 1980 and 1990, yen issues on European markets grew by 32 percent, compared with an overall European market expansion of 16.7 percent.[43] To assist with the sale of government bonds, Japan also encouraged foreign bankers and dealers to enter Tokyo's market. For the first time in the 1980s, Japan issued licenses to foreigners to operate trust companies.

It all seemed very practical and mostly technical, but the implications for Japan's system of control were far-reaching. As the government became dependent on corporate funds and securities dealers to conduct its financial affairs, it also became ever more vulnerable to pressure from these firms. American and British bankers and brokers showed none of the compliant, accommodating characteristics of their Japanese colleagues. Unlike the members of the Iron Triangle, outsiders had no awareness of Japan's bureaucratic agenda, and if some did, they cared less about it than did the Japanese. The foreigners began to demand more open Japanese markets and more license to use new financial techniques and instruments. And because they helped with the government's finances, the Japanese regulators had to yield. For the first time since the end of World War II, control became a two-way street. At the same time, as foreign dealers thwarted bureaucratic power, Japan's involvement in the world's financial markets began to place her under tremendous pressure to abandon the arbitrary controls used by the Ministry of Finance and the Bank of Japan, and to harmonize her procedures and regulations with those of other countries. Japanese banks had to meet world standards on capital ratios and other financial measures that determine how much they set aside against different sorts of loans or deposits. As these international rules took an element of discretion from Japan's bureaucrats, their power suffered further erosion because the financial crisis of the 1990s forced her weakened banks to borrow and seek deposits from abroad. Once they were involved overseas, Japanese banks began to pay as much attention to foreign credit rating agencies as to their regulators in Tokyo. They started to insist that these bureaucrats consider the reactions of foreign credit agencies to their policies. As all these forces gained momentum over the 1990s, it has become difficult to determine who controlled whom.

THE DISINTEGRATION OF CUSTOMS

While undermining the Iron Triangle's once powerful system of control, all these pressures—the immediate ones of recession and financial loss and their root causes of economic maturation and globalization—have begun to break down long-standing Japanese customs and institutions. The cohesion within Japan's *keiretsu* families of firms has loosened noticeably, while Japan's famous system of lifetime employment and its corollary, the strict seniority system of promotion, have lost their hold on employees' and firms' loyalties. The complex web of Japan's wholesale and retail distribution systems, which America trade negotiators have complained about for years, has begun to come unstrung. These and other practices were once touted to be the basic difference between Japanese culture and that of the West, but it is becoming apparent that such claims were exaggerated.

The once-powerful cohesion in Japan's famous *keiretsu* groups of firms has begun to unravel for the same reason that companies have begun to resist the bureaucracy's "administrative guidance." From the beginning, the *keiretsu* formed one of the basic building blocks of Japan's centralized system. Descendants of the prewar industrial conglomerates (called *zaibatsu*), the *keiretsu,* usually led by a bank or major trading firm, have served as business' major link to the bureaucracy in the Iron Triangle. The firms within the family have held shares in one another, have tried to buy from one another, and, most importantly, have helped one another in troubled times. The *keiretsu* support relationships were vital in the early postwar period, when there was a great shortage of physical and financial capital and firms had nothing to fall back on when the going got tough. This kind of group insurance actually mirrored the overall Japanese system in miniature, with the senior companies in their *keiretsu* playing the role of the civil service bureaucrats, directing investment, determining the allocation capital and credit, rewarding cooperation, and punishing recalcitrance. But as the cutbacks in capital spending have enlarged the surplus cash flows of the stronger firms, they have acquired a greater measure of financial independence than in the past. Having more to lose, they have become less cooperative and less willing to put themselves at risk in the old mutual support system. Not surprisingly, they have begun refusing support to weaker members of their *keiretsu*. Although firms try to suppress news of such an un-Japanese failure to cooperate, the trend is evident nonetheless. Japan's Long-Term Credit Bank revealed not too long ago that, in order to protect its capital base, it would divest itself of shares in Japanese corporations.[44] At Matsushita Electric, the need to compete globally and to protect earnings has led this leader in the *keiretsu* to turn away from other members. Kazaburo Shikata, chairman of the subcontractors association within the *keiretsu*, revealed that Matsushita has sought better prices by shopping elsewhere so that other members of the *keiretsu* can no longer rely on Matsushita for business. A decade ago, the subcontractors' entire output was dedicated to Matsushita, now only half sells within the *keiretsu*.[45] Nissan Motor and Hitachi recently refused to help their *keiretsu* colleague, Nissan Life, and the insurer failed as a consequence.[46]

Relations between employers and employees, once the envy of the world, also seem to have broken down under the pressure. Slower growth, a need to bolster productivity, the intensity of global competition, and the desire to protect newfound corporate equity have all prompted companies to entertain what is popularly known in the West as "downsizing." Managements have reconsidered the viability of the Japanese custom of lifetime employment. At one time, the widely known and often admired practice of never firing or even laying off employees was a given in Japanese corporate life. It not only was easy to support in the previous decades, it was advantageous. Firms had little equity at risk, and all had confidence that the bureaucrats in control of the system could keep the economy growing rapidly without serious interruption. Lifetime employment was, in fact, the only rational response, because rapid growth often made it difficult for firms to find capable staff, or any staff at all for that matter. Between the late 1950s and the early 1990s, job markets in Japan were so tight that statisticians gave short shrift to the unemployment statistics watched so closely in the West. They developed a uniquely Japanese measure that compared the number of job offerings with the number of job seekers. Through much of the country's long period of rapid growth, offerings usually exceeded seekers, sometimes by as much as 40 percent.[47] In that environment, companies saw no gain in letting workers go, even during brief economic slowdowns. History and faith in the system had convinced them that the periods of bad business would pass quickly and that good workers would be scarce when business picked up again. Even a nearly incompetent employee was better kept on the job, because firing him might mean going without help altogether. The bureaucracy fostered the system for its own purposes—it prevented unrestrained competition in the job market by employees or employers, and so made the job of top-down control easier.

When the 1990s' recession began, companies, encouraged by MITI and other ministries, tried to retain the lifetime employment system. They resorted to the old practice of cutting bonuses (as much as 50 percent of workers' pay) and idling people on the job. Japan's Labor Ministry estimates that during the worst of the recession, paid jobs without work exceeded the official unemployment rate by a wide margin, totaling perhaps 14 percent of the workforce.[48] But supporting these many idle workers began to erode profits, which was unacceptable even to firms that believed strongly in the old system. Directly following the halt of economic growth in 1992, corporate profits in Japan fell by nearly half. As the recession wore on, the old concerns about the ability to find future workers began to dissipate, especially as firms became aware of the fundamental forces slowing the pace of economic growth. The practice of hiring in anticipation of future needs stopped. In 1993, Ministry of Labor figures showed only seventy-five job offerings for every one hundred job seekers. By the mid-to-late-1990s, those one hundred seekers competed for only sixty-three offerings, and that adverse situation has persisted into the closing years of the decade.[49] In some cases, continued adherence to lifetime employment threatened a company's survival. Even when bankruptcy was a distant concern, firms moved away from lifetime employment in order to protect the new equity they had attained through their retained profits.

Then layoffs began. They started in the small, undercapitalized companies, but spread quickly to the large well-known firms. In 1992, Nissan, the huge auto manufacturer, announced the closing of its Zama plant outside Tokyo, causing serious labor dislocation. As the first closing of a major manufacturing facility since the Second World War, it had an immediate and widespread psychological effect. But the significance of the Zama plant closing went far beyond the fact that it was first. For years, it was considered the model of Japanese efficiency, and hence, economic success. Its proximity to Tokyo made it a must-see on tours for Western businessmen, investors, and government officials. Its closing signaled not only the breaking of an important social contract, but also the end of an era of Japanese dominance and growth under the old system. In addition to the plant closing, Nissan also announced its decision to phase out 5,000 jobs.[50] Japanese steel producers followed with layoffs by the thousands. Soon, the list of firms making layoff announcements read like a Who's Who of Japanese Industry and Commerce. Nippon Telephone & Telegraph Corporation (NTT) cut 33,000 jobs or 14 percent of its workforce during the four years after the recession began. Toshiba let 5,000 workers go from its 75,000-person workforce.[51] And the downsizing has not been confined to industry. Seiyu, a major Japanese retailer, discharged or forced early retirement on 15 percent of its workforce.[52] Japan's Ministry of Labor reported that since 1992 more than one-third of all Japanese firms have fired, laid off, or forced employees into early retirement.[53] The number of workers in Japanese manufacturing fell by 4 percent in just the first phase of the cutbacks, some by attrition, many by layoffs.[54] The corporate giant Toyota, which at first made much of adhering to lifetime employment, in time began to allude to the possibility of future layoffs in its press releases. Even as Toyota's management kept to the letter of the old system, it prepared for potential relief by violating its spirit. By the second half of the decade, it transferred 10 percent of its white-collar staff from regular employee status to "contract positions."[55] If at some future date management sees the need to shed these people, it can claim to have just canceled contracts, without laying off or firing anyone. Even the state-owned postal savings and insurance system caught the new approach and, in the interest of efficiency and profitability, planned cuts amounting to 20 percent of its workforce of nearly 40,000.[56]

Attitudes did not revert back to those of the old system during a brief economic surge after 1995. Even as profits rebounded for a time, companies knew that the strength was due in part to the changing approach toward employment and *keiretsu* ties. Rather than turn back, management signaled its understanding of the new economic fundamentals. Without explicitly mentioning the forces of economic maturation or the globalization of markets, these firms acknowledged them nonetheless, and continued to break down old patterns, even during this more prosperous interlude. Downsizing then began to focus on more tenured, higher paid workers. Pioneer Electric, for example, forced twenty-five high-ranking managers to either retire early or face dismissal.[57] The number is small, but by Japanese standards it reflected a revolution in thinking. The firings announced by the Osaka retailer Hankyo in 1995 focused entirely on the managerial staff, which the firm cut by more than half.[58]

Having adopted a new, hard-nosed approach to employment, Japanese businesses began to rethink another hallmark of the established system: seniority-based wage policies. Under Japan's old "way," raises came only with tenure on the job. The practice supported the lifetime employment system by binding workers to the firms that were bound to them. The bureaucrats, always interested in suppressing competition and securing control, fostered the approach for the same reasons that they promoted lifetime employment. But now, with the commitment to lifetime employment declining and the employment market becoming more fluid, firms had to find new ways to bind their valued workers to them. So they have jettisoned the old seniority-based wage structure in favor of the Western practice of paying higher wages to more valuable employees. On the cutting edge, Honda, Sony, Fujitsu, and several department stores have begun to adopt the American idea of negotiating wages individually with their senior employees.[59] Japanese firms have even begun to look at the very un-Japanese practice of offering stock options to retain and motivate valued people. The fact that recent national wage offensives of all production workers produced different agreements with different firms, even those in the same industry, indicates how the old uniform, seniority-based approach has begun to disappear.[60]

The slowed pace of growth and the threat of layoffs have changed Japanese attitudes toward consumption as well. As with so much else in Japan, the old system of retailing has begun to come apart. When Japan was growing fast, it had little trouble maintaining its unusual and costly system for the distribution of goods. Unlike other nations, Japan's wholesalers and retailers avoided price competition. With the active support of the bureaucracy and its Iron Triangle, they engaged in a kind of wealth-sharing arrangement, in which they segmented the market into little monopolies at each stage of distribution from producer to final consumer. Participants at each level took their cut and passed the product along to the next stage, its price increasing with each step. As per the old system's priorities, this structure kept foreign sellers and products out through its complexity and opacity, and helped suppress consumption by keeping prices high, consumer choices few, and the chore of shopping remarkably unpleasant. As long as the country's rapid growth persisted, people felt richer and complained little despite this strange approach, and the bureaucrats were happy. The system also appealed to the strong Japanese sense of community. People knew that the high prices supported the small shops and the countless layers of the distribution network. The knowledge of having helped find work for everyone compensated for the minor hardships of higher prices.

But as confidence in perpetually rapid growth dissipated, the Japanese consumer grew less willing to pay for this system. In the 1990s Japanese merchants offered discounts for the first time, and, as in Western countries years before, discounting began to change the ways of retailing and consumption. Significant inroads have occurred in the sale of rice, that most symbolic of Japanese commodities. In the last few years alone, warehouses and storefronts dedicated to the very un-Japanese practice of selling both domestic and imported rice at reduced prices have opened in Tokyo and other cities. Since the bureaucratic officials had always implemented their restrictive practices through informal understandings, they found themselves at a loss when merchants started defying them.[61] The discounters' profits on each kilo of rice fall well below the fat margins of the old system, but as with discounters everywhere, lower prices have brought additional customers and with them, sales volumes to enhance returns. Traditional stores have reacted to this competition by discarding traditional ways. Established supermarkets have introduced American-style, low-priced, generic products and imported goods that were not available in Japan a few years ago.

The change has benefited the Japanese consumer, even though it has cut into the profits of traditional wholesalers and retailers. The price of all food, not just rice, has dropped, although it still remains high by world standards. One Japanese housewife in a Tokyo working-class district exclaimed how "rich" she felt, pointing out, almost conspiratorially, that generic soy sauce cost 40 percent less than Kikkoman, once her only choice.[62] The whole effect of the generics, the discounters, and the imports has helped bring more of the good life to many Japanese consumers, despite the sluggish pace of economic growth and in the face of the still strong anti-consumer bias of the old system. In 1992, for instance, food cost the average Tokyo area family 18.1 percent of its disposable income. At last count, that figure had fallen to 16.7 percent.[63] The new attitudes toward consumption and toward bureaucratic rules have encouraged merchants to discount and import not just food but a whole range of consumer items. Leading the pack are the larger retailers, who deal in volumes sufficient enough to give them bargaining power with the manufacturers and to make importing worthwhile. Despite still-restrictive regulations, the average store size in Japan has grown by more than 16 percent since the 1980s, and even MITI has bowed to the pressure in the mid-1990s, shortening its approval time for large store licensing from thirty-five to eighteen months.[64] It has become even less restrictive in recent years. Perhaps even more telling, in 1997 the Japanese consulting firm Funai announced a deal with an American commercial developer, Koll, and a real estate company, World Premier Investment, to build a series of "megamalls" across Japan. At the same time, a group of six firms, called MGJ Japan, revealed similar plans for the Tokyo, Yokahama, and Osaka areas.[65] Clearly, the system that has worked steadfastly for over fifty years to suppress consumption is losing ground.

While these new attitudes and practices seem, at least on the surface, to grow from the immediate pressures of the recession and economic stagnation of the 1990s, it is evident that their roots lie in the longer-term trends of economic maturation and globalization. It is even possible to trace the first signs of these changes back to the 1970s, when these fundamental trends were just gaining force. Even then, the economy had sufficient wealth to prompt people to begin to question the single-minded focus on growth. They sought to "rehumanize" society, and began what was called the "consumer movement."[66] At the time, the government reacted by raising social spending. Many municipalities responded to the movement by turning from an exclusive focus on development projects to a concern over industrial waste. The Iron Triangle was shocked when municipalities that had previously courted development canceled projects over pollution or quality-of-life concerns. Under the sway of this change, huge, much-heralded development plans in Matsu Ogawara, Tomokomai, and Shibushi Bay never reached fruition.[67] In 1972, the country elected Kakuei Tanaka Prime Minister after a campaign in which he promised to improve the lives of the people, not just industry. Under the slogan "Rebuilding the Japanese Archipelago," Tanaka planned massive public works spending for the Japanese people, including expansion of the bullet train "to move people, not exports."[68] He even proposed radical new measures to improve the social safety net by doubling retirement incomes and increasing national medical coverage by 40 percent.[69] His motivation may have been cynically political, as many observers have suggested, but the pressure on him to adjust national priorities came from a genuine change in the climate of opinion at the time.

The civil service bureaucracy resisted Tanaka and his "consumer movement," and was eventually rid of him when a bribery scandal connected to the Lockheed Corporation in the United States destroyed his political power base.[70] Some observers suggest that the press campaign against him was inspired and informed by Japan's civil service. Whether or not the bureaucracy assisted in Tanaka's downfall will doubtless remain a mystery. But the depth of bureaucratic resistance is hardly mysterious. Then, as now, the old system gave them great power that they did not and do not want to lose. The pressure on the bureaucrats is much greater today than in Tanaka's day. With the recession and the financial crisis of the 1990s revealing more clearly than ever the old system's inability to cope with a mature economy and globalization, more Japanese have turned against the idea of bureaucratic control and begun to question the old approach and its priorities. As the next chapter will show, a reform movement is growing that is eager to accelerate Japan's inevitable changes away from her centralized system, its bias against consumption, and its single-minded focus on production and exports.

THE WAR
BETWEEN
REFORMERS
AND
BUREAUCRATS

THE REFORMERS OF THE 1990S HAVE exhibited much more power—and have enjoyed much wider public support—than did their predecessors in the 1970s and 1980s. The financial strains of the decade have raised so many doubts about Japan's "way" that a liberalizing, decentralizing reform agenda now dominates public debate. Japan's crucial 1996 elections for the lower, more powerful house of the Diet primarily revolved around reform issues, as have subsequent votes and major policy debates. All political parties, even the long-dominant Liberal Democratic Party (LDP), have campaigned on and positioned themselves around a reform platform. Still, a fifty-year-old system with deep roots and notable historic achievements does not change easily. Japan's civil service bureaucracy remains powerful and much of it stands fundamentally opposed to any substantive change. So too, do many politicians and interest groups who will lose to liberalizing reforms. Certainly, reform in Japan has proceeded at an uneven pace and doubtless will continue to do so. Time, however, is clearly on the reformers' side. Although few explicitly acknowledge the forces of globalization and maturation, these trends will make it difficult to resist the proposed changes, whatever the personal preferences and party biases of those currently in power or of those who might replace them in the future.

THE CHORUS FOR REFORM

Today's reformers are hardly a uniform or homogeneous group. Within the Diet, the party alignments keep shifting as do the names of their champions. Outside the Diet, reform is well represented in academic, media, and business circles, though each spokesman has his own particular priorities, and many have no obvious party allegiances. Nonetheless, the reformers basically agree that Japan must abandon her old system of centralized control exercised by a close, secretive government bureaucracy in Tokyo, and replace it with a more liberal approach that will deregulate the economy, decentralize control, and create structures to ensure public accountability for those who exercise power.

Each element in the reform movement has a slightly different emphasis. Some stress the need for increased economic flexibility and seek to achieve it through deregulation and the reduction of red tape—the rules, licensing procedures, and approvals by which the civil service controls and directs the economy. They would liberalize the system to encourage new business development and free trade within Japan as well as between Japan and other countries. The reformers also seek to simplify Japan's tax code, make it more equitable, eliminate the subsidies that favor businesses over households, and generally make it less biased toward big business. Other reformers would go beyond economics to strike at the heart of the old "way" by insisting on accountability and disclosure by the government and civil service. They want to limit the abuse and arrogance that were so evident in the aftermath of Kobe. These reformers promote public debate over the insider consensus that has typified the Iron Triangle and its domination of the economy. They want to establish clear lines of responsibility. Remarkably, given that not too long ago the Japanese universally touted their "way" as superior to Western capitalism, reformers of all stripes seem anxious to move Japan toward Western practices in order to, in the words of one commentator, bring her approach "into harmony with those of other nations."[1] Stating the position with un-Japanese bluntness, Yoshihiko Miyauchi, president of Orix, Japan's large nonbanking financial institution, put it this way: "We won't become like America, but we will move some way toward the American model."[2]

Virtually all the reformers pay homage to the remarkable economic success of the old system. But in the same breath each notes that the new, more complex environment demands change. Diet member Ichiro Ozawa, a one-time power in the LDP and early founder of the reformist opposition in the Diet, reflects this attitude. His best-selling reform manifesto, *Blueprint for a New Japan,* notes that the old system "greatly assisted" the country's growth in the past but now has become untenable and is "no longer able to respond adequately to the changes taking place at home and abroad."[3] The respected University of Tokyo economist, Masahiro Okuno, has also taken this common attitude and clarified its links to the fundamental forces pressuring Japan: "The Japanese system worked very well at a time of high growth," he said, speaking to a business and political audience in Tokyo in the mid-1990s, but "considering the progress in information, internationalization, and social maturity, the system has reached the limits of its effectiveness."[4] This reform attitude has become so pervasive that it has even found its way into reports issued by the guardians of the old order, the civil service bureaucracy. A recent missive from the Industrial Structure Council of MITI's Subcommittee for Long-Range Issues (just the designation reveals the ponderousness of Japan's bureaucracy) urged that Japan adopt a "new paradigm" to "abandon existing policies, management styles, and ideas about living standards and embark upon structural reforms of historic magnitude."[5]

The "new paradigm" described by most reformers has a very un-Japanese freewheeling quality. Ozawa's work simply calls for the adoption of "fundamentally laissez-faire policies" and the abolition of "excess regulations." It encourages efforts to "[chop] down the thicket of rules and regulations" that he and other reformers blame for "choking initiative, creativity, and economic growth."[6] Ozawa's position, like that of so many other reformers, condemns continued bureaucratic guidance as entirely inappropriate now that Japan's economy has become a "fluid entity and not something that can be managed by a handful of administrative organizations," in other words, the Iron Triangle.[7] Another prominent reformer, Kenichi Ohamae, business consultant, author of *The End of the Nation State,* and one-time candidate for mayor of Tokyo, has echoed the same feelings about the incapacity of bureaucratic direction. He has argued that the bureaucracy's control of the national interest is "little more than a cloak for subsidy and protection" and that in the fast-moving globalized economic environment, "no policy can substitute for the efforts of individual managers in individual institutions to link their activities to the global economy."[8] Masao Miyamoto, ex-bureaucrat and author of *Straitjacket Society,* a best-selling critique of Japan's civil service, refers in his writing to the "totalitarianism" of the old system and argues that opening and deregulating markets "would enrich the lives of consumers in both Japan and the West."[9]

The reformers have strengthened their hand considerably with the increasing support of Japan's powerful business community. Business' desire to dismantle the old system might at first blush seem contrary to its interests. After all, the old system has always favored, even coddled Japanese business. It has strived to maintain high prices for its products in the domestic market, subsidized business' costs, protected it from imports, and helped it compete against foreigners in export markets. But business has come to see the cost of this coddling as too high. In Japan's now mature economy, there are fewer opportunities to develop along the obvious channels favored by the bureaucrats, and companies have chafed at the system's reluctance to allow them to experiment freely with new products and new markets. Faced with a complex and dynamic global economy, they want to develop the novel corporate structures and joint ventures on which Japan's old bureaucratic system has always frowned. Even large, well-established firms have balked at the rigidity imposed by the old bureaucratically directed system. In order to deal with global competition and new technological developments, they want more flexibility than the old system can give. They have come to resist the old system's arbitrary decisions on licensing and approvals, and its constraining rules on financial arrangements, especially now that Japan's beleaguered banks cannot fulfill business' financing needs.

Corporate Japan has turned toward reform also because it feels what is popularly called the "scissors effect." Coined by Paul Kennedy in his book, *The Rise and Fall of Great Powers,* the phrase refers to two "blades" of pressure on Japan's established export-driven system: One is the backlash from the industrialized world against Japanese exports and its protected domestic market, the other is the challenge from the newly industrialized economies of Asia, outperforming Japan in such basic manufacturing as steel, shipbuilding, and auto assembly.[10] Despite recent economic turmoil, Japanese exporters have become aware of these dual threats and see reform as a way to garner maneuvering room for dealing with them. Beyond the "scissors effect," Japanese businesses have turned to reform as a way to overcome their difficulties with foreign lenders. Because foreign lenders fear that Japanese firms will lose viability should bureaucratic coddling stop, they have protected themselves by imposing a special premium interest rate on Japanese borrowers. Japanese firms, naturally, would like to avoid this extra interest charge, and have seized on national progress toward deregulation and liberalizing reforms as a way to show foreigners that such fears are groundless.

Japanese business and commercial people have become so taken with the reformist agenda that *Japanese Business Today,* a popular English-language monthly of big business in Japan, has identified "the complete reform" of Japan's economic structure as "unquestionably the most important task facing the nation."[11] It was business support for reform that encouraged MITI to publish its endorsement of the "new paradigm." In fact, that report was authored by a group headed by Gaishi Hiraiwa, formerly chairman of Japan's prestigious Keidanren or Federation of Economic Organizations, the main industrial employers group. The report pointedly advances an agenda of deregulation to help Japanese businesses become more competitive internationally, particularly the service sector. To facilitate the restructuring of older firms, it advocates easing stock market restrictions to allow the creation of new companies and novel corporate links.[12] Takao Kichiro, while president of Nikko Securities, added his voice to the chorus, calling for an end to the "old methods which distorted the price mechanism, over-regulation, *keiretsu* and rigged construction bids."[13] More recently, Shochiro Toyoda, while serving as chairman of Keidanren and also of Toyota Motor Corporation, expanded this line of thinking by advocating reforms in what he termed the "Keidanren vision" of a more "open" and "vigorous" society. In his discussions of this reform vision, he, like so many others, noted that "Japan's economic and social systems—which supported its postwar economic development—have become largely inefficient and irrelevant." His work in this area calls on Japan to dismantle regulations, remove barriers to imports, and make structural changes to allow small business to grow. Toyoda would even move all major government offices—effectively, the capital—from Tokyo to reduce congestion. Far from shrinking from the reform agenda, he has called on Japan to "undertake Draconian reforms comparable to the changes that the nation effected in the Meiji Era and after World War II."[14] This is powerful stuff, especially coming from a conservative chairman of a powerful institution that virtually constitutes one bar of the Iron Triangle.

Beyond such calls for a general easing of the old centralized, controlling approach, this diverse group of reformers has singled out specific aspects of the old system as requiring special attention. Much of their concern has centered on Japan's financial markets, which are most vulnerable to the forces of globalization as well as to direct competition from Singapore, Hong Kong, New York, and London. The reformers have argued that in the present dynamic environment, Japan urgently needs deregulation and liberalization to allow the financial market, instead of the ministries, to determine where funds flow and at what price. "To turn back [from financial liberalization]," pleaded

Johsen Takahashi, research counsel to the Mitsubishi Research Institute, would bring "ruin for the Tokyo markets."[15] But the reformers have also gone beyond financial concerns and singled out specific industrial policies and practices as well. They have made it clear that they would welcome an end to the practice of lifetime employment and the seniority wage system, both of which they have identified as impediments to the economic efficiency that comes from labor's freedom "to migrate among economic activities."[16] In this same spirit, the reformers have sought to end restrictions on land use and to transfer authority over zoning and real estate development from the central government in Tokyo to local governments. Reaching farther still, they have pushed to open up the wholesale and retail distribution systems by ending subsidies for certain business uses of water, power, and other utilities, repealing most transportation regulation, and, of course, simplifying the tax code while making it less pro-business and more equitable.

Moving the attack from bureaucratic regulations to public policy, reformers have criticized the government's heavy reliance on public works spending to implement fiscal policy. They have argued that not only has this practice failed to help Japan out of the 1990s recession, but it has for years served to enhance the bureaucratic power that is the antithesis of the liberalization they seek. Without explicitly mentioning the general maturation of Japan's economy, their arguments have referred to it by pointing out Japan's reduced need for industrial infrastructure. Kozo Koide, senior economist for the Industrial Bank of Japan, has argued that government spending on public works continues long after any economic need has been met. He has claimed it is a reflection of each ministry's desire to increase its own influence and that of its political allies. "[T]here's a fishing port every seven or eight miles on average all along the Japanese coast," he wrote, "and still the Ministry of Transportation plans to expand [their number]."[17] Joining the criticism, Shoji Sumita, a senior civil servant who recently retired from the offending Ministry of Transportation, has argued that much of the public works spending is undertaken purely for political payoffs or bureaucratic power. He has pointed out that Japan spends an inordinate 6.9 percent of her GDP on public works, compared with less than 3 percent in the United States and most European countries.[18]

In order to shut down these corrupt and wasteful practices, reformers have put forth plans for thorough administrative and fiscal change. Their aim is not just to reduce the unwieldy government budget deficit and check bureaucratic control, but also to redirect spending away from industrial infrastructure into areas that better suit the needs of a mature economy, such as communications and technological research. Ozawa has linked such efforts to weaken centralized direction with the devolution of decision-making power away from Tokyo, arguing that "except when absolutely necessary, power should be transferred from the national to the local governments" or away from government altogether.[19] Ken Moroi, vice president of Nikkeiren, Japan's Federation of Employers' Associations, has echoed this sentiment: "Centralization in Tokyo serves no interests except those of senior bureaucrats and those who want to buy votes. Local government is much closer to people's needs and can better allocate for people and for business interests."[20] Taking a slightly different tack, another leading reformer, Hiroshi Kato, president of Chiba University of Commerce, has criticized Tokyo for ignoring local government budgets in its policies. His writing supports dramatic cutbacks in spending by the national government as well as deregulation. He, too, has spoken directly in favor of moving away from the old system's tremendous emphasis on spending for public works toward support for "'software' sectors, such as education and medical care, with a slant to the twenty-first century."[21]

The reformers received powerful intellectual support from the work of Professor Yukio Noguchi of Japan's Hitotsubashi University. His recent book, *1940 Taisei* (The 1940 System), argues persuasively that most of Japan's approach or "way" does not have its roots in Japan's ancient culture, as many of its supporters have argued, but actually originated in the war plans of Japan's military government of the 1940s.[22] As one reviewer put it: "All of the system's main features—industrial cartels, bureaucratic regulation, *keiretsu,* government involvement in business, restrictions on competition, barriers to market entry, etc.—were set in place…to prepare the nation for all-out war. The bullets may have stopped flying half a century ago, but in some respects Japan is still fighting World War II."[23] Among the extensive evidence for its argument, Noguchi's work takes pains to show that until recent reform measures, the laws governing the Bank of Japan remained largely unaltered since the 1930s, when they were written in conscious imitation of Nazi Germany's Reichsebank, complete with instructions to "fulfill state obligations" beyond the straightforward management of government finances.[24] His research identifies the roots of the bureaucratic control of credit in the Bank of Japan's 1942 establishment of the National Financial Control Association. That body, his book argues, organized finance around a select group of banks that now are clearly identified with existing *keiretsu.*[25] Noguchi's analysis looks at long-standing corporate practices, such as lifetime employment, the emphasis on production over shareholder interests, and the seniority wage structure, and demonstrates their clear links to the National General Mobilization Law of 1938, and the 1940 Outline for the Establishment of a New Economic Order. More than any cultural imperative, these pieces of wartime legislation established the now classic Japanese approach to industry, ordering that "capital, management, and labor should become a single organic whole and raise productivity."[26]

This is ominous reading, especially for today's Japanese, who typically associate the wartime government only with destruction, defeat, and failure. Of course, considerable debate surrounds Professor Noguchi's contentions. But his analysis—right or wrong—has advanced the reform movement in several ways. First, the great publicity given his thesis has raised the profile of reform issues. Second, by associating the present system with the despised wartime government, his discussion has made it easier for Japanese from all walks of life to break the link—long cultivated by bureaucrats—between Japan's system on the one hand and national and cultural loyalties on the other. Finally, by arguing that prior to 1940 Japan's system was more like the capitalist West, with less centralized control, less regulatory interference, and less rigid structures, Noguchi's work and the similar efforts of other reformers like him have shown that Japan can and has functioned in a system different from the present one. In so doing, they have helped dispel much of the anxiety that such recommendations have created in citizens wedded to tradition.

With this perspective, reformers have extended their agenda beyond economic and fiscal change to political reform. They have attacked the underlying secretiveness and lack of accountability in the old system, its trust in bureaucratic power, its preference for economic growth above public well-being, and its assumption that these biases will serve the long-term interests of the Japanese people. Ozawa's *Blueprint for a New Japan* certainly goes back to first principles with a very un-Japanese emphasis on the individual. Speaking for many in the reform movement, Ozawa's book claims that "[r]eal democracy begins with...the autonomy of the individual."[27] Ozawa's work tops its reform suggestions with critiques of the efficacy of bureaucratic control, which he and other reformers would replace with an insistence on "self-reliance and creativity for the individual and the firm."[28] The reformist calls for "political leadership" to hold the civil service accountable to the people—as it has never been—speak volumes to the basic dissatisfactions driving this movement. So do the calls to "ensure that the policy-making process is clear and shows citizens and the world who bears political responsibility in Japan, what they think, and what their larger visions are."[29] Joining Ozawa and many other reformers in this insistence on transparency regarding public decision making, Minoru Tada, professor of Japanese politics at Nisho Gakusha University, has stressed the need for a "reliable opposition" in the Diet.[30] Ozawa has made similar noises, though strange for a politician, seeking "alternations in governments between two parties that will compete with each other [openly] on the basis of policy, not of factions or personalities."[31]

The reformers have sought to achieve their ambitious political goals in two ways: through promoting freedom of information and through electoral reform. The former, they have argued, is a critical antidote to the secretiveness of the old system. According to Diet member Yukio Edano of the reformist Democratic Party, "[o]nce a freedom-of-information law is put into effect, then 90 percent of reform is done."[32] This might overstate things, but few who know Japan's system can doubt that greater transparency will advance other aspects of reform substantially by making the government and the civil service accountable to the public for their actions. The effort to gain a freer flow of information certainly has received a lot of support from the general public. As a distrust of the bureaucracy has grown in the 1990s, increased numbers have filed formal requests for information about official bodies and actions. The actual statistics are impressive. Such requests exploded from 1,000 in 1990 to 10,492 in 1996, the last year for which reliable data are available.[33] This is a 949 percent rise in six years or a 48 percent annual rate of increase. Local government has felt compelled to respond to the public will. When the Kanagawa prefecture south of Tokyo passed its Freedom of Information Act in 1983, giving citizens a legal right to official documents, it was an anomaly. Since then, forty-four other local governments or almost 95 percent of the prefectional and major city administrations have bowed to public pressure and passed similar statutes, most quite recently.[34] According to Kunikatsu Tomoi, director of public information for Kanagawa prefecture, the freedom-of-information rules force local officials to "care about what our residents need and want."[35] Diet member Edano and other reformers have lobbied continually to persuade the Tokyo government to yield to this pressure and pass a national law. As of this writing, Japan still has no national freedom-of-information law, but the success at the local and prefectural levels testifies to the reformers' growing power as well as the national direction.

The most significant reform achievement to date has been the radical change in Japan's electoral system brought about by the Political Reform Law of 1994. In framing this successful piece of legislation, the reformers aimed to force political accountability and open debate in two ways: first, by ensuring that the Diet would have the viable, active opposition that Japanese politics had lacked since the LDP was founded in 1955, and second, by refocusing political debate on national issues and away from the local pork-barrel issues

that had dominated under the old approach. To accomplish this, the reform
legislation first redistricted Japan to reflect the huge increase in urbanization
during the past thirty years. Because the farm lobby had so dominated the
LDP and policy, it was argued that the redistricting would weaken LDP hegemony and help create a viable opposition. The new law also abolished Japan's
old system of multiseat districts, where electoral districts had between three
and six representatives in the Diet depending on their size. Under the old system, a group of candidates from each district ran for whatever seats were available, but each citizen could vote for only one candidate. The seats were then
filled according to which candidates received the most votes. If there were five
candidates and three seats, the candidates taking the second and third seats
might win with as little as 20 percent of the vote each, even less if the first candidate won a large plurality. The reformers argued that this old system invited
candidates to campaign by promising specific favors to small but substantial
local constituencies. The new law replaced the multiseat districts with a combination of 300 single-seat districts and 200 seats determined by proportional
vote for parties at the national level. Since winning in a single-seat district
would take a greater proportion of votes, reformers claimed that the new system would reduce the temptation to focus on specific local constituencies and
instead create an inducement for candidates to deal with national issues or at
least local issues of widespread concern. The proportional seats, based as they
are on a national vote, would refocus debate on each party's national campaign
as opposed to local issues.

At this writing, Japan has had only one major election under this new law,
the 1996 vote for the lower, more powerful house of the Diet. The Western
press was disappointed in the results, which returned the LDP to power. Certainly the outcome fell short of electoral reform's greatest hopes. Still, much of
the law's promise was fulfilled. The campaign seemed to focus more on
national issues than in past elections—reforms of the structures governing politics, economics, and finance were major topics. While the Liberal Democratic Party won a plurality and formed the next government, it failed, for the first
time since it was founded, to secure an absolute majority in an election. Furthermore, the vote did return an active and reformist—if highly balkanized—
opposition to the Diet. While neither side of the reformist debate can claim
clear success or failure in this, the battle goes on, and that, after all, was an
objective of the 1994 law. Certainly the groundwork for more substantial
future reform was laid. In the 1998 election for the upper, less powerful house
of the Diet, the LDP lost its dominance, with a significant plurality going to
the reformist Democratic Party of Japan.

BUREAUCRATIC RESISTANCE, SCANDAL, AND POLITICAL INEPTITUDE

While the reform movement has gained adherents and widespread public support, particular vested interests, especially Japan's civil service bureaucrats, have steadfastly opposed most proposed changes, slowing or stopping many fundamental initiatives. In the words of one prominent reformer, "it will be an enormous task [to achieve] fundamental political and social reform [because many] have built up vested interests under the [present] system,"[36] especially the bureaucrats who administer it. The civil servants have defended their resistance to change on the basis of the economic and social pain that would accompany the deregulation and liberalization demanded by the reformers. As one senior bureaucrat put it, these old bureaucratic managers want to "hold the economy together [in a system that has] served Japan well for many years."[37] Speaking from the Ministry of Finance, Dr. Eisuke Sakakibara, vice minister for international affairs, described the bureaucrats' concern that there be a balance not a "conflict between stability and proper supervision."[38] His comments revealed worry over the consequences of a "situation of cold turkey [such as] they have in Russia." The alternative, he claimed, is "sound surveillance" of markets and market participants.[39]

Whatever other motivations are present, caution and resistance to change are natural reflections of the approach taken by civil servants the world over. Wherever they are, they seem instinctively to place stability above other goals. This priority draws them to the profession and sustains them in it. A go-slow approach to deregulation and liberalization characterizes even those bureaucrats who have sympathy for reform and recognize the powerful pressures for change in Japan. The pace of such reform is sometimes so slow that progress seems imperceptible. The bureaucratic attitude shines through with special clarity in a slightly dated article from 1984 entitled "Orderly Liberalization of Financial Markets," by Bunji Kure, who at the time headed the research department of the Bank of Japan.[40] Typical of bureaucratic resistance, Kure's article argues against an early push for financial deregulation, not by promoting the merits of "going slow" but by dwelling on peripheral details. The essay, in fact, manages to avoid addressing the issue of deregulation entirely. At the time, Japan's financial markets were more heavily regulated than they are now. Reformers were pushing for the abolition of administered interest rates on time deposits at banks. Kure acknowledged the virtues of market rates, but he focused his entire discussion on the scale of administered rates allowed on deposits of various sizes. His concern was whether the system should allow

greater latitude in rates paid on ¥500 million deposits than on ¥50 million
deposits, or whether the rules should apply on a uniform scale. He never considered deregulation and allowing the market to set the rates. His only concession to the market came in the form of a suggestion to rewrite the rules so
officials could "regulate interest rates closer to…market rates." Mr. Kure's
approach was vintage bureaucrat. Although he tried, he failed to disguise his
lack of responsiveness to reform, his complete distrust of the market, and his
underlying desire to retain bureaucratic controls and prerogatives. Japan has
long since passed this issue. The reformers won: the rates were deregulated.
This discourse from the 1980s has relevance today, however, because the
bureaucratic bias, approach, and style remain, and come through much more
clearly in hindsight than in the complexities of current debate.

    This old, bureaucratic approach is certainly evident in the present debate,
though it is more sophisticated and a bit harder to pin down than it was in
Kure's effort. For instance, the former vice minister for international affairs at
the Ministry of Finance, Toyoo Gyohten, responded to proposed reforms,
which would enable customers and investors to obtain more information about
banks by saying, "if depositors come to know all the details about the financial
conditions of the banks, then the too-sudden expansion of information would
not help depositors to formulate the most objective view of the soundness of
the institution."[41] The presumption here is not that information enables good
judgment but rather that the MOF knows better than the public what is good
for depositors and should, therefore, retain the information. Sakakibara has
also fit into the pattern, though he has an appealingly flamboyant style that frequently disguises his steadfast support for the old system. Though he stated
bluntly that "Japan's postwar system…is rotting and it is good that the process
of correction should be accelerated by more competition," he still has advocated a go-slow approach to deregulation.[42] "If they [market participants] fin-
ish," he argued, referring to reforms, "we'll give them another dish." For all his
stated desire to "accelerate" change, he has resisted reforms that allow Japanese investors more latitude regarding how and where they invest funds. Dr.
Sakakibara has argued that these rules should still contain limits "on the
amount to be invested without a guarantee of principal."[43] Makoto Utsumi,
business professor at Keio University and former MOF official, has taken the
same bureaucratic perspective. Private investors, he said, "might jeopardize the
principal itself—very risky."[44] All this sounds appropriately protective, but in
practice would entirely limit one's freedom of action. Unless investors can take
reasonable risks with investments and responsibility for them, they might as
well leave the entire decision with the bureaucrats, which of course, is what the

civil service wants. Furthermore, the "guarantee" to which both Sakakibara and Utsumi refer is not a simple deposit insurance scheme, such as the one Japan has in common with the United States and other developed countries. It reflects an arrogance that assumes the Japanese bureaucracy can devise a system to protect investments from loss, in this case, pension funds.

Many bureaucrats are sincere in their beliefs that caution is needed to protect financial security and that the ministries have the greatest wisdom about such matters, but reformers take a more cynical view of the bureaucratic resistance to change. These critics scoff at allusions to guaranteeing investment principal by pointing to the events of the 1990s as an unmistakable lesson that the principal is always at risk, and that bureaucratic cautions and restrictions protect nothing except the continuing power of the civil service bureaucracy. Everyone on both sides of the debate knows that deregulation, liberalization, and increased accountability in government will shrink the power of the civil service, and that the first law of bureaucracy, as the reformers have frequently pointed out, is self-preservation. Akio Mikuni, president of Mikuni & Co., a credit rating agency, has, in his comments on the nature of Japanese finance, described what bureaucrats stand to lose if reform goes forward: "banking...is a franchise like the McDonald's hamburger chain—the head office is the MOF." The civil servants at this and other ministries do not want to lose the power and prestige conferred by that kind of control. They will do whatever they can to keep it. "Besides," Mikuni added, "they really do think they can do better than the market."[45] Atsuo Hirano, senior managing director of Mitsubishi Bank, has put bureaucratic concerns in a starker light: "To deregulate means that eventually some bureaucrats will lose their jobs."[46]

Whatever the motivation of the bureaucrats—risk aversion for the overall society or self-interest—they have used their ample power to slow or block reform efforts. As with so many other things in Japan that are associated with the Iron Triangle, the bureaucracy's most effective efforts to fight reform have relied less on engaging in direct confrontation on the issues than on the subtle practice of day-to-day business and administration. Turf wars and petty claims between and within ministries, even those unrelated to antireform agendas, have held up changes indefinitely, despite senior civil servants' support. It is widely known, in and out of government, that within the Ministry of Finance, the securities, banking, and international finance bureaus act as separate fiefdoms, each protecting its own interests and sector. One will try to block anything the other does, if that action will intrude in the least on any prerogative. If these bureaucratic adversaries cannot reach a consensus, nothing gets done at this powerful "ministry of ministries." Such disputes within the MOF, and between it and other agencies, have stymied movement on even the smallest technical points, let alone the fundamental issues of reform. During a minor consideration of how to manage certain financial futures, for example, all progress stopped while the MOF and MITI split hairs over whether financial futures are securities or commodities. The former would regulate the one, while the latter would have jurisdiction over the other. Complicating things further, the Ministry of Justice entered the fray to assess whether these common financial products run afoul of gambling laws. Other issues on deregulation have come under the jurisdictions of the Ministries of Agriculture, Construction, Transportation, and Health and Welfare, which administers pensions. Frequently, half a dozen ministries have disputed small points of a reform issue, while a different group disputed other aspects of the same issue, all on narrow technical grounds and never on a substantive consideration of the proposal's overall objectives. Also blocking efforts at reform are the frequent rotations of ministry staffs—so frequent that decisions are held up while the new regulators learn the issues, conduct their own studies, and reopen negotiations with other ever-changing power groups within and between ministries. That anything gets done at all is a testimony to the strenuous efforts, earnestness, and good will of some civil servants who push decisions through.

It is this bureaucratic power—petty and grand—to thwart reform that has raised skepticism among Western Japan-watchers about the prospects for fundamental change in Japan. Despite their shared pessimism, not all Western observers arrive at their skepticism in the same way. One group includes such notable students of Japan as Chalmers Johnson, James Fallows, Clyde Prestowitz, Eamonn Fingleton, and Leon Hollerman, all of whom agree with the premise that Japan's civil service is in a commanding position. According to them, this bureaucracy, with its Iron Triangle, has directed Japan successfully for years, has things going pretty much according to plan, and continues to support the old system, its practices, and its priorities. This entrenched power, they have argued, has neither a desire for change nor any need to yield to pressure from reformers. Hollerman referred, almost with awe, to the Iron Triangle as a "collusive oligarchy" that seeks "comprehensive security," certainly for itself and presumably for every person and business in Japan.[47] Eamonn Fingleton has suggested that neither the reformers nor any political power could "rein in the prerogatives of the bureaucracy, particularly the MOF." Rather, he has argued that the Finance Ministry is "playing along [with reform ideas]...[but] retain[s] the power to change its mind."[48]

The second camp, led by Karol van Wolferen and including R. Taggert Murphy, expresses skepticism about the prospects for reform but for very different reasons. They do not believe that the civil service is an all-powerful monolith. Instead they have argued that there is little prospect of progress because Japan's political institutions and elected leadership cannot provide a true national direction capable of overcoming narrow bureaucratic interests and those of other power groups. Without any group to oversee it all, including the Ministry of Finance, those narrow and contending interests will forever thwart any effort at change. In his writing, van Wolferen's claims that the nation's bureaucratic elite "permanently confuse Japan's national interest with the prosperity and perpetuation of their own organizations."[49] Certainly, all the bureaucratic infighting and turf wars would seem to support his viewpoint over those of Hollerman, Fingleton, and others who have spoken of a comprehensive overarching bureaucratic power. But from either perspective, most Westerners remain skeptical about reform's prospects.[50]

If, however, van Wolferen is correct about the nature of the system, as it seems he is in light of all the bureaucratic bickering, then there is more reason for optimism about change. The problem he sees facing reform is inadequate political leadership, not an unassailable adversary in the civil service. The implication is that a strong elected government and clear direction could overcome bureaucratic resistance, either by inspiring the civil servants to pull together and form a new set of priorities or, failing that, by playing the narrow interests of the bureaus and ministries off each other. Unfortunately for those who want change, Japan has enjoyed little reliable political direction through most of the time that the reform movement has been gaining momentum. Quite the contrary, for much of the late 1980s and throughout the 1990s, the war between the reformers and the bureaucrats has created an awful political muddle that no leader or group has been able to overcome fully. Compounding the problem, the ongoing turf wars, failures, and gross ethical lapses during this time have spawned a great cynicism among the Japanese public. It has come to distrust anyone with power and has acted accordingly. During the initial eight years of upheaval, between 1988 and the important 1996 election, resignations and a lack of voter confidence brought down eight prime ministers.

Unfortunately, Japanese cynicism about their own leadership during this time was justified. These years provided the citizens of Japan with a series of sad revelations and scandals. However corrupt people thought Japanese politics might have been, the reality proved to be worse. The Japanese were scandalized especially because, prior to these exposures, they had held their leadership in remarkably high regard, both the politicians and the bureaucrats. The painting of this unsavory picture began in 1988, when the Recruit insider trading scandal broke on the scene. The Japanese people learned that the

Recruit-Cosmos Company, a publisher of magazines for job seekers, had bribed politicians and civil servants with the company's own stock as well as huge sums of cash in order to gain protection for the company from competition. The scandal forced Noboru Takeshita, Prime Minister at the time, to resign. Revelations that corruption had reached its highest levels turned enough voters against the Liberal Democratic Party that it lost the upper, weaker house of the Diet for the first time since 1955, when it was formed through a union of the Liberal and Democratic Parties.[51] The Recruit scandal was so shocking that both the company and its former chairman, Hermosa Ezoe, remained the subject of press coverage and editorials right through the late 1990s.[52]

In 1991, before the shock of the Recruit fiasco had passed, the Japanese public got a second dose of scandal when the press revealed that Nomura Securities and the three other major brokers, Daiwa, Nikko, and Yamaichi, were compensating their major clients for stock losses in the falling Japanese market. The incident embarrassed the Ministry of Finance, which was in charge of supervising brokers. It was especially embarrassing when, upon his resignation, the disgraced president of Nomura, Yoshihisa Tabuchi, implied that Ministry officials knew all along what was going on. Fortunately for the government, these events reflected more on the bureaucrats than on the Diet, which was able to hold on. But there was more scandal to come. In 1992, the first press reports emerged that a leader of the LDP, Shin Kanemaru, had used political donations from a construction company to buy ¥3.4 billion ($27 million at the exchange rate of the day) in discount bonds for himself. More shocking still, when the police searched his office, they found large amounts of cash and even a safe full of gold bars. The whole LDP was tarred by this blatant display of personal greed. The picture of wide-ranging corruption struck the public with disturbing force. By the summer of 1993, the scandal had split the LDP, aided by the economic and financial setbacks of the day, as well as the growing realization that more fundamental changes were straining Japan's system. Disciples of Kanemaru, including Ichiro Ozawa and Tsutomu Hata, tried to take over his faction in the LDP, and when they failed, they left the party, donning the mantle of reform. Ozawa published his *Blueprint for a New Japan,* while Hata gave rousing speeches about the need for a more open and sophisticated Japan. They and their colleagues sided with a no-confidence motion against then LDP Prime Minister Kiichi Miyazawa. It carried. The lower, more powerful house of the Diet dissolved, and thirty-eight unbroken years of single-party LDP rule in Japan came to an end.[53]

When the government fell, Ozawa cobbled together a coalition of eight opposition parties under Prime Minister Morhiro Hosokawa. It promised rapid reform and for a time was widely popular. The new Prime Minister received approval ratings of 70 to 80 percent from the Japanese public, the highest ever recorded for that office.[54] This coalition managed to pass the landmark election reform law in January of 1994. By spring of that year, however, another scandal created political havoc and disheartened the Japanese people still further. This scandal raised questions about Hosokawa's personal finances and, given the people's strained patience, forced his resignation. Tsutomu Hata stepped into the prime minister's office as head of the now shaky reformist coalition. This government fell only two months later, when the Socialists left it to side with the LDP. Hosokawa's resignation and the collapse of Hata's government caused despair about reform's prospects, both in Japan and in the West. *The New York Times* identified Hosokawa's resignation as a "sharp blow to Japanese hopes for a more responsive politics and American hopes for a less bureaucratic and regulation-bound Japan."[55]

When Hata fell in 1994, an LDP-Socialist coalition formed a new government, controlled by the LDP but under the Socialist Prime Minister, Tomiichi Murayama. This ridiculous link between the conservative, pro-business LDP and the old Socialist Party convinced the Japanese public that the politicians had no principles, ideology, or agenda except securing and maintaining power. The coalition was a marriage of such opposites that it could not deal with any substantive issues, least of all fundamental reform. This government's obvious problems were compounded by the growing sense of the intractability of Japan's recession and the seriousness of her financial crisis. While the shock of these setbacks helped propel the reform movement, it also froze the government's ability to respond by destroying what little confidence the Japanese had in their leadership and that the leadership had in itself. The politicians had believed the rhetoric about the system's ability to forestall economic and financial problems, as well as maintain rapid growth and "guaranteeing the principal" indefinitely. At the time, the setbacks rendered politicians incapable of responding even rhetorically to the rising chorus for reform. Under Murayama matters drifted. The reformers became more vocal and more frustrated by the lack of response. The man on the street in Tokyo, Osaka, or Sapporo became increasingly cynical. After the one important victory on electoral reform, it looked like Japan could go no further.

SIGNS OF NEW DIRECTION

But to the deep chagrin of politicians the world over, politics is not a closed game. Outcomes and advantages depend on more than the skills of the

players and can shift decidedly in response to the outside pressures of economic, financial, and social realities. In Japan's case, the effects of her immediate economic and financial difficulties, as well as their underlying causes—
the pressures of globalization and economic maturation—have continued to
tip the balance of power toward the side of change and reform, and will continue to do so for some time into the future.

These forces, along with the antibureaucratic mood they fed, signaled the
ultimate demise of the status quo approach of Prime Minister Murayama.
After the Kobe Earthquake and the other distressing events of 1995, the Prime
Minister's approval ratings dropped to all-time lows. Murayama resigned on
September 21, 1995, at which time the LDP took over the coalition, placing
the then Minister for International Trade and Industry, Ryutaro Hashimoto
into the Prime Minister's office. More skilled than Murayama at making a pretense of action, Hashimoto was also aware that merely posing could not work
for long, nor could drifting or the old ways. The public mood had changed,
and even with its sad cynicism, it provided the LDP and its strange ruling
coalition with a real, pro-reform opposition in the Diet.

The inability to turn back the clock or to continue to drift was actually
evident before Murayama resigned. In 1995, an attempt to reverse the electoral reform and reestablish the old multiseat districts failed to pass in a Diet
vote, despite LDP-Socialist support.[56] If this was not enough to convince
Hashimoto and other members of the LDP establishment that the environment was changing, subsequent efforts to bail out a group of failed real estate
lenders certainly provided an additional lesson about the new political climate.
Shortly after taking office, Hashimoto was confronted with the failure of a specialized group of real estate lenders called *jusen.* They were the brainchild of
big banks and the Ministry of Finance and so their failure was especially
embarrassing to the Iron Triangle. Whatever their origins, the government simply could not allow them to go under without jeopardizing the country's financial system. On MOF advice, just as in the old days, the government decided
to channel tax money to alleviate the problem. The public outcry was deafen-
ing. The people had suffered from the recession and losses in the stock market. Now the government wanted to earmark their taxes to bail out profligate
lenders of the 1980s bubble years. The opposition in the Diet, led by Ozawa,
staged a sit-in to block the vote on this use of tax money. There was extensive
press coverage of the story, in Japan as well as the West, including undignified
photos of opposition Diet members sitting cross-legged on lobby floors or
camped in stairwells. In the end, Hashimoto and the government forced the
issue. The tax money was used to bail out the lenders. The government got its

way even as it fueled public resentment. The episode hurt Ozawa and other opposition members too. They lost both the exchange and their dignity. Though these events made no winners, they taught a lesson that the old days of simply following the MOF's sage advice, regardless of opposition or public preference, were gone.

Once the *jusen* issue was behind him, Hashimoto's forceful manner came as a welcome relief to a public that had become simultaneously cynical about the political drift and terrified by it. The Prime Minister's popularity ratings rose, and Hashimoto called an election for the fall of 1996 in order to solidify the LDP's dominance. This was the first vote under the new election law. Despite the cynicism among the Japanese, and skepticism among Western observers, all watched for some change to emanate from the new rules, and all expressed disappointment when the voting resulted in an LDP government. But this reaction misread the results. Although much that came out of this important election did indeed favor the bureaucracy against the reformers, other aspects offered a hint of encouragement to those who were seeking change in Japan's system.

On the side of the status quo, the public showed a clear reluctance to give the government to the reformers yet. The LDP and its old-line politicians took a strong plurality of 239 seats, 32 more than in the previous Diet but still 12 short of a majority. The new ruling coalition was still heavily dominated by the LDP under Prime Minister Hashimoto.[57] Neither Hashimoto nor his party colleagues showed much sympathy for those who wanted to move Japan away from her old, centrally controlled system. Hashimoto's book, *A Vision of Japan: A Realistic Direction for the 21st Century,* stands as a conservative contrast to Ozawa's reformist *Blueprint* and was described by Japan-watchers at *The Economist* as "a limp agglomeration of self-justifying anecdotes and turgidly excessive detail, pushing no platform more radical than tinkering with the status quo."[58, 59] Position papers written by the LDP before the election failed to give much hope of compromise with reformers either. The Coalition Policy Accord, issued by the LDP coalition in the summer of that year, failed even to mention the deregulation of basic industries and markets that loom so large in reformist agendas.

Hashimoto's initial cabinet appointments also worried reformers. All were old-style LDP leaders—the selections aimed to balance major party factions, and following time-honored party tradition, were based on seniority instead of aptitude for the post. His selection for Minister of Finance was Hiroshi Mitsuzuka, who was described by Japan-watchers at *The Financial Times* as the "archetypical LDP heavyweight."[60] The Cabinet Secretary, the seventy-year-old Seiroku Kajiyama, was said to embody the old LDP in its glory days. Other new ministers showed an explicit resistance to liberalizing reforms. All were steeped in traditional LDP politics and had worked for many years with the bureaucracy in the Iron Triangle. Most troubling from a reformist perspective was that the new cabinet failed to include the Minister for Administrative Reform, which Hashimoto had referred to as a means of changing the bureaucracy.[61] Subsequent cabinet reshuffling failed either to elevate reformers or show any particular sympathy for the reform agenda. At one point, Hashimoto exhibited a remarkable lack of sensitivity to public sensibilities by appointing Koko Sato—a man notorious for his role in the Lockheed scandal that brought down Prime Minister Tanaka—to head the influential Management and Coordination Agency. The ensuing public outcry forced a reversal of that decision.[62]

While the media, especially the Western press, jumped on these results and declared Japanese reform dead, it soon became clear that issues more important than just the preferences of Prime Minister Hashimoto or the old guard of the LDP were gaining recognition. In that 1996 election and the maneuvering immediately following, the first signs of a changing Japanese politics emerged and have gained momentum since. By then, practical politics began demanding concessions to the reform agenda. However much the old guard at the LDP wanted to carry on in the old way, the events and pressures of the 1990s were too important to ignore. The public's mood had changed, and politicians, even the cynical ones, could see that the ground rules had shifted from the years of complete LDP hegemony. Japanese leaders began to recognize that in order to retain power they would have to support at least pieces of the popular reform agenda, whatever their personal preferences. Cynical as this might sound, the pattern of gratifying public desires over institutional interests is in itself new for Japan and a sign of a major shift in Japanese democracy. It displays a much greater responsiveness to the people than has ever been shown in the past. It also suggests that government will have to continue to recognize at least the moderate aspects of the reform agenda, regardless of the parties in power or opposition, or the individuals heading them. As it turns out, that is exactly how the LDP behaved.

The change was evident in the tone of the campaign and the patterns of voting. The results of the first election under the reformed election law were indeed promising. While the LDP won an expanded plurality, it failed to secure a majority. This might seem a small victory to those steeped in Western practices, but in Japan it was remarkable. It was the first time in the forty-year history of the Liberal Democratic Party that it failed to secure an absolute majority in an election. (The loss of power in 1992 was caused by parliamentary defections and not a setback at the polls.) As the reformers had hoped, the new electoral rules also helped to elect a real opposition, which was also a dramatic change from the past. Reformist opposition remained fragmented, to be sure, but the two main reform parties at the time, the Democrats and the New Frontier or Shinshinto Party, won 208 seats between them, only 31 seats short of the LDP position.[63] This made it clear that the LDP could no longer ignore the opposition. The Diet now had a potent counterbalance to LDP business as usual. Furthermore, the new election law achieved its goal of refocusing voters from local pork barrel issues to national concerns, not the least of which was reform. According to all press reports out of Asia, reform stood out as a primary voter concern, sharing top billing with the bread-and-butter issue of taxes.

In addition to pushing national issues onto Japan's political agenda, the campaign's emphasis on reform spoke volumes to the growing force for substantive change in the country. Despite his personal ambivalence, while on the stump Hashimoto had to compete with his reformist opponents by promising to cut bureaucratic power and deregulate the economy. In fact, every major party in the campaign used such language as "administrative reform," "smaller government," and "deregulation" in its platform. At times the competition became almost comic. When early in the campaign Ozawa's New Frontier Party promised to cut the number of ministries from twenty-two to fifteen, Hashimoto countered by promising to cut the bureaucracy back to fourteen ministries. As the election approached and the debate became more intense and acrimonious—rather un-Japanese characteristics, and indicative of change—Hashimoto cut his number to eleven and then ten.[64] He and politicians of all stripes acknowledged that the public's preferences and the popularity of reform were clear enough.

A sure sign that Hashimoto knew times had changed occurred on election night. Noting the low voter turnout, less than 60 percent of the electorate, he commented on the intense public dissatisfaction with the current politics and the urgent need to develop greater sensitivity to the public's wishes. Of his plurality, he told his party associates: "Maybe it is a victory, if you want to call it that," but he added, "we have not been given full marks," using the Japanese student's expression for a good test score.[65] Only days after the election, he signaled his and the party's new responsiveness when, instead of backpedaling on his campaign reform promises, which everyone in Japan and in the West expected, he announced his intention to pursue deregulation and liberalization of the economy. It is doubtful there was much personal or party conviction in this continued reform drive. More likely, it was a practical politician's effort to stay ahead of the electorate. But, as mentioned above, this was something new for Japanese politics and, in the morass of interests that is Tokyo, was probably a more reliable engine for reform than a principled dedication.

Hashimoto focused first on financial reform. This choice showed more responsiveness to the public's particular disdain for the Ministry of Finance—which it held responsible for the financial crisis as well as a string of embarrassing scandals—than it did sensitivity to the reformers' preference to concentrate on this issue. By pushing financial reform that would limit the scope and weaken the power of this unpopular ministry, Hashimoto could count on a political return. Actually, his and the LDP's political instincts were responding to the public disdain for the MOF even before the 1996 election. In February of that year, the party initiated a study on the possibility of breaking the Ministry up into three separate entities.[66] Studies and commissions in public life are frequently a means for delaying action. This is true on both sides of the globe. But the Prime Minister's willingness to target this "ministry of ministries" signaled both an end to the myth of the MOF's invincibility and the widespread awareness of the need to respond to the powerful pressure for reform. By late spring of 1996, the old LDP-Socialist coalition had gone beyond commissions and studies and actually drafted a bill to break up the Ministry, make the Bank of Japan independent of the MOF, and weaken the Ministry's power by splitting off a separate agency to handle licensing functions, which had long provided a means for the MOF to enforce its "informal guidance." In a significant bow to reformist sentiment, the government announced that the aim of the proposed breakup was to make regulation more "transparent" and to increase "accountability."[67] All candidates supported this proposed law during the campaign. The MOF naturally fought it and managed to water down the proposals from the radical first drafts.[68] It failed to come to a vote, however, because the call to an election dissolved the Diet. But since the election, the ideas have reemerged.

Hashimoto and his party showed even more clearly that they understood the strong popularity of reform by extending the attack on the Ministry of Finance into a raft of deregulation and liberalization measures under the heading "big bang," or "*bigu ban*" in an official Japanese announcement. Named after the massive British liberalization of London's financial markets ten years before, these measures included much that was promised in the election but was dismissed at the time as mere rhetoric. Negotiations in early 1998 between the government and the civil service produced agreement to revisit the plans for weakening the Ministry of Finance. These discussions outlined measures to strip the Ministry of its responsibility to supervise financial markets, a major source of its long-standing controlling power.[69] The new law also freed the governor of the Bank of Japan from review by the more political Ministry of Finance. In so doing, it shifted Japan's approach to the formation of monetary policy and the supervision of financial institutions closer to the model of the Federal Reserve System in the United States, and central banks in other developed nations, including the new European Central Bank.[70] This piece of reform legislation carried special significance. It was the first action to change the law governing the MOF and the Bank of Japan since 1942, when their structures were established in conscious imitation of Nazi Germany's Reichsebank.[71] In addition to this significant change, the "big bang" freed brokerage commissions from the fixed schedule that had prevailed for half a century, tore down the barriers between brokering and banking, brought Japanese accounting practices more into line with international norms, and lifted Japan's more than fifty-year ban on holding companies, a shift that allowed firms greater flexibility than in the past.[72] As a further indication of the pressure to accommodate reform, the "big bang" measures actually went into effect on schedule in spring 1998, despite the ready excuses for delay in Japan's continuing financial trouble and Asia's financial and currency crisis that was becoming particularly acute at the time.

Still bowing to public pressure, even the old guard LDP showed a willingness to entertain reforms beyond financial market deregulation. In fact, the otherwise antireform cabinets—from both just prior to the election and immediately following it—gave their blessings to nearly 3,000 economic, financial, and administrative reforms to deregulate and weaken the control mechanisms exercised by the bureaucracy for the entire postwar period.[73] The Diet even approved legislation to repeal the earlier ban on companies issuing stock options.[74] Because stock options invite management to focus closely on stock values, the elimination of this ban will accelerate the recent pattern for firms to balk at cooperating with bureaucrats or other firms in their own *keiretsu*. Further reducing the Finance Ministry's power to allocate credit, this new legislation forced the Ministry to rewrite old guidelines. Now firms will have more latitude when issuing shares in the market and floating bonds, which will free companies from their former dependence on banks and other ministry-controlled institutions.[75] To continue the advance of liberalization, the new rules abolished the tax on securities trades as well as the permissions, filings, and reports formerly required for foreign exchange transactions.[76, 77]

The new government began the process of shifting power away from Tokyo toward local government entities and extended past liberalizations in matters of domestic and international trade.[78] In the area of everyday economic activity, it implemented a "Deregulation Action Program" to remove direct barriers to foreign trade, but more significantly, it removed internal barriers that had made Japan's economy rigid and kept out imports.[79] This initial effort and subsequent measures lifted controls on rail freight charges; abolished all restrictions on telecommunications services so that carriers could now supply telephone, television, and cable on a single line (something not yet done in the United States); repealed the government monopoly on job placement agencies; relaxed restrictions on imports of refined petroleum products; decontrolled the price of refined oil products at wholesale and retail levels; repealed the old monopoly on electric power to reduce prices and allow firms like Kobe Steel, Hitachi Zosen Shipbuilding, and Toyota to enter the market and sell their surplus power; abolished limits and price restrictions on transportation services, which, among other things, will increase the number of taxis on city streets; removed restrictions so that four new airlines could enter the domestic market; relaxed construction rules to allow builders greater flexibility in meeting safety and strength standards; abolished rate-setting standards on insurance; and eased some of the zoning restrictions and tax differentials that had tied up the real estate market for years.[80, 81, 82, 83]

For all these efforts, however, the public evidently decided that Hashimoto and his cabinet had not done enough and, in the 1998 vote for the upper, weaker house of the Diet, delivered their message in a most brutal fashion. When the results of the July 12, 1998 poll were final, the LDP won a mere 44 seats of the 126 available, down from the 61 that it held previously and far short of a majority. In addition, the LDP failed to win a single seat from Japan's four largest cities, Tokyo, Yokohama, Osaka, and Nagoya. Worse still, the message was delivered by a huge turnout, at least when compared with past upper house elections. Exit polls showed that most of the additional votes came out to protest the inadequate reform progress of the LDP leadership. The main opposition Democratic Party of Japan gained, winning 47 seats compared with its previous 38. But the extent of dissatisfaction was most obvious in the gains of the independents, who won 25 seats, almost double the 13 that they held before the election.

The public's ongoing and insistent demands for reform could not have been clearer. The message to the LDP was that it must gratify the public desire for reform in order to retain power in the lower, stronger house of the Diet. For the new LDP leadership it was the same reading Hashimoto had in 1996, except writ large. They seemed to receive it. In the initial scramble for power after Hashimoto resigned, the candidates for his vacated post, Keizo Obuchi, former Foreign Minister in the Hashimoto cabinet; Junichiro Koizuni, former

Welfare Minister; and Seiroku Kajiyama, former Chief Cabinet Secretary; made clear their pro-reform agendas. The fact that the power struggle within the LDP occurred publicly, including televised debates, was a major change in Japanese politics. In the past, such struggles were settled behind closed doors among party faction leaders and powerful interest groups with no attempt to win over party rank and file, much less the general public, as the debates of 1998 aimed to do.

Once Obuchi secured the LDP presidency and so the Prime Minister's office, he went out of his way to show that he had heard the reform message. His first utterances as Prime Minister were pledges to step up the pace of economic deregulation and financial rationalization. He voiced a willingness to compromise with the opposition parties, another novel aspect to recent Japanese politics that also spoke to the rising power of the forces for change. His first gesture was to build what he called his "economic reconstruction" cabinet. Although Obuchi continued in the time-honored LDP fashion to balance cabinet appointments among the party's three largest factions, his selections showed a sensitivity to the reform pressure that had caused the election defeat. Obuchi chose the well-regarded academic, Akito Arimo, as Education Minister and Seiko Noda as Minister of Posts and Telecommunications. Appointing a woman to control the huge postal savings system was new enough, but Noda is also known for her insight and not for her connections to party factions. The appointment of Kiichi Miyazawa to head the Finance Ministry gratified old-line LDP faction members. But drawing on Miyazawa's well-regarded reputation in financial circles also displayed a recognition of the need to bow to a reform-minded electorate that had clearly become impatient with Hashimoto's less technically qualified choices. Obuchi and his new government have continued their efforts to gain public approval by proceeding strongly along these pro-reform lines, refusing to backtrack on liberalizations, despite the convenient excuse offered by the Asian financial crisis.

But for all the progress that has been and continues to be made, liberalizing reform and deregulation still have a long way to go. The "thicket" of rules referred to in Ozawa's book remains mighty tangled. Many reformers have clearly expressed their dissatisfaction with the effort thus far, and probably will for some time to come. The reformers, despite their recent victories, worry that the Bank of Japan's independence is a sham because the Finance Ministry still has the power to approve its budget, or that the new permission to form holding companies may be ineffective since Japan's Fair Trade Commission can still set limits on company size.[84] Some reformers suspect that the new real estate rules will do little to ease practical restrictions because the Ministry of Finance and the Bank of Japan can still prevent banks from foreclosing on mortgages to relieve the burden of bad real estate loans.[85] Still other reformers have expressed frustration with the authorities for having done nothing to privatize the management of the vast investments in the post office savings plan or public pension funds. Most troubling to those who seek administrative reform has been the Diet's inability to pass a bill establishing a Japanese equivalent of the General Accounting Office in the United States to audit the ministries and thereby ensure accountability.[86] Some of these concerns may be addressed soon in the present reform momentum, though others may fester for some time.

For all the forceful impetus behind change, there still remains great power in the civil service bureaucracy to resist reform and the strong conservative elements in the Diet will fight to preserve as much of the old system as they can. Despite all the emphasis and debate on reform since Japan's problems emerged in the early 1990s, the decade draws to a close with the Bank of Japan still in control of credit allocation, and the Ministry of Finance still administering Japan's complex tax code and writing the nation's budget, which is passed by the Diet largely undebated and unopposed. The Finance Ministry has not suffered the thorough dismemberment that so many reformers demanded and so many politicians promised. It has thus far resisted the major tax cut proposed by reformers. The Ministry of International Trade and Industry continues to exert tremendous influence over industrial policy, subsidies, licenses, and critical approvals for industry and commerce. The Ministries of Transportation and Construction maintain full discretion in the handling of contracts for public works, which are, of course, of great importance to businesses and politicians alike. And, as described earlier, the ministries continue to use the media to put their spin on events and ideas, and to contain critics, if not discredit them entirely. Though the old system has ceded much of its power in recent years, much remains nonetheless.

Another frustration for reformers is the strong conservative streak that persists among the Japanese public and its leadership. Despite a basic sympathy with the reform agenda, conservatism has fostered concerns that the reforms might come too fast. It is feared that "collateral damage" will further harm the already weak Japanese financial institutions when the reformers expose them to stiffer competition from other domestic and foreign players.[87] Other conservatives doubt the ability of Japanese institutions to cope with a liberalized regime. A political cartoon that ran right after the "big bang" reforms were announced captured this feeling well. Labeled "Reluctant to Fly High," it showed then Prime Minister Hashimoto standing on an ice flow pointing to a flock of high-flying geese and imploring the penguins at his feet, labeled "Japanese banks," to follow the example.[88] In some respects, this rather sympathetic resistance has presented a more difficult obstacle to reformers than the bureaucratic blocking, for there is always the chance that it might contain some truth. Against this, the cynicism of politicians might prove to be an important asset to advancing reform. After all, promoting change only to please voters should instill a willingness to forge ahead with no regard for the risks that are always present and always offer a reason for inaction.

Doubtless, the ascendancy in this war between the reformers on the one side and the conservatives and bureaucrats on the other, will swing back and forth for a long time to come. The specifics of each battle will create a conflicting mix of news that will frustrate advocates on either side. Politicians will change their stripes, or at least their tones, to suit whichever side is popular at the moment. In 1997, for example, a panel to advise the Prime Minister on administrative change laid out a formal plan to fulfill campaign promises and cut the bureaucracy from twenty-two to thirteen ministries, even abolishing MITI. This panel seemed very pro-reform. But at the same time, under pressure from influential civil servants, the panel also suggested the dilution of earlier proposals to weaken the Ministry of Finance.[89]

Never in any democracy does movement continue smoothly in a single direction. Japan is no exception. But even so, the direction of change is clear. All the underlying forces in the immediate and long-term economic situation push toward liberalization and other such reforms. For all the deviation, failures, and backtracking of recent years, the strides to liberalize Japan's economic and financial environment stand as a remarkable achievement, especially given the attitudes and concerns of just a few years ago. In light of what she has already done, Japan clearly has begun a sea change. The developing political environment certainly speaks to the prospects of future reform along these lines. Open debate, opposition in the Diet, and responsiveness to public wishes might seem familiar to Westerners, but are new to Japan. It is clear that Japan has begun the political adjustments demanded by the inexorable pressures of economic maturation and globalization, regardless of whether today's political personalities continue in power or even in prominence. Although the adjustment has progressed too slowly for some reformers, the pace will pick up in the near future as Japan faces even greater pressure for radical change from the rapid aging of her population.

GROWING OLD
IN
YOUTHFUL
ASIA

MORE THAN ANY OTHER INFLUENCE, the aging of Japan's population will pull the nation away from the patterns, practices, and priorities of the past. The number of elderly is growing fast—faster, in fact, than anywhere else on earth. By the year 2010, one Japanese in five will exceed sixty-five years of age. By 2020, one in four will fit into that category. The burden of this immense population of retirees on a proportionately diminished working population will force a series of difficult adjustments on Japan that will change the face of the nation. Some will exaggerate trends already in place as a consequence of globalization, the economy's maturation, and other more immediate pressures, both political and economic. Others will take the country in new directions entirely. Generally the shortage of labor at home will force Japan to integrate more with Asia than in the past, for there she will find the labor and other economic resources that she lacks. This shift, in turn, will force her to reorient her domestic economy away from its former emphasis on manufacturing toward the service, financing, and managerial functions that she will need to manage her overseas interests. Unavoidably, these changes will necessitate still more difficult adjustments. Japan eventually will have to take on the role of regional leadership, a development that will shift the entire political-economic balance in Asia.

THE DEMOGRAPHIC PROBLEM

Even a casual tourist in Japan can observe the extreme extent of her developing demographic trouble. There is a dearth of children and young adults but
an abundance of the middle-aged and elderly. A Sunday visitor to Tokyo's
Meiji Shrine park can see this in the families that come out to view the green-
ery and visit the Shinto temple there. These groups typically consist of a single child accompanied by a phalanx of adults: two parents, an aunt or uncle
or several, a number of grandparents, perhaps a great-grandparent or two. The
expense of the children's clothing—traditional costumes sometimes—and the
doting nature of the adults exhibit more than the mere affection of parents and
relatives; it speaks to the preciousness that comes from rarity. The working-
class neighborhoods of Tokyo or Osaka or even the small country villages show
this stark trend more clearly. While it is true that in the developed world today
there are not the convoys of prams or flocks of schoolchildren that were so
prevalent in the 1950s and 1960s, in Japan, the prams and children have all
but disappeared.

Japan's aging trend reflects developments at both ends of the demographic distribution curve. Not only are her birthrates low but her elderly have
enjoyed a great increase in life expectancy. Tables 5.1 and 5.2 offer statistics
on both phenomena. Japan's patterns throughout the post-World War II
period exaggerate the demographic ebbs and flows experienced by the rest of
the developed world. Like the United States and Europe, Japan experienced
a baby boom in the late 1940s and the early 1950s, but it was more extreme
and of shorter duration than in other nations. In the 1960s and 1970s,
birthrates fell all over the developed world, but in Japan they plummeted, and
have fallen further since. By 1980, Japan's birthrate was barely half of what it
was in 1950. In the United States, the decline was a third less. At last count,
the average Japanese woman had only 1.42 children in her lifetime, far below
her U.S. counterparts at 2.05 and well below the 2.1 rate commonly identified
as the pace needed to maintain population levels. Nor is there any sign of a
change in attitude that might reverse this pattern. A recent Japanese government survey indicated that only 22.6 percent of Japanese mothers claim to
enjoy child rearing. That compares with 71.6 percent who claim to enjoy it in
the United States.[1] While a low birthrate once helped Japan's economy by
allowing her to concentrate on production instead of child care, education,
and other youth services, it has now left Japan with a severe shortage of young
workers to replace the large number of older workers who soon will retire.

While babies have become scarce, improved nutrition and health care have

TABLE 5.1
BIRTHRATES
(Live births per 1,000 people)

	Japan	USA
1950	25.5	24.1
1960	14.7	23.7
1970	15.3	18.4
1980	12.8	15.9
1990	10.2	16.0
1995	10.5	14.9

Sources: Japan: Ministry of Health and Welfare, *Japan Statistical Yearbook,* 1997. USA: Bureau of the Census, *Current Population Reports,* 1997.

TABLE 5.2
LIFE EXPECTANCY OF THE POPULATION
(Years)

	At Birth		At 65 Years	
	Japan	USA	Japan	USA
1950	54.0	68.2	11.2	13.9
1960	68.0	69.7	13.1	14.5
1970	72.0	70.9	13.9	15.0
1980	76.0	73.7	16.1	16.3
1990	79.1	73.7	18.1	17.0
1995	80.0	74.8	18.6	17.2

Sources: Japan: Ministry of Health and Welfare, *Japan Statistical Yearbook,* 1997. USA: Bureau of the Census, *Current Population Reports,* 1997.

made the Japanese the longest-living people on the planet. Other nations have increased their populations' life expectancies too, but not as dramatically as Japan has. The average Japanese baby born in 1995 could expect to live for eighty years, almost 1½ times as long as in 1950 and 1⅕ times as long as in 1960. That same Japanese child can, on average, expect to live five years longer than an American child born in the same year, whereas in 1950, the American child's life expectancy was more than fourteen years longer than the Japanese child's, and in 1960, almost two years longer. This means that Japanese workers must support retirees for longer than anywhere else. Today, when the average Japanese retires at sixty-five, he can expect to live for almost nineteen more years. (Life expectancy at sixty-five averages a higher age of death than expectancy of birth because it is unaffected by youthful deaths.) His American peer can expect to live only seventeen more years. Two years may seem like a minor difference, but it means that Japan must support her pensioners about 10 percent longer than the U.S., or Europe, whose population's life expectancy is similar to America's.

These demographic changes are just beginning to impact the relative productive capacities of these nations. As Table 5.3 shows, in the 1960s and 1970s Japan's population was predominantly young, with few retirees and many in the prime working age group of twenty to sixty-four. She had a large proportion of young people ready to join the labor force and so had good reason to enlarge the country's industrial base rapidly. With a relatively greater number of workers and youth ready for work, Japan had both more working hands relative to her needs than either Europe or the United States, and greater growth potential in her young once they joined the workforce. These factors gave her a competitive advantage. But the low birthrates and the growing life expectancy of the aged over the past twenty years have erased much of this advantage. Japan's population profile has moved much closer to those of her competitors in the developed world. Her younger population has dropped to a smaller percentage of the whole than that of the United States or Europe, and the proportion of her population at the prime working age, though still greater than her Western competitors, has lost much of its former dominance. Her retired population, which was once small when compared to the Western world, has grown to 14.1 percent of the whole. This proportion matches Europe's and is larger than America's at 12.6 percent of the population.

Though these relative population profiles are moving toward parity, the trends inherent in Japan's situation will put her at a competitive disadvantage. Long-term forecasts are generally suspect, but in the area of demographics, projections from the available data are quite a bit more reliable than most socioeconomic forecasts. After all, everyone who will be involved in the workplace or retired within the next twenty years has already been born, and no exertion of policy can change the aging process. Japan's Ministry of Health and Welfare, the U.S. Census Bureau, and comparable official bodies throughout the world make accurate, long-term forecasts of their national population profiles. Using those official projections, Table 5.4 (p. 92) reveals Japan's absolute and relative demographic predicament. The Japanese population is expected

TABLE 5.3
DISTRIBUTION OF AGES
(Percentage of Population)

	Japan				United States			
	0–19	20–64	65–74	75+	0–19	20–64	65–74	75+
1950	45.8	49.3	3.7	1.3	33.9	57.9	5.6	2.6
1960	40.2	54.1	4.0	1.8	38.5	52.3	6.1	3.1
1970	32.8	60.2	4.9	2.1	37.7	52.5	6.1	3.7
1980	30.6	60.3	5.9	3.1	31.8	56.9	6.9	4.4
1990	26.5	61.5	7.2	4.8	28.8	58.7	7.3	5.3
1995	23.1	62.7	8.7	5.4	28.7	58.6	7.1	5.5

	Western Europe			
	0–19	20–64	65–74	75+
1950	30.7	59.2	7.0	3.1
1960	30.7	58.0	7.5	3.9
1970	31.6	55.4	8.6	4.5
1980	28.6	56.9	8.6	6.0
1990	24.3	61.3	7.7	6.8
1995	23.6	61.5	8.8	6.1

Source: The United Nations, *Sex and Age Distribution of the World's Populations*, 1994.

to age so that by 2010, over 20 percent of the nation will exceed sixty-five years of age and nearly 10 percent will exceed seventy-five years. In that year, the proportion of dependent retirees in the Youithed States will not exceed that which presently faces Japan. By then, Japan's population will have a slightly smaller percentage of working-age individuals than either Europe or the United States. By 2020, more than 25 percent of the Japanese population will exceed sixty-five years, and over 12 percent will exceed seventy-five years, while those of working age will fall below 55 percent. Meanwhile, by the same year, the proportion of people available to work in Europe and the United States will have dropped only marginally, certainly far less than in Japan.

Not only will this growing population of pensioners put Japan at a disadvantage as a manufacturer and exporter in the global marketplace, it will also place a tremendous burden on her economy. Demographics alone cannot

TABLE 5.4
PROJECTED AGE DISTRIBUTION
(Percentage of Population)

	Japan				United States			
	0–19	20–64	65–74	75+	0–19	20–64	65–74	75+
2000	21.4	62.1	10.2	6.3	28.5	59.0	6.7	5.8
2010	20.0	58.9	11.7	9.4	27.1	59.4	7.4	6.2
2020	19.8	54.6	13.5	12.1	25.2	57.3	10.4	7.1
2030	20.3	53.6	11.4	14.7	24.7	53.5	11.8	10.0

	Western Europe			
	0–19	20–64	65–74	75+
2000	25.0	60.3	8.9	5.9
2010	22.8	61.1	8.9	7.3
2020	22.6	58.4	10.9	8.1
2030	22.8	54.8	12.3	10.2

Sources: Japan: Ministry of Health and Welfare, *Japan Statistical Yearbook*, 1997. USA: Bureau of the Census, *Current Population Reports*, 1997. Europe: United Nations, *World Population Prospects*, 1996.

predict an economy's general productive or competitive ability, but they are a critical part of the equation. These pensioners will strain the economy by continuing to consume its products, even though they have ceased to produce (at least in the conventional sense of the word). Regardless of whether they draw on well-funded pension plans, pools of past savings, or public support programs, the goods and services that they consume must be produced largely in the present by the existing workforce. The pool of workers (now shrinking relative to the population of pensioners), will find it increasingly difficult to support these retirees while simultaneously providing for their own needs, those of their families, and continuing to produce the surplus output on which Japan's export machine depends. Compounding the problem, the inevitable demands for increased medical care and other special needs of the elderly population will shift the nation's scarcer labor resources away from the general production of products suited to global exports.

To gauge the economic burden on the working population created by these population shifts, as well as the implications for a nation's competitive

TABLE 5.5

RECENT AND PROJECTED DEPENDENCY RATIOS[a] FOR JAPAN AND HER CHIEF COMPETITORS

	Japan	*USA*	*Western Europe*	*China*[b]	*Southeast Asia*[c]
1990	5.2	4.7	4.2	9.7	14.9
2000	3.8	4.7	4.1	8.7	13.5
2010	2.8	4.4	3.8	8.2	12.3
2020	2.1	3.3	3.1	8.1	10.3
2030	2.1	2.5	2.4	4.1	7.3

[a] Ratio of the proportion of the working age (20–64) population to the proportion of those older than 65.

[b] Includes Hong Kong, but excludes Taiwan.

[c] Includes Brunei, Cambodia, East Timor, Indonesia, Laos, Malaysia, Burma, the Philippines, Singapore, Thailand, and Vietnam.

Sources: Japan: Ministry of Health and Welfare, *Japan Statistical Yearbook,* 1997. USA: Bureau of the Census, *Current Population Reports,* 1997. Western Europe: United Nations, *World Population Prospects,* 1996. China: State Statistical Bureau, *China Statistical Yearbook,* 1994. Southeast Asia: United Nations, *World Population Prospects,* 1996.

ability, demographers rely on a statistic called the "dependency ratio." It has diverse uses, but in this context it simply measures the number of people of working age available to support each pensioner. Table 5.5 looks at recent dependency ratios as well as projections made by government agencies in Japan, the United States, and Western Europe. The table includes figures for China and Southeast Asian nations as well. Though other Asian nations offered little competitive challenge to Japan in the past, their demographic advantages warrant attention now that they have come of age economically, and will compete with Japan and the West in manufacturing and exporting in the future. Japan's growing disadvantages in the coming decades can be shown dramatically when stated in terms of this ratio. By 2020, she will have barely two working-age people for each retiree. That is less than half of the mid-1990s ratio. Even though all the nations represented will face an increased burden of retirees, in the same year, Europe and America will have three workers per retiree—one-and-a-half times that of Japan. China will have four times as many (eight) and Southeast Asia will have five times as many (ten). With each passing year, the demographic advantage enjoyed by the rest of Asia will increase, because despite recent setbacks these nations are building up their economic

infrastructures, enhancing their technological prowess, and improving education so that their abundant labor forces will produce more efficiently.

These official demographic figures, dramatic as they are, actually under-
estimate the potential economic strain on Japan. Her labor shortage will be
worse than predicted, because not all working age people want to work or can
find it. According to Japan's Ministry of Labor, 69 percent of the working age
population today, men and women combined, participate in the workforce
outside the home.[2] If this rate holds into the next century, by 2020 the country will have a mere 1.5 people at work for each retiree. Circumstances will further limit those available for production because the growth of the elderly population will divert human resources in order to fill the need for medical and
hospice services required by the aged. In this respect, it is significant that the
fastest growing age group in Japan is seventy-five years or older. According to
the Ministry of Health and Welfare, this very elderly group will increase from
just over 5 percent of the total population in the late 1990s to 15 percent by
2025. According to calculations from The Population Research Institute of
Tokyo's Nihon University, this growth of the elderly population will cause
Japan to reallocate 1 to 2 percent of her workforce away from general production and into activities dedicated to the care of these elderly.[3] Taking this
reallocation into account, realistically Japan will have only 1.4 workers in general production for every dependent pensioner by 2020.

If left to develop without taking compensating measures, this situation
will impose significantly on the average Japanese working man or woman. And
since the burden will be nationwide, there will be no way to shift it elsewhere
within the society through government interventions or insurance schemes.
One way or another, on average, each pair of Japanese workers will have to
bear the support of more than one pensioner. The proverbial Mr. Tanaka—the
Japanese equivalent of America's Joe Smith and well known to anyone who has
ever taken a Japanese-language course—will struggle to support himself, his
wife, his one or two children, and his obligation for the complete upkeep of
about three-quarters of a pensioner. The burden of meeting this obligation will
go well beyond that of a dutiful son or daughter caring for aging parents (of
which there are many in Japan). It will require funds for room, board, travel,
a dignified amount of pocket money, and medical expenses (not just insurance
premiums or deductibles, but everything). Of course, Japan would never actually house retirees with the Tanakas and their neighbors. But unless Japan can
find a way to leverage her dwindling labor resources, the economic burden on
Japanese working men or women will be no less onerous than if things were
arranged that way. However productive Mr. Tanaka is, his budget, strained by

the burden of this elderly population, will have little excess available to contribute to Japan's famously high rate of savings or to invest in Japan's economic future.

Within the constraints of Japan's present system, with its emphasis on domestic manufacturing, the country has little maneuvering room to meet this challenge. A rise in birthrates, which is unlikely given Japan's present social climate, would do little to help the labor situation for at least twenty years, and in the meantime, would simply add to the burden of dependents on the already beleaguered workforce. Nor can Japan look for help from an increase in immigration of younger workers. Indeed, she has always discouraged immigration and continues to do so. For instance, to become Japanese citizens, the law requires candidates to take Japanese names and to immerse themselves in the Japanese culture. Koreans living in Japan for several generations are neither accepted in Japanese society nor granted citizenship. According to the Ministries of Justice and Labor, in its largest year on record, immigration accounted for a mere 5 percent of new workers.[4] By contrast, in the United States, the Department of Labor estimates that immigrants, though still only a small portion of the existing population, have greatly impacted the margin of growth. In recent years they have accounted for 28 percent of the expansion of the population and a higher proportion of the expansion of the labor force.[5] Even if the Japanese were to change and welcome immigrants, it is not apparent that they could attract the kinds of talented workers needed. Except for a small group of Western executives, Japan's reluctance to accept foreigners makes an immigrant's life in Japan rather lonely and unappealing.

In addition, there is not much hope of finding working hands by increasing participation in the labor force. With 88 percent of men of working age either employed or seeking work, there is little chance to squeeze more workers out of the male population. Though women's current participation rate of about 50 percent would seem to leave room for significant additions to the workforce, Japanese culture makes that difficult.[6] For years, it has been the Japanese pattern for young women to enter the workforce and stay until married. Those who do continue beyond their weddings usually quit after their first child to care for the family and home full time. There is no evidence that this pattern is changing or will change. The Japanese government has not tried to encourage women to go to work. While in the future the need for workers might lure married women back to the workplace by raising wages, the situation is as likely to encourage wives to stay at home, because the labor shortage will also raise their husbands' wages. More importantly, the growth in the numbers of the aged will increase the need for more women to stay at home to care for elderly parents and other relatives, as per Japanese custom. Presently, some 6 to 7 percent of Japanese women provide this care, but according to detailed studies by N. Ogawa, the head of Nihon University's Population Research Institute, given current customs, the aging trend could cause that number to rise to 40 percent by 2025.[7] While the practice of caring for an aged parent at a son or daughter's home has great social value and will also relieve the medical establishment of some of the financial burden of caring for the growing elderly population, its tendency to remove workers from the job market will only exacerbate the problems facing Japan's labor-deprived future. Even in the unlikely event that the employment rate of Japanese women was to rise to the nearly 60 percent that exists among American women, the change would do little to moderate the effect of the impending labor shortage.[8, 9]

Rather than asking women to return to the job market, Japan's economic agencies have looked for help in this developing demographic situation by encouraging people to work beyond retirement age. Under the slogan *hataroku ikigai hachi-ju nan,* or "eighty productive years" (slogans are even more important to Japanese and other Asian officials than to their Western counterparts), the government aims to convince employers to allow older employees to remain on the job longer than before and also to induce them to work part-time after formally relinquishing their old positions. The program promotes liberal work rules and health-building measures, and has established centers for retraining called *korei sha koyo tysako,* or "silver manpower centers."[10] Since elderly Japanese already participate in the labor force in greater numbers than in most developed nations—37 percent of the male population over sixty-five compared with only 16 percent in the United States, and even fewer in Europe—this campaign offers only modest prospects of success.[11] And, indeed, this has been the experience to date. Of the small number of pensioners who have registered at the centers, only 60 percent have actually found work and then for only brief periods.[12] Japanese corporate cultures do not lend themselves to the flexibility required to cope with part-time help from returning retirees, despite recent downsizing efforts and changes in seniority-based wage systems. Japan still permits mandatory retirement, which most corporations actively enforce. According to surveys from the early 1990s, almost 85 percent of Japanese firms have mandatory retirement rules and only 4 percent of them permit workers to stay on past the age of sixty.[13] Although there are no more recent comprehensive surveys, anecdotal evidence suggests that little or nothing has changed in this regard. Extensive research by Japan's Life Insurance Culture Center concluded that to increase the reemployment of the elderly significantly, Japanese culture must change in ways that are "highly unlikely to occur."[14]

Without much chance of greatly increasing participation in the labor force, productivity growth among existing workers would seem to offer some relief for Japan's future labor shortage, but here too prospects are limited. Productivity growth has always been Japan's answer to economic obstacles. She rebounded after the oil shortages and price increases of the 1970s by revamping her industry and increasing the average output per worker at the fantastic rate of 5.3 percent annually for a sustained period of ten years between 1970 and 1980.[15] But this option is much more limited than in the past. The economy's maturation and the impact of globalization have made rapid economic advances much more problematic than in Japan's earlier years of development, and preclude any return to the old astronomical productivity growth rates. Indeed, the slowdown is already evident in the historical data. Even in the boom years of the 1980s, output per worker in Japan increased by only 4.1 percent per year, less than in the 1970s and a far cry from the near 8 percent rates of productivity expansion in the 1960s. During the first three quarters of the 1990s, output per worker increased only 0.6 percent per year.[16] Since the pressures of maturation and globalization will intensify rather than recede, future growth in Japanese productivity will more likely resemble the 1990s than any earlier period, especially because acute labor shortages will limit the ability of business to enhance productivity by quickly retooling and restructuring in response to changing market needs.

ASSESSING THE STRAIN

Because Japan has limited means to enlarge the labor pool, and few possibilities of increasing productivity rapidly enough, the demographic situation will be a huge imposition on her economic well-being—unless, of course, she can compensate by altering her economic structure. Difficult as that will be after so many years with her present structures, Japan will make the necessary adjustments, because she is not willing to suffer the economic losses that would almost certainly accompany a failure to change. As part of the effort, she will expand her industry overseas to take advantage of the ample labor resources elsewhere in Asia. To control the new environment, she will transform her domestic economy away from manufacturing toward services, finance, and management. In effect, she will establish herself as the headquarters of a web of economic connections that she will build throughout Asia. It will be a radical shift from the Japan the world has come to know, but she will make it because of the tremendous pressure to protect her economic position and standard of living.

A calculation of the potential loss she could suffer in the absence of such alternative adjustments gives a sense of the extreme economic pressure implicit in this demographic situation, and assurance as to why she will find it in herself to engineer this radical change. Such a calculation is necessarily a tenuous exercise, given the size and complexity of Japan's economy, as well as the long span of time over which events will unfold. There are three ways to approach this matter: (1) by estimating the economic shortfall from the relative loss of workers; (2) by estimating the cost of financing the retirement and health care of the growing number of aged; and (3) by measuring the tax and governmental borrowing implications of the demographic trends. These approaches arrive at slightly different figures but suggest, with remarkable consistency, that in the absence of a major adjustment to Japan's economy, the aging trend could force a 15 to 20 percent decline in the country's standard of living. This is an impressive figure, even with a generous allowance for miscalculation, and it implies the kind of severe economic hardship that can prompt radical change. As a percent of GDP, it equals about one year's savings and about three years' exports. It is equivalent to almost four years' growth in the boom decade of the 1980s, and over a decade's growth at the slower pace of the 1990s.[17] Clearly, the stakes are high.

Approaching the calculation directly from a labor perspective must account both for the drop in the relative size of Japan's working population and the proportion of workers that circumstances will draw from general production into vocations dedicated exclusively to the elderly.[18] As Tables 5.3 and 5.4 show (see pp. 91, 92), official Japanese government figures anticipate an 8.1 percentage point drop in the proportion of the working-age population from 62.7 percent of the total population in the mid-1990s to 54.6 percent by around 2020. This implies a 13 percent drop in the relative number of Japanese available for work and a proportionate loss in output relative to the needs of the overall population.[19] Furthermore, the work at Nihon University's Population Research Institute calculates that circumstances will divert an additional 2 percent of the working population from general production to geriatric care, implying an additional drop in those available for general production. Combined, these rudimentary calculations suggest a staggering 15 percent shortfall in production compared with needs or an equivalent drop in Japan's general standard of living. In time, of course, a very gradual increase in worker productivity could compensate for the difference. But at recent rates of productivity growth, this would take a long while, about twenty-five years, in fact.[20] In the meantime, Japan's population would be struggling just to maintain its former living standard, let alone to see it increase. Such a setback would be especially hard for the Japanese, since they have become accustomed to a rapidly rising standard of living.

The second alternative calculation of the strain examines the matter from the perspective of financing the aging trend. This method must account for a few more elements than the labor approach did, but overall, it suggests that the demographic pressure will hurt living standards by about as much. In addition, it indicates that the demographic strain will erase one of the great hallmarks of Japan's past economic success: her huge flow of savings. For years, Japan has relied on a high tide of savings to finance her extensive industrial development and her powerful export machine. Without this financial support, Japan could not have sustained the heavy emphasis on domestically based production and exports, the keys to her past economic success. But the aging trend will change all this, and quickly too, absorbing savings from households, corporate pension schemes, and government-run social security. It will make further demands on national income by increasing the need for public and private health care spending. Combined, the financing demands of the aging trend will not only reduce this savings flow, they will also tap into the existing wealth from past saving.

For individuals, the impact of aging on savings is straightforward and predictable enough. When people retire, their income usually drops, leaving them with fewer resources from which to save. So they slow the flow into savings or cease it altogether. Retirees will frequently sustain their level of consumption by drawing down the assets accumulated over a lifetime of saving. When a large proportion of the population shifts from middle age to retirement, as it will in Japan, these factors cause average savings flows for the nation as a whole to fall, even if the young and middle aged continue to save at their previously high rates. Pension plans at corporations follow a similar pattern. When the firm's workforce is young, management sets funds aside to invest in securities, a kind of corporate investment account, to build their pension pool for the day when workers will retire and draw on it. Then, as a significant portion of employees pass from middle age into retirement, these firms—like individuals with their own retirement nest eggs—withdraw funds from their pension asset pools or allocate the investment income from them to their retired staff. The inflow can become an outflow, if the size of the working population shrinks at the same time. The combined effect of these individual and corporate adjustments could halve Japan's private savings rate of 18 percent of income.[21]

As a direct result of this anticipated future draw on savings, individuals and firms recently have begun to beef up their immediate savings flows. Some company management has exhibited near panic about securing retirement funds for the demographic onslaught. Japan's limited disclosure rules make statistics in this area sketchy, but Hitachi, Tokyo Electric Power, and New Oji Paper have all made headlines in the Japanese press for recent sizable contributions to their pension plans. A random survey of sixteen large Japanese corporations by Goldman Sachs (Japan) Ltd. found fifteen increasing investments in their pension asset pools, because they were not adequately funded for the surge in pensioners expected in coming years.[22] In the mid-1990s, the electronic giant, NEC, deposited a whopping 109 percent of net profits into its pension plans, up from 30 percent in 1992.[23] But this will not solve Japan's demographic dilemma. While this preparation has ballooned recent savings figures, the inflow will slow once the pension funds reach adequate size and are "fully funded." Then, when the workers retire and draw on existing funds, corporations will allow their asset pools to dwindle.

The government in Tokyo has failed as yet to follow the household and corporate sectors by making anticipatory increases into public retirement funds. Yet the future increase in retirees will, if anything, burden Japan's public finances more than it will her corporate pension funds. The legitimate demands of retirees will draw the government budget deeper into deficit and further drain the nation's overall savings flows. While Japan's Social Security system has its own complex and historically unique institutional structure, it is fundamentally similar to the pay-as-you-go approach of the United States. Contributions from those working are used to pay those who are retired. The "trust fund," to which both systems refer, is more of an accounting device than a pool of assets. The "fund" is used to offset shortfalls elsewhere in the government budget. Effectively, it invests entirely in government debt and will eventually become a current obligation of government, that is, the taxpayers, who, by and large, are the workers and companies making the contributions in the first place. In this structure, the aging trend's onslaught on government finances will come from three directions: (1) from the increase in Japan's Social Security pension obligations; (2) from the added burden on Japan's national health plans; and (3) from the reduced flow of tax contributions into both areas. The prospective cost for Social Security alone is mind-boggling. And the pressure has already begun. Since 1970, the pension obligations of the system have soared by 16.5 percent per year, compared to the 8.8 percent nominal growth for the economy as a whole. Social Security obligations have increased from 1 percent of GDP to 6 percent, in the same time period.[24] The Organization for Economic Cooperation and Development (OECD) has made calculations to extend this link between aging and pension obligations into the future. It has estimated that by early in the twenty-first century, public pension obligations will approach 18 percent of GDP.[25]

On top of the cost of pensions, medical expenses associated with the aging trend will also strain public and private finances. Outlays for Japan's comprehensive national health plans have already exploded, multiplying thirteen-fold between 1960 and 1998, largely because of the greater cost of improved medical technology, but also due to the start of the aging trend. In 1973, medical care for the elderly comprised 11 percent of Japan's overall health care spending; by the early 1990s, it had expanded to 38 percent of such spending, public and private, and absorbed half of all funding for the national health system.[26] This pressure will intensify as the aging trend gains momentum. According to the Ministry of Health and Welfare, the national health system spends four times as much on a person over sixty-five than it does on the average citizen. The Ministry projects that the number of bedridden in Japan will increase from 700,000 earlier in the 1990s to over 1 million by 2010, and over 2½ million by 2025. This is a 260 percent increase. Those suffering from senile dementia will go from 1 million to 1½ million by 2010, and to about 3½ million by 2025, a 230 percent increase.[27] The Population Research Institute of Nihon University in Tokyo has estimated that the cost of caring for the aged will grow from ¥30 trillion in the mid-1990s ($260 billion at the exchange rate of the time) to over ¥119 trillion ($950 million at the average exchange rate of the late 1990s) by 2025. Based on these figures, medical funding for the elderly will grow from 38 percent of the nation's current public health costs to about 60 percent in the early decades of the twenty-first century. These data suggest that the increase associated with the cost of the aging trend will amount to at least 1 percent of GDP, raising the total cost of this one group's medical care to a full 6 percent of GDP.[28]

This figure, however, underestimates the full extent of the medical financing burden. For instance, the cost of nursing homes is not included in official medical spending figures, yet they will surely become one of the most rapidly expanding areas of Japan's health care system, and this expansion will require financing from the government and/or the private sector. Though omitted from cost estimates, Japanese officials at the Ministry of Health and Welfare have acknowledged this growing need by implementing what they call the "Gold Plan" (strangely enough, they use the English-language phrase in their official announcements). The "Gold Plan" calls for adding 300,000 beds to special nursing homes and upgrading their staffing—currently only slightly more than two-thirds of Japan's nursing homes offer a night nurse.[29, 30] At the same time, the government has sought to avoid additional expense by encouraging its citizens to continue the tradition of caring for elderly relatives at home. Sixty percent of Japan's elderly live with their children or other relatives. To prevent this figure from falling to the American level of 33 percent and thereby further burdening government resources, the "Gold Plan" also aims to enlist 100,000 new home health care workers. Those workers will assist in family caregiving so that the Japanese homemaker can continue to house her elderly relatives in her spare room, thus avoiding the need for transfer to nursing homes.[31] The "Gold Plan" may be sparing the public purse from even greater burdens, but it still imposes a hefty expense on top of those already projected by the Ministry.

Combining these spending estimates yields a slightly larger overall assessment of the demographic burden on Japan's standard of living than does the calculation based on the decline in the relative workforce. The expected halving of the rates of individual savings and corporate pension contributions suggests a 9 percent loss to the general economy. In addition, the official figures on the increased public outlays for Social Security, medical care, nursing home care, and supporting home care, approach 11 percent of GDP. In total, these calculations suggest an economic burden of almost 20 percent of GDP, if Japan fails to make major structural adjustments to compensate for the aging trend. This differs some from the first figure of 15 percent, but in reality, it is remarkably close, given that the approaches are so different and the estimates extend over a period of decades.

The third means to assess this demographic burden considers the tax and public borrowing implications of Japan's aging trend. The Ministry of Health and Welfare has estimated that the cost of financing government expenditures for both pensions and health care will require a mammoth increase in payroll contributions, from 17.4 percent of wages currently, to about 35 percent by 2025. This is a brutally large figure, considering that there are many other taxes in Japan as well. The Ministry of Finance estimates that the highest payroll tax it could realistically impose is 30 percent, a jump of 12.5 percentage points from recent levels.[32] Since this will fall short of the amount required to meet obligations to the elderly, it suggests that the government will have to borrow the difference. According to the MOF's figures, Japan's budget deficit in the late 1990s already exceeded 8 percent of GDP,—Japanese accounting practices tend to understate deficits when compared with international accounting conventions.[33, 34] Even at this understated level, Japan's present deficit is dangerously large. It compares unfavorably to the United States' deficit in the mid-

1990s of 1.5 to 2 percent of GDP and a surplus toward the end of the decade.[35] The OECD has estimated that without a tax increase, the heightened costs of pensions and medical care resulting from the aging trend in Japan will increase the already existing deficit to a whopping 20 percent of GDP.[36] Even with the substantial hike in payroll taxes—the 30 percent alluded to by the Ministry of Finance as an upper limit—the budget deficit will approach 13 percent of GDP. The hike in payroll taxes of 12.5 percentage points indicated by the MOF would amount to 7 to 8 percent of GDP, since payrolls comprise about two-thirds of GDP. Adding the tax and borrowing figures to calculate a single estimate of the potential economic shortfall yields a figure similar to the labor-based estimate of a 15 percent setback in the standard of living.

In these projections, there is no pretense of accounting precision. But the fact that these various approaches seem to arrive at similar results does produce a measure of confidence in the general reliability of the estimates. Even though there is ample room to argue with the calculations and the specific underlying estimates, the important issue is less the exact computations than the clear picture that they paint of the potential for great economic hardship if Japan faces her demographic trends with her present economic structure. Whether measured in terms of the relative size of the labor force; the dramatic slowdown in the domestic rate of savings and the associated drain on the government-run Social Security pension scheme; or the unavoidable hike in health care spending, which has substantial tax and public borrowing implications, the picture portrays tremendous economic pressure that will gobble up the savings surplus on which the nation has depended to sustain its growth for over fifty years. Unless she makes major structural adjustments, it is clear that the demographic pressure will bring Japan down from the upper ranks of industrial nations, a status she has strived for since the middle of the nineteenth century.

JAPAN WILL NOT ACCEPT THE SETBACK

Of course, Japan will make the necessary changes, for no people, not even the ever-patient and long-suffering Japanese, can accept a setback of this magnitude. Their samurai concept of *gaman,* which exhorts them to bear all with equanimity, can go only so far. If increased participation in the workforce or productivity growth within her old system can no longer protect Japan's high standard of living, the Japanese will actively and ardently seek other means to retain their prosperity. These other means will necessarily lie overseas. Since her problem arises from a domestic deficiency, Japan will naturally try to compensate by gaining command over foreign economic resources, in this case, labor. It would not be the first time a nation has made such a substitution. Britain did this to obtain natural resources and even manufactured goods in the nineteenth century. Indeed, Japan has used foreign natural resources for years to substitute for her domestic shortages. Now she will have to extend that use to labor as well. This step is more complicated than for materials or products, but feasible nonetheless.

To accomplish the substitution, Japan will have to reverse many points of her old system. She will have to abandon her long-standing emphasis on home-based manufacturing and export. She will have to transplant much of her manufacturing might abroad, where it can find plentiful labor to substitute for the lack at home. She will have to reorient her economy away from the old emphasis on production toward management, finance, and other "headquarters" functions that can help her secure the profits of her overseas interests and to best utilize her limited number of well-educated workers. She will have to open herself up more to imports in order to supplement her declining domestic production and allow her people to benefit from the production of foreign labor. Reformers have already begun to move Japan in some of these directions in response to the twin trends of economic maturation and globalization. They have pressed hard to open Japan's economy to the world, cease the single-minded focus on manufacturing exports, and liberalize her financial arrangements. But the changes will need to go farther than most reformers now envision. In order to cope, Japan will need to take a series of steps that ultimately will change the entire character of her economy and her society.

Fortunately for Japan, the impetus for this transformation will not have to come entirely from the top. Without much in the way of official direction, the pressures of the aging trend—as well as globalization and the economy's maturation—will create individual incentives for many of the required moves simply through the efforts of Japanese households and businesses to deal with the exigencies of the changing environment. Much will occur naturally, even if her bureaucrats resist the change. A big step in this process of adjustment will be her industry's move overseas. Without a conscious realization of the larger picture, Japanese manufacturing will move in reaction to Japan's labor shortage and the rising costs that it will bring. They simply will seek cheaper alternatives abroad. So without any guidance from the government or civil service, each firm will contribute to the general migration simply to sustain its competitive position.

In this great move, the rest of Asia will have a special allure. The relative demographic advantages of China and Southeast Asia will continue to produce a siren call for Japanese industry. While the dearth of Japanese workers will raise wages and other costs in Japan, other Asian countries will continue to offer a cheap, abundant, and youthful workforce. While the expense of pensions and health care will raise Japanese taxes, the rest of Asia, hungry for investments, will continue to offer special incentives. Asia will further its appeal by improving its physical infrastructure and human capabilities, especially by raising education levels. The effort, of course, will not bring China, Malaysia, or other Asian countries up to Japanese levels, but, barring political upheaval, time is on the side of the rest of Asia, and any improvement will add to the attraction of leaving Japan to relocate there. The recent problems in Korea and Southeast Asia have temporarily increased risks and given Japanese business planners pause in contemplating a move. But over the long term, these troubles will only enhance Asia's allure by reducing relative wages, land prices, and the general costs of doing business, as well as by making these countries that much hungrier for Japanese investments. Adding still further to the attraction, Asia will retain well-established trade links to Japan, the promise of a large, rapidly growing market, and a cultural affinity that other regions cannot match.

Actually, Japanese industry has long since seen the advantages of an Asian base for manufacturing. For some time, production costs in Japan have run higher than in most places on earth, and especially the rest of Asia. Japan's MITI recently reported that while Japanese firms struggle at home and many of their subsidiaries in Europe and America lose money, their Asian affiliates have become the most profitable operations by far for the long term. On occasion the cost advantages have already enabled Asian competitors to surpass their Japanese counterparts. The earnings of South Korea's Samsung Electronics or the Philippines' San Miguel Brewing have from time to time exceeded those of Japan's auto giant, Toyota. Samsung has actually produced more DRAM computer memory chips for the world market than Japan's electronics powerhouse, NEC. Singapore Airlines, which successfully privatized and listed on Singapore's stock exchange in 1985, has reported strong profits, while Japan Airlines has only recently emerged from the red after a massive cost reduction program. South Korea's Pohary Iron & Steel Company long ago showed its clout by surpassing the once dominant Nippon Steel of Japan in both profits and output.[37]

The list goes on, with Asian companies surpassing their Japanese counterparts, and Japanese subsidiaries in Asia reporting rates of profitability superior to their parent companies. Although Asia's crisis has partly interrupted this pattern, Japanese businesspeople can see the fundamental trends beneath such occasional setbacks. These fundamentals have become so obvious that Nippon Steel highlighted the issue with a slogan to encourage employee effort. In Japanese they say, "*costo sakugen de katchi nuko,*" which means roughly, "overtaking the competition despite high costs."[38] Faced with these comparisons, it is easy to see why Japanese firms have begun to respond to the advantages available elsewhere in Asia (even before their impending labor shortage develops) and will continue to do so more thoroughly as the demographic pressure increases in the future.

While this news of inferior domestic profitability might chagrin the members of Japan's business community, it should hardly surprise them. Businesspeople have known for years that Japanese labor costs are astronomical compared to most of the rest of the world. The difference between Japanese hourly wages and those in Europe and the United States are great, but these differences pale when compared with wages in China, Malaysia, the Philippines, and other Asian countries. According to a survey made by Morgan Guaranty Singapore, hourly manufacturing wages in Japan averaged (the equivalent of) $20 an hour in 1996. Compare this with $16.88 an hour in Western Europe; $13.44 in the United States—gaps of nearly 20 and 50 percent respectively. But these differences are small compared with average hourly wage rates of $5.62 in Hong Kong, South Korea, Singapore and Taiwan; 91¢ in Southeast Asia generally; and only 35¢ in China.[39] Pay differences off the shop floor are less pronounced but still significant. According to the *World Competitiveness Yearbook* of 1996, the average Japanese engineer earned the equivalent of $130,500 a year; his American counterpart earned $60,000; his South Korean or Philippines peer earned $45,000; his Malaysian or Indonesian colleague earned $40,000; and his equally well-trained Indian counterpart earned only $25,000.[40] Although more current data does not exist, Asia's recent problems surely have exaggerated these differences by temporarily depressing labor markets and rates of compensation, too. Doubtless, wages will rise again in other Asian nations, but Japan's imminent labor shortage will ensure that in the future, Japanese labor will still be much more expensive.

To be sure, wage differences do not tell the whole story of labor expense. Overall labor cost comparisons also depend on levels of efficiency and job competence, both of which can vary greatly from one country to another and from one industry to another within a country. Frequently such differences can compensate for wage differentials. There is no denying that Japan still has the edge over the rest of Asia when it comes to efficiency and competence, and by a wide margin. Her commercial and production infrastructures, both physical and human—especially the education and training of her average worker—are far superior to most other nations, particularly those elsewhere in Asia. While these Japanese superiorities stand out at every level, straightforward comparisons of literacy rates illustrate the differences well. None of Japan's Asian competitors has her 100 percent adult literacy rate. Some are pretty close though. Hong Kong, Singapore, and the Philippines boast rates of over 90 percent, close to the 95 percent rate in the United States. Of course, this still means that about one worker in ten in these other Asian nations cannot read the instructions that his Japanese counterpart can. Indonesia is at a greater disadvantage in this regard, with an adult literacy rate of only 84 percent and China's rate is as low as 80 percent.[41] Along with workers of superior education and training, physical facilities in Japan—ports, trucking and rail links, as well as the reliability of the mail, electric power, and telecommunications services—also counterbalance some of Asia's other obvious wage cost advantages. Moreover, other Asian countries have pronounced disparities between their urban and rural workforces, and among services available in different regions. Any and all of these calculations might cause a Japanese firm to hesitate in moving its facilities.

But Japan's Asian competitors are taking these points seriously and making strenuous efforts to correct their deficiencies, efforts that in most cases have continued throughout the recent turmoil. To hurry the process, many nations in Asia have sidestepped their own rules and regulations. It is rumored that officials in poor internal Chinese provinces have turned a blind eye to the law that would force Japanese subsidiaries in their regions to use the unreliable local phone hookups, and instead have allowed them to use their own (illegal) satellite links.[42] In other instances, local authorities and national governments have altered former policies and moved to upgrade their power grids to satisfy the Japanese and other foreign subsidiaries. Recently, Mitsubishi Heavy Industries and its parent, Mitsubishi Corporation, made a deal with China's Guangdong province to build a $1.2 billion coal-burning furnace electric power plant to serve the local population and, of course, the Japanese operations in the region. To facilitate this project, the Chinese reversed their former insistence on local control of public utilities and will let the Japanese operate the plant for twenty years before turning it over to the Chinese. This accommodation will not only support existing Japanese investment in a very practical day-to-day engineering sense, but expressly reassures Japanese subsidiaries already operating in the area, and those considering a move, that they will have a reliable power supply. This is not the only such arrangement. Before the Guangdong venture, Japan's Marubeni Trading Company made a similar but slightly smaller deal to build and maintain a power generating plant to serve an industrial park in the Philippines. The trading companies Nisho Iwai and Itochu became involved in industrial parks based on similar deals to lure Japanese industry to Indonesia and Malaysia as well. Japan's Mitsui Company has even set up an industrial park of this sort in the political pariah Myanmar (Burma). Certain Japanese firms have taken steps to upgrade Asia's level of education as well, and with it, their attractiveness as potential sites of relocation. Following the lead of the American auto giant General Motors, which set up a college to train engineers and technicians in the Philippines, Japanese firms have attached schools and training centers to their production facilities throughout Asia.[43]

In addition to low wages and efforts to improve the value of workers in these Asian destinations, other cost benefits to business have offered an unequivocal lure to Japanese producers. Japan's huge consumer electronics firm, Sharp, put figures to many of these attractions when, in 1996, the firm's operating chief, Taizo Katsura, asked his business planning unit to compare the relative advantages of placing facilities at home in Japan versus Thailand or China.[44] According to the unit's calculations, the hourly wage differentials were indeed significant. They placed Thai wages at only 6 percent of Japanese equivalents, and Chinese wages at 4 percent. But the report writers also highlighted property prices for plant siting as an area for savings. The Sharp staffers estimated China's price to be 10 percent and Thailand's only 1 percent of the Japanese equivalent. They rated construction costs in Thailand at less than half, and transportation costs at about one-quarter of their Japanese levels. (Chinese figures in these areas were not available for the study.) Warehouse space in either location was estimated at about one-fifth the cost of Japan's. Electric power costs were pegged at 45 percent of Japanese levels in Thailand and about 33 percent in China. Taxes were also determined to be much friendlier in Asia than in the Japanese home islands. Sharp's staffers found Thai and Chinese corporate taxes to be about 20 percent less than Japan's. But these tax estimates focused purely on statutory rates. A simultaneous survey conducted by the *Japan Times* included all the special breaks made available by Asian governments to lure Japanese investment into their countries. It calculated the effective corporate marginal tax rates in Asia to be between one-half and one-third of Japan's rate.[45] In fact, the only cost burden that either study could identify as higher than Japan's were excise taxes in China, which Sharp's researchers estimated at 30 percent higher. As with the Morgan study, updated figures do not exist, but since Sharp made its comparisons, surely Asia's troubles have depressed prices there and heightened government efforts to lure industry. These factors can only widen the gap between Japan and other Asian nations.

Beyond all the cost advantages, Japanese business can feel the attraction of the potentially substantial market in Asia. East Asia, excluding Japan, has approximately two billion inhabitants. Even excluding China, the region's population amounts to some five hundred million, which exceeds that of the United States, the United Kingdom, France, and Germany combined. To be sure, East Asians have less buying power than their Western and Japanese counterparts, are less educated, are less productive workers, and have recently suffered serious economic and financial setbacks. But even the most unimaginative businessperson can see in these census figures a lot of potential consumers and willing workers. Despite their recent reverses, there is no denying that these countries are developing for the long run. For much of the 1990s, Asian economies as a whole grew at a pace of 6 percent per year, excluding the effects of inflation. For social reasons, China, with its immense human and natural resources, made an effort to cool its long-term annual growth rate to under 10 percent even before the Asia crisis erupted. By contrast, the United States has led the developed world with an annual growth rate of about 3 percent on average, after inflation. Japan's economy has barely grown at all. The crisis has slowed the pace of growth in Asia, but only a few pessimists expect the problems to persist indefinitely. Even with the effects of the recent economic troubles, the growth of trade in the region has still managed to dwarf the impressive overall economic comparisons. Intra-Asian trade has expanded by 20 percent per year through most of this decade. This is four times as fast as the showing for the developed world. In 1996, Asian trade with Japan surpassed Japan's trade with America and Europe combined.[46] Japan's Ministry of Finance noted a telling juxtaposition between their trade with the West and with Asia: Based on long-term trends, the size of the decline in Japan's surplus with America and Europe almost equaled the rise in the overall Asian surplus.[47] While no one has specifically linked these parallel movements, it appears to Japanese eyes that the previous advantages they had relative to America and Europe are migrating to the rest of Asia. Naturally, they want to follow these advantages in order to exploit them.

Recognizing that their overall size and rapid growth are attractions to Japanese and other foreign businesses, Asian nations have brightened the allure by forming regional associations to create an image of a single, rapidly growing market of immense proportions. Indonesia, the Philippines, and Malaysia are each large markets in their own right. There is justification for a firm to set up in each country to serve that particular national market. But Japanese and other foreign developers prefer the prospect of investing in one nation on a scale that can satisfy a larger regional market. China, perhaps, is the only nation that can ignore this logic: It offers a potential megamarket in itself. Other Asian powers, to create the compelling regional argument, have exhibited remarkable foresight and joined in the Association of South East Asian Nations (ASEAN), comprised of Brunei, Indonesia, Malaysia, the Philippines, Singapore, Thailand, Vietnam, and, recently, Laos and Mynamar (Burma). Its oft-used and somewhat exaggerated slogan brags of "one billion consumers." And though the group has moved slowly, ASEAN has nonetheless pursued the strategy of one vast market to entice Japanese and other foreign transplants. To make what it calls the "borderless zone" a reality, ASEAN has created the ASEAN Free Trade Area (AFTA). Not only has this arrangement achieved the remarkable feat of including one acronym in another (something before thought only possible within the Washington beltway) but the group has actually moved toward its objective of a single large market, a pattern that continued uninterrupted, even through the height of Asia's crisis. It has begun to reduce duties and plans to abolish tariffs on most manufactured and agricultural goods by 2003. An even more attractive feature for Japanese producers looking to escape their home-based disadvantages, are AFTA's plans to replace individual national investment rules with a single, liberal, pan-ASEAN policy.[48]

Certainly, the shift of Japanese industry into Asia has different roots than its earlier moves into Europe and America. Japan's efforts in the West were less reflections of the fundamental advantages and disadvantages for production than attempts to mollify foreign political resistance to Japanese exports, or to maneuver around efforts to exclude Japanese products. Japan's auto and electronics manufacturers moved into Europe with trillions of yen, not because Europe provided critical cost advantages but simply to establish themselves in the nations of the European Economic Union before it could exclude them. This motivation is still very much alive. Hiroshi Okuda, president of Toyota, displayed it clearly in early 1997 when he threatened to cease investments in Britain and to move them to the continent if London decided against full integration with the rest of Europe. For similar reasons, Japanese manufacturers turned to the United States in order to gain a foothold against various threats at retaliation against Japanese imports. Japanese industry also moved into Mexico, when the North American Free Trade Association (NAFTA) raised the prospect of an exclusive trading bloc. Table 5.6 presents the results of a study by Japan's Export-Import Bank that clarifies the differing motivations between the move West and the one into Asia. Over three-quarters of the firms with subsidiaries in Europe and America cite the protection of existing markets abroad as a reason. Reducing currency risk is also a significant factor in Western investment. But with regard to Asia, the motivations clearly are basic

TABLE 5.6
STATED REASONS FOR JAPANESE FIRMS
LOCATING OVERSEAS[a]

	North America	Western and Eastern Europe	Newly Independent Asia[b]	ASEAN[c]	China[d]
Secure low wages	2.3	7.8	11.4	40.1	59.0
Maintain and expand market shares	77.3	78.4	69.7	64.5	48.1
Access to new markets	25.0	29.4	23.5	31.5	54.1
Export to Japan	16.7	7.8	22.7	36.0	36.6
Export elsewhere	13.6	25.5	31.8	42.6	32.2
Avoid currency risk	24.2	24.5	20.5	21.8	13.7

[a] Figures show the percent of Japanese managers citing each reason and its relation to the move in each region.
[b] Hong Kong, Singapore, South Korea, and Taiwan.
[c] Brunei, Indonesia, Malaysia, the Philippines, Singapore, Thailand, Vietnam, and Myanmar.
[d] Excludes Hong Kong and Taiwan.

Source: Export-Import Bank of Japan, December 1995.

to the business of production. Respondents to the Export-Import Bank study bluntly stated that their quest in Asia was to lower wages, and to use the improved cost structure there to export to markets elsewhere in Asia, outside of Asia, and back to Japan herself.

Responding to these many lures, Japanese investment in Asia has already skyrocketed, even before the demographic strain has had a chance to become intense. In just the past few years, according to MITI, Japanese firms have poured the equivalent of about $1.5 trillion into overseas facilities worldwide, increasing the amount by 12.5 percent a year for the five years ended in 1996—the last year for which complete, reliable data are available. Of this amount, the share going to Asia doubled, translating to a growth rate of close to 25 percent a year. By 1996, Asia attracted over 60 percent of all overseas investments by Japanese manufacturers. The MITI figures show that over 10 percent of all Japanese manufacturing was already taking place overseas, though this number was over 25 percent for her larger manufacturers.[49] Every Japanese auto producer has facilities in South Korea or Taiwan or has tied itself to a

South Korean or Taiwanese producer.[50] Singapore has attracted subsidiaries from all of the significant electronics firms in Japan. Increasingly, Japanese electrical appliances are made in China, Thailand, Malaysia, and Indonesia. Japanese firms already manufacture three times more television sets overseas than they do in Japan. In 1996, 60 percent of color television sets sold in Japan—once the flagship of Japanese exports—were imports largely from Asian subsidiaries. Videocassette recorders, another more recent symbol of Japan's exporting strength, are fast becoming imported goods as well. At last count, 28 percent were imported from Asia.[51] By 1996, Japan also imported 89 percent of her calculators, 55 percent of her hairdryers, and 30 percent of her photocopy machines, mostly from Asia.[52] Of the 2,478 foreign deals involving Japanese firms in 1994, the last year for which reliable data are available, 1,305 were with firms located in Asia.[53]

The Japanese influence in Asia already outweighs that of other foreigners. While in the 1980s, Japan and the United States held parity in Asian investment, the recent acceleration in Japan's spending has elevated it to, in the words of prominent Asia-watcher Edward J. Lincoln of the Brookings Institution, a "substantially larger absolute and relative presence in...Asian countries."[54] As early as 1989, Japan's Economic Planning Agency noted that Japanese investment was dominant in South Korea, Thailand, Malaysia, and Indonesia.[55] Japan's presence has expanded further since. A drive through Shanghai's industrial suburbs reveals gate after gate with Japanese flags flying over them. According to the Shanghai Foreign Investment Commission, cumulative Japanese investment in the area tops America's by almost 25 percent and Europe's by more than half.[56] Visitors to Manchuria in China, Japan's prewar colony, report the prevalence of Japanese industry and managers in the region. Similar reports come from visitors to Thailand, where Japanese manufacturing has long been concentrated, but also from areas in Indonesia, Malaysia, and the Philippines, where the interest is more recent. Japanese retailing permeates Asia. Set up to serve Japanese tourists and expatriots in Asian facilities, Japanese retail chains are now a major part of local scenes. Japan's Saison retailing group has created ties across the region with major retailers in Indonesia, Thailand, Taiwan, Hong Kong, and Malaysia, through its *Azia Kouri Chein Nettowaku* (Asian Retailing Affiliation Network). Takashimaya, another Japanese retail giant, has extended its subsidiaries through its *Han Azia Tiaheiyo Nettowaku* (Trans-Asia-Pacific Network). Quoting the number of stores in these chains is pointless: they are growing too fast.[57] Matsushita, which already has twenty-nine businesses in China (eighteen are manufacturers, and eleven are wholesalers or retailers with a total of one hundred outlets), has announced plans to open 3,000 more outlets and production facilities.

Sony has also announced plans to produce one million mobile phones per year in Beijing. Daiwa Research Institute, one of Japan's largest think tanks, has conservatively projected that by the year 2000, the proportion of Japanese manufacturing abroad will have doubled from its 1996 level, with almost all the growth in Asia.[58] Based on the results of a mid-1996 survey by the Japan External Trade Organization (JETRO), one-quarter of all Japanese manufacturing—and a greater portion of the larger, more significant firms—will move overseas, with the bulk going to Asia.[59]

Though much of this Asian industrial presence still consists of assembling parts—originally made in Japan—for re-export to America, Europe, other markets, and back to Japan, this old pattern is changing. The assembly function is safe for Japanese businesses because it keeps the Asian subsidiaries dependent on the home-based parent. In this structure, Asia has imported as much product from Japan as Japan has purchased from it. While some 20 percent of Japan's total imports have come from transplanted Japanese enterprises (and a much larger portion of finished goods imports), Japan has balanced this by selling its Asian subsidiaries parts for assembly as well as machinery for initial plant construction and modernization.[60] But as the impending labor shortage impels Japanese businesses to move into Asia, this old practice will dissipate and the nature of these Asian subsidiaries will change, creating more sophisticated problems for management and control. Matsushita's Chinese operation is indicative of what may happen. For years, Matsushita's Chinese subsidiaries, in Manchuria and elsewhere in China, were sent Japanese parts and worked to assemble air conditioners and small television tubes for re-export back to Japan or to supply the American and European markets. More recently, however, these subsidiaries have moved into the more high-tech area of VCR construction. In addition, Matsushita's policy goal is to sell these products in the domestic Chinese and Southeast Asian markets. The current strategy effectively has the Chinese subsidiary completely bypassing Japanese input and seeking its own markets wherever it can find them, independent of the domestic Japanese operation. Another indication of expansion, Matsushita has begun to use its Chinese facilities for researching multimedia and voice training technology. Until now, this kind of skilled work was reserved exclusively for the firm's Japanese workforce. Matsushita, in short order, has developed ten such overseas research facilities, though not all in China.[61]

Asia's recent crisis has interrupted the trend, though all recognize that the long-term fundamentals for the migration of industry are still in place. In the meantime, the recognition of the underlying strength of this movement—even before domestic Japanese manufacturing finds itself weakened by the country's aging trend—has absorbed Japanese interest and awakened fear. A

Brookings Institution study in the early 1990s notes that, even back then, concerns had produced a dramatic increase in newspaper and government commentary on Japan's role in Asia. Facing the inevitable optimistically, that discussion resurrected the old Japanese notion of the "*tobu kamo no mure*" or "flying geese" pattern of development in Asia with Japan at the head.[62] But the beginnings of the movement of Japanese manufacturing into Asia have also raised concerns in business and government circles about what the Japanese refer to as *kudoka,* literally the "hollowing out" of its industry. The Japanese are beginning to fret that they will undergo a loss of manufacturing capacity comparable to the American decline in manufacturing in the late 1970s and early 1980s. The hollowing-out issue has elicited book-length discussions from Japanese agencies and think tanks.[63] Whatever the concerns, there is little the nation can do to shift the balance back in favor of Japan or to prevent industry's movement, especially in a few years when the country's labor shortage begins to have its effect. However much the pattern upsets those who prefer to maintain the old system, industry's shift abroad will proceed inevitably, as each individual firm weighs the pros and cons of the inexorable demographic pressures, as well as the maturation and globalization trends. The effect will likely resemble that suffered by the United States in the 1970s, when it faced a similar exodus of industry (though for different reasons).

However worrisome, Japan should resist this migration of manufacturing or even a "hollowing out" of industry. The move, after all, is a crucial adjustment that will enable her to acquire wealth and income from foreign resources to replace those lost at home as a consequence of her shrinking labor force. As such, it will form a pivotal part of her effort to protect her standard of living in the face of the increasing burden of her aging population. At the same time, the shift of industry overseas will also help meet the challenges of globalization and the economy's maturation. The rest of Asia, unlike well-developed Japan, is still desperate for the tools of industry. Like the salad days of Japanese development, capital investment there will yield much greater returns in profitability and productivity than at home, where the abundance of advanced equipment has diminished the impact of capital investments. The Asia move will also help "globalize" Japanese production, enabling it to meet the competition of other multinational firms better by reducing costs generally, providing increased flexibly for responding to market and price fluctuations, and most importantly, reducing the vulnerability of Japanese industry to fluctuations in the yen's value. But however great the promise of this overseas move, to use it effectively to meet all the economic and demographic challenges facing Japan, the country will have to change more than just the location of her factories.

SIX

FINANCING CHANGE

ULTIMATELY, THE CHANGES NEEDED TO cope with all the pressures of globalization, economic maturation, and especially the population's aging will transform Japan's entire domestic economy and its priorities. Moving factories offshore to tap foreign labor will be only one step in the process. In time, the nation will have to abandon her long-standing emphasis on domestic mass production for export and turn her focus instead to high-level services—finance, management, design, and research. These services will enable Japan to leverage the talents of her small but well-educated labor force to control her foreign interests to her best advantage, and ensure that she can bring home as much as possible of the surplus wealth produced abroad. She will become an importer instead of an exporter of goods, as her future labor shortage forces her to turn increasingly to foreign products to meet her people's material needs. In the process, her proud trade surplus will fall into deficit, though she will have an opportunity to make up the difference by exporting the services that she will also have to develop. Radical as this may seem, the changes will have to extend even further. The nation's need to enlarge her web of interests overseas will eventually force Japan to dispense with her long-standing reluctance to assert herself diplomatically. She will begin to assume economic and financial leadership in Asia and the world. To use a phrase that has recently gained popularity in Tokyo, Japan will become Asia's "headquarters nation."[1] In support of that role, she will have to break with other practices of the past, leave behind her long-held reservations about financial power, and drive the yen and her financial markets to global prominence as never before. Many Japanese and other Asians will dislike the changes, but this new and unfamiliar Japan will emerge as she responds to the developing economic and demographic imperatives.

SHIFTING DOMESTIC GEARS

Anticipating the greater changes to come in trade policy and the orientation of her domestic economy, Japan has begun tentatively to ease her old restrictive posture on imports. Previous chapters have touched on some of the reforms already implemented. In time however, Japan will need to go well beyond simply easing her former stance; she will have to effect a complete turn in her long-standing trade policies. With domestic production constrained by labor shortages and increasing amounts of her manufacturing located abroad, Japan simply will no longer have her old ability to promote exports and restrict imports. Instead, she will have to facilitate the flow of imports in order to procure the foreign production needed to support her people, especially her huge retired population.

The preceding chapter gave a general idea of the odds facing Japan if she tries to continue as a trade competitor while her retired population grows relative to her working population and her "dependency ratio" rises. The demographics are dire; they will, in fact, reverse the past advantage on which Japan's impressive trade performance was based. Fifty years ago, when she embarked on her famous "way," with its great emphasis on exports, her dependency ratios gave her a clear edge over her Western competitors. At the time, Japan had many more workers relative to her dependent retired population than did Europe or the United States. It took a long time to lose that edge but it is lost and eroding further. By the mid 1990s, each major developed region in the world was on almost equal footing in this regard, and could field about 60 percent of its population for work, with the remainder being either young or old dependents. In coming years, this balance will shift decisively against Japan. By 2020, her extreme aging trend will give Europe one more worker per pensioner than Japan, about a 50 percent relative advantage, and the United States 1.25 more workers than Japan, or nearly a 60 percent advantage in its labor supply. (By 2030 the forecasted odds begin to even out again, but those official projections depend on heroic assumptions about future birth rates in Japan and other nations, expectations that have only a negligible influence on workforce projections for the next twenty years.)[2] Elsewhere in Asia, these important demographic advantages are astronomical when compared to Japan. In the mid 1990s (the last period for which data are available) China had more than twice the workers available to support its aged than Japan, and Southeast

Asia had more than three times as many. By 2020, China will have almost four times as many workers per pensioner as Japan, and Southeast Asia more than five times as many. To fight for trade dominance in such an environment would be wasteful and doomed to fail.

In addition to these relative disadvantages, Japan's extreme demographic pressure will begin to impose a severe physical constraint on her export potential. With a shortage of workers and a large dependent population of retirees to support, Japan simply will have a smaller part of her overall output available to sell abroad. The migration of her productive capacity overseas, which itself will reflect her labor shortage, will only intensify this shortfall. Of course, in time productivity growth can enlarge the potential output of this reduced workforce, even as industry migrates. But at any moment, there is a limit to the amount that each worker can produce in a week, a month, a year. That production must go to support the worker and his dependents, including the elderly. Only after meeting these essential obligations is any excess product available for sale overseas. Japan had remarkable trade success in past years because she produced well in excess of her modest domestic needs, which the bureaucracy held down by suppressing consumption. But the aging trend will surely make this old approach untenable. With limited numbers of workers and a growing dependent population, her domestic needs will absorb an increasing proportion of domestic production, leaving less and less for export. Indeed, domestic needs will so press her constrained domestic output that Japan will have to step up her importing to cover the shortfall and meet her aging population's material needs.

Japan's shortage of goods for export and her need for imports will not occur across the board. Every nation has areas of comparative advantage on which it concentrates and from which it exports even when general shortages develop. Japan will draw on her areas of special advantage and continue to export electronic equipment, computers, fine machine tools, and other such products for which she is well known. But her relative labor shortage will cause exports to dwindle in other, less dominant areas, such as chemicals, textiles, and consumer goods. Increasingly she will import more in these areas so that the overall trade surplus will shrink.

In time, these circumstances will turn the proud trade surplus to deficit. How long this will take is difficult to pinpoint, but it is virtually certain to happen. To accommodate the 15–20 percent shortfall in productive power estimated earlier suggests a need to cut exports or increase imports well in excess of Japan's present trade surplus. By 2010, the red ink could approach ¥73 trillion at today's prices ($60 billion at the average exchange rate prevailing in the late 1990s) or about 9 percent of GDP. Of course, in any year, the exact state of Japan's foreign account will depend on other factors in addition to the demographic pressure. A weak yen on foreign exchange markets, for example, could ameliorate the effect by making Japanese products cheap to foreigners and making imports dear to the Japanese. Conversely, a strong yen on foreign exchange markets could exacerbate the problem for a period of time. A surge or slowdown in economic activity in Japan or abroad could cause similar effects. But whatever the impact of these relatively transitory factors, they cannot and will not counteract the inexorable power of Japan's growing demographic pressure to curtail her ability to export and increase her dependence on imports.

This outcome will be hard on Japanese pride, but even so, changing Japan's system to facilitate an increased flow of imports is the only way that her people will ever get the product and thus see any benefit from industry's move abroad. Of course, Japanese business can sell its Chinese or Malaysian output elsewhere and use the proceeds to purchase what Japan needs in imports, but in the end, there will be little benefit for Japan unless this new output can flow back to her people and replace the goods that she will no longer be able to produce domestically. Public need, then, will require Japan to relax her old view of trade, stop pushing exports, and ease restrictions to welcome an increased flow of imports. Otherwise, the movement of industrial facilities overseas will help no one in Japan but some company executives and their stockholders. No doubt conservatives and old-line bureaucrats will resist a change in long-standing trade policies. But the pressure of public need, and the ensuing outcry if it is ignored, will force the policy change. For without it, standards of living for the average Japanese will surely suffer.

An opening to imports and a de-emphasis on exports will come as a wrenching change and make for a very different Japan than the one to which the world has grown accustomed. Even so, there are already signs that Japan can make the adjustment and is moving in these directions. In a 1994 paper, the renowned Japanese economist Shigeto Tsuru identified two historic stages in this process. He placed the first stage as early as the 1960s, when the country finally reached a satisfactory level of prosperity. It was then that the urgency to export lessened, and an incipient consumer movement prompted a selective opening to imports. At the time, the bureaucrats moved cautiously, using great care to minimize the competitive disadvantages to significant domestic industries. Tsuru placed the second stage in the mid-to-late 1970s, when Japan liberalized import restrictions a bit less selectively than in the 1960s.[3] Since Tsuro wrote, a third stage in this process has emerged. As described earlier, since the late 1980s Japan has yielded to pressure from Europe and particularly the United States to reduce her emphasis on exporting. She has lowered import barriers, if only marginally, and made changes to allow imports to move more freely through her domestic retail and wholesale distribution networks. Some of the restraints previously imposed by the *keiretsu* families of firms have lessened as well. Much of the recent movement has developed less from top-down policy than from the forces of Western pressure, domestic business reactions to the recent economic setbacks, and intense competition from emerging economies elsewhere in Asia. Whatever the causes or timing, however, these changes offer signs that Japan can take the directions on trade that she must in the future when she will come under even more intense pressure, especially from her demographic imperatives.

The gradual policy shift has had a reflection in official economic statistics as well. Clearly, exports have declined as an engine of growth. In the mid-to-late 1990s, exports accounted for 10 percent of Japanese GDP, slightly more than exports mean to the United States economy, but far less than their 12 percent share in Japan in the mid 1980s and 15 percent share in the early 1980s.[4] Perhaps even more significant as a harbinger of the future is the changing mix of Japanese imports. In its heyday, the Japanese economic machine almost exclusively imported only those raw materials needed for its manufacturing—iron ore to turn into steel and then into machinery and autos, crude oil for distillation into fuels and chemicals, and cotton and other fibers to feed Japan's textile industry—all products that supported her export drive at its various stages. The authorities discouraged the import of manufactured goods because they competed with Japan's industrial development plans. But in more recent years, this stance has softened. Imports of raw materials have taken a back seat to those of manufactured goods, mostly consumer items. Manufactured items have risen to 60 percent of all Japanese imports.[5] This difference is quite recent, too. As early as 1985, imported raw materials still dominated by a large margin; then, finished manufactured goods made up only 28 percent of total imports.[6]

Of course, Japanese and American trade negotiators disagree on the significance of these trends. The Americans believe it is necessary to distinguish between imports from Japanese transplants and those from truly foreign firms. A recent report from the Office of the U.S. Trade Representative insists that the imports are entirely from transplanted Japanese firms, and that there is only "limited statistical evidence that corporate Japan's claimed buy-national-at-any-cost is becoming a thing of the past."[7] There may be truth in this conclusion, but, of course, the American trade representative has a negotiating position to support. The Office wants to pry open markets for American products. On the other side, the Japan External Trade Organization (JETRO) has its own negotiating position to support. Its report notes that even during the worst years of the 1990s recession, when domestic sales stagnated and Japanese firms were cutting payrolls, the sales outlets of foreign makers showed growth and more than one-third of them increased employment.[8] This is a hot debate, and these distinctions are important to government negotiators. However, they miss the more critical point about Japan's future—her growing willingness to take imports from any source.

As Japan's aging trend gains momentum and her labor shortage becomes a reality, the pressure to continue in this direction will intensify. But even as these developments drive Japan's great trade surplus into deficit, the nation need not lose her economic prominence. As other nations have before her, Japan can and will find alternative sources of economic strength.

These alternatives will emerge from her responses to the other fundamental pressures of globalization, economic maturation, and, most critically, the aging population. As one shift prompts another, Japan will begin to reorient her entire domestic economic emphasis away from manufacturing, and that change will serve this purpose. Thus as Japan's need to control her growing array of overseas facilities becomes more prominent, her domestic economy will naturally shift its focus toward management functions, design, research, and finance. These services—the very best that the East has to offer—will give Japan something valuable in place of manufactured goods to sell abroad so that she can pay for the necessary flow of imported goods. The shift toward these new, high-value endeavors will suit her limited but highly skilled and educated workforce better than her old preference for mass manufacturing. This plan will follow the path taken in part by the United States decades ago and by Great Britain before that.

There are signs, too, that Japan is already moving to reorient her economy in these ways, even before the demographic pressure has had a chance to create a domestic labor shortage. The percentage of Japanese workers involved in mass manufacturing has declined, as has manufacturing's share of the Japanese economy. Services have gained. In just the last few years, employment in manufacturing has dropped by more than 10 percent, while employment in services has risen by 12 percent. Since 1993, Japan has employed more people in services than in manufacturing.[9] By the mid 1990s, manufacturing accounted for only about one-quarter of Japan's total GDP, half of the 50 percent that it amounted to in the 1960s and 1970s.[10] These figures still exceed manufacturing's comparable position in the United States, where it occupies barely more than 17 percent of total GDP,[11] but the difference between the two countries is a lot less than it once was. Japan's powerful industry association, the Keidanren, has forecast a dramatic further decline in manufacturing's share of GDP and employment.[12] No doubt some of the recent shift reflects the influence of Japan's recession and immediate currency fluctuations, both of which set back manufacturing more than services. But such cyclical considerations cannot account for the full extent of this change over ten years. It must also reflect the longer-term, fundamental pressures described here, economic maturation and globalization, if not yet the demographic trends.

In the West, the shift away from manufacturing and toward services typically carries an ominous tone, with allusions to displaced, disgruntled workers and a weakening economic structure. The Western pattern typically develops as increased investments in plant and equipment raise the productivity of each manufacturing worker, thereby lowering the number of workers the nation needs. As productivity rises, so do wages, pushing companies to send lower level production jobs overseas in search of cheap labor. In the popular Western conception, workers displaced from manufacturing in this way tend to gravitate to low-paying service sector jobs. This pattern creates concerns embodied in the disparaging comment popular a few years ago that described America as becoming a nation of hamburger flippers.

Whether or not this harsh characterization is applicable to the United States (and that was always debatable), Japan's move away from domestic manufacturing will have none of these characteristics. Japan's aging trend will create a shortage of labor, displaced workers will be rare, except on a more or less temporary basis. Far from threatening jobs, the shift of manufacturing overseas will provide a needed supplement to limited domestic production. Also, the service jobs created in Japan will have none of the Western characteristics of poorly paid, low-skilled repositories for otherwise unemployable production workers. Quite the contrary, service jobs will be a positive response to the growing need for skilled "headquarters staff" to control and direct extensive overseas facilities. Of course, Japan's economic transformation will create a class of displaced workers similar to those in the West. Without belittling the personal hardships or the social problems they will bring, the larger trends, especially the generalized labor shortage, will render this effect but a minor crosscurrent in the overall flood of Japan's transition.

Far from a sign of economic weakness, Japan's headquarters service functions will form a critical part of her effort to maintain a high standard of living in the face of the pressures straining her economy. By deciding at home what is produced, where it is produced, where it is sold, and at what price, Japan will retain the means to control a substantial portion of the wealth she will create overseas. These headquarters service functions—in management, research, design, and finance—will constitute Japan's new export, to her overseas transplants, and other companies abroad as well. Through the sale of knowledge, skill, coordination, and innovation, Japan's reduced labor force will have a way to earn income to take the place of the flow of exports on which her economy had previously depended. It might seem that such service exports will not generate adequate income for this purpose, but with an array of transplants throughout Asia, it should fill the need well. By charging each external affiliate even a small percentage for such critical services, headquarters in Japan will net a healthy income in addition to the usual ownership dividend. Effectively, Japanese managers, researchers, designers, and support staffers will have vastly increased productivity, because their contributions to the productive process will multiply over a host of foreign workers. This sort of productivity expansion is not easily rendered into statistics, but just because it is unmeasurable does not mean that it is insignificant. These headquarters functions will, in fact, create a highly profitable return to Japan. They will sustain a considerable number and range of high- and mid-level personnel and give them the wherewithal to pay the cost not only of the surge in imports but also of other domestic functions in a Japan, where prices will surely rise as the shortage of labor raises the average wage.

As Japan transplants much of her manufacturing abroad and reorients her domestic economy in these ways in order to manage it, she will create a kind of regional division of labor in Asia. The management control, research, and direction will come from Japan, while the bulk of production will occur elswhere in Asia. In many ways, this is a natural division based on relative advantages. Japan is more thoroughly developed than other Asian nations and has a more sophisticated, better educated pool of labor from which to staff the headquarters as well as the finance, research, and design functions. The rest of Asia has an ample and eager workforce in need of industrial facilities, training, and direction. This notion of such an allocation is not a new concept. As early as the 1970s, the prominent Japanese economist Kiyoshi Kojima argued the case for a national division of labor and specialization in Asia.[13] More recently, in the early 1990s, a report from the Economic Planning Agency of Japan's Ministry of Finance alluded to just such a regional allocation and coordination of talent and resources.[14] Since such a division of labor is an economically rational approach to the relative strengths and weaknesses in the region, it should create the most wealth for the most people in Asia, at least until the rest of Asia reaches a comparable level of development. As the securities analysts like to say, there is a natural synergy at work here.

Whatever the idea's rationality or pedigree, this regional division of labor will inevitably meet with official disapproval as it develops. Governments and their bureaucracies always want their economic functions housed in their own jurisdictions. Japanese bureaucrats will lament the loss of raw productive power, while officials in Japan's client states will resent control from a foreign headquarters. Especially for non-Japanese, the new order will resemble an empire too much for comfort. It will remind many of Japan's wartime domination of her neighbors under the ostensibly economic Greater East Asia Co-Prosperity Sphere. The language of the Economic Planning Agency's reports does little to lessen such fears. It employs a rhetoric that is disturbingly similar to that used during the war, calling the unfolding relationship between Japan and Asia *"kyochoteki han ei kankei"* (a cooperative prosperity relationship). Although for the time being that is an accurate description, and although nothing in this situation or modern Japanese attitudes even hints that Japan will repeat her behavior of the 1930s and 1940s, the memory and the rhetoric are already creating objections. Nonetheless, all of Asia will have an interest in adjusting. Japan will embrace the situation because she will not have the alternative of producing for herself, and this arrangement will offer a means to protect her standard of living. Japan's client states will tolerate the situation because Japanese investment will bring them development and wealth.

While the new order in Asia will undoubtedly evoke unpleasant comparisons to the aggressive Japanese empire of the 1930s and 1940s, it will more closely resemble the British Empire of the nineteenth century. A huge foreign workforce spread over a vast region will sustain an educated managerial class in Japan that will develop the kinds of services at home that will support and help perpetuate its privileged position. Of course, there are differences between the historic British model and Japan's future in Asia. Britain's empire had a powerful political and legal core, which Japan's Asian influence will lack, at least in a formal way. Also, Britain never suffered from a labor shortage as Japan will. Early in its empire, Britain retained much of the manufacturing, relying on the empire for raw materials. But by late in the nineteenth century, even the manufacturing, which had been cutting-edge, had begun to migrate out into British possessions or British-owned properties in the United States. As a result, it was the financial, administrative, commercial, and research functions, not the production itself, that increasingly sustained British consumption of the product of its vast foreign holdings. The Bank of Japan has noted these historical parallels, and recently completed a report that compares Japan with Great Britain at the turn of the nineteenth century. It notes how Britain had passed the peak of its industrial power, and in order to gain advantage from growth and a development outside its borders, was reorienting itself away from heavy manufacturing and export competition toward finance and other services. The Bank of Japan's *Annual Report* of 1995 summarizes that study and refers to the British experience as a guide for Japan's future. The report even points out how Britain lost its basic steel industry to operations overseas and sustained its presence only by making specialty products—like spring steel—that in the context of the late nineteenth century were more akin to research and design projects than basic production.[15]

Although the Asian division of labor will ensure the economic future of Japan, the radical nature of the necessary change understandably raises doubts about the country's ability to make the adjustment. After all, Japan has long focused exclusively on mass production and exports, and done nothing to foster the service sector that her future will require. Her Iron Triangle has squelched entrepreneurial endeavor, innovation outside of the large corporate structures, and experimentation of any kind with management structures or specialty products. In an effort to provide her mass production industries with an earnest, disciplined workforce, her education and training systems have long ignored the cultivation of leadership and innovation that will become prized in this new Japanese future. Nonetheless, there are already strong signs that Japan can and will make the necessary adjustments, as she always does when the pressure becomes great enough and her survival is at stake. The statistics quoted earlier on the decreased relative importance of manufacturing speak to the direction of change and Japan's ability to make it. In recent years, she has also begun to enlarge her research functions, enhance her managerial abilities beyond those needed simply to maintain an efficient shop floor, change her educational emphasis, and even shift her business philosophies to achieve the flexibility needed to cope with smaller, more specialized, and more service-oriented activities. Konosuke Matsushita, founder of the electronics firm that bears his name, set the direction for his company specifically, and Japanese business generally, when he insisted that Japan's emphasis must and will shift toward information and services, from "*ju ko cho dai* [heavy, thick, long and big] to *kei haku tan sho* [light, thin, short and small]."[16]

One of the surest signs of Japan's willingness to make the necessary adjustments is her sudden interest in educational reform. Japan's lack of Nobel laureates has become a symbol to the Japanese of their nation's educational shortcomings. Numerous popular publications and government studies have compared Japan's half dozen or so scientific Nobel Prize winners with more than 180 for America and over 60 for Germany.[17] It especially seems to rankle that one Japanese researcher won his Nobel for work that he did in America. Noting this shortfall, commentators speak of the need to shift the emphasis of Japanese education and training, despite justifiable pride in the high average level of education in Japan and the large number of new patents secured by business each year. The concern centers on the system's seeming inability to produce the excellence and leadership in science and the managerial fields that the country will need in the future. Critics of the status quo claim that Japanese schools, though remarkably successful in many ways, are poorly suited to this new future. For instance, the critics admit that the enforcement of conformity was once useful in creating a disciplined workforce, but today it suppresses the imagination and initiative that Japan needs. Leo Esaki, president of Tsukuba University, frequently billed as Japan's M.I.T., captured the new feeling when he said: "The Japanese system is already equipped to produce followers," now it needs to cultivate the "diversity" that can produce an "intellectual elite."[18] The Ministry of Education has already responded by launching a program in June 1997 to do nothing less than "turn Japanese education on its head," in the worlds of one observer.[19] As of this writing, the details of that plan still remain vague. It will disappoint Leo Esaki and others who want change immediately, but nonetheless the pressure for change is clear and coincides with the need to realign the domestic economy for the country's new headquarters function.

Along with educational reform, Japan has begun to serve her future needs with a renewed interest in pure scientific research. The Diet recently passed so-called "basic law," calling on the Prime Minister's Council for Science and Technology to search for ways to promote pure research.[20] This emphasis would develop even without the need to reorient the domestic economy away from old-line mass production. As noted earlier, having reached economic maturity and caught up with the West, Japan can no longer use the West as a model and needs now to do her own research to guide future development. This consideration forms the fundamental motivation behind MITI's stepped-up government spending on basic research. But the coming need to reorient the domestic economy toward research and management services will overlay that effort, reinforce it, and add urgency as well. So far, the research effort has had mixed results. Japan's National Space Development Agency (NASDA) has created the well-respected and successful Rocket System Corporation to act as a general contractor for satellite and space technology.[21] But not all the work has produced tangible results. Critics explain that research in Japan faces an impediment because Japanese university labs fail to communicate and cooperate in the ways that support such efforts in the United States.[22] This surely is one of many other issues to overcome if Japan is to make the adjustments necessary to cope in the future. But the direction of change is already clear and, whatever the immediate motivations, it will support the longer-term, fundamental transformation that Japan's new future interests will demand.

An even more significant sign of Japan's future reorientation is her new openness to joint ventures with foreign firms. After years of resisting foreign links as a threat to Japan's "way," with their responsiveness to centralized bureaucratic control, Japanese companies have begun to develop all kinds of research sharing, joint ventures and affiliations with foreign firms. The stated reasons for these links are telling, and show that Japan is moving away from the old exclusive emphasis on mass manufacturing and is turning toward those economic functions that will support the knowledge-based headquarters that she needs to become. Japanese partners have made clear that their objective is to gain the technical, design, and managerial skills that they lack, and know they will need to succeed in the future. In the area of space, for instance, Mitsubishi Electric, contracting for Japan's Rocket System Corporation and in concert with the Society of Japanese Aerospace Companies, has sought and gained a strong relationship with the Russian rocket and space industry in order to absorb Russian engineering and design expertise.[23] On the other side of the economic and business spectrum, another part of Mitsubishi has linked up with CUC International, Inc., of Stamford, Connecticut to learn the ins and outs of on-line retailing.[24]

Various moves taking place in Japan's domestic market have assisted this joint-venture effort, including the deregulation of the telecommunications industry. Under pressure from the United States and complaints from domestic business about telecommunications costs, Japan recently privatized the long-protected Nippon Telephone and Telegraph (NTT) and opened the field to competition. That change prompted the Japanese trading company Itochu and the Japanese electronics maker Toshiba to enter the industry via a joint venture with U.S. West and the Time Warner Group. The joint firm, called Titus Communications, was established as a cable TV company but later received approval to enter the telecommunications market and meet NTT head on.[25] Deregulation prompted the auto giant Toyota to enter the arena. Toyota also sees a Japanese future that lies away from the mass production of cars, and has indicated its intention to link up with an unnamed German telecommunications company.[26] It is especially significant that the Japanese partners in both of these ventures hope not only to sharpen their technical and marketing skills, but also to gain the managerial skills to enable them to operate profitably in this highly competitive global market. To be sure, Japan's deregulation in this area has had little to do with any explicit national policy to help the domestic economy reorient itself, but nonetheless the responses of these firms show an eagerness to shift focus for the future.

The coming move away from mass production toward knowledge-based functions is also reflected in Japan's receptiveness to venture capital. During most of the post-World War II period, when Japan's Iron Triangle believed, with good reason, that it could look abroad for the proper direction of industrial development, there was little interest in new ventures. Start-up firms, particularly in specialized areas, were viewed as distractions from bureaucratic planning and, worse, as siphoners of credit and other economic resources that could be better used by larger, mass-production firms. But the success of venture capitalists in the United States has turned heads in Japan. Many have come to view these entrepreneurs as offering the economy the flexibility that it will need to cope with future pressures. Japan has suddenly recognized how venture capitalists can keep the economy on the cutting edge of product and business technology, and provide a crucial kind of economic leadership and direction. Comments by Toru Takahashi, director of research and development for Canon, a major producer of photographic and office equipment, exemplify the new thinking. He has complained that American venture capital has continually stolen a march on the larger Japanese firms, by investing in companies that design new technology, outsource production (frequently abroad), and saturate the market before Canon and other large Japanese players can even present their products to the consumer.[27] In contrast to the universal disdain of the not-too-distant past, business powers in Japan today regard new ventures as the tools with which the Japanese economy can pursue its new economic interests and acquire critical skills for its future.

Remarkably, some of Japan's giant trading companies have shown the greatest enthusiasm for venture capital. Mitsui & Co. has even established a subsidiary, MVC Corp., devoted entirely to it. According to Misuo Kurobe, once a Mitsui director and now managing director for Salomon Brothers in Tokyo, the trading companies (including his former employer) are new to venture capital but are already pouring "tens of millions of dollars" into small start-up firms.[28] Even Japanese banks, never known for innovative thinking, have begun to back entrepreneurs. It is a striking sign of the new future that Masayoshi Son, an ethnic Korean living in Japan, was able to get bank financing for a new venture in software distribution, Softbank Corp., with neither collateral nor a large backer, but simply on the basis of a promising business plan.[29] His success is an awesome sign of change in a Japan that not too long ago would have dismissed his efforts immediately on the basis of risk and ethnicity.

Further evidence of Japan's ability to embrace this fundamental economic reorientation has mounted with the long list of venture start-ups that have received financing and become successful in recent years, despite the general economic setbacks of the 1990s. Yasuyuki Nambu took advantage of deregulation to set up a temporary employment agency, a class of business that did

not exist in Japan a few years ago, but one that is certain to thrive as the service economy, which will require staffing flexibility, begins to develop. Kenichi
Ozaki was able to finance his business, Bekkoame, an Internet service provider,
even before the Internet was widely available in the country. The venture firm
H.I.S. began by offering cut-rate airline tickets and is now on the verge of challenging Japan's three established domestic air carriers. Shinobu Osako, a former mapmaker, found financing for his firm, Zenrin, which has developed successful software for car navigation systems.[30] Perhaps most indicative of Japan's
new emphasis is the success of the venture firm D. Brain Securities. (The company uses the English language name.) Founded by Yoshita Denawa, this firm
provides a market to trade the shares of otherwise unlisted, small, growth companies. It is effectively a technologically advanced capital market services company designed to help finance service companies in other areas.[31]

The signs of breakdown in the old *keiretsu* ties also stand as a harbinger
of this kind of change. Chapter Three showed how the economic setbacks of
the 1990s have already disrupted the ties in these families of firms that hold
shares in one another and have long strived to support one another through
their buying patterns. The growth of small venture operations and the movement of manufacturing overseas have intensified this rift. In China, for
instance, Asin Seiki Co., an affiliate of Toyota, the largest auto group in Japan,
and Unisia Jecs Corp., an affiliate of Nissan, Toyota's largest competitor, have
set up a joint subsidiary to manufacture clutches in Nanjing.[32] In some cases,
the whole *keiretsu* system has turned on its head. The recent action of three
small personal computer makers—Altus, Akia, and Sangi—is indicative. Each
of these companies was set up without any *keiretsu* ties or even manufacturing facilities. With only management and design, they contracted out the manufacturing of their product to the giants within Japan and with overseas transplants, and arranged distribution through large retailers and wholesalers.[33]
Eventually, they outsold the giants, NEC, Toshiba, and IBM (Japan). Effectively, these small firms with no established backing have successfully subcon-
tracted their production and distribution work to the senior *keiretsu* members,
who for decades have controlled contracting in Japan. Through it all, these
headquarters firms have remained purely management and design centers.

The upheaval across such a broad front has begun to impose a combination of flexibility and a hardheaded attitude toward business relationships that
is unlike the old "way" with its long-standing emphasis on size, mass production, consensus, and cooperation within *keiretsu* families of firms. Management
has begun to abandon the old insistence on market share above all else. At one
time, of course, the pursuit of market share had strong, rational business under-

pinnings. When mass manufacturing was the obvious way for Japan to develop, size gave firms the economies of scale that were so important to competitiveness. But in the future, when Japan herself will no longer be the site of production, this old equation will no longer work. Instead of churning out product, Japan's workers will coordinate numbers of products produced in numerous locations around the world. In such an environment, size and economies of scale will take on entirely different meanings. Sensing the beginnings of this change, management has begun to adjust its thinking. They call the change *risutora,* a Japanizing of the English word "restructuring." Instead of sheer size, Japanese firms, as their Western counterparts did long ago, have begun to think in terms of the firm's profitability as measured by its returns on equity or capital or investment. This new approach to gauging business success is far more useful to the emerging breed of managers and planners—the headquarters staff—whose job it will increasingly be to evaluate and compare otherwise disparate operations in order to determine where income comes from and, more importantly, where best they should channel corporate funds. Whereas a few years ago virtually all Japanese companies thought in terms of overall revenues and market share, a recent survey by Japan's premier business publication, *The Nikkei Weekly,* revealed that one company in five now considers profitability, as measured by return on equity, a critical target.[34] Anticipating many of the future changes described here, from the economy's needed reorientation to the coming Asian division of labor, Mitsubishi has referred to this new approach to business as critical to developing a "sound global strategy."[35]

THE RISE OF FINANCE AND THE YEN

In the chemistry of Japan's transformation into the headquarters of a new economic network throughout Asia, finance will play a singular role. Whereas in the past, Japanese banks gained prominence from sheer size, the new environment will demand a more subtle, talent-based rise in Japanese finance. Coordinating global or regional economic networks, as Japan will have to do, will require the consummate financial skill of deciding which activities and which subsidiaries are good business risks and so require the additional financing for expansion. The enlarged role of Japanese finance will also enable Japan to sell headquarters functions beyond the Japanese transplants by lending to, insuring, issuing securities for, and advising Asian and other foreign enterprise, even where there is no other significant Japanese affiliation. That is what the United States and Great Britain have done in their own ways in Asia and elsewhere. Japan's effort will in time take her well beyond the straightforward projection of banking power, as it did Great Britain and the United States, and force her to overhaul all her old policies and attitudes toward currency and finance. As Japan abandons its old "way" and embraces the new, she will see a need to drive aggressively toward the internationalization of the yen and toward making her financial markets a truly global center that will suit her developing role as headquarters.

This transformation will completely reverse past policy. For most of the last half century, Japan has downplayed finance, using it almost exclusively as the handmaiden of her export-led industrial policy. Unlike other dominant countries, which count on finance to enhance national wealth and power in their own right, Japan's economic leadership has relied on international finance expressly to promote goods exports by keeping the yen as cheap as possible on foreign exchange markets. That effort has developed on two fronts. First, Japan has promoted huge financial outflows in an effort to flood the world with yen and thereby more than meet the demands of foreigners who want the currency in order to buy Japanese exports. In the second strategy to keep the yen cheap, official Japan has resisted anything that would raise financial demands for her currency. In this effort, Tokyo has shown an extreme reluctance to allow the yen's "internationalization," that is, its extensive use as a medium of international exchange for trade or between central banks. To further impede the internationalization of the yen and otherwise discourage financial demands for the currency, Japanese officials have worked to restrict Tokyo's financial markets and keep them from achieving global status.

Future pressures, however, will turn around all these long-standing forces. As the labor shortage causes Japan to de-emphasize exports, it will also eliminate the primary reason for the cheap yen policy in the first place. Indeed, Japan will develop reason to want a strong yen to give her buying power, first, for the imports she will need to supplement her domestic production, and second, to build production facilities abroad for her overseas transplants. But even as the new circumstances prompt Japan to want a rise in the yen, pressures will weaken the engine that once propelled the yen upward. Indeed, they will put that engine into reverse, as Japan's trade balance swings from surplus to deficit, and funds begin to flow out of the country to buy foreign products, whether they are made by Japanese transplants or others. Again, Japan will turn to financial policy as a counterbalance, this time in the opposite direction. In this future environment Japan will still need to put financial capital out of the country to invest in new overseas facilities, but she will reject the notion of offsetting the effects of trade by promoting a direct investment inflow, from either Japanese or foreigners. (Facing a labor shortage she would have a difficult time convincing businesses to make such a commitment anyway.) Instead, Japan will create her counterbalance by promoting the financial demands for the yen that she once eschewed. Tokyo will promote her yen as an international currency by advocating its use as a medium of exchange between other nations, as the United States dollar is used today. With this same objective in mind, she will promote a global role for her financial markets so that they can provide the necessary foundation for the internationalization of the yen, as well as attract foreign financial capital and financial dealings into the country and the currency in other ways. It will be a difficult adjustment; after all, for over fifty years Japan has followed exactly the opposite tack.

The long-standing cheap yen financial policy has always been key to Japan's overall industrial development strategy. The pattern was evident even in the earliest stages of Japanese reconstruction under the American occupation. At the 1949 negotiations to set the value of the yen in the then American-dominated Bretton Woods system of fixed currency rates, the Japanese bargained fiercely to keep the currency as cheap as possible. The Americans, who wanted ¥300 to the dollar, met Ministry of Finance intransigence and finally settled for a 20 percent discount from their initial bargaining position, setting the rate at ¥360 to the dollar. This cheap yen served Japan well. By giving Japanese product an attractive price to foreigners and making foreign goods expensive for the Japanese, it promoted export-led growth through the 1950s and 1960s until 1971, when the Bretton Woods system fell apart. This export economy cost the Japanese people by denying them the array of affordable products that Americans, among others, enjoyed. But to the Iron Triangle, that was a small price to pay for Japan's rapid industrial development.

Even by the 1960s and '70s, when Japan's development strategy had proved itself and the country was running chronic, large trade surpluses, she still resisted pressure to revalue the yen upward. In retrospect, many present-day reformers note that pressure in the late 1960s was the first sign that Japan's system of export-led development was running itself out. The upward pressure then on the yen, wrote one Japanese financial commentator, should have moved Japan's policy elite to "shift the driving force of the economy from exports to domestic demand."[36] But that is not what happened. Instead, Japan continued to fight the yen's rise through the 1970s and '80s, long after the Bretton Woods system of fixed exchange rates ended. Even as late as the '80s, when most of the rest of the world's central bankers and finance ministers had long adjusted to a regime of floating currency rates, Takashi Hosomi, when vice minister of international affairs at the Ministry of Finance, desperately tried to develop a scheme to prevent yen appreciation by pushing for limits on how far each currency could float up or down before concerted central bank action would bring it back into alignment. This arrangement, referred to in currency circles as a "snake" because of the shape that these shifting limits make on a chart, was proposed in 1983 by Prime Minister Nakasone to then United States Treasury Secretary James Baker.[37] Ostensibly, Japan made the proposal as a means of bringing order to chaotic currency markets, but since the yen was under intense pressure to rise at the time, its adoption would also have helped keep Japan's currency cheaper than if it had floated freely. The proposal came to nothing because the central bankers and finance ministers of the rest of the world had no desire to institutionalize a cheap yen to give Japan the special export advantage that she wanted.

Seemingly in contradiction to her cheap yen policy, Japan did join the Plaza Accord among central bankers in 1985 to coordinate a decline in the foreign exchange value of the dollar, and by implication a rise in the yen. But she did so only because the United States dollar had risen sufficiently between 1983 and 1985 to offer a cushion that allowed Japan to cooperate without jeopardizing her basic cheap yen/pro-export strategy. And even then, the subsequent rise in the value of the yen caused consternation. The modest slowdown in the growth of exports and the economy that followed the yen's rise in 1985 and 1986 was referred to popularly as the *endaka fukyo,* or high yen recession, and was viewed popularly in Japan as the result of American interference in basic Japanese policy. Japan's major daily, the *Asahi Shimbun,* worried over the "rebellion of the market"[38] and *The Nikkei Weekly* noted that it heard "no applause" to Prime Minister Nakasone's reassurances.[39] One Japanese journalist summed up both Japan's long-standing motivation and bitterness at the yen's rise: "Neither the Japanese general public nor the business community in particular viewed the situation as just another recession in the usual sense. For them, the whole process was an affront to national identity, because it appeared that *gaiatsu* [foreign pressure] was trying to contain the export might, upon which Japan had so heavily relied to catch up with Western countries."[40] Indeed, the commitment to weakening the yen again remained so fervent that, at the time, Japan refused to stimulate her slowed economy through government spending, relying only on the reduction of interest rates, which also tended to reduce the yen's value by discouraging foreigners from using yen deposits and encouraging the Japanese to seek deposits in other currencies.[41]

Lacking the cooperation among central bankers to meet her currency ends, Japan turned to fight the yen's rise during this time by pressuring Japanese firms and individuals to invest overseas, particularly in the West, and especially in America, where the trade imbalance was greatest. In this effort, the huge budget deficits of the United States government that persisted through the 1980s and early '90s served Japan's purpose well. By buying a large proportion of the notes and bonds issued by Washington, Japan pushed yen out of Ministry of Finance coffers and her domestic market, and onto the international exchanges, where they relieved some of the upward price pressure that the trade surplus had placed on the currency. According to Kenichi Ohmae, a confidant of former Prime Minister Nakasone, the Ministry of Finance at this time actively bullied Japanese banks and insurance companies into buying dollar assets against their better judgment. It also bullied them out of taking profits in American securities because a repatriation of the funds would create an undesirable flow back into yen.[42] Nomura Securities economist Richard C. Koo has actually noted counterbalancing financial flows on a month-by-month basis during difficult times for the currency. When the yen got particularly strong in the spring of 1995 and fell toward 80 to the dollar, his firm noted record Japanese purchases of $19.2 billion United States government bonds in a three-month period. Later in September of that year when the pressure on the yen eased a bit, his sources reported record sales of American assets of $16.8 billion by the Japanese between September and December, a larger figure than during the New York stock market crash of October 1987.[43] These countervailing financial flows did not entirely counteract the tendency for the yen to rise on foreign exchange markets, but they moderated the upward move considerably. As R. Taggert Murphy's insightful book, *The Weight of the Yen,* points out, the pattern created a perverse sort of interaction between Japan and the United States, in which Japan effectively lent America the money to buy Japanese exports.[44] There are those in America who have condemned this pattern of behavior, claiming that Japan has fostered an American dependence on Japanese product even as she has bought up the wealth of the United States.[45] The Americans who see this as a conspiracy to undermine their economy are overreacting, but the point of long-standing Japanese policy to use investment flows to manage her currency is clear, even if it is not aimed particularly at America.

As part of this fight to keep the yen cheap, during this time the Japanese authorities discouraged the yen's use as an international currency. Definitions of what constitutes an international currency are slippery, but the United States dollar has for years stood as the prime example. Currencies are benchmarked to it, trade contracts are denominated in dollars even when they do not concern Americans, and investors price and hold assets in dollars, regardless of whether they live in the United States or deal in American products. According to the Federal Reserve Bank of New York, the dollar is used in half of all international trade transactions and 80 percent of world financial transactions.[46] The deutschemark acquired this role within Europe, if not the world at large, and held it through to the introduction of the euro. In both cases, the international uses of these currencies prompted traders and dealers to hold greater balances in them than they might otherwise, and the accompanying demand has pushed their value above where it would have settled in the market. The Japanese, especially the Ministry of Finance, have wanted none of this. They have, therefore, discouraged the yen's use in contracts and financial dealings, and have succeeded in keeping the international community from using the yen in these ways. Their accomplishment is remarkable given the vast size of Japan's economy and the reach of her commerce.

Primarily, the MOF and others in the Iron Triangle have battled to stop the internationalization of the yen by resisting overseas contracting in yen. Typically, each party to a trade contract prefers it denominated in its home currency to prevent currency fluctuations from shifting the contract's value away from basic costs, which typically are in the home currency. But since only one party can have the contract in its own currency, the nod usually goes to the stronger party. Having grown to the point of dominance in many industries, Japan would seem to enjoy that kind of leverage in negotiating contracts. But under pressure from the authorities, few firms have availed themselves of this power. Even in exports from Japan, where Japanese firms would seem undisputedly to have the upper hand, only 34 percent of contracts have been priced in yen. Yen-denominated imports have accounted for a mere 3 percent of the total.[47] Using similar reasoning, Japanese authorities have also resisted the natural tendency to price Japan's foreign loans in yen. As with trade agreements, most parties prefer loans denominated in their home currency because it reduces the chance that currency fluctuations will cause the values of their assets and liabilities to diverge. Usually, the lender is the stronger party and so gets international loans denominated in its currency. Thus in the nineteenth century, British loans to the financially insecure Russian, Turkish, and Chinese governments were denominated in sterling. In the early twentieth century, American loans to Britain were denominated in United States dollars. But even though Japan has made huge loans to the United States and other countries, she has refused to denominate them in yen. When the United States government suggested issuing yen-denominated bonds in the late 1980s, Japanese authorities actively discouraged the idea.[48]

Aside from applying direct pressure against contracting in yen, the Ministry of Finance has led in this effort to discourage an international role for the currency by using its regulatory powers to make it difficult for traders and investors to deal in Japanese financial and currency markets. For a currency to serve an international role, it must be backed by broad, liquid financial markets that enable an array of domestic and foreign operators to trade the currency, trade assets denominated in that currency, hold deposits as well as investments denominated in it, and hedge positions in forward, futures, and options markets. The MOF and allied ministries have fought the yen's rise by denying it this kind of backing. As with so much else in Japan, the details of how the ministry bureaucrats have accomplished this reach a complexity that defies straightforward description. The Finance Ministry has, of course, relied on the maze of restrictions and controls that it has long imposed on Japan's financial markets. Earlier discussion touched on some of the licensing and reporting rules as well as the host of controls and limits. In general, restrictions on the types of instruments available to investors and dealers, together with the power to determine which institution can issue which instruments to which buyers, have conspired to discourage foreigners from dealing in Japan's financial markets and thus holding yen deposits and yen-denominated assets. The lack of an extensive market for derivatives—futures, forwards, options—has made it especially difficult for traders and investors to hedge their positions against volatility, and has made them reluctant to deal in yen in the Tokyo market. Singapore's well-developed currency futures market has provided a convenient regional alternative to Tokyo, and that has helped the Finance Ministry discourage currency and financial operators from entering the Tokyo market. Japan's chronically low money-market rates and steep schedule of tax withholding has discouraged participants further. Even as Japan has made strides recently in deregulating her financial markets, the MOF has made efforts to retain many of these strictures to keep it inconvenient or expensive to deal in Tokyo. According to Eamonn Fingleton, the Ministry has resisted deregulation as much to keep the yen cheap as to serve its natural desire to control internal flows of credit.[49] Fingleton may have overstated, but nonetheless caught the MOF's efforts to persist in the old pattern of fostering a cheap yen to support export-led growth.

Japan has not managed to hide the basis of her financial policy. In the early 1980s, Ezra Salomon, in a paper prepared for American negotiators under the Reagan administration, concluded that Japan was keeping the yen low, and identified the financial means by which she was holding back the currency despite that nation's huge trade surplus.[50] American negotiators, alerted to Japan's tactics, tried to thwart these practices by pushing Japan to internationalize the yen, and have continued to do so since. The initial pressure from the United States created the U.S.-Japan Yen-Dollar Committee. The Ministry of Finance, true to its long-standing policy, resisted the American push. Under pressure, however, the Ministry did yield some ground. As part of an "internationalization," it allowed foreign banks to enter Japan and win trust bank licenses, and it permitted the issuing of yen-denominated securities outside Japan, giving birth to the Euro-yen market.[51] Since then, Japanese authorities have gradually yielded to pressure for other market liberalizations, leading up to the "big bang" reform measures. Over time these concessions have allowed full currency convertibility; permitted foreign issuance of yen-dominated bonds, called Samurai bonds, in the Tokyo market; allowed a wider range of deposits at Japanese banks and deregulated the rates paid on them; established the Japan Offshore Market; allowed foreign securities investments by Japanese pension funds as well as the postal insurance fund; permitted the issuance of convertible bonds, called warrant bonds in Japan; and implemented a stream of like accommodations, some even permitting the use of financial and currency derivatives.[52] A few of these measures appealed to the bureaucrats at the MOF because initially they facilitated an outflow of financial capital from Japan, and so fed one financial effort used to hold back the yen's rise on foreign exchange markets. But all of these and other liberalizations have gradually set the stage for raising the international status of the yen and Japanese financial markets, and so have run fundamentally counter to long-standing MOF desires to keep the currency weak.

The building demographic problems surely will intensify the pressure on the MOF and her sister agencies to extend and enlarge upon these policy reversals. As the labor shortage limits Japan's ability to export, even the Finance Ministry will see the irrationality of its cheap yen strategy. Further relieving the authorities of their long-standing currency concerns, Japan's move to emphasize the export of high-value services instead of goods will make what she sells the world less price sensitive than goods exports have been, and so less vulnerable to shifts in relative currency values. Japanese leadership also will begin to see the usefulness of a high-priced yen in meeting the country's increasing need for imports and in supporting the foreign spending needed to transplant Japanese industry overseas. It will, of course, take time to realize the differences, but as the demographic pressure increases in coming years and the chain of other responses plays out, the wisdom of a reversal in existing policy will assert itself. Instead of playing down the yen, Japan will want to cultivate financial demand for it, especially as her trade balance slips into deficit. In direct contradiction of the old emphases, Japanese officials will seek the internationalization of the yen. They will induce Japanese business to insist on denominating both import and export contracts and loan arrangements in yen. Policy will encourage other traders and lenders to denominate their deals in yen, even when the Japanese are not involved. Policy will also foster the internationalization of the yen by promoting it as a reserve currency for central banks, especially in Asia, and as a general medium of international exchange, whether or not the Japanese are involved. Japan might, by some definitions, even seek to create a yen bloc in Asia. Though the meaning of currency bloc varies with the user of the words, certainly it would involve the use of the yen to denominate contracts throughout the region, whether the Japanese are a party to them or not, and the dominance of the yen as a reserve currency in the region for central bankers and business people. There is even a chance that in time Japan will seek to benchmark regional currencies to the yen, as in Europe they were effectively benchmarked to the deutschemark until the launch of the euro. Actually, Japan will begin to secure the yen's internationalization as soon as she ends her old policies of resisting it. As a powerful worldwide trader that is especially strong in Asia, the yen naturally will lean toward a dominant position.

The Asian currency crisis of 1997 gave a hint of one way that Japan might pursue the new policy. Just before the crisis broke, then Prime Minister Hashimoto was promoting Europe's economic and monetary union and the use of the euro as a "major currency" largely to ensure that the yen would not rise into that role and have its price bid up on foreign exchange markets.[53] When the Asian crisis broke, Japan offered to support the Thai baht and assured Korea and all the Southeast Asian states suffering currency devaluations that Japanese bank lending would continue to support them.[54] Her motivations included the stated desire to avoid a widening crisis and to avoid currency market chaos. But they also stemmed from her constant fear about a rise in the value of the yen. If she allowed other currencies in the region to decline against the yen, then she would find herself at a competitive disadvantage for exporting. By continuing to pump yen out into the region she might forestall such a development. To these extents, Japan was following her old, cheap yen policy line. But Japan surprised the world in the crisis by also proposing a regional emergency fund to deal with this and future crises.[55] In one respect, of course, the fund idea, by supporting these other currencies, simply extended the cheap yen strategy by a different route. But, in another respect, such a fund could go a long way toward "internationalizing" the yen into at least a regional currency, and even lay the foundations for a yen bloc. Indeed, the success of such a fund could have enticed some Southeast Asian nations to peg their currencies to the yen as Hong Kong has to the U.S. dollar. The Japanese who proposed the fund surely were aware of this potential, and certainly the reaction of Western leadership showed that it saw a clear link. Some accused Japan of trying to undercut the International Monetary Fund or exclude it from the region.[56] Western central bankers and finance ministers became quite defensive, suggesting that such a fund, if it were established, must have some non-Asian management.[57]

Ambiguous as the intentions of the proposed fund were, it nonetheless offered another sign of change. To cope fully with future pressures, the internationalization effort will have to go further and become clearer too. Of course, there are innumerable ways in which Japan might seek her new objective and promote the yen's internationalization, all dependent on specific conditions of the moment. Reform of the Tokyo financial markets, however, will be essential. Japan's reforms to date have come from foreign pressure or, more recently, the ascent of reformers within her power structure. But as the demographic situation intensifies Japan's need to support the yen, a consensus will emerge in favor of financial reform to develop the broad, liquid, diverse financial markets that are a critical foundation for an international currency. As this push gains momentum, Japan will have to cultivate an openness that in the past she has labeled disruptive or risky. She might still worry over the risks, but she will have to change in order to get global market participants to include Tokyo on an equal footing with London and New York. Ultimately, Tokyo will have to offer the full range of financial instruments, activities, and the free flow of funds that characterize other well-developed financial markets. Tokyo will have to permit the hedging and speculation, the trading in futures, options, and options on futures that Japan has frowned on and forbidden in the past. Her old way proceeded on the principle that things not expressly permitted were forbidden. In the new way, she will effectively have to move to the principle that things not expressly forbidden are permissible. And the list of forbidden practices will have to remain small, at least if New York and London permit them. Japan will have turned the corner of the needed change when Tokyo's or Osaka's markets overshadow Singapore's futures market for yen and other currencies.

Not only will the development of financial markets help Japan with the needed reversal of her old, cheap yen currency policy, it will also respond to future pressures from another critical perspective: It will provide her with desperately needed financial capital. Since the 1950s, Japan's ongoing savings flow has allowed her to ignore foreign financial capital and neglect the development of her financial markets. When a population pours excess savings into simple post-office savings plans, as Japan's people have done for years, there is little need to develop attractive, diverse financial vehicles to coax savings from her own people and to lure it from abroad. But, as described earlier, the aging of Japan's population will deprive her of the huge flow of savings on which she built her past economic success. She will need to encourage her people to save.

She also will need foreign financial capital to supplement domestic savings, something she has not needed since the late 1940s and early '50s. Her drive to rebuild her manufacturing capacity abroad will multiply that need, as will the retooling at home to support the reorientation of her domestic economy.

The upgrade of Japan's financial markets will provide a critical means to squeeze the additional savings out of her own people and lure foreign financial capital to Japan. For this reason, in addition to the growing need to internationalize the yen, Japan will work to make those markets broader, more liquid, more open, more sophisticated, and allow them to offer a greater diversity of financial products than in the past. Certainly, her own people will have a greater inclination to put money aside if they have the option of placing it in attractive instruments tailored to their savings and investment needs, such as Western financial markets offer their populations. She might not have needed these attractions in the past, but in the savings-short future she will, and her regulators will have to ease restrictions to allow her brokers, dealers, and mutual funds to develop such attractive financial products. These efforts will also help bring the nation more foreign financial capital as well. Of course, Japan will also get foreign capital directly by going to overseas markets to float loans and securities issues. But more than this kind of internationalization, she will get command of foreign capital by luring the foreign money to Tokyo through better developed, more liquid and sophisticated financial markets. If anything, the freedom to develop and trade a diversity of financial instruments and products is even more important to this effort than as an appeal to the individual Japanese saver. After all, foreign financial capital has more options in other markets, and so the effort to lure it requires even more competitive financial practices and vehicles.

When it comes to foreign capital, only direct flows to loans or the purchases of Japanese stocks and bonds will directly supplement Japanese savings. But luring the trading funds of dealers and speculators and their deposits through Tokyo will also help serve Japan's future financing needs by giving Japanese financial institutions a measure of control over foreign funds. For example, if an array of attractive financial instruments brings foreign deposits to Japanese banks or investment accounts to dealers, it will allow Japanese bankers, dealers, and fund managers to channel these funds to Japanese objectives. There need be no hint of impropriety in this. Simply increasing the relative proportion of Japanese financial players will bring a Japanese perspective that will identify worthy investments in Japanese interests that would otherwise go begging if the money were controlled purely from Western centers. Gaining advantage in this way from the control of other people's money is not quite the classic case of what economists and central bankers call *seigniorage,* in which a government or bank controlling a nation's supply of money gets to command wealth that it has not earned. But it has a similar quality that Japan can acquire by developing her financial markets and that she will appreciate in her relatively savings-short future.

Such changes will mark a radical departure from the financial policies of the Japan that the world has come to know. As should be clear from previous discussion, Japan will have to overcome a lot of external and internal resistance to make the change. While that prospect might engender a skepticism about her ability to accomplish the adjustment, it is worth noting that not too long ago, Japan made a similar shift, if only on a temporary basis. Each of the two energy crises of the 1970s created a financial environment that was similar to the future that Japan now faces. They threw her trade account into deficit and forced on her a need for additional international capital inflows in order to finance purchases of imported oil and otherwise meet the needs of her people. Faced with such a situation, Japan's bureaucrats simply reversed field.[58] Strictures quickly came off foreign purchases of Japanese stocks and bonds, even though they had stood since the late 1940s. Officials also removed the special reserve requirements that had long been imposed on nonresident yen deposits. When the crisis passed and Japan ceased to need the foreign capital, official policy reverted. Japan again restricted capital inflows and promoted capital outflows as she had previously. In the second oil crisis in the late 1970s, Japan again turned policy 180 degrees. Reserve requirements on foreigners' yen deposits were again removed and rules on foreign financial transactions were eased. This effort led directly to the amendment of Japan's Foreign Exchange Law in 1980, which promoted much freer flows of currency, effectively systematizing the ad hoc changes of the 1970s.[59]

Of course, the energy crises were temporary, and future pressures will have a more enduring quality. But Japan's ability to shift focus and emphasis in the past, even if only for a brief while, shows her responsiveness to the changing needs of the times and creates confidence in her ability to shift again in response to the longer-lived and fundamental demands of globalization, economic maturation, and the aging of her population. Indeed, given the depth and power of these forces, Japan should exhibit a thoroughgoing response— in currency, financial policy, and, necessarily, the orientation of her economy. Once the change gains momentum, the practical, business character of the country will bear little resemblance to the Japan of the last fifty-some years. But as radical as these changes will be, the needed adjustments will demand still other shifts in policies and priorities, and in realms beyond economics, business, and finance.

DIPLOMACY, ARMS, AND ASIAN INVESTMENTS

JAPAN FACES AN ESPECIALLY DIFFICULT adjustment as the momentum of change forces her to raise her diplomatic and military profiles. For decades, Japan has enjoyed almost an invisible approach to foreign affairs. This has left her more flexible than most nations in her international business dealings. But as adjustments to the new environment force her into a greater economic and financial integration with Asia, Japan will find it impossible to continue in her old, retiring way. If only to secure her overseas investments, she will feel a heightened need to influence policy in those foreign nations where she locates her factories. Her growing dependence on imports and global finance will also demand that she exercise more diplomatic muscle. If this were not motivation enough, Japan will also have to face the growing security issues of tense, post-Cold War Asia. Actually, Tokyo has already begun to recognize the need for a more engaged foreign policy, and has made efforts to become more active diplomatically, both at the United Nations and independently. Though these efforts have helped lay the foundations for a new Japanese diplomacy, she will soon need to go beyond them. She will have to step out from America's diplomatic and military shadow, where she has stood comfortably for so long. Eventually, her diplomatic profile will rise to levels not seen since the Second World War, and, because an active diplomacy requires it, so will her military profile. These changes will strain relations between Japan and the United States, between

Japan and her Asian neighbors, and within Japan herself. The change will involve risk, but from Japan's perspective, the risks of not changing will be far greater.

THE CHALLENGE OF DIPLOMACY

Diplomatic leadership will not come easily to Japan. For over fifty years, she has subordinated her foreign policy almost entirely to American Cold War strategies, and otherwise taken a passive approach to foreign relations. Right after World War II, her position in the world was controlled entirely by the United States, which had occupied the islands. Horrified by the ravages of the world conflict, at first the Americans wanted to create an agrarian Japan, incapable of making war. The Cold War, however, produced a shift in policy. Instead of pastoral helplessness, the United States promoted Japanese industrial development in order to make her a bulwark of the American policy of containment—first of the Soviet Union, later of China—and to forestall any Communist movement within Japan. But since the United States and its allies were still afraid of reemergent Japanese military power, a unique Japanese-American security arrangement developed. The occupation forces dictated a new Japanese constitution, including an Article 9 that strictly denied Japan recourse to military force, except in defense of the home islands. America put Japan under its nuclear umbrella. Japan effectively ceded her defense and many of her diplomatic prerogatives to the United States, and concentrated on economic development.

For a long time, the arrangement suited just about everyone. Those parts of Asia that had suffered at the hands of Japan's imperial army found relief in Japanese disarmament and what seemed to be a permanent American check on her freedom of action. The United States got a critical forward base in Asia—in effect, an unsinkable aircraft carrier from which to project power for the pursuit of its Cold War containment strategy. And by making Japan a diplomatic and military client, the United States got considerable control over this growing economic power. America held Japan's diplomatic proxy in geostrategy and effectively dictated Japan's votes at the United Nations and other international bodies. Although Japan lost a lot of independence in the arrangement, it did not seem difficult to give up at the time. Since the Japanese people blamed the devastation of the war on the pursuit of international power politics, they wanted none of it. At the same time, the arrangement offered Japan distinct economic advantages. By guaranteeing the integrity of the Japanese home islands and the all-important shipping lanes for Japanese trade, the United

States relieved Japan of huge defense-related expenses as well as the distraction from economic development that an independent foreign policy would impose. The arrangement obligated Japan to focus herself on the United States, but that, too, was easy, at least for a while. America was Japan's main market for exports, overwhelmingly so in those early post-war years. Subordination to the United States helped Japan into the European market, too. The rest of Asia offered little at the time. It only began to develop in earnest in the 1980s, and for much of the post-World War II period was just emerging from colonial status.

Throughout the 1950s, '60s, and '70s, this remarkable arrangement with the United States kept Japan out of the international arena, except in those very narrow areas that concerned business. During this time, Japan played her subordinate role faithfully. Even in Asia, she followed America's lead. Japan normalized relations with Beijing in 1972, only after the United States did in 1971; relations with Vietnam opened after the United States pulled out in 1973.[1] It suited Japan to follow. In the heavily armed, tense milieu of the Cold War, Japan's diplomatic and military impotence simplified her relations with the world. Recognizing these advantages, in the 1970s Prime Minister Takeo Fukuda laid out the ground rules for Japanese diplomacy. His "Fukuda Doctrine" simply foreclosed discussion of any large diplomatic or security issues, and prevailed for twenty years.[2] Helpful as it was, Japan's passivity was at times humiliating, as a popular story from the 1960s (told in Japan to this day) illustrates. A group of Japanese diplomats on a state visit to Europe stopped in Paris to pay their respects to Charles de Gaulle. He refused to see them, dismissing the whole mission as a group of "transistor salesmen."[3] The insult stung Japan, because there was truth in it. She could not have it both ways. By accepting the arrangement with the United States, Japan had excluded herself from equal standing among the powers, and de Gaulle, who always had a keen sense for where power resided, was the perfect person to point out that truth. Still, Japan willingly accepted the slights because the economic advantages of the American treaty were tremendous.

As useful as the American arrangement was, however, it became increasingly difficult for Japan to sustain her purely subordinate status as her economy grew in complexity and began to weave a web of foreign associations. The multiplication of Japan's foreign economic interests demanded high-level diplomatic skills to smooth the way for trade relations and business ventures. The pressure became more intense as Asia developed and Japan became more involved in the region. However, in the 1970s, when Japan first began tentatively to act for herself diplomatically, the impetus came not from Asia but from world financial markets and from the Middle East. Of course, her vulnerability to an increasingly globalized economic environment became painfully clear when the yen began to rise against other currencies in the wake of President Nixon's 1971 decision to put an end to fixed exchange rates. But it was the first energy crisis in 1973 that pointed up Japan's need to develop the means to affect policies and events beyond her borders.

Official Japan responded with the first stirrings of an independent Japanese foreign policy since 1945. The new doctrine was referred to as *sogo anzen hosho,* or "comprehensive national security." It took a broader view of Japan's security than straightforward defense of the home islands, extending the notion to securing vital Japanese interests in the world, including the protection of sea-lanes for trade as well as Japanese access to export markets and raw materials for her industry. Though some observers have made much of the novelty of this approach, it was hardly new. Such notions of national security were a major motivation (though not the only one) for the Japanese aggression that led to the Second World War. Even in the nineteenth century, just after modernization, Japanese attitudes explicitly identified national security in this broad light. Indeed, at the time, Japanese thinkers referenced the American historian Alfred Thayer Mahan, who characterized national security as "not merely defense of our territory, but defense of our just national interests, whatever they may be and wherever they are."[4] Later in the 1970s, as world events began to impinge on Japan and Asia, Japanese policy makers further clarified the doctrine, claiming that it was "the duty of Japan as the advanced country in Asia to stabilize the area and establish a constructive order."[5] But since security arrangements with the United States and the Fukuda Doctrine precluded Japan's use of the usual diplomatic and military channels, she compromised, serving her diplomatic needs through the manipulation of foreign aid.

Given the special pressures of the 1970s, Japan's then nascent aid program focused on the Middle East, with the aim of securing a constant supply of oil. Japanese aid rose and fell with the price of oil. When oil was in short supply and its price was high, Japan poured resources into the region. In the 1980s, when oil supplies again became plentiful and prices fell, Japan lost interest in the Middle East and it disappeared from her aid agenda.[6] But by then, Japan's growing interest in Asia opened another ultimately broader avenue for aid to serve her foreign policy needs. Because aid was virtually Japan's only diplomatic tool, it acquired a much greater importance to her than it had to the United States and other aid-giving nations. Her budget for this foreign assistance expanded at a dramatic 8 percent per year throughout the 1980s. By the early 1990s, it amounted to a full 2 percent of all government spending and exceeded the total amount of aid given by the United States, which has both a larger economy and a larger overall government budget. In the early 1990s, the Japanese government budgeted to give the equivalent of $150 billion in foreign aid, growing it throughout the decade by 3 to 4 percent per year, though recent economic setbacks have delayed some outlays compared with the budgeted schedule.[7]

As with so much else in Japan, the Iron Triangle, with its cooperative relationship between government and business, has set the aid agenda. Though aid is administered by government agencies—the Japan International Cooperation Agency (JICA) for direct grants, the Overseas Economic Cooperation Fund (OECF) for subsidized "soft" loans, and the Export-Import Bank for direct, trade-related "hard" loans—business interests have considerable say in the process. The Keidanren, for example, sponsors the Japanese International Development Organization (JAIDO) that joins the government's OECF to subsidize Japanese business in countries where the risks might preclude a purely private venture. Similarly, the Japan Overseas Development Corporation (JODC) is a joint business-government financial operation that provides financing for small Japanese firms investing abroad. And the Association for Overseas Technical Scholarships (AOTS) combines MITI funds with private money to train Asian technicians in Japan.[8] Determined in this way, Japanese aid naturally has promoted the same kind of business-government cooperation among the recipients of loans and grants. The idea is "deeply embedded in Japan's philosophy of development," wrote a Foreign Ministry spokesman, "that the public and private sectors must work not as adversaries but as partners."[9]

However diverse the sources and recipients of the aid, Japan's pattern of giving has always converged on her broader foreign policy interests. These, of course, have focused on those countries that mean the most to her from a commercial or economic perspective. But Japan has refined her selection process still further, focusing on those commercially important countries where the United States has the least influence or is least reliable. For example, Japan has always depended heavily on raw materials from the Americas, particularly Mexico and Brazil, but has channeled little aid there because the influence of the United States has secured those needs for her. Instead, she has concentrated on Asia, where America has comparatively less influence, but which she also needs greatly, as a source of raw materials, a target for investments, and, ultimately, a potential labor pool. Since the 1980s, Japanese aid to Asia has averaged 2.5 times that of the United States.[10] Her top four aid recipients have been Indonesia, China, the Philippines, and Thailand, in that order.[11] Nearly two-thirds of all Japan's bilateral aid has gone to Asia, and two-thirds of that has gone to Southeast Asia.[12] By the mid-1990s, Japanese money accounted for slightly over 50 percent of all aid received by China, almost 60 percent of that received by Thailand, about 66 percent of all aid received by the Philippines and Indonesia, and about 80 percent of that received by South Korea and Malaysia.[13]

Being the primary provider of aid to Asia has given Japan a measure of influence in the region, and she has enhanced her leverage by carefully controlling how the aid is used. As in Japan's domestic economy, the restrictions are determined by the civil service bureaucracy. The Ministry of Foreign Affairs has established the post of Ambassador for Asia-Pacific Cooperation to coordinate all aid efforts.[14] MITI has placed personnel at embassies. They coordinate with local officials, other Japanese government agencies, and Japanese firms in the area in order to maximize the aid's influence over the host government.[15] To maintain control, Japan has arranged fully 80 percent of her aid on a strictly bilateral basis.[16] Because a bilateral arrangement is just between Japan and the receiving nation, she has retained much more say in how the funds are spent than if the aid went through multilateral channels. Those channels typically involve pools of donors with the giving administered by international bodies like the World Bank. Japan's Foreign Ministry made its strategy crystal clear early in the 1990s, stating that "in view of the imperative of aid as a foreign policy tool for Japan, it is likely that bilateral aid will continue to account for the majority of Japan's aid activities."[17] For similar reasons, Japan has shown a distinct preference for subsidized loans over direct grants. The client nation's obligation to repay the loan gives Japan more influence in how the money is used than if it were granted outright. According to the Development Assistance Committee of the Organization for Economic Cooperation and Development (OECD), Japan has disbursed over half her foreign aid through loans, far more than other countries. The Committee noted that Japan ranked twentieth out of 20 nations in the proportion of grants in overall aid.[18] In the Asian Development Bank, for example, Japan and the United States have shared equally in contributions, but Japan has provided about 40 percent of the bank's subsidized loans, compared with America's 17 percent.[19] Consistent with this pattern, Japan also has insisted on control by placing severe conditions on her lending. The same OECD Development Assistance Committee noted that Japan ranked twentieth out of 21 nations as to the flexibility and accommodation in the terms of her aid loans.[20] Recently, Japan has backed off from her old practice of tying aid to specific purchases of Japanese goods and services, but the control has continued as a consequence of her size as a giver and the nature of her giving. The bulk of the contracting in Japanese aid projects has continued to go to Japanese firms. Non-Japanese companies have received less than 10 percent of the work financed by Japanese aid in loans or grants.[21]

The power and single-mindedness of Japan's aid program has gone far to substitute for the diplomatic latitude otherwise lost to her security arrangements with the United States. Her manipulation of aid has enhanced her political ties and influence, especially in Asia. Japanese bureaucrats are playing an ever larger role in making policy in recipient countries, successfully shaping it to serve Japan's ends.[22] Indeed, Japanese bureaucrats have authored the long-term industrial policies of Thailand and Malaysia.[23] Asia's recent economic and financial setbacks have interrupted Japanese timetables, but still MITI has grown sufficiently confident of its influence in Asia to set up a "master plan," for *sogo kyorkaku* (comprehensive cooperation.)[24] Under this plan, MITI will strategically direct Japanese foreign aid toward those infrastructure projects that it believes will benefit Japanese business abroad and, in the end, will support the region's division of labor. A remarkable 40 percent of Japanese aid has been earmarked for infrastructure, compared with only 3.5 percent of American aid, which has not been managed nearly so diligently or closely.[25] Certainly, Japan has shown no timidity in wielding the influence it has acquired from her aid programs. Some years ago, Japanese threats to cut off aid to Thailand resulted in an end to complaints there about too many Japanese contractors. In the mid 1990s, Japan's ambassador in Bangkok persuaded the Thai government to defy the World Bank when prudence demanded that Thailand scale back spending on a large Japanese-sponsored project.[26] K.S. Nathan of the University of Malaysia observed as early as 1990 that the Japanese were "calling the shots in all of the Asia Pacific."[27] Chung Moon Jong, a member of South Korea's National Assembly and the son of Hyundai's founder, was even more blunt. According to him, by manipulating their foreign aid grants and loans, "the Japanese have already conquered Asia."[28]

For all the influence that aid has earned Japan, it will nonetheless fail to meet future diplomatic needs. Her increasingly complex economic interests in Asia will demand greater diplomatic flexibility and subtlety than the mere manipulation of grants and loans can provide. As Japan's economic and demographic pressures intensify her "comprehensive cooperation" with the rest of Asia, she will face ever-increasing needs to wield national power in ways that she has not since the Second World War. And while the economic pressures to enhance influence beyond her borders would be sufficient to force change on Japan, Asian political and security tensions will add their own strong incentive for Japan to increase her diplomatic prowess. The fall of the Soviet Union has eliminated an old Cold War check on China, which, as a consequence, has begun to exhibit a disconcerting aggressiveness to match its remarkable economic growth. The collapse of North Korea's economy has made that country even more volatile and dangerous than it was. Petty border disputes crop up frequently, and Asia's recent currency and financial crises have caused internal political problems in several major countries. Having to deal with this increasing regional tension on top of her expanding economic interests will make it even more plain to Japan that she can no longer afford to cede her foreign policy to the United States. Reluctant as she is to take on a heightened diplomatic and military profile, she will have to do so.

As Japan responds to these urgent pressures, the small practicalities of her industrial expansion into Asia will assist in the process, acting as natural diplomatic catalysts that would raise Japan's foreign policy profile in any case. Japanese firms in pursuit of business advantage will lobby Tokyo on behalf of the host market and the host government as well as lobby the host government on behalf of Tokyo. These firms will provide a natural entrée for Japanese officials to bring their influence to bear on foreign markets and the governments that have jurisdiction over them. The need for these Japanese firms to hire workers and deal with labor unions abroad, get construction permits and licenses, and engage in other basic business activities will drive them to seek the assistance of their own government officials and thereby force Tokyo's involvement with Asian government officials. Asia's underdeveloped legal framework will heighten the tendency for Tokyo to become involved diplomatically there. In Europe and the United States, where Japanese businesses can exercise legal remedies for grievances, they have little need to call on Tokyo for protection or assistance. But in much of Asia, legal remedies are rare, and political power is the only means to redress grievances—or to get anything accomplished, for that matter. Japanese businesses will increasingly demand Tokyo's help as they have already in China and elsewhere. Japan's embassy in Beijing is always telling the Chinese to honor their agreements in an effort to protect her businesses from the obstructions and other difficulties that almost certainly would befall them without official help from Tokyo.[29] In Vietnam, where there is hardly any legal system, it is virtually impossible to do business without a strong sponsor from the embassy. The stronger the national sponsor, the greater the advantage.[30] Not all other Asian nations are as difficult as China and Vietnam, but diplomatic clout helps nonetheless.

This kind of involvement will intensify and become more extensive as the Asian division of labor develops and Japan becomes more integrated with and dependent on overseas facilities in Asia. Much will stem from Japan's realization of how vulnerable this integration could make her. She cannot miss the

point that while each plant built in China or Southeast Asia, each joint venture, and each trading facility will produce wealth for Japan, it will also be a
hostage to foreign economic and social conditions and the policies of foreign
governments. As much as Japan's national welfare will depend on overseas
expansion, the effort also will place it at risk to a foreign government's potential economic mismanagement, a government's inability to secure domestic stability, or even to the possibility that foreign authorities will expropriate Japanese facilities. Tokyo cannot and will not remain passive in the face of such
vulnerability. Since Japan's economic and demographic circumstances will prevent her from simply taking it all home, she will have to develop all her diplomatic capabilities to gain that needed influence. No nation can allow its production facilities to move into foreign jurisdictions as Japan will have to do,
and not exercise the means to protect those overseas sources of wealth.
According to one Japanese diplomat, quoted anonymously in a recent issue of
the *Far Eastern Economic Review,* the country is keenly aware of her developing predicament and feels a "sense of anxiety...over what type of tools, or
leverage, [she will] have over [the host] countries."[31] These will involve a
heightened diplomatic profile, and necessarily will include military strength to
support that diplomacy and, in extreme situations, protect Japanese interests.

As part of her new efforts to build an active foreign policy, Japan has also
begun to feel a growing pressure from the rest of Asia to act as the region's
spokesperson in matters of world trade. Southeast Asia in particular has
become concerned about Western trading blocs that would exclude them,
including the European Union and the North American Free Trade Area. The
ASEAN nations especially feel a shared interest with Japan to promote global
trade.[32] They know that, though they trade among themselves more now than
they ever did, they still sell a great deal to the United States and Europe.[33] As
a group they run a huge surplus with the United States, and rely on America
as their chief export market.[34] Along with Japan, these ASEAN states, in the
words of the Malaysian *Business Times,* are "investment-driven and export-ori-
ented, inward looking in terms of production networking but outward looking in terms of exports."[35] In that commonality, they have singled out Japan as
their voice, because her economy is the largest, and she is the only Asian member of the Group of Seven (G-7). The G-7 comprises the world's most
advanced economic and financial powers: the United States, Germany, France,
Britain, Italy, Canada, and Japan. The ASEAN states know that individually
they have little bargaining power with richer nations, and even as a group, their
power is limited without Japan.

Although these economic considerations alone are forcing Japan to develop an active, independent foreign policy, perhaps the frightening prospects of Korean instability and Chinese assertiveness are applying a more urgent pressure. For a long time Japan seemed completely unconcerned about the possibility of hostilities so close to her shore. As in so many areas, she relied on the United States to contain any conflict and acted as if she were invulnerable behind the American shield. But with the possible presence of nuclear missiles in North Korea, and an equivocating American stance toward the unpredictable and increasingly desperate government in Pyongyang, Japan's complacency has dissipated. Especially threatening to Japanese security is North Korea's possession of the Nodong-1 intermediate-range ballistic missile, which can reach most of the western islands, and the probability that Korea has perfected the longer-range Taepo Dong missile, which will be able to reach Tokyo.[36] The extent of the threat became clear in 1998 when North Korea used one of its longer-range missiles to overshoot the Japanese islands and put a payload into the Pacific. Pyongyang claimed that it was a failed space shot, but the serious security implications were clear to all.[37]

The first signs of a Japanese awakening to these threats appeared in 1992, when a white paper from her Defense Agency made much of the North Korean missile threat.[38] In response, Japan took an active role in the negotiations that resulted in the U.S.-Korean accord of 1994. Japan agreed to finance North Korea's switch from its old nuclear reactors, which could produce weapons-grade material, to new, less threatening light-water reactors. Since then, she has retained her new sensitivity to events on the Korean peninsula and become heavily involved in the provision of food aid to North Korea. This aid has nothing in common with her other, economically linked aid maneuvers.[39]

China adds more pressure for a heightened Japanese foreign policy response. Certainly, Japan is aware of China's great and increasing economic and military power and that nation's willingness to use it. The Japanese seem more alert to danger from China than the Western nations. According to a recent Nikkei-Dow Jones survey, twice as many Japanese see China as a threat than do Americans.[40] In a 1996 white paper, Tokyo's Defense Agency abandoned Japan's old complacency and raised atypical alarm over China's military buildup, particularly its aggressiveness in the Taiwan Strait and over the potentially oil-rich Spratly Islands in the South China Sea.[41] According to Robyn Lim, professor of international relations at Hiroshima Shuda University, it is not China's growing economic strength or even its increasing presence as a continental military power that is most critical to Japan, but rather that China is also developing "a serious oceangoing navy."[42]

Precise figures on China's military are hard to come by, but a recent paper prepared jointly by Japan and the United States supports a measure of Japanese concern. According to that paper, China maintains a standing army of over three million men and has increased defense spending by 10 percent a year on average since 1989.[43] Perhaps most ominously, China has begun a massive modernization of its military. In the early 1990s, China purchased a number of Russian MiG-31 fighter-interceptors, and more than seventy of the sophisticated Russian SU-27 long-range fighters. As of this writing, Chinese aircraft are the only ones in Asia equipped with sophisticated Archer air-to-air missiles, and the country has also negotiated to purchase the still impressive land-based surface-to-air SAM300 missiles. China's navy has procured sophisticated antisubmarine helicopters, and added to its own submarine fleet with the purchase of several Russian Kilo-class conventional submarines. The modernization drive has already equipped China's ample fleet of destroyers and other surface vessels with ship-to-ship as well as surface-to-air missiles. Perhaps most upsetting to Japanese observers, Chinese military authorities are investigating the purchase and development of satellite technology for command and control as well as for spying.[44] It also appears that China has begun to enhance its nuclear capabilities. Obviously, China is especially secretive in this area, but in addition to the troublesome testing of a few years ago, analysts in the United States have alerted allies to an "increase in activity." Writing recently in *International Security,* Iain Johnstone of Harvard University noted this increase and argued that China has significantly stepped up its nuclear posture from its previous doctrine of "minimal deterrence."[45] Summing up China's advances in these areas, a recent Rand study put China's "military capital"—which Rand defines as the accumulated cost of new equipment plus research and development less depreciation—up to about half that of the United States and well above any other Asian nation.[46]

Compounding Japanese fears, China has launched a diplomatic offensive in Southeast Asia that threatens Japan's dominant position, at least indirectly. Speaking at recent ASEAN meetings and in bilateral talks, Beijing has promoted what it calls a "new order" in Asia, centered on cooperation with China, and implicitly slanted to exclude the United States and its long-term ally, Japan.[47] Such a bid for primacy, if not outright hegemony, is upsetting enough from a Japanese perspective. But even more troubling is the Chinese nationalism that has helped fuel the diplomatic aggressiveness and support heightened military capabilities. It seems that the Chinese authorities have turned to nationalism as a substitute for communism to bind the huge country together. Chinese writers and academics have backed the trend, producing an array of books and pamphlets to bolster what they call China's "spiritual civilization."[48]

Some writers are more belligerent than others, and Chinese nationalism comes in all stripes, but the memory of World War II gives it all an anti-Japanese tone. Perhaps more troubling still, the nationalism speaks to the population's willingness to support the use of China's new powers—economic, political, diplomatic, and military. Meanwhile, a recent report by Washington's Center for Strategic and International Studies points to other reasons why China might want to achieve sway in the rest of Asia. The study notes that China's growth rates will create a great future need for imported food and oil. By 2010, it estimates, China will have to import oil equal to half of Saudi Arabia's present production.[49] This coming need to procure resources makes the future China look even more dangerous and aggressive than the present one.

To complicate the situation further, the United States has shown less willingness than it once did to shoulder the entire burden of Japanese security. While the Cold War's end has done nothing to make Asia safer, it has instilled a desire in America and Europe to enjoy a "peace dividend." Accordingly, American defense spending fell by well over 30 percent between 1990 and 1997, with further cuts planned.[50] After 1992, the United States Department of Defense reduced military personnel in East Asia from 135,000 to 100,000, and in 1992, the navy vacated its huge naval base at Subic Bay in the Philippines.[51, 52] Despite American assurances of a continued commitment to Asian stability and the security of its sea-lanes, these actions have raised concerns in Japan and elsewhere in Asia. The navy may have left Subic Bay only because the Philippines requested it, and the United States Pacific Command may still include 300,000 soldiers, sailors, and airmen, as well as a powerful fleet, but anxiety among Asians about American disengagement has grown and so has the fear that the United States ultimately will yield position to China in Asia.[53] As one Japanese commentator put it, the concern is that the departure of America will give China a position in Asia "like that of the United States to the rest of the Americas."[54] In the face of such a prospect, Japan has begun to question her old assumptions, as have other Asian nations that have to deal with China. Japan is their only alternative, despite lingering bad feelings from the Second World War. They have pressured Japan to make herself capable of filling the gap should the United States leave or pare down its commitment. Malaysian Prime Minister Mahathir Mohamad has been most vocal. "We accept that Japan has very close relations with the U.S.," he said, "but for how long will Japan ask the U.S. to protect it?"[55]

All the factors that have raised Japanese angst—Korean threats, Chinese bullying, questions about America's commitment in Asia—have also raised security concerns throughout Asia, creating something of an arms race that, in its turn, has only heightened each country's feeling of insecurity. The nations of Asia have raised defense spending, even as the United States and Europe have cut it. As indicated earlier, China has increased its outlays rapidly. Taiwan jumped its own defense spending by 30 percent in the first half of the 1990s, South Korea by 35 percent, and Indonesia by 60 percent.[56] The push has grown strong enough to prompt Valeri Kartavtser of the huge Russian state-run arms producer, Rosvoorouztsenic, to characterize "Asia, particularly Southeast Asia and the Pacific Rim, [as] one of the most promising export markets for defense products."[57] Recent economic and financial setbacks in Asia have upset procurement plans and timetables, but the purpose of these governments remains, as does the trend to build their defense capabilities. Indeed, the political instability brought on by the crisis has only strengthened their resolve. The danger implicit in this general demand for arms has, in turn, added yet another pressure on Japan to enhance her own diplomatic and military capabilities, and pursue a more active, independent foreign policy. She has followed the general Asian pattern, expanding her military spending by about 50 percent during this time.[58]

Although each nation has its own particular motive in this recent arms buildup, the regional pattern is unmistakable. Taiwan, which, admittedly, is in a particularly tight spot, kicked off massive war games in the spring of 1997, just before Britain turned Hong Kong over to China. In front of 200 reporters, Taiwanese President Lee Teng-hui made an ostentatious show of the island's military power. He made a special point of stressing Taiwan's weapons-producing capability, lest anyone think that it could not cope with Chinese attempts to isolate it.[59] South Korea has responded to North Korea's nuclear and missile capabilities by redoubling its own missile development program.[60] Vietnam has appealed to ASEAN ambassadors to help it in its dispute with China.[61] While no one has yet responded with support for Vietnam, the request itself has added to the general concerns that have fed this turn to arms. The Philippines has actually sent naval ships to back up claims contested with China in the area around Mischief Reef in the South China Sea.[62] Although no shots were fired, the incident showed how regional tensions could easily lead to combat. Indeed, Burma and Thailand have actually exchanged shots in a dispute over fishing rights.[63] Jakarta's Center for Strategic and International Studies has noted the growing tension throughout the region and its increasing military component. Though Indonesia is as involved as any other nation, the Center nonetheless expressed concerns about the "politicization of military affairs" that has developed in the 1990s.[64] The region's recent financial and currency losses might have reduced each nation's ability to buy arms, but the economic turmoil has also increased tensions, suspicions, and exacerbated the fears that have inspired the arms race.

Though it did not involve Japan directly, an Indonesian action of 1996 illustrates the questions and concerns facing Japan in the future. In September of that year, Indonesia mounted its largest military maneuvers in years, involving air, land, and naval forces. The maneuvers centered on the natural gas-rich Natuna Islands in the South China Sea and aimed unmistakably at a tenuous Chinese claim to the area. According to military observers, the maneuvers were primarily a demonstration of Indonesia's "capability of projecting…battalions and support ships into trouble spots" for the many invited members of Asia's diplomatic corps, the press, and the Chinese.[65] While Japan makes no claim to the region, the episode was nonetheless instructive to Japanese diplomats and defense planners. Indonesia's goal was to show its ability to protect its vital economic interests at the extremes of its far-flung archipelago. Japan knows that she, too, will need to protect far-flung interests, many beyond the extremes of her own archipelago throughout Asia and the Pacific Rim, including, significantly, inside China. Just like Indonesia, Japan will need an active diplomacy with military backing to secure these interests. She will also need to make a display of military might, less for fighting than for assuming the lead in the ongoing diplomatic dance in which she will have to engage in order to manage her growing international position in tense, unstable Asia.

DIPLOMATIC AND MILITARY RENAISSANCE

In developing these critical capabilities, Japan will face a huge adjustment from her long-standing role as the pacifist subordinate of American policy. She will make the wrenching change because the preservation of her standard of living will require foreign ventures, and they will demand an active, independent foreign policy and a strong, modern military. Without this more active foreign policy, all the other necessary responses to the developing economic and demographic imperatives—the move of industry overseas, the development of an Asian division of labor, and the reorientation of her domestic economy—will fail to support Japanese prosperity securely.

Japan has already shown an ability to make the needed change. It is evident in the gradual (if largely disguised) move away from the passivity that has characterized her underlying policies for years. Actually, the first signs appeared very early on, even while American troops were still occupying the country. During the Korean war, though Article 9 of her new, postwar constitution forbade her any armed force, Japan saw her own vulnerability to foreign aggression and recruited military personnel to help with the American war effort. In deference to her new constitution, Japanese recruits avoided direct combat, but Japan did provide extensive logistical support and suffered casualties. Japanese laborers were sent to Korea to unload war material. Forty-six Japanese minesweepers were added to the fleet to keep Korean ports clear. Some were sunk. At the Inchon landings, Japanese crews manned one-third of the support ships at the scene.[66] Although Japanese diplomatic activity at the time was entirely controlled by the American occupation authorities, the recruitment of an armed force was a first step away from the original idea that Japan was entirely unarmed and inactive in power politics.

During the long Cold War period following the Korean conflict, Japan kept moving, though slowly, toward a more positive defense posture and an active foreign policy. Her caution was due in part to a concern for the sensibilities of other Asian nations, but mostly it reflected a need to consider the strong domestic tendencies toward pacifism. The Socialist Party, which from the mid-1950s until very recently was the only significant Diet opposition to the Liberal Democratic Party, had a strictly pacifist plank in its permanent campaign platform. (In the mid-1990s the Socialists jettisoned this plank to join the LDP government.) Many Japanese sympathized with that party's original position. These citizens associated international power politics and the military with the devastation of the war and simply wanted no more of it. Others, in order to cope with feelings of personal or national guilt, cast themselves as victims of their own military. Their revulsion against the military showed in open hostility. For years after the war, Japanese military personnel had to wear civilian dress in public or risk ridicule or worse. Hajime Sakuna, who eventually became the Defense Agency's senior counsel, remembered people spitting at him when he was a student at Japan's defense academy.[67] Chalmers Johnson, the doyen of American Japan-watchers, noted that many Japanese came to equate democracy with pacifism and an inactive foreign policy.[68] The Japanese developed pride in their country's pacifism and her low-profile approach to foreign affairs, viewing it as a leadership innovation that only Japan could claim. Intellectuals referenced the great Japanese novelist of the late nineteenth century, Natsume Soseki (1868–1912), who criticized the goal of international leadership as a "Western idea that is naturally confining and frustrating to Japanese."[69]

Yet Japanese foreign policy gradually gained initiative. After the Korean War ended, Japanese leadership successfully resisted a movement to disband the limited military that she had pulled together under American tutelage. The

Cold War and continuing tension on the Korean peninsula raised enough security concerns that even the pacifists had to yield. In 1954, after the American occupation ended, Japan formally organized her self-defense forces (SDF).[70] The name reflected the nation's pacifism. Japan was to have no army, navy, or air force. Instead, she organized a ground self-defense force (GSDF), a maritime self-defense force (MSDF), and an air self-defense force (ASDF). Showing a more substantive interpretation of the constitution's pacifist spirit, these forces were limited purely to defensive activity and were geared mostly to maintaining domestic order—a significant difference from the armed forces of other nations. But even at that early stage, the very existence of these forces belied the purely pacifist state that the founders of postwar Japan envisaged. Further, the presence of the SDF spoke to a potential to develop an active ability to participate in international power politics should the need or desire develop.

During the Vietnam war, Japan again managed to do what she needed to cope with the exigencies of the situation. Despite the letter and spirit of the pacifist Article 9 and the clear preference of much of her population to eschew involvement in foreign political and military affairs, Japan's leaders saw cooperation with the United States to be in the nation's interest. They willingly opened Japanese facilities to support the American war effort. Japanese help in Vietnam was less complete than in Korea and further from the action; Vietnam was of less vital interest to Japan than was Korea. Nonetheless, Japan helped America move some 400,000 tons of military supplies a month. Kedena air base averaged a takeoff or landing every three minutes around the clock between 1965 and 1973, for more than one million military flights.[71] Despite these efforts, Japan still had no independent foreign policy. She still stood willingly in the shadow of the United States.

That began to change with the oil embargo of 1973. The startling action of the Organization of Petroleum Exporting Countries showed not only Japan's vulnerability to an interruption in oil supplies, but also the limits of American power. Japan suddenly saw a need to develop foreign policy tools to do for herself what the United States could not do for her. Because her hands were tied by Article 9 and her still important security treaty with the United States, she focused on the manipulation of foreign aid, as described earlier, but she also began to consider the possibility of a more active diplomacy. In 1976, for the first time since the Second World War, Japan organized her defense strategy and foreign policy around an explicit doctrine, the National Defense Program Outline (NDPO).[72] Part of that plan called for a campaign to get public support for military modernization. Efforts to raise public awareness in

Japan of the altered world environment paid off with the beginnings of a change in sentiment. Whereas in the 1950s more than half the population resisted the SDF and the security treaty with the United States because it drew Japan too much into international power politics, by the 1970s the opposition had dropped to less than a third of the population.[73] At that time, the Diet set a ceiling on defense spending at 1 percent of GDP per year. On the surface this seemed to continue a commitment to Japan's retiring, pacifist approach, and it placated the opposition in the Diet as well as most of the pacifist elements of the public. But it was, in fact, far more defense spending than Japan had engaged in previously, and gave the foreign policy and defense people more latitude than they had enjoyed since 1945. Most important, however, the plan's mere existence signaled that Japan was beginning to think strategically and actively about foreign policy.

As part of the surge in activity that grew out of this new political environment, Japan and the United States began to reconsider their strategic and defense arrangements. In 1978, they jointly issued the "Guidelines for Japan-U.S. Defense Cooperation." It expanded Japan's role as a support to the United States in Asia and enlarged her responsibilities for her own self-defense.[74] By the 1980s, Japan was reconsidering her ban on weapons exports. Largely in response to the military potential of Japanese technology, she had initiated the ban in 1967 and extended it in 1976.[75] She began to loosen the strictures with the Joint Military Technology Commission (JMTC) established with the United States in the 1980s. By then, the Japanese public had taken another step toward accepting Japanese power. Surveys showed that by the 1980s, only a fifth of the population still objected to the SDF.[76] Japan was regularly allowing American nuclear submarines and American ships with nuclear weapons to use her port facilities in direct violation of her old nuclear weapons bans.[77] And in the 1980s, as Japan's Asian relationships became more important and her interest in the region became more intense, she readily agreed to patrol sea-lanes out to 1,000 nautical miles from her coast, and have battle groups from her maritime self-defense force accompany American aircraft carriers on Pacific maneuvers.[78] By 1985, Japan had changed enough to allow the United States to station two squadrons of F-16 fighters with nuclear strike capabilities openly on her soil.[79] In the late 1980s, she overcame old-line pacifist resistance to participate in the American Strategic Defense Initiative (SDI).[80]

The Gulf War of 1991 accelerated the nation's transition toward a more active approach to foreign affairs. More than any other incident, this war made clear to her policy makers that Japan could no longer shield herself behind her security treaty with the United States. Initially, Japan approached the conflict in her accustomed manner—as someone else's problem. Focusing as usual on the economic and trade issues, she took the stand that she could procure oil from an Iraqi-occupied Kuwait as well as she could from an independent Kuwait. When pressured to participate in the coalition against Saddam Hussein, she declined, as she had frequently done in the past, citing her "peace constitution." The United States and its allies refused to accept this. Japan was shocked. At last, after much vacillation, Japan contributed $13 billion to the war's financing and reluctantly provided a fleet of mine-sweepers.[81] She felt improperly thanked for her generosity. She also felt embarrassed; she had clearly missed the world's expectations of a major power. Her inability to respond decisively on political issues reflected badly on her legitimacy as a member of the club of most advanced nations, a group with which she wanted to identify. The embarrassment intensified when Japanese diplomacy failed to get Saddam to release Japanese hostages. For those policy people in Tokyo who had not already seen the need to adopt a more active, decisive approach to foreign affairs, these events sounded the alarm.

Under the influence of Japan's frustration and embarrassment, public opinion changed further. An increasing number of Japanese were coming to agree with the comments of former United States Ambassador to Japan Edwin O. Reischauer that "there is something unhealthy about a country as economically powerful and technologically advanced as Japan attempting to remain politically out of sight."[82] The foreign policy debate was coming into the open, and Japan started to abandon her former passive diplomatic attitude. Still, she hesitated to begin a complete transition to world power status. As in the past, deference to her pacifist principles and the still large pacifist segment of her population made her search for a way to soften the image of increasing power and assertiveness.

She fixed on the United Nations (UN) as a means to raise her foreign policy capabilities without appearing to contradict past manners and ideals. Thus in the 1990s, she began to work hard to get Japanese military personnel involved in UN peacekeeping operations. In 1992, Japan's foreign policy establishment at the Foreign Ministry and the Defense Agency fought to get the legislation through the Diet to allow the participation of Japanese troops. When the so-called "PKO" bill (for peacekeeping operations and not to be confused with Ministry of Finance price keeping operations) passed, it stood as a remarkable break from the past. It enabled personnel from Japan's self-defense forces to participate in a limited way in UN operations in Cambodia, Somalia, Mozambique, and in the Middle East.[83, 84] To advance her diplomatic status further, Japan also began to push very hard to obtain a permanent seat on the UN Security Council. This desire for a UN link carries an expression of Japan's sincere, idealistic support for the organization and its agencies, but it serves a more Machiavellian national objective as well. The UN affiliation will offer Japan a fine, relatively safe platform on which to develop her diplomatic and military profiles, create a fully independent foreign policy, and serve her fundamental economic needs.

Certainly, the prestige of leadership at the UN will give Japan an invaluable asset as she asserts herself as the "headquarters nation" in Asia. Not only will stature at the world body gain the respect of other nations in the region, but it will also lend an air of legitimacy to Japan's elevated status. As mentioned earlier, the members of ASEAN have already chosen Japan as a spokesperson for the region on some issues. They have effectively acknowledged Japanese leadership as a result of her position as the only Asian member of the rich nations' club, the Group of Seven. A permanent seat on the UN Security Council would round out the impression of Japan as a natural leader for Asia. The seat is especially important because China already has one. As of this writing, the permanent seats in the Security Council belong to the major allies from World War II: the United States, Britain, Russia, France, and China. In the contest to claim leadership in Asia, China's permanent Security Council seat at the UN offers a counterbalance to Japan's G-7 status. If Japan could get her permanent seat on the Council as well, it would definitely tip the leadership scales in her favor. Then, in the words of one Japanese policy maker, Japan would have a means to "augment [her] responsibility for the management—if not the solution—of international political issues."[85] Or in the words of former Japanese Prime Minister Hashimoto, Japanese representatives would be "treated more appropriately so we can fulfill our international obligations."[86] Showing considerable diplomatic acumen, Japan has used her position as part of the prestigious G-7 to help get the desired influence at the United Nations. She has insisted that the G-7 explicitly support the UN, and pressed G-7 meetings to include a political agenda as well as the usual economic and financial focuses. In the early 1990s, Japan demanded and got the G-7 to endorse the United Nations as the means to world "stability" and "prosperity."[87] While Japan's lobbying doubtless had a principled motivation, it also fit nicely with her national self-interest, part of which, at the moment, is to ingratiate herself to the United Nations in order to elevate herself there.

In addition to the important element of prestige and the very real influence that it can create, the UN affiliation will help neutralize both internal and external resistance to a more active Japanese foreign policy, at least for a time while everyone adjusts to the idea. It will also help with a legal problem. The pacifist Article 9 of Japan's constitution states:

> [T]he Japanese people forever renounce war as a sovereign right
> of the nation and the threat or use of force as a means of settling
> international disputes.
>
> In order to accomplish the aim of the preceding paragraph, land,
> sea, and air forces, as well as other war potential, will never be
> maintained. The right of belligerency of the state will not be
> recognized.[88]

The spirit here is clear enough. Not only does it preclude the maintenance of any armed forces, but also any diplomatic activity that requires a military threat, explicit or implicit, and that encompasses most international power policies. As is evident from this quick historic review, in the past Japan has pushed the boundaries of the Article many times in order to deal with the pressures of the moment. It is easy to argue that the very existence of the self-defense forces violates the law. But no matter how far she has pushed the envelope at other times, the constitution still constrains an active foreign policy. Ultimately there will be a confrontation between Japan's new needs and the admirable ideals of Article 9. By keeping a focus on the UN, Japan can delay that unpleasant event. This is precisely the argument used by Diet leader Ichiro Ozawa, author of Japan's electoral reform of the early 1990s and advocate of a stronger Japanese posture in diplomacy, defense, and finance. His influential book, *Blueprint for a New Japan,* argues that by putting Japanese troops "entirely under command of the United Nations" there is not a "sovereign use of force," and Japanese troops can "act, even in combat," without violating the constitution.[89] The Peace Keeping Operations Bill of 1992 was the first step in the process. It will go on from there.

As this approach to Article 9 will, for the time being, quell domestic resistance to a more active Japanese foreign policy, the UN link will also help quiet objections elsewhere in Asia. It will not placate all who resist Japanese power, but it will help legitimize it and at the same time offer Japan's neighbors a sense that there is some check on it. A recent editorial in the prestigious Bangkok *Asia Times* endorsed this particular approach. "[G]iven Asian neighbors' sensibilities," it said, "gradualism may be the most appropriate policy for now."[90] Of course, different countries and groups in the region have different attitudes. Lee Kuan Yew, the founder of Singapore as an independent city-state, sees problems almost regardless of Japan's affiliations. He characterized the use of

Japanese defense forces overseas, under any auspices, as equivalent to "giving liqueur chocolates to an alcoholic."[91] Similarly, in almost every country in the region there are vocal, organized groups who distrust Japanese power. They see a pathology in Japan's inability to acknowledge her war guilt. They have protested the Ministry of Education's sanitizing of the war in Japanese text-books and shown displeasure with Japanese politicians honoring Japanese war dead, some of whom, these people have pointed out, were war criminals. War crimes groups from Asia have even protested in front of the UN building in New York to counter Japan's bid for a Security Council seat.[92, 93]

Some in Asia, however, welcome greater Japanese strength, and see the United Nations affiliation simply as an aid in gaining acceptance among their more suspicious countrymen and women. Time has helped heal old war wounds. Anwar Ibrahim, once the Deputy Prime Minister of Malaysia, noted that fear and resentment of Japan resided in his "father's generation...This is a different world." Malaysian Prime Minster Mahathir has gone so far as to encourage greater Japanese presence and power. When Japan worried over join-ing his proposed East Asian Economic Caucus because it would exclude the United States, he dared the Japanese to take care of themselves, and went on to ask why Japan worried over losing American nuclear protection because it would not last anyway.[94] A new, more favorable perspective on Japan's war role has emerged. Though people in Malaysia and Indonesia suffered under Japan-ese occupation, they have credited the Japanese with reducing Asia's awe of European colonial powers and thus helping to stimulate nationalist movements that brought independence to these countries. Economics has also helped mod-erate resistance. Even Lee Kuan Yew—at the same time as he worried over liqueur-filled chocolates—saw a Japanese role in securing Asia's sea-lanes should the United States withdraw. In the early 1990s, he was ready to encour-age Japan to "carry more of its own defense, which will eventually include the protection of sea lanes beyond a thousand nautical miles" of Japan.[95]

However ambivalent other Asian nations feel about the issue of Japan-ese power, China remains implacable. The Chinese leadership has some of the most bitter personal memories of the war, as the fighting and the Japanese occupation there were particularly savage. But scars from long ago are only part of the story. Japan is the only East Asian power that can challenge ulti-mate Chinese primacy or hegemony in the region—economic, financial, or political. On that basis alone, the Chinese will resist any extension of Japanese power in any realm. Japanese affiliations with the UN and the G-7 rankle fur-ther because they are high-profile acknowledgements of the reality of Japan-ese strength, and they reinforce it. To be sure, China had less trouble with Japanese troops in Cambodia as UN peacekeepers than it would have had if the troops were there on strictly Japanese business. But it was entirely a matter of the lesser of two evils. China has objected and will continue to object to any sign of an influential Japanese foreign policy under any auspices. But even if the UN link cannot soften Chinese attitudes, it still is useful to Japan in dealing with China, for it will make it awkward for China to oppose Japan as publicly or as vociferously as it might want. In this sense, the UN link will also serve Japan by helping to quell objections elsewhere in Asia that stem from fear of what China might do in response to Japan assertiveness. And these are significant. Singapore's Prime Minister, Goh Chok Tong, for example, has implored Japan to soften her stance and use "constructive engagement" with China for the sake of regional stability.[96] By helping to quiet China, the UN affiliation will offer something of an answer to him and others who take a similar line.

As action under a UN affiliation softens objections to the growth of Japanese power, it will at the same time help Japan develop and refine her diplomatic and military capabilities for the time when she will have to exercise them independently. Most important in this respect, United Nations action will permit Japan to safely develop a reputation (which she does not currently have) for sophisticated diplomacy and an effective military. Anticipating this, perhaps, some in Japan have proposed an "Asian Standby Force" for the United Nations. Modeled on the long-standing "Nordic Standby Force," it would assign mostly Japanese troops permanently for United Nations operations all over the world.[97] Doubtless, the UN would put such a force to good use for the world's benefit. It would also suit Japan's future needs by training her troops and giving them experience that they could not get otherwise, at least not without raising significant foreign policy risks. This advantage must provide at least a partial explanation of why Japan is so interested in having her troops used in peacekeeping operations of almost any kind. By earning a reputation for an effective and efficient military in these non-inflammatory ways, Japan will gain an asset that can bolster any future international diplomatic effort without the need to use the force.

As Japan gains from her UN affiliation, she will also smooth her transition to more complete power status by expanding her role within her treaty with the United States. And, indeed, that process has already begun. The treaty's first incarnation, signed right at the end of the American occupation, created perceptions about the relationship that have endured, despite the subsequent enlargement of Japan's role and elevation of her stature within it. Originally the agreement severely limited Japan. The first Japanese negotiators, Prime Minister Yoshida and Foreign Minister Ashida, saw the United States taking responsibility for all external defense of Japan and for securing sea-lanes as well as foreign Japanese interests, such as they were at the time. Any Japanese armed force was aimed at "policing against communist insurrections,"[98] which was a legitimate concern in the late 1940s and early 1950s. But soon after, Japan's military responsibilities expanded. By the mid-1950s, after Japanese assistance to the United States in the Korean War and the creation of the self-defense forces, Japan's role in the security treaty began to take on some of the qualities of a conventional partnership with the United States. The treaty had its first formal revision in 1960, at which time it codified the changes that had taken place in the late 1950s, making the pact "more reciprocal" than it had been, in the words of the negotiators, and implicitly giving Japan a heightened "measure of self-determination."[99] This expanded role was made still more explicit in the Guidelines for Japan-U.S. Defense Cooperation issued in November 1978. Actually, Japan was able, during the negotiation of the Guidelines, to exercise the kind of diplomatic maneuvering for which she had no place during the previous thirty years. Though Japan clearly was ready for the change, she claimed sensitivity to her still largely pacifist population and made a show of reluctance in expanding her role in the treaty. Making the changes seem like a concession to the United States helped her sell her heightened diplomatic and military posture to the reluctant elements in her own population as well as to her anxious Asian neighbors. It also helped Japan exact "compensation" from the United States: the return first of Iwo Jima island and then Okinawa.[100]

During the 1980s, the implication of Japan's expanded role in the treaty became clear. The Americans no longer were meant to do the whole job of defense. Japanese armed forces were positioned for external threats, not internal order. The ground self-defense force expanded. Eight divisions moved from populous regions, where an internally oriented security force would naturally reside, north to Hokkaido Island, where they faced the then external threat of the Soviet Union. Japan reinforced these divisions with her new M90 tank, which she produced from her own designs that improved on the American M1 tank. The self-defense forces began to upgrade their communications, command, control, and intelligence capability—what military people call C³I. By the late 1980s, Japanese armed services were operating according to what they called the "seashore" or "forward" defense posture, which effectively moved border defense out one thousand nautical miles from Japan's coast, and explicitly took responsibility for defending the straits around Japan. It put the SDF potentially into direct confrontation with the Russian navy, which uses these sea-lanes to gain access to the Pacific. By the early 1990s, Japan had fully abandoned her traditional focus on "defensive defense" and adopted what she called an "offensive defense" backed with the latest high-tech weapons.[101]

In 1997, the security treaty with the United States changed again, taking yet another step to increase Japan's reciprocal responsibilities and, in effect, her diplomatic independence and military power. The new treaty does not yet commit Japan to a full partnership in defense with the United States; while the United States remains bound to defend Japan, Japan is not yet bound to defend the United States. The new agreement, however, breaks dramatically with the past by offering a number of ways in which Japan would assist American forces in Asia, even if Japan herself were not directly under attack. According to the treaty's language, Japan has committed herself in certain "situations" in "areas surrounding Japan" to: engage in minesweeping operations for her own shores; conduct search and rescue operations; provide extensive logistical support for American troops; evacuate noncombatants from points of danger; perform high-seas inspections to enforce economic sanctions; and, of course, defend herself.[102] This might seem routine in Western agreements, but it is a major step for Japan. Any of these obligations would have been questionable, and some objectionable, under past agreements. And some could put Japanese lives on the line.

The 1997 agreement expanded the latitude for Japanese diplomatic and military action in new ways. Past treaties, in deference to sensibilities in Japan and elsewhere in Asia, always made the terms and the areas of Japanese involvement crystal clear. This agreement is very different. It defines neither the "situations" in which Japan might get involved, nor the "areas" in which her involvement might take place. This difference has given Japanese diplomacy more maneuvering room than it has had for over fifty years. It will help Japan deal with the particular security issues of post-Cold War Asia as well as help her secure her far-flung economic interests. According to Tetsuo Maeda, professor of international relations at Tokyo International University, the whole "aim is to extend the activities of the SDF beyond Japanese territory."[103] But the effect will be subtler than that. By making the treaty hinge on an assessment of the situation instead of the geographical parameters used in the past, it makes it easy for Japan to interpret her field of interest within the treaty as extending from Siberia in the north, to Korea, to the Taiwan Strait, all the way into Southeast Asia, wherever, in fact, she might need diplomatic leverage to pursue her expanding interests. Making the whole purpose quite explicit, Makoto Sakuma, one-time chief of staff of the maritime self-defense force and chairman of the joint staff council, applauded the treaty as supporting the increasing need to "give Japanese overseas a sense of security."[104]

Japan got to enjoy her newfound diplomatic strength as soon as the treaty's provisions were announced, even before the Japanese Diet or the American Congress could ratify it. Anticipating a reaction in Asia, Japan and the United States mounted parallel efforts to reassure other Asian powers, at least on the surface. Instead of Japan tagging along with America, as happened in the past, this time each nation independently explained the treaty in terms of its bilateral relationship with each Asian country. Most of Asia seemed cautiously positive about the new treaty. Given its history, South Korea understandably asked Japan expressly to reaffirm her constitutional position against using force to settle disputes.[105] But for most, an editorial in Bangkok's prestigious English-language journal, *Nation,* summed up the region's measured feelings. By welcoming the "improved security in the face of China's increasing power," it showed support. By also remembering "the havoc wreaked by Japan's military adventures in World War II," it alerted its readers to remaining "reservations among Asia-Pacific countries about the expansion of Japan's security role." Aside from lingering memories of World War II, the major concern in Singapore, the Philippines, and elsewhere was not how Japan might use the expanded latitude but rather how the treaty might precipitate a dangerous confrontation with China.[106]

China, of course, was not pleased, and as might be expected, presented the greatest challenge for the diplomatic arts. In dealing with China, however, Japan found immediate use for the expanded diplomatic leverage that the new treaty gave her. China suspected that the U.S.-Japanese agreement aimed at containment. Even before the treaty's announcement, Shen Guo Fang, a Chinese Foreign Ministry spokesman, expressed concerns that an "arrangement" that went "beyond its bilateral dimension...would complicate the situation in the region."[107] Taiwan, naturally, was another point of concern. Chinese Prime Minister Li Peng described any consideration of Japanese interference in Taiwan as "utterly unacceptable." And at the United Nations, Chinese Foreign Minister Qian Qichen harassed Japan's then Foreign Minister Keizo Obuchi over Taiwan.[108] Japanese diplomats had no desire to inflame the Chinese, but neither did they want to give blanket assurances, and in this case, unlike so many times in the past, they could avoid that. Foreign Minister Obuchi could easily assure China that the new guidelines were intended, as always, "strictly for the security of Japan" and that the country would maintain its exclusively "defense oriented policy."[109] But at the same time, Japan could disguise exactly what she would or would not forbid herself. Past treaties were so clear and limiting that foreign powers knew where Japan would have to stop even before they asked. This time, she could make room for herself. Then Prime Minister

Hashimoto asserted that the guidelines did not specifically target Taiwan, but still he refused to rule out a Japanese role. "This isn't the sort of situation where we draw a line on the globe and say, 'up to here.' It's not that simple," he said.[110] At one time for Japan it was that simple, leaving her diplomats with little negotiating room.

Anticipating her ultimate need to move beyond the UN and American security relationships, Japan recently has begun to engage in more truly independent diplomatic activity than in the past. Since 1992, she has developed what her policy makers have referred to as a "two-track" approach to strengthening her influence: one track deals bilaterally with individual countries of interest, especially to promote stability, and the second track promotes parallel policy discussions on a region-wide basis. As an expression of how seriously she takes the effort, Japan has established a very public "Prime Minister's Council on Japan and the Asia-Pacific Region for the 21st Century."[111] The Council's aim, and consequently Japan's, is to use this two-track process to establish an Asian equivalent of Europe's Conference on Security and Cooperation in Europe (CSCE). The plans exclude the United States, as does the European Conference, and place Japan in a position of leadership. With these goals in mind, Japan has pushed a political and security agenda at the once purely economic ASEAN summit meetings since the early 1990s.[112] And, after initial hesitation, she placed considerable support behind Malaysian Prime Minister Mahathir's proposal for an exclusive East Asian Economic Caucus.[113] As part of the effort, Japan has stepped up state visits and taken action at home to develop the institutions to support a more independent and active foreign policy. In 1997, the ruling Liberal Democratic Party set up a parliamentary group to study ways either to repeal the pacifist Article 9 of the constitution or to find some legal device to reconcile it to Japan's new manner, needs, and objectives.[114]

Recently, Japan has done more to distance herself from her timid past than just convene councils and set new objectives and policy guidelines, although these actions alone were radical departures from her old, diplomatically retiring self. In 1997, without waiting for any formalities, she sent air self-defense force planes to Thailand to evacuate Japanese nationals caught in that year's round of Cambodian bloodletting.[115] In the past, she might have counted on the United States Air Force or just sat out the situation. The year before her mini-airlift and even before much talk of revising Japan's security treaty with the United States, then Prime Minster Hashimoto made a five-nation tour of Southeast Asia to deal with security issues as well as the usual economics and trade topics. In a significant change from the old Japanese approach to diplomacy, he stressed bilateral relations with each country over multilateral arrangements. To bolster Hashimoto's effect, Japan's then Minister of Defense, Naoki Murata, took a similar tour a month or two later.[116] While such a clearly security-oriented follow-up seems common enough by Western standards, for pacifist, America-dominated Japan, the willingness to deal with her own security at that level was something of a diplomatic watershed.

Japan's emerging diplomatic independence has extended beyond Southeast Asia to Europe, Russia, and China. In 1996, Japan sent then Foreign Minister, Yukihiko Ikeda, to the European Commission in Brussels. He addressed the usual trade, economic, and finance issues, but Minister Ikeda also shocked his hosts by expanding the agenda, saying that the usual economic issues were "inseparably connected with international politics and security-related topics." In a remarkable break with past Japanese practice, he put forward Japan's positions and pressed the Europeans on the Balkans, the former Soviet Union, and North Korea. The European diplomats spoke openly of their surprise that Japan was willing to deal with these issues. Ikeda then added to the novelty of the meetings. As a way of advertising Japan's new diplomatic posture, he went out of his way to stress the rapport that he had developed elsewhere with his Russian counterpart, Yevgeny Primakov, even though the Russian had not attended the Brussels meeting.[117]

And, indeed, Japan, in advancing toward her new, higher profile diplomacy, has stepped up her contacts with Russia. As a natural first step, she has focused on finally signing a treaty of peace for World War II. The sticking point has been a small group of islands stretching north toward Siberia that the Japanese call the Northern Territories and the Russians call the Kurile Islands. Soviet troops occupied the islands during the closing days of the war and conflicting claims have persisted. The Cold War and American domination of Japanese diplomacy held back negotiations. But in this short, recent period of more active independent Japanese policy, she has struck an agreement with Russia that both sides expect will result in a final peace treaty by the year 2000.[118] But Japanese-Russian talks have had a broader agenda than the unfinished business of World War II. In what observers have begun to refer to as the "multifaceted approach" of Japanese diplomacy, Japanese-Russian talks have examined prospects for military as well as economic cooperation.[119] Japan has emerged from these talks advocating Russian admission to the Asia-Pacific Economic Cooperation (APEC) forum, which includes the United States, Canada, Japan, and Southeast Asia. She has signed agreements in which Russia will guarantee Japanese economic interests there against appropriation.[120] On the security side of the equation, defense ministers from each country have visited the other's capital, and, in a landmark protocol, the two nations agreed to: notify each other about upcoming military exercises, exchange information on basic defense policies as well as protections against chemical and biological weapons, and arrange a continuing dialogue between their respective defense establishments.[121] In this short time, agreements have progressed so fast that one British observer characterized the Japanese/ Russian relationship as her "widest ongoing security accord with any country apart from...the U.S."[122] And Japanese officials have described the new Russian relationship as "profoundly affecting the balance of power in Asia."[123] In a symbolic but nonetheless significant gesture, Russia invited Japanese naval participation in the celebrations for the three hundredth anniversary of the Russian navy, and so in the summer of 1996 Japanese warships, flying the rising sun flag, entered Vladivostok for the first time since 1895, when Japan entered the port as victors in the Russo-Japanese War.[124]

While much of Japan's recent warmth toward Russia doubtless stems from her concerns about China, Japan has not stinted on extending her new diplomacy toward that nation either. Japanese efforts in China have gone a lot further than being coy over her new security treaty with the United States. Of course, Japan has long tried to manipulate her relations with China through aid. In 1995, she suspended aid grants, but not loans, to protest Chinese nuclear testing. Early in 1997, after China signed the comprehensive nuclear test ban treaty, Japan offered a carrot by making public the recommendation of a group within her government to resume grant aid. But Japan held off actually resuming aid in order to pry agreements on fishing out of the Chinese, and advance Japan's desire that China destroy the chemical weapons left behind by the Japanese after World War II.[125] Aspects of Japan's Chinese diplomacy have also followed her old, largely economic and trade-oriented approach, such as pressing China's admission to the World Trade Organization. Indeed, Japan pressed this point so aggressively that Europe accused Japan of watering down the entry requirements for China's sake.[126] But in other respects, Japan's China diplomacy has haltingly begun to anticipate the more active role that she will have to pursue in the future. In 1997, before the announcement of the new security treaty with the United States, a group of Diet members, who were responsible for defense policy, met for substantive talks with China's Foreign Minister, Qian Qichen, and its Defense Minister, Chi Haotian. They briefed the Chinese generally on Japanese defense policy, and specifically on arrangements with the United States.[127] At the same time, Japan atypically took a stand on internal political repression in China, instructing her ambassador in Beijing, Hideaki Ueda, to make that position clear to China's government.[128]

But then in a throwback to her old, timid approach, Japan agonized over attending the ceremonies in which Britain handed Hong Kong over to China. To go would offend the United States, which boycotted the ceremonies over Chinese human rights issues; to stay away would offend China.[129] She compromised, sending a low-profile delegation.

Although all this diplomatic maneuvering on two continents is a significant break with Japan's past and a sign for the future, the most dramatic illustration to date of Japan's more active foreign policy revolves around some otherwise insignificant, uninhabited islands in the East China Sea. Claimed by Japan, which calls them Senkakus, and by China, which calls them Daioyu, and by Taiwan, which calls them Tiaoyutai, these islands became the source of tension in 1996. A private group of Japanese nationalists, called the Japan Youth Federation, placed what they called a lighthouse on one of the islands, and then settled in it to secure the Japanese claim. The Chinese and Taiwanese governments protested (separately, of course) but otherwise did little. A private group of Chinese nationalists chartered a ship in Hong Kong and set out for the islands to counter the Japanese lighthouse keepers. The conflict was hardly worth notice, yet the previously passive Japan sent out a flotilla from her maritime self-defense forces. Without doing anything to remove the Japanese nationalists encamped around the lighthouse, this fully armed Japanese naval contingent kept the private Chinese group from closing on the island. One Chinese, either in protest or out of frustration in the face of the Japanese gunboats, leapt into the sea and began to swim toward the island. He drowned. Eventually, the Chinese withdrew, as did the representatives of Japan's maritime self-defense force. The Youth Federation people remained in place, although subsequently, in an attempt to advance other negotiations with China, Japanese police raided the Youth Federation Headquarters in Tokyo and seized records.[130] While the incident is of minor significance in itself, it does starkly illustrate the change in Japan. Here Japan willingly risked relations with two neighboring states for a nationalist gesture. She quickly resorted to a military approach, and was willing to project significant naval force far from her home islands. Such an action would have been unthinkable for the Japan that hesitated and equivocated at the time of the Gulf War in the early 1990s, let alone during the Cold War.

As Japan has anticipated her ultimate needs by stepping up her independent diplomatic initiatives, she has also anticipated the military support required for such a diplomatic effort. According to the 1997 budget, spending for Japan's Defense Agency equaled just under five trillion yen (about $40 billion at that year's exchange rates). While this is well below the $250 billion budgeted for defense by the United States, it is large compared to most nations. It rivals the defense budgets of Britain, France, and Germany combined.[131] After the United States and Russia, Japan probably ranks third in military spending in the world—perhaps, fourth, after China, though reliable figures on China and Russia are hard to come by.[132] And, as indicated earlier, while Europe, America, and Russia are cutting their defense spending, Japan's is rising rapidly along with the rest of Asia. Japan also has great potential to step up such spending in the future. At present, she spends only 1 percent of GDP on arms, compared with about 3.5 to 4 percent for the United States and Britain, some 3.5 percent for France, about 3 percent for Germany, an estimated 5 percent plus for China, and a figure approaching 9 or 10 percent for Russia.[133] Even if Japan's economy continues to grow slowly or stalls altogether, she could double or triple her defense budget with less strain than most countries face to maintain existing levels.

Whatever its future potential, Japan's military is already an impressive force. True to her postwar tradition, Japan has kept her profile low, but appearance should not be confused with reality. The self-defense forces have one quarter of a million men under arms. Although that is a small figure compared to the United States (with over one million), and certainly Russia or China (with several million each), it is not a small figure compared to most other nations.[134] More significantly, what Japan lacks in numbers she makes up in the most advanced, technologically sophisticated equipment and systems. She began the latest modernization in the 1980s in response to the "Hiyuchi Report" from the government's Advisory Panel on Defense Policy, which stressed the need to upgrade the military. According to Susan Willett, senior research fellow at the University of London's Center for Defense Studies, Japan's military equipment is "among the most modern in the world," a match for any, clearly superior to China's, and, in most respects, Russia's as well.[135] What is perhaps most significant to Japan's new diplomatic posture and her future needs is that the application of high-tech equipment has blurred the line between defensive and offensive capabilities. Japan's ground self-defense force consists of thirteen heavily armored divisions backed by over one thousand state-of-the-art tanks, an array of other infantry fighting vehicles, and mobile surface-to-air missiles. The air self-defense force has 450 aircraft at the last publicly available count. Its operating radius will expand dramatically as the new F-2 long-range fighter (formerly the FS-X developed jointly with the United States) comes on line in the year 2000. The maritime self-defense force has more than 350 thousand tons of warships: 8 destroyers, some equipped with newest Aegis fleet-to-air defense system developed by the United States;

55 fast frigates; 18 submarines; 100 P-3C Orion antisubmarine patrol aircraft; and a flotilla of service, supply, and tanker ships. It is still what naval people call a small-ship navy, but it is changing from the purely defensive coastal force of some years ago to one that can project power abroad. There are no aircraft carriers yet. Still, it rivals the Chinese navy—which includes 18 destroyers, 52 frigates, and 52 submarines—that has inspired so much fear in Asia. China clearly has a marginally more offensive force, especially the submarines, but ship for ship, China's navy has much less offensive capability than Japan's.[136]

Building on this significant base, Japan has plans to improve her self-defense forces in ways that will make it still more capable of projecting power. She has ordered AWACS (Airborne Early Warnings and Control) aircraft, which, though useful in defense, can also help direct an attack on distant targets.[137] She is considering joining the United States in the joint development of an advanced ballistic missile defense system.[138] Although defensive in nature, this system would make the home islands more secure from attack, and thereby free Japan to pursue a more active foreign policy. Perhaps even more significant, Japan has stepped up her intelligence capabilities. In 1996 the Diet voted to consolidate the intelligence arms of each branch of the self-defense forces into a single Defense Intelligence Agency, a Japanese CIA.[139] With it, Japan has begun to upgrade her entire military reconnaissance network. Combining the needs of the Foreign Ministry with the Defense Agency, this new agency has taken a first step toward building and operating a "constellation" of ten low-earth-orbit imaging (spy) satellites for twenty-four hour operations, which, though very useful for purely defensive purposes, can be equally useful in offense.[140] Enhancing Japan's ability to project power most directly, her Defense Agency, in preparation for peacekeeping operations with the UN, is expanding its airlift capacity, adding significantly to its fleet of tankers, air and maritime, and other naval support, including four flatbed, 8,900 ton amphibious landing ships that could, with certain technical provisions, even serve as mini-aircraft carriers for Harrier jump jets.[141]

In a short time, Japan's diplomats and military have made great strides toward developing the active and independent foreign policy. It is apparent that she sees the need in Asia's unsettled security environment. Whether or not Japanese leadership makes the link explicit, the development will also provide a necessary support for the dramatic economic and financial measures that Japan will have to take in order to cope with her economic and demographic pressures. The nation has begun to move out of the shadow of the United States. Though still tied to America, Japan is far from the retiring diplomatic and military client of the United States that she once was. She has not yet completed her transformation. To deal with the insecurities and tensions that have beset Asia since the end of the Cold War, Japan must continue to upgrade her diplomatic and military capabilities. To protect her ever more complex and subtle interests in Asia, she will need more diplomatic and military flexibility. To secure her position as the headquarters nation in Asia's division of labor, she will have to exercise more leadership, especially in light of the Chinese competition. No doubt all these changes will diminish her special relationship with the United States as they elevate her position in Asia.

An independently minded, strong Japan will raise fears within the country, elsewhere in Asia, and in the West as well. These concerns are easy to exaggerate. Just because Japan will develop her foreign policy capabilities does not necessarily mean that she will become aggressive, as she was in the 1930s and 1940s, or that she will become involved in a military conflict. But the dangers should not be ignored either. Japan is undergoing a sea change, and when such a change concerns international power politics, it always carries profound risks. Indeed, as the next chapter will discuss, in addition to all these obvious risks and concerns, Japan's unique group culture introduces some unusual uncertainties and dangers into this situation.

RISK IN THE TRANSITION
TO A MORE
POWERFUL JAPAN

THE TRANSITION FACING JAPAN TODAY IS as significant, as profound, as any of the great shifts of her past: opening to the world in the mid-nineteenth century, the descent into militarism in the 1930s, and the great turn from militarism to commerce after World War II. The prospective demographic, economic, diplomatic, and military shifts are clearly of this magnitude.

Although there is good reason to expect Japan to manage these huge adjustments in an orderly and constructive way, there is still tremendous risk involved in a transformation this profound. The aging of Japan's population and the reorientation of her economy will place a great strain on Japanese society. There is even the potential for social disintegration. In all this powerful change, there is no denying that the legacy of World War II will haunt Japan and her neighbors. Events of that brutal time present an unsettling parallel to the forthcoming extension of Japanese political and economic interests into the rest of Asia, especially with her growing military power. Although a return to the aggressive behavior of sixty years ago is not especially likely, these changes have the potential to bring Japan into a tense and possibly violent confrontation with China, or to create a complete break with the United States. The potential for trouble certainly extends beyond the realm of national security (though risks in this area are the most frightening). A little imagination could easily expand the list of fears and potential problems. In the words of former United States Ambassador to Japan, Michael H. Armacost, "as Japan's capabilities increase, uncertainties about future intentions will grow and with that, so also will possibilities for miscalculation."[1]

While there is a wide open field for speculation about possible risks and uncertainties, policy makers, planners, and others who need to deal with potential problems would do well to identify those fears that can be dismissed and concentrate on the contours of more likely potential problem areas. These will lie primarily where people have come to count on constancy but where the new future will witness a major change. For example, an aggressive, nuclear Japan, though the exciting stuff of book jackets, can be dismissed as a remote possibility, as can like concerns. Instead, there are three areas worthy of consideration. Two are related and pertain to the strains on Japan's long-standing alliance with the United States and Japan's continuing commitment to pacifism. These two realities have remained constant in Asia for so long—more than half a century—that any weakening or dissolution would unavoidably excite anxieties, in Japan or elsewhere, that might derail or distort Japan's constructive transformation to her new, more powerful status. Eventually Japan will have to distance herself from America and rethink her pacifism, but in the meantime, too precipitous a change would put a smooth transformation at risk, and raise dangers in Asia and the world accordingly.

The third great "uncertainty" concerns Japanese culture. On the surface, its remarkable cohesiveness would seem to offer a shield against many kinds of risk, including civil unrest—and it does. But in other respects, her powerful orientation toward the group makes Japan vulnerable. Because Japanese culture discourages individuality and stresses service to joint objectives, transition periods, such as the current one, are more disconcerting to the Japanese than they are to other cultures. The Japanese can become almost desperate when they lack national purpose, a basis for group action. At such times, their urgent search for a new plan of action can lead to an unfortunate, or even self-destructive turn, as it did in the 1930s when Japan chose the path to militarism. The possibility of this or some other irrational act is, admittedly, distant, but not remote enough to dismiss out of hand.

FEARS OF AN ARMED
AND INDEPENDENT JAPAN

Despite a great temptation to draw parallels to Japan's last tragic experiment in becoming Asia's headquarters nation, it is important to keep in mind that

Japan fundamentally is a very different country today than she was during World War II. She is highly unlikely to repeat her behavior of the 1930s and 1940s or anything like it. Nonetheless, the carnage brought by the ostensibly economic "Greater East Asia Co-Prosperity Sphere" still haunts the shadows of Asia's consciousness. And it does not help dispel such ghosts that the basic motivation for Japan's modern expansion is the same now as in the 1930s and 1940s: She is searching for a hinterland to support her well-developed but limited island base. Earlier in the century, her drive into Asia aimed at raw materials, whereas this time it aims at finding labor resources to work her transplanted factories. Still, both cases show a Japan looking to maintain her power by using Asia to meet those needs that she cannot fulfill herself. There are enough similarities to raise legitimate concerns that Japan might radically subordinate other nations' interests as she becomes the headquarters nation in Asia's developing division of labor. But there remains little reason to fear a repeat of that terrible time of sixty years ago.

One reason to dismiss fear of a militarily aggressive Japan is her acute consciousness of her own history. This will prompt her to proceed with special care in exercising power in Asia. She is well aware of the legacy of distrust bequeathed by her brutal past. Her utter failure during the war to use military power successfully to acquire her hinterland has taught her the danger and futility of trying to subjugate others by force. Japan is well aware that she will need the cooperation, even the enthusiasm, of other governments and peoples in Asia to man her transplanted factories and make an effective transformation to the headquarters nation. Further, today's Japan faces two major checks on military aggression that were not in place in the bad old days: China and the United States. In the 1930s and '40s, China had too little power and the United States too little presence in Asia to intimidate Japan before the shooting started. Finally, Japanese industry has less interest in military business today than in did before the war. In the '30s and '40s, Japanese industry promoted militarism because it depended on arms sales to its own army and navy for a large portion of its revenues. Today, no major Japanese company depends on arms sales for more than 10 percent of its revenues.[2] Even if Japanese defense sales doubled, this pressure still would fall far short of what it was sixty years ago.

Neither is there reason to fear a nuclear Japan. Few doubt that the Japanese could develop a nuclear capability quickly. And with the nation's space program already capable of putting satellites into orbit, there is no question that Japan could develop a regional or even global missile delivery system. Certainly the temptation exists; there has long been a sense that a nation must possess a nuclear threat to enter the highest ranks of international power. The strenuous efforts of France and China to join the nuclear powers testify to this temptation. Some even suggest that a nuclear Japan would help stabilize Asia.[3] Despite these factors, the nuclear option for Japan remains highly unlikely. As the only people ever to suffer a nuclear attack, there is a deep feeling among Japanese at almost all levels of society that they simply will not brook nuclear arms. The antinuclear lobby draws from both the left and the right of the political spectrum, and is much stronger than the general pacifist lobby, which remains stronger than in most nations. Even that small group of extremists who would reassert the emperor's divinity and return to an overseas empire rejects the nuclear option. When France tested bombs in the Pacific in the mid-1990s, Japanese protests were by far the loudest and largest of any nation's, as was the case when China, India, and Pakistan did their testing.[4] Even prominent nationalists, Shintaro Ishihara and Jun Eto, both of whom have advocated aggressive rearmament and a break with the United States, have spoken out against a Japanese nuclear capability.[5] But more compelling than even the fundamental and understandable Japanese horror of "the bomb" is the fact that a nuclear capacity would make Japan more vulnerable than she is without it. Unlike the United States, China, and other continental powers, Japan's small size makes it difficult for her to present a credible threat of retaliation after a first strike. That would make her a more tempting target than other nations. She cannot avoid this, whether she builds a nuclear arsenal or not. But Japan also knows that if she had such an arsenal, it would certainly be targeted.

Unlike the questions of an aggressive or a nuclear Japan, the risks to the Japanese-American alliance are not be so easily minimized. To date, anxieties about weakness in this long-standing constant of the Asian scene have remained vague. Each time friction arises between the two nations, both sides rush to reassure each other and the world of their continued commitment to their alliance. Except in selected instances, Japan's diplomatic and military renaissance has remained largely disguised, partly out of Japan's desire to retain as much of her old, low-profile image as possible, and partly because the world has not yet changed its way of thinking about Japan. Both Japan and the United States have worked hard to bolster the appearance that Japanese military power is circumscribed by the alliance, even though the newly renegotiated mutual defense treaty clearly gives Japan much greater responsibility than before. But, as the earlier discussion emphasized, this circumstance cannot last. Japan's new, more powerful position will become increasingly evident, and it will become apparent that Japanese foreign policy will ultimately move away from the priorities and guidance of the United States, or the United Nations

for that matter. With that weakening of the alliance, a great and long-lived constant in Asia's power balance will begin to dissipate, and that surely will raise
the sense of uncertainty in Asia and elsewhere, even if there are no direct signs
of trouble.

While Japan still regularly signals her desire to remain firmly in her
American alliance, hints of her resistance to—on occasion almost a defiance
of—American wishes have signaled a change. Elements of a new Japanese attitude were evident even as early as 1992, when Japan took the United States to
task at the World Bank for insisting on free market reforms as a condition for
other nations to receive aid.[6] Japan's position was well known long before the
dispute with the Americans. What is significant is that she advanced her own
position against her old mentor instead of allowing other Asian nations to
plead the case, as she would have done previously. Likewise, Japan has in
recent years resisted following America's lead on China. After the Tiananmen
Square incident in 1989, Japan pointedly refused to use the word "massacre"
as the United States and several European powers insisted on doing. At the
same time, Japan's Foreign Ministry published reports of internal discussions
that were highly critical of Western nations, chiding the United States in particular for overreacting to and interfering with China's internal affairs. This
was something of a compromise with Japan's new position. She did not chide
America *officially* on this point, but rather let it be known that some policy
makers wanted to make the criticism. Still, Japan showed far more defiance
than she would have dared in previous years. The Foreign Ministry made it
clear that it considered the "human-rights diplomacy" of the United States
entirely inappropriate.[7] Later, on the issue of Iran, the Foreign Ministry sided
with Europe's desire for a dialogue against the American policy of isolating the
Islamic regime.[8] In the same vein, in the 1990s Japan has voted against the
United States several times at the UN, much more frequently than in previous
years, and even pushed an agenda for UN agencies to endorse a greater governmental role in market and industrial development than the United States
favors.[9] These small points would mean little for any other nation, and do not
necessarily reflect a weakening in the alliance. But because in the past Japan
set her foreign policy almost entirely to please the United States, they raise
doubt about the durability of what once seemed to be a certainty.

Recent trade negotiations hint of a weakening bond between Japan and
the United States. To be sure, for some time Japan has refused to acquiesce
entirely to American demands. But until recently, she has never done
so directly and publicly. In deference to her subordinate diplomatic status,
she preferred vaguely worded agreements of principle that left her room to

maneuver in practice. Recently, she has abandoned such oblique tactics, refusing to work from America's trade agenda or accept American criteria for success or failure. The United States, for its own reasons, has also become less solicitous. Neither nation is as cordial as it once was, nor is there the old urgency to reach a compromise or accommodation from either side.

For the United States, the discord stems in part from genuine impatience about the persistent trade deficit with Japan. Mostly, however, it grows from a new attitude brought by the end of the Cold War. When the United States was in the business of containing the Soviet Union and communist China, it willingly provided Japan with trade advantages and economic leverage. Economic concessions cemented Japan in the Western camp, and Japan's economic strength made her that much more valuable an ally. Today, however, America has no reason to offer Japan special economic advantages, and its approach to dealing with Japan has changed accordingly.

Meanwhile the Japanese disenchantment has paralleled that of the United States, though from different motivations. During the Cold War, Japan saw America's "nuclear umbrella" as well worth any minor concessions on trade or economics, especially if she could deal in appearances and limit the real extent of any adjustment to American demands. Today, however, the nuclear umbrella is worth less than it once was, even as other security concerns have become more important. As the United States has shown signs of reducing its security guarantees anyway, Japan has come to see fewer reasons to accommodate American wishes, or to humiliate herself in creating the appearance of doing so. At the same time, other economic pressures have given her reason to pursue her own interests independent of the United States.

The differences between the Bush and Clinton trade missions to Japan illustrate the dramatic changes that have taken place in a rather short time. In the late 1980s, President George Bush's trade negotiators quickly settled a semiconductor agreement that included American sales quotas in the domestic Japanese market. At the same time, Bush's team advanced what it called the Strategic Impediments Initiative (SII) to "harmonize" the economic structures of Japan and the United States, presumably to boost American sales in Japan. The Japanese had no desire to make the adjustments pressed by the Americans, but the symbiotic spirit that prevailed during the Cold War pushed them to make at least a pretense of acquiescing to American desires. By contrast, President Bill Clinton's team of negotiators came on much stronger than did the Cold War-era missions. They made strident demands for quotas of American sales in Japan, which they referred to as "objective measures" to track progress on American access to the Japanese economy. The negotiators wanted to renew Bush's semiconductor agreement and extend a like arrangement for autos. In her old subordinate role, Japan would have acted quickly to accommodate such insistent American demands. Certainly, there would have been no open defiance. But in the new environment, the Japanese displayed a previously unseen resistance to match the new aggressiveness of the American negotiators. They charged Washington with pursuing "managed trade" and ironically assumed the role of champions of free trade, declaring, reasonably if disingenuously, that adhering to quotas for the purchase of American goods would interfere with efforts to deregulate their domestic economy. Clinton's team failed to meet its objectives.[10] In rejecting the demands of the United States, Japan advanced her independent posture further by rejecting the long-standing bilateral approach favored by the United States. The Japanese insisted not only that the old quotas be scrapped, but also that aggrieved parties put issues of bias before a new multilateral, private sector forum, which the Japanese called the Semiconductor Council.[11] Japan's insistence on such a body signaled less about practical trade matters than it did a new stand on resisting American leadership.

Since the failure of the Clinton negotiating effort, Japan has continued to present an independent diplomatic stature. When the United States recently pressured Japan to extend an agreement with NTT (Nippon Telephone and Telegraph) to procure material from American contractors, Japan countered by refusing until the United States Federal Communications Commission agreed to license two Japanese carriers, NTT and NDD, to provide international telecommunications service from an American base. This would be a common enough quid pro quo in dealings between other developed nations, but it was remarkable compared with past Japanese practice. Certainly, the United States saw nothing of the kind when it reached its original NTT procurement agreement with Japan in the 1980s.[12] In a confrontation over port practices, Japan, unlike her old self, enlisted the support of European and other Asian trading nations to pressure the United States to lift temporary sanctions.[13] Japan has shown a similar independence and toughness in negotiating the recent airline agreement with the United States as well. She yielded more places for American carriers in more Japanese cities than previously, but Japanese negotiators entirely thwarted the American insistence on a complete opening, what they called "open skies."[14]

A particularly dramatic and unnerving sign of a growing distance in the relationship came in the spring of 1997, when then Prime Minister Hashimoto bluntly threatened American financial markets. Speaking at Columbia University in New York, the Prime Minister suggested that continuing intense

American trade pressure might prompt Japan to sell her vast holdings of U.S. government bonds. As if to confirm Japan's power to unbalance the market, New York's stock and bond markets fell precipitously the day following Hashimoto's remarks.[15] Few national leaders, even very aggressive ones, make such blunt threats. Japanese diplomats immediately jumped in, explaining the threat as the lapse of a jet-lagged man. But the symbolism was clear—even though such an action would actually hurt Japanese sellers as much Americans—and doubtless calculated.

Also hinting that the future might lack the old certitude of strong Japanese-American ties, Japan has shown clear signs of seeking a military capability that could survive a break with the United States. The buildup and modernization of her forces discussed earlier is, of course, a significant element in this picture, as is the change to a less purely defensive nature for Japan's land, sea, and air forces. Both make Japan better able than in the past to project power without American support. But still, these changes alone do not necessarily point to a dissolution or even a distancing in Japan's relationship with the United States. Japan's recent insistence on making her own weaponry, however, introduces a more ominous factor into the equation. It speaks directly to the possibility of, and perhaps preparation for, a break in the alliance or a widening distance in it. In the past, Japan's self-defense forces depended heavily on American contractors, and for years made no sign of wanting to alter the situation. These days, Japan has begun to insist on her own way. Even when she cannot avoid using American defense technology, Japan has pressed for privileges within licensing agreements that permit her to modify the design and make it her own. This emphasis on her own production from her own designs has gained such prominence that the Japanese have named it *kokusanka,* or "indigenous procurement." Japan has redesigned the American M-1 tank and begun to design and produce her own armored vehicles, warships, radar, guidance and control systems, as well as missiles. Even when working to American specifications, she has insisted on incorporating as much domestic content as possible. Almost all the components of Japanese production of Raytheon's Patriot missile are made domestically. Japan has already abandoned the American scout helicopter and produces her own, the OH-X, at Kawasaki Heavy Industries. Fuji Industries supplies the air self-defense forces with its own T-5 primary pilot trainer. Kawasaki now manufactures the UP-3D electronic warfare trainer under license from Lockheed Martin, but is already advancing its own design, P-3, for the turn of the century.[16] Ironically, the much ballyhooed joint venture with Lockheed Martin to produce the F-2 (formerly FS-X) fighter, based on the American F-16, suffered tremendous delays and cost overruns, because the Japanese insisted on controlling the project and keeping it as domestic as possible.[17]

As Japanese independence of the American alliance raises general feelings of uncertainty, perceptions of risk will get a jolt when Japan officially reconsiders the pacifist Article 9 of her constitution, as she almost certainly will have to do. So far, Japan has made great strides toward independent power without having to deal directly with the Article. Her affiliation with the UN, as described earlier, has enabled her to avoid addressing the limits imposed by a strict interpretation of the Article. The effort has kept the still huge pacifist element in her population at bay. Even so, the pacifists see the change coming. Speaking for them, Minoru Tada, professor of politics at Nisho Gakusha University, has, in his widely read columns, given voice to the despair about the change, and decried Japan's expanding military role.[18] It is clear that time is on the side of change. Many of the Japanese pacifists come from the aging generation that can remember World War II and its immediate aftermath, and now they are passing out of positions of power and influence. Surveys show the Japanese, particularly younger people, are less committed to the highly pacifist aspects of their constitution. Sixty percent of the Diet has already come out in favor of softening the language of Article 9, and, as mentioned earlier, the Diet has set up a group to consider amending the constitution on this point.[19] Some, led by Masashi Nishihara, professor of international relations at the National Defense Academy, believe that there is no need to abolish or amend the constitution in order to allow Japan to increase her military role.[20] But there is a growing feeling that Japan will have to face the issue at some point in the not-too-distant future. The widely read daily *Yomiuri Shimbun* has editorialized boldly since 1994 about the need to "expunge" the constitution of its pacifist clauses.[21] Whether the politicians make a stand on the issue, or, as some suggest, it comes down to a referendum, the consideration alone will signal the end of another former, long-standing certainty in the body politic of Asia and the world.

With the passing of each old certainty, anxieties will grow, and, even without specific dangers, the growth of uncertainty alone will alter Asian power relationships, which in turn will produce new independent uncertainties and the potential for the "miscalculations" about which Ambassador Armacost has warned. Japan's need for maneuvering room will demand either modifications in the American treaty or its dissolution. The former is, of course, less threatening and unsettling than the latter, but it still will change Asia's power balance. Japan's increased prominence at the UN will affect risk calculations in similar ways. Procuring a seat in the Security Council and the rising profile of her armed forces in peacekeeping operations surely will signal an end to old assurances of Japan's former, limited role. A stronger signal will emerge from Japan's efforts, independent both of the United States and the UN, to secure her expanding international economic and security interests. Even if the nations involved can avoid dangerous confrontations, Japan's clear need to work out her own arrangements with China, Russia, ASEAN, and even Europe, will unbalance previous power assumptions and heighten everyone's sense of future uncertainty. None of this is necessarily threatening. Aside from historical allusions, a powerful, active Japan offers as much potential for a secure Asia, and consequently the world, as it offers danger. Certainly, this new Japan could stand as a check on China's hegemonic ambitions. The issue of risk in this context has less to do with identifiable dangers than the creation of huge unknowns, as Japan's new needs and new powers emerge to sweep away old assurances and assumptions—and the calculations based on them.

THE CULTURAL WILD CARD

Few of the uncertainties created by Japan's rise to power are as unpredictable as those built into her remarkable and singular group culture. While on the surface Japan resembles any other Western society, few could deny that she has always reacted differently to success and adversity than Western cultures have. In assessing the special risks implicit in this difference, the issues revolve around the intense need in the Japanese culture for concerted group action. It offers reason for both optimism and pessimism in the face of the profound, coming changes.

The great capacity for Japan's group culture to marshal people behind the national purpose has often served Japan well. It has also led to disaster. Once the Japanese form a consensus on direction, they follow it with a will that few other societies can muster, except, perhaps, in time of war. This powerful resolve enabled Japan to make marvelous strides in development during the late nineteenth century and following the destruction of World War II. The danger arises in times of transition, such as the present, when Japan abandons an old consensus goal and seeks a new direction. Then, her urgent desire to form a new consensus about a new group mission can, in the words of Japanese social critic Robert Ozaki, cause her to "grab any idea which happens to be currently fashionable," whether or not it is constructive or rational, and pursue the goals of that idea with a zeal bordering on "fanaticism" and at times "hysteria."[22] Much in the present situation, of course, suggests that Japan will take a constructive approach to her transformation to a full-fledged political-economic power. But, as her history shows, the risks of something less desirable remain, especially under the profound pressures that she faces.

This distinctive character of Japanese culture issues primarily from its emphasis of the group over the individual, and the corollary need to feel that each member of the group is working toward a larger, noble purpose. These traits, in turn, have their origin in Japanese notions of a fundamental debt, or *on.* There are several kinds of *on,* but together they impose on all Japanese an obligation that they can never fully discharge to one another and to their ancestors for having civilized the world and made it a habitable, safe, and comfortable place. In traditional Japanese culture, people carry a debt of *gimu* to their family and ancestors, a filial devotion that, no matter how ardently followed, a person "never pays more than one ten-thousandth of [it.]"[23, 24] The culture also identifies the debt of *giri,* which the individual owes to fellow Japanese in society at large. Unlike *gimu, giri,* theoretically, can be repaid, but since a person lives in society, the debt is constantly being renewed and so, in practice, is never ending. The pressure of these debts is powerful, very real, and immediate to Japanese. People will even speak of *giri* having so much weight that it prevents them doing what is right, *gi.*[25] Together these obligations impel all Japanese individuals to place themselves second to the larger society. This is very unlike Westerners, and particularly Americans, who see themselves as individuals whose first obligation is to themselves or their family. To Japanese, the group directs virtually all action and purpose.

With each Japanese person obligated in this way to family and fellows in the larger society, individuals easily and willingly subordinate their wishes to those of the group. Indeed, the Japanese word *giri* is frequently translated simply as "conformity to public opinion."[26] Owing so much to everyone else, Japanese do not mind others sitting in judgment, as Westerners would. Quite the contrary, they accept the judgment, almost welcome it in order to test for themselves whether they have successfully discharged their deep obligations. The effect is so powerful, in fact, that the Japanese derive their feeling of self-respect, *jicho,* entirely from the opinions of others in the group. In direct contradiction to Western notions, little esteem comes from within the individual. "If there were no society," explained one old Japanese man in an interview with the great scholar of Japanese culture, Ruth Benedict, "one would not need to respect oneself"—that is, cultivate *jicho.*[27] Western regard for a person who defies the group on a point of principle has little place among these Japanese notions. Western ideas of individualism and the individual pursuit of happiness, so dear to Americans especially, strike the Japanese as selfish and a little immoral. In the Japanese language, the word "individualist," *kojinshugisha,* says nothing flattering. It commonly suggests an egotistical, self-ish person. The phrase "independent personality," *dokuritsushin,* refers to an uncooperative soul with an attitude of "stiff-necked defiance and a lack of con-cern for others."[28] Japanese virtue stresses mutual dependence. According to Robert Ozaki, Japanese crave the "we" feeling, identifying with the group and subordinating their individuality to the point that "they and the group are fused into oneness."[29] The language captures the link, speaking of *giri-ninjo,* which combines the notion of debt with the word for human feelings, kind-ness, and generosity. Expressing this kinship, the Japanese always introduce themselves with their corporate or institutional affiliation immediately; only later will they reveal their status within that group, whether professor, pro-duction-line worker, accountant, janitor, or chief executive.

Of course, Japan has moved a long way toward Western values and respect for the individual over the years. Certainly, the group is less powerful today than when the American Lafcadio Hearn first described the severe group emphasis of Japanese culture in the late nineteenth century, or even since Ruth Benedict published her remarkable anthropological study of Japan-ese culture, *The Chrysanthemum and the Sword,* in the late 1940s. But still, by common Western standards, Japan remains highly group oriented, and indi-viduals remain group directed. Certainly, the issue comes up frequently enough among modern observers of Japan. Karel van Wolferen described the still powerful influence in his now classic 1989 work, *The Enigma of Japanese Power,* and on the lighter, more personal side, so did Masao Miyamoto in his Japanese bestseller, *Oya Kusho no Okite* (Straitjacket Society), about life in Japan's Ministry of Health and Welfare.[30] Shuichi Kato, a prominent social and literary critic, frequently writes about Japan's fundamental "groupism" and has repeatedly observed that "[w]hen an individual conflicts with the group, the resolution is for the individual to adapt, not for the group to change."[31]

This cultural reverence for the group remains a staple of the public pos-tures of politicians, bureaucrats, and most social commentators. Recent dis-cussions in the daily press about Japan's 1990s recession and its effect on social cohesion frequently come back to questions of *giri* and obligations to the larger society.[32] In 1987, Japan's Ministry of Education publicly explained the nation's need to shift emphasis from the Western stress on guarantees of individual rights to social and national responsibilities.[33] One of Japan's more powerful Prime Ministers, Yasuhiro Nakasone, frequently paid homage to Japan's cul-tural reverence for the group. In a 1986 speech, for example, he referred to Western principles of individualism as coming from the "desert culture" of the Middle East. In Judeo-Christian belief, he claimed, individuals are like hard separate grains of sand. But the Japanese come from what he called a "monsoon culture" and stick together like the glutinous rice of which they are so fond.[34] In this same spirit, notions of subordination to the larger group even carry over into Japanese notions of race. Their word for race, *mizoko,* conveys a sense beyond straightforward anthropological classifications, or even the old-fashioned Western notion of a people that share a common culture and heritage. Rather, as Japanese use it, the word refers to an "organismal" and "familiar" solidarity. It is this bond to the group that the Japanese feel and to which they refer in their frequently used expression when communicating with foreigners, *ware ware Nihonjn,* "we Japanese."[35]

Obligation to the group is so great that in the workplace it can literally drive people into the grave. The phenomenon is common enough to warrant a word of its own, *karashi,* or "death from overwork." In 1997, when a Japanese court found that group pressure at the advertising agency Dentsu had brought on an employee's suicide, it used the label *karashi.*[36] This was a rare case in which the Japanese courts sympathized with an individual. Usually they bow to the power of the group. In the early 1990s, for instance, a society of war veterans sued a widow on the disposition of her husband's burial site. Being Christian, the dead man had indicated in his will the desire to be interred in a Christian cemetery, a desire that his widow shared. But since he was also a war veteran, his old comrades wanted him in their "regimental plot." Finding in favor of the veterans, the judge accused the widow of selfishness and insensitivity.[37]

"Groupism" is so fundamental to Japanese life that the word for "sincerity," *makoto,* has an almost entirely different meaning from its common English translation. To the Japanese, *makoto* has nothing to do with the Western notion of a genuine reflection of an individual's inner feelings. The Japanese respond to the idea of self-expression in the words of a once common but now somewhat old-fashioned expression: "Behold the frog who when he opens his mouth displays his whole inside."[38] Instead, the Japanese relate ideas of sincerity to the group's expectations of the person. People are considered sincere when they internalize the group's expectations and goals. The Japanese see *makoto* as the stuff that gets each member of the group to follow the "way" or *ryu,* mapped out by the whole. A somewhat old-fashioned expression holds that "*makoto* is what makes it stick," with the "it" referring to the will or way of the group.[39] Thus, in Japanese, *makoto* is always used with an external object. Individuals are "sincere" or "true" to something, their firm, their nation, their profession, their group. In the Japanese context, there is little sense in having *makoto* to oneself.

Because this subordination to the group requires ongoing self-denial, it leaves the Japanese with an intense personal need for the group effort to have a noble mission, something greater than any single member. Otherwise, the sacrifice of self would involve suffering to no purpose. Japanese corporations show a sensitivity to this aspect of Japanese character (and indirectly take advantage of it) by making the job seem like part of a great team endeavor. Work is never done strictly for profit or earning a wage, as it typically is in Western companies. Japanese firms present themselves as going beyond such mundane concerns. They talk of the "company spirit," *shafu* in Japanese, and sometimes even put a Shinto shrine on the roof of their office buildings or plants to make clear the association with something larger and more noble than the workaday world. Every major firm has a company song that speaks to high-minded goals of serving the national purpose. Having become a member of the company group, the employees can feel that they are working for something bigger than their paycheck or even their family's security and comfort; they can acquire the sense that they are working in a "benevolent family" that is producing something of "intrinsic value" for the nation.[40] By successfully feeding this basic cultural need, Japanese companies have enjoyed a loyal, disciplined, earnest, and hardworking labor force that has been the envy of the economic world for years.

Of course, every person, in Eastern or Western culture, can find fulfillment in joining a group and working toward noble goals that go beyond self. But the Japanese, with little individualism to offer alternative satisfactions, harbor an especially desperate need for the larger mission. In the United States or Europe, when the common cause loses its savor or purpose, people can fall back on self-improvement or the notion of effort for ego's or family's sake. But in group-oriented Japan, these motivations fail as viable alternatives for most of the population. Tied to the group, people need the common cause to avoid the despair of having no purpose at all. And herein lies the special risk in Japanese culture relative to the West. When an old way breaks down and the Japanese lose that desperately needed sense of common mission, they may clutch at whatever course is most appealing at the moment in order to regain that treasured feeling, even if that new "way" is irrational or destructive. And because few in that culture can stand apart from the group to counter its direction, the movement, once started, can go to extremes.

Japanese literature and history are replete with illustrations of this remarkable character and the dangers implicit in it. They show the tremendous cooperation, self-sacrifice, discipline, energy, and even fanaticism when the individual has a "mission" within the group or the nation as a whole. And they show the feeling of aimlessness and desperation to find something new, when the mission dissipates and the consensus behind it fails. Again and again, over hundreds of years Japanese novels begin by describing the lassitude and despair of their protagonists with life itself. But in these stories the malaise evaporates when the heroes find a great mission (no matter how distant the goal) to justify their submission to the group.[41] In the novels, the characters' period of transition, when the new mission is not yet clear, carries the highest drama. Historically for the whole nation, too, that is also the time of greatest drama, and also of greatest danger. Japan's history shows that when the consensus forms around something positive, the genius of her culture for concerted action has enabled her to accomplish great things. But her history also shows periods when her culture's great needs have impelled her to follow irrational answers zealously to extremes and to her own to ruin.

Japan's success stories are familiar. The opening pages of this book briefly describe her remarkably concerted response to the Western challenge in the mid-nineteenth century. Confronted with undeniably superior Western power, the Japanese jettisoned the old medieval isolationist approach of the Shoguns that had prevailed for 250 years. Japan suffered a civil war in the late 1860s before she completed the transition. She then formed a new consensus to make the West a model for future development. Once that was done, her group culture embraced the new goals completely. Her people focused on the singular effort required to catch up to the West, and they did. Within thirty years, she went from feudalism to industrialism and by the end of the nineteenth century could count herself the economic and military equal of most Western powers.[42] The pattern following World War II is even more illustrative of these marvelous cultural traits. When the militarism that brought the war failed, the Japanese lost their old group mission. Without the all-important group purpose, they first fell into the sort of malaise of which her literature and history eloquently speak. Unlike Westerners, their depression was not so much due to a sense of failure, as to a longing for that lost sense of common purpose. As one anonymous Japanese was quoted as saying at the time: "No more bombs any more, the relief is wonderful. But we are not fighting anymore and *there is no purpose.*"[43] Concerned with the complete lack of energy that accompanied this culturally induced feeling, in 1946 the authorities used Japan's public radio to chide the people for not cleaning up the rubble of war as fast as the Germans did.[44] Of course, Japan soon found the new consensus that gave her the all-important common cause. With new purpose for her group feeling, she embarked on her second catch-up with the West described elsewhere in this book (and in great detail in countless other works).[45] Like the first catch-up in the nineteenth century, it suited the needs of her group culture well. In it, the Japanese rose to the challenge, giving Japan's leaders and managers an eager, loyal, hardworking and disciplined people, who produced the widely known economic miracle that took about thirty years to bring Japan to parity with the first rank of Western powers.

But not all her choices for concerted action have served Japan as well as her missions in the nineteenth century and after World War II. After the First World War, for instance, Japan realized that she had achieved her goal of economic and military parity with the West. Her great objective of the nineteenth century accomplished, her group culture found itself at a loss. True to past cultural patterns, the 1920s witnessed something of a "psychic shipwreck" in Japan.[46] There was widespread feeling that the country had lost direction. Rather than see her plight as a natural outgrowth of a culture that desperately needs missions, it was popular for intellectuals and moral thinkers to blame "modernity" for corrupting Japan. The "patriotic societies" that began to spring up in the 1920s had better instincts than the intellectuals. They knew, implicitly at least, what Japanese people needed. They gave the nation a mission, calling on her to embark on another "restoration," using the Japanese expression for the great national transformation in the late nineteenth century, which couched itself in terms of "restoring" the emperor to power. In the 1920s, Japan had no need to catch up industrially or to "restore" the emperor to his rightful place. But she did need to restore the noble feeling of having a great group mission.

Claiming to return Japan "to a new sense of purpose," the "patriots" of the 1920s cast about for a new cause.[47] By the early 1930s, they began to find it in a peculiarly Japanese brand of militarism and imperial ambition. Their attempted coups and political assassinations put off the average Japanese, but the "patriots" gained sympathy nonetheless, because they were providing that larger purpose that Japan so desperately wanted. That sympathy was palpable. In a 1931 failed coup attempt, the conspirators received comparatively light sentences, even though they killed the Prime Minister. When Japan was regularly executing common criminals, the worst sentence given to the conspirators was life imprisonment for its leader. Some participants in the failed coup received prison sentences of only four years.[48] The judges explained themselves by remarking on the "patriotic motivations" of the defendants. By the mid 1930s, the new militarist consensus had formed to feed the culture's need.[49] It was irrational and culminated in the insanity of the war with the United States, Great Britain, and other allies. Not only was the war unwinnable, but to make it worse, the (militarist) credo embraced by Japan's culture had gone to such extremes of stressing courage and "spirit" that it frequently eschewed heavy armament in its tactics, effectively maximizing the country's casualties and pain.

The horrors of the 1930s and the Second World War seem very far indeed from modern, sophisticated Japan, and they are. It would be foolish and irresponsible to suggest that Japan will repeat that experience. But at the same time, she is undeniably in a period of transition to which her culture is especially vulnerable. Despite the economic and financial setbacks of the 1990s, there is no question that Japan has again accomplished her goal of catching up to the West, and again is under pressure to find a new group commitment. Certainly there are signs of the lassitude and despair that beset her in the past when she lost her common goal. As earlier discussion showed, the sense of failure in the 1990s has grown intense. Many Japanese feel that it is "over for Japan"—suicide rates are up, and employers see none of the earnest enthusiasm from young recruits that was so common when Japan had her catch-up goal. There is, as the *Japan Economic Almanac* averred, a sense that the nation has reached "a watershed, marking the end of an era and jarring the foundations of confidence in the country's post-war political, economic and social systems."[50] Others have fretted about the possibility that Japan's economic competitiveness will suffer from the erosion of the "belief among employees that they are working toward a common corporate goal."[51] Popular novels, such as the *Coin Locker Babies,* examine the seamier side of Japanese life, criticize popular culture, and speak despairingly of a country that has lost its bearings.[52] There are even signs of a return to the nationalism that so disastrously filled Japan's cultural needs in the 1930s. She has seen the growth of the Japan Youth Federation, which consciously imitates the "patriotic" associations of the 1920s and 1930s.[53] This is the same group whose lighthouse on disputed islands in the East China Sea caused an international incident in 1996 involving Japan's maritime self-defense force. Professor Nobukatsu Fujioka wrote a surprise bestseller about how Japan should stop apologizing for World War II; in 1990 an extremist shot and wounded the mayor of Nagasaki for criticizing the late Emperor Hirohito's role in the war.[54] The year 1998 saw success for the film *Pride* that painted Japan's wartime prime minister Tojo in a flattering light. And recent years have seen a renewed interest in novelist Yukio Mishima, who in the 1960s railed about Japan's loss of soul and then killed himself after exhorting SDF troops to mount a 1930s-style coup.[55]

These isolated events in no way suggest a return to irrationality. At most, they are scattered warnings and perhaps not even that. But they do highlight the fact that the present period of transition, in addition to all the economic, financial, and foreign policy risks, also introduces uniquely Japanese cultural risks that cannot be ignored by the Japanese or by others. Most likely, a modern, sophisticated Japan will find a new common purpose that will help her cope constructively with her economic and demographic pressures. By reorienting her domestic economy, striving in a cooperative way to become the headquarters nation in Asia's division of labor, and taking on a responsible leadership role, Japan's new purpose will benefit herself, Asia, and the world. But still, the strategies and contingency plans of government, business, and investors alike should not dismiss these risks and uncertainties, including the potential effect of Japan's unique cultural imperatives.

NINE

GAINING
PRACTICAL
ADVANTAGE

WHETHER OR NOT JAPAN HAS A ROUGH time with her transition, and however great the cultural or foreign policy risks, there is no mistaking that her social and economic transformation will create rich business and investment opportunities, the richest, in fact, since her last great transition right after World War II. Japanese leadership can enhance this business potential and, in the process, smooth the path of change by adopting reforms to facilitate it instead of fighting it. Resistance will confuse market participants, create false starts, and inappropriate judgments. But by pursuing reform and thereby clarifying future direction, the nation's leaders can enlist the scrappy world of moneymaking to serve the country's long-term fundamental needs. After all, it will be the individual efforts of businesses and investors to "cash in" on the new environment more than direct action from above that will create the needed new economic practices and financial structures.

The recession and financial weaknesses of the 1990s have disguised a lot of this business opportunity, but an economy need not boom to create moneymaking prospects. Closer inspection indicates that, despite recession, the bonanza seems already to have begun in some areas. This chapter explores these and future opportunities and how they will assist Japan's fundamental metamorphosis even as they enrich the firms and individuals involved, both Japanese and foreign. It previews the opportunities that will become available to exporters from the United States, Europe, and the rest of the world, as they find it easier and more profitable to penetrate the domestic Japanese market. It investigates Japan's changing approach to business management, explains why it will suit her better in her new role of headquarters nation, and discusses how the adoption of that new approach will present opportunities for consultants, systems specialists, and firms with management expertise, especially American and other Western firms. These pages review how efforts to bring Tokyo's financial markets up to world standards will open other prospects for imaginative individuals and firms to profit from a vast array of new financial products and practices. It will become clear that even those not involved directly in Japanese trade or Japanese business should find tremendous investment opportunities as the prices and returns on Japanese stocks, bonds, and more exotic financial products adjust to the new environment.

TRADE

Some of the most straightforward business opportunities will develop in the shifting patterns of trade as the ongoing pressure of Japan's aging population, globalization, and the maturation of the economy force her to welcome imports. The advantages from this trend will develop across a broad front, but not universally. Those who compete with Japanese imports in their own domestic markets will see no relief. Japan's factories abroad will work from Japanese designs, using Japanese quality control, to produce updated versions of the same Japanese products that have presented a difficult challenge for so long. If anything, Japanese products from elsewhere in Asia will have superior cost advantages to the old, Japanese-made items, making them even more competitive. But, as Japan comes to rely on imports to meet her population's demands, those who seek to penetrate the Japanese retail market or find buyers among Japanese business should see a range of new options.

The sale of medical products would seem to offer obvious opportunities as Japan's elderly population burgeons. In the past, Japan has imported few foreign medical supplies and pharmaceuticals, claiming, at times ridiculously, that Japanese anatomy and physiology are so different that virtually any product made abroad is unsuitable for Japanese. But the aging trend will create such urgent needs that old attitudes will change, and since this growing market has been so closed, the slightest opening should offer great potential to foreign sellers. Medical imports could double in the early years of the next century. The greatest growth potential lies less in the areas of drugs and surgical equipment than in the sale of fixtures and supplies for nursing homes. Not only is an increasing segment of the population destined to need these services, but existing nursing home facilities need upgrading. According to MITI, the sales of specialized nursing home equipment in Japan—special lifts, adjustable beds, wheelchairs, sinks and showers designed to accommodate wheelchairs, horizontal transfers, and the like—have already begun to approach one trillion yen annually ($8 billion at the average exchange rate of the late 1990s) and are growing at about 16 percent a year.[1] Foreigners are well positioned to profit from this trend, because Japanese in the medical business recognize not only the longer experience of Europeans and Americans in the institutionalized care of the aged, but also the greater sophistication and superior design of their products. Many Japanese companies that build and upgrade domestic nursing homes have already begun to look abroad for many of their fixtures and furniture.[2] Opportunities for foreigners in this "silver industry," as the Japanese call it, will surely multiply as the aging trend gains momentum. Japanese respect for Western expertise will also extend opportunities to the architects and designers of nursing homes and their interiors, as well as to consultants and managers who can develop and maintain such health care facilities in a cost-effective way.

How consistently reform will facilitate these and other changes remains an open question. Earlier discussion described the recent, uneven progress. But, on balance, the effort has been encouraging. As indicated, in the 1990s Japan has taken steps with a five-year "Deregulation Action Program" to remove direct barriers to foreign trade as well as internal barriers that by 1998 had made 3,000 "steps" for deregulation.[3] Especially important in this context is the reduction of tariffs, generally, and on food particularly, where they had previously approached 20 to 30 percent. Old technical barriers have come down as well; Japan has begun to make her rules about food additives, as well as her metallurgical and mechanical tests, conform to those used in Europe and America.[4] The liberalization of her Large Retail Store Law, which has proceeded in steps over a number of years, has allowed Japanese retail outlets to reach a size sufficient to source from imports, thereby removing what was a great impediment to the introduction of large foreign retail chains. Business responded quickly to even the preliminary liberalization steps, especially considering the poor economic climate that had already developed in Japan. From the law's change until early 1998, the number of large stores has quadrupled.[5] And the effect on retail imports has just begun. Though this is only a small start in clearing the terrible thicket of rules and impediments in Japanese economic life, the market for imports should open more widely with future reforms as her demographic and economic pressures become more acute.

Although reforms like these will make it easier than it once was to penetrate the Japanese market, Japan will remain a difficult place for foreigners to
do business. Markets for imports (and cutbacks in Japanese exports for that
matter) will not materialize on all fronts. Japanese manufacturing will remain
a formidable global competitor in many areas—such as autos and electronics—that will blunt foreign penetration into the Japanese domestic market,
and she will continue to export effectively in such areas of special expertise.
Both Japanese business and the Japanese consumer will remain exacting buyers, demanding durability, reliability, and consistent quality. Even with more
open markets, foreign firms will continue to need one or more of three critical characteristics to succeed in Japan: first, tremendous cost advantages; second, a recognized and respected brand name; or third, a reputation for special expertise or technology. Simply being there will not be enough. Even with
the desperate need for imports in Japan, each foreign supplier will face intense
competition from exporters from across the world, all of whom will want a
piece of Japan's large, rich, and newly receptive market.

Among those exporters hoping to succeed through cost advantages,
American agriculture could prove one of the big winners. For years, taste and
trumped-up health issues have kept American food imports out of Japan. As
with medical supplies, at times Japanese authorities have even claimed that a
unique anatomy rendered Japanese unable to consume American beef, rice,
apples, and a host of other products. But the recent reforms in tariffs and technical impediments have made American cost and pricing advantages obvious,
as they have for other efficient agricultural exporters, such as Canada and Australia. Business has seen the impact even in the midst of Japan's recession. Agricultural imports by Japan increased by 30 percent in the years immediately following the initial deregulatory reforms of 1995–96. Perhaps most indicative of
change and a special harbinger of the future, the growth in imports has gone
beyond simple grains and fruits. Imports of more refined or processed products, such as beer, wine, and coffee, have soared by 60 to 80 percent. Ironically
for that great fishing nation, so too have imports of fishmeal, which grew by over
100 percent.[6] This latest surge in sales to Japan has made her one of the world's
leading purchasers of American agricultural products. By the late 1990s, 20 percent of all agricultural exports from the United States went to Japan. Japanese
purchases exceed the next largest buyer by a factor of two.[7]

A complete list of firms and industries with cost advantages over Japanese domestic competition is, of course, beyond the scope of this book, and is
always changing. But in addition to agriculture, American furniture and pre-
fab housing stand out as having sufficient advantages to last for some time.

American furniture manufacturers have benefited particularly from the liberalization of the Large Store Law, which has offered them venues to display the quality and design of their products. Remarkably low-priced compared to domestically made products, American furniture imports to Japan have lately surged by 20 percent a year.[8] The growth is especially impressive, because Japan was in recession during this time, and usually furniture sales and other big-ticket items suffer disproportionately in periods of economic difficulty. At the same time, the pre-fab housing industry, particularly in the United States, has leveraged its significant cost advantages to increase sales in Japan. After the 1996 reforms harmonized Japanese standards with American and European conventions on the strength and the configuration of walls and other structures, Japanese imports of manufactured housing grew by nearly 100 percent in just over twelve months. Even log cabins took off. Michigan-based Town & Country Cedar Homes recently reported selling as much as one-quarter of its timber homes and log cabins in Japan.[9] And since manufactured housing is just getting known in that country, there is still great potential, enough to provide growth for American exporters even in a Japanese housing market that will likely remain stagnant overall.

If the foreign seller lacks significant cost advantages, an established brand name will serve as an alternative basis for success in Japan's increasingly liberalized markets. Of course, brand name recognition will help anywhere, but it is especially important in Japan. Unlike America and Europe, where a significant part of the consuming public passes up brand names to find products that are rare, unique, or alternatively, generic, Japan's group culture drives consumers to seek out recognized names, effectively goods that the group has endorsed. For example, Chrysler has failed in selling the efficient, inexpensive Neon. The Neon had the support of Honda's retail network in Japan and is the most Japanese-like car in Chrysler's line. With only a modest price advantage, it has failed to sell well against the domestic competition. By contrast, Chrysler's Jeep sells very well, even though it costs more and is not well suited to Japanese roads or most Japanese lifestyles, as are the Neon or most Japanese-made cars.[10] The difference is purely the appeal of the Jeep name and whatever imagery goes with it. Indeed, even as Chrysler has begun to pull back on Neon, the Jeep brand has caught on so well that in late 1997 Chrysler ended Honda's seven year contract to retail Jeep in Honda showrooms. Chrysler will now offer the vehicle directly to Japanese buyers.[11] Similarly, the well known and widely respected German auto companies have used name recognition to leverage recent reforms and penetrate the domestic Japanese market. Even in the face of recession in Japan and currency fluctuations, sales of Mercedes, Audi, BMW, and Volkswagen have expanded. Japan's big German car importer, Volkswagen Audi Nippon (VAN), reported bringing in over 5,000 cars a month even during the worst of Japan's recession. The company's president, Mitsuro Sato, noted the growth in an otherwise difficult economic environment, commenting: "Japanese consumers have only just started to exercise [their] choices…I can't see them going back."[12] With trade reform continuing, they will not have to go back to old ways, and will continue to buy imports, at least those that have brand names or cost advantages.

Certainly name recognition explains the list of other foreign retailers who have managed to penetrate Japan's marketplace since the reforms began. Toys Я Us quickly established almost 40 successful outlets right after MITI earnestly began to liberalize the Large Store Law in the mid-1990s. Since then, the company has successfully added ten stores a year to the chain. Gap Stores, J. Crew, Eddie Bauer, and L.L. Bean have grown more slowly than Toys Я Us, but still have managed to use their well-known brands to go from zero presence in Japan to an impressive success with short chains in the Tokyo area. Texas-based Pier 1 Imports combined two critical characteristics, name recognition and cost advantages, to establish itself quickly after deregulation began. This American company is well on its way to building its planned 100 outlets by the year 2000.[13] But as these primary brand names have leveraged reform to make impressive gains, even in the teeth of Japan's recession, the general principle has held with the secondary brands, such as Chrysler's Neon. They have failed in those few instances when they have tried to enter the market, even after the deregulation began.

The last of the three criteria for foreign sales in Japan, a reputation for special expertise or technological advantage, will remain essential to success, especially in supplying Japanese industry. Of course, given the speed at which technology changes, such sales edges will come and go, but some should persist for a time. In environmentally friendly products and techniques, for instance, the Japanese recognize the longer experience of American and European firms, and, not unreasonably, associate it with a special expertise. In response to tighter environmental laws, Japan now uses more biodegradable packaging and has gone to the United States and, to a lesser extent, Italy for at least half its imports. The recognition of expertise in this and other environmental areas should prompt the Japanese to continue to use foreign sources for supplies, equipment, and advice in solving problems. Japan recognizes foreign talent elsewhere as well. Although Japanese cable or satellite television has little to concede to American or European technical ability, Japanese business has recognized American experience and ability in broadcast marketing. Motivated by this, Japan's first satellite broadcaster, Perfect TV, sought out a link with Florida-based Home Shopping Network, while other cable broadcasters have turned to links with QVC, the Philadelphia-based mail-order company.[14] America's Motorola, Inc. has traded on its pioneering role and reputation for expertise in mobile communications to win market share in Japan directly through its subsidiary, Nippon Motorola, Ltd., and indirectly by contracting extensively with Japanese vendors. Japan's mobile communications provider, DDI, for example, relied entirely on Motorola's system to expand its network by a factor of four in recent years.[15] In 1997, Motorola's reputation won it multibillion dollar, multiyear contracts with a group of Japanese cellular telephone providers, which included DDI, Nippon Idou Tsushin Corp., and IDO. (The equally good reputation of Motorola's usual partner, DSC Communications, won it the contract to manufacture many of the switches and much of the hardware for this new system.)[16] In the early 1990s, Sweden's Ericsson Corp. and Finland's mobile phone producer Nokia Inc., recognizing the value of such a reputation in Japan, sought to emphasize their special technological prowess by establishing themselves in Japan's Yokosuka Research Park. Having earned this coveted reputation, they were well positioned to benefit when the deregulatory reforms went into effect. Ericsson, with the added edge of a well-known brand name, did better than Nokia. It received orders from Japan's Digital Phone Group and Digital Tu-Ka Group and saw a 250 percent surge in orders.[17]

This need to have and sustain one or more of these critical criteria—price advantages, brand name, or special expertise—comes through most clearly in the story of Compaq Computer's relative failure. The number one personal computer maker in the world, America's Compaq Computer, Inc., entered the Japanese market through its subsidiary, Compaq K.K., just before the Deregulation Action Program began. At first, it did well, trading on its low-cost hardware, and its reputation for global prominence. But its price advantage rapidly disappeared. The better-known Japanese producers, Fujitsu, Hitachi, NEC, even IBM Japan, all of which had been overcharging in the domestic Japanese market, quickly countered Compaq's price advantages by bringing their prices down, and Compaq had no other advantage to fall back on. There was nothing wrong with the Compaq product, but to the Japanese, it offered nothing special next to the better-known Japanese names. Compaq quickly lost the ground that it had won, and has not risen above sixth place in the Japanese personal computer market since.[18] Some analysts suggest that Compaq could have forestalled its slide if it had a Japanese partner. Perhaps, but the companies with success stories are no more likely to have a Japanese partner. In the end, Compaq had neither special cost advantages, nor sufficient brand appeal, nor the reputation of a special technological edge or expertise.

In addition to using such advantages for selling directly into Japan, the changing circumstances should also offer new opportunities from the growth of intra-Asian trade. Until the late 1997 collapse of many Asian currencies and financial markets, trade within Asia had grown more rapidly than trade between Asia and other nations. That growth suffered a setback as Thailand, Malaysia, Indonesia, the Philippines, and Korea suffered varying degrees of economic and financial confusion. They tightened their economic policies to deal with their respective currency and financial problems, as well as to abide by the strictures imposed by the International Monetary Fund (IMF). The crisis was severe and continues to have ramifications. But it became apparent, even in the worst of the crisis, that the pace of trade within the region would in time regain its old momentum and continue the old, impressive growth trends. As shown earlier, Japan's need to rely increasingly on Asia will support this trend in the future and will likely accelerate it. Cyclical economic setbacks will not change Japan's need to move her industry abroad in order to cope with her developing fundamental labor shortage. And her need to establish herself as the headquarters nation in Asia will sustain Asian integration. Under this powerful influence, Asian business should offer as good a place to gain advantage from Japan's change as in Japan herself.

Ironically, the economic and financial setbacks in Korea and Southeast Asia may in time accelerate the regional integration with all its attendant opportunities. Even as the crisis has slowed the pace of investment and the growth of trade, the collapse of other Asian currencies in 1997–98 has heightened cost advantages to the Japanese for locating industry there, and thereby intensified Japan's push into Asia. Furthermore, the nations involved seem to have responded to their setbacks by reaching out to one another. In late 1997, at the height of the financial and currency crises, the Association of South East Asian Nations (ASEAN) agreed to accelerate its long-standing plans to reduce intraregional tariffs and trade barriers. Perhaps even more significant as a motivator for Japan, the crisis has raised China's leadership profile, thereby challenging Japanese primacy. The ASEAN meetings at which the tariff liberalization plans were announced included representatives of China, Korea, and Japan. It was the first time Asia's most powerful nations met without the participation of the United States. China stressed its idea of a "regional economic structure," a notion with which Japan felt compelled to concur. Most of the larger states, Japan prominent among them, warned against the temptation of protectionism during the momentary pressure of the crisis. All renewed their commitment to regional integration in "mutually complementary, non-exclusive and non-discriminating" terms, to use the words of the meeting's communiqué.[19]

While the crisis is not yet resolved, and there is still time for the pressure to undo the trend toward Asian integration, Japan's increasingly intense need to move out into Asia suggests that over the long haul local Asian firms will enjoy a growing market in serving Japanese industry located in their countries. Of course, Japanese producers, even those located abroad, will try to bypass the locals and look to their old domestic supply network as they have in the past. In many instances they have persuaded their domestic suppliers to relocate with them. The pattern was once so common among Japanese auto producers in the United States that it became an issue in trade negotiations. But Japanese producers will not have the luxury of relying exclusively on old domestic suppliers, and therein lies a new opportunity. The Japanese will have to source from the locals, and they in turn will welcome the products and advice—from the West and elsewhere—that can help them in selling to the Japanese. China, for instance, has inaugurated a number of huge projects with Japanese companies, ranging from the modernization of Chinese agriculture to the construction of a high-speed rail link between Beijing and Shanghai.[20] These projects clearly will enrich the primary Japanese contractors, but they will also improve prospects for local firms and for non-Chinese firms who either supply the locals or have interests in them. Indeed, beyond straightforward supply arrangements, these particular Japanese-Chinese projects, as well as the move of Japanese industry into Asia generally, should spur local firms to upgrade their operations and products in order to capture the new, Japanese-linked business. These developments should offer additional opportunities, especially to the sophisticated Western consultants, engineering operations, systems and computer people, who can sell these Asian firms advice, supplies, and systems—who, in sum, can upgrade the local firms to enable them to meet the notoriously exacting standards of Japanese business.

Parallel opportunities should develop with the Asian companies that will migrate to Japan as part of Asia's economic integration. As Japan becomes the headquarters nation, other Asian firms will look to extend the relationship with the Japanese transplants by exporting directly to Japan or by setting up offices, sales, and service operations in Japan. Many already have.[21] Through the 1990s, for example, Korea's Samsung has beefed up its two Japanese subsidiaries, despite Japan's recession, and Kia Motors of Korea has enlarged its research operation at Inzai in Japan's Chiba prefecture.[22, 23] Taiwan's Precision Casting Manufacturing Company, a major producer of golf equipment, has traded on the Asian integration to expand its mail-order business in Japan.[24] As these Asian firms focus on Japan in order to take advantage of the opportunities in that changing environment, they will provide opportunities to other firms in Asia—and in Europe and America. Working with these Asian firms should have particular appeal to companies that might otherwise have no route into Japan. As with the Asian locals who will supply the Japanese transplants and projects, so these Asian firms in Japan will offer opportunities to other suppliers, as well as to the consultants, engineering concerns, and other business support operations that will help them refine their products and upgrade their efficiency sufficiently to prosper in Japan's demanding marketplace.

DOMESTIC JAPANESE REORIENTATION

The reorientation of Japan's domestic economy should create still more subtle new business and investment prospects. As described earlier, Japan will need to shift away from her old, almost exclusive focus on mass manufacturing for export toward the management, design, and finance activities that will suit her growing role as the headquarters nation in Asia. Such a massive shift in emphasis naturally will require a retooling of Japanese skills and business practices that, in turn, should yield diverse opportunities for individuals and Western firms, who have greater experience and expertise than Japanese in the areas of coordination, communication, and control. Even greater opportunities will emerge because Japan's reorientation will also require her firms to change their ways of managing their business—to prize efficiency, control, and profitability over size and market share, and decisive management over the old consensus system. Few existing Japanese management teams have much experience in these new approaches. Assessing management's efforts to come up to speed in these ways will yield other investment and business opportunities. Helping Japanese management adjust to the global environment, and especially to manage Japan's growing interests in Asia, will involve new types of businesses and businesspeople and new business opportunities both at home and abroad.

Elements of this changing approach to business and hence the basis of these opportunities are already becoming apparent. Even the most hidebound Japanese manager has become troubled by the loss of efficiency and profitability caused by the long-standing quest for size and market share above all else, and by the associated commitment to lifetime employment. Of course, in the fast growth years from the 1950s until well into the 1980s, when Japan was rebuilding herself and her immature economy was catching up to the West, there was little distinction between size, market share, and profitability. Expansion brought power and profits, and because Japan began from such a low base, increased size inevitably brought economies of scale that enhanced profitability. Building staff and binding it to the firm with lifetime employment and a seniority-based pay scale seemed reasonable and rational. But the maturation of Japan's economy, as discussed earlier, has rendered this old approach obsolete. No longer can firms assume that sheer size and enlarged market share will enhance profits. The economic setbacks of the 1990s have brought that point home dramatically and viciously to Japanese business.

In response, Japanese management, after long years of neglect, has begun to focus directly on profitability, particularly that critical gauge, return on equity (ROE). This measure of a company's earnings as a percent of the firm's net worth is especially popular among analysts and businesspeople in the West because it relates profits directly to the stockholder's ownership interest. Japan's new business focus on this and similar measures has brought home to Japanese management and shareholders how relatively poorly their old approach has done. According to a study by the Daiwa Institute of Research, the average return on equity of a Japanese firm recently averaged around 5 to 6 percent, less than one-third the ROE of the average American counterpart, at 17 to 18 percent.[25] Of course, some of the difference reflected the relatively sluggish state of Japan's economy and the relatively robust state of America's. But that could not explain all, or even most of, the difference. Japanese businesspeople accept that much of their shortfall results from the obsolete arrangements and perspectives used to structure their businesses, guide them, and set their priorities.

Concern over this huge difference naturally has become an engine of change. Firms have begun to focus on cutting costs. Layoffs and plant closings, unthinkable only a few years ago, have become commonplace. Japanese banks, being particularly hard-pressed, have joined in this pattern. Fuji Bank has announced its intention to close forty overseas units, mostly in Europe and America, and thirty-one branches in Japan. The Long-Term Credit Bank announced a 20 percent staff reduction and plans to close half its overseas branches in an effort to cut overall costs by 25 percent.[26] The giant broker/dealer, Nomura Securities, reacting with uncommon speed to poor profit results, announced layoffs of two thousand employees.[27] But these gross solutions are only part of the story, and Japanese management knows that. Companies have begun to try to increase profitability by making longer-term, more fundamental adjustments in their management structures. Taking their cue from Western strategies, increasing numbers of Japanese firms have begun to streamline their decision making, put control systems in place, and impose efficiencies. According to Takanori Matsura, a respected expert on Japanese corporate culture, the once-revered "consensus approach" is now seen as a cause of deadlock. It is being replaced by clear direction and accountability in both the legal and business sense.[28] Instead of large groups of senior people who have been granted board member status in honor of their long, loyal service, companies are beginning to insist that board members set practical strategies, take responsibility, and provide clear direction for company policy. Sony has already streamlined its decision-making hierarchy, replacing its unwieldy board of thirty-eight directors with a trim group of ten. Taking a further step away from time-honored Japanese practice, three of the ten current Sony board members come from outside the firm.[29] According to the new Japanese reasoning (and common American practice) these outside directors will help impose accountability and bring new perspectives that a purely management-based board could not develop on its own. Fuji Bank has followed Sony's lead partway in this, cutting its board from twenty-eight members to six.[30] Toshiba has approached the same streamlining questions differently. It reasoned that the company's broad diversification was impeding good decision making and efficiency. Its management has set out, American style, to sell off its less profitable areas and focus on the company's strengths in information and technology. So has the computer giant NEC under its president, Yoshihiro Suzuki, whose succinct slogan, "Specialization Brings Success," has made that very un-Japanese approach crystal clear.[31] Honda Motors has adopted a raft of American-style management disciplines that stress individual responsibility over group consensus, put clear reporting relationships in place, insist on individual performance assessments, and impose strict standards to control costs."[32] All this is new to Japan and was exceedingly rare only a few years ago.

The new emphasis on profitability has also begun to feed on itself by altering relationships within the *keiretsu* families of firms. Earlier discussion showed how the ties in these groups have begun to loosen as a consequence of the maturing of Japan's economy and the economic setbacks of the 1990s. Firms have refused family members' help, something that would not have happened even five years ago. As mentioned earlier, in spring 1997, Nissan Motor and Hitachi refused to help their *keiretsu* member Nissan Life out of its financial difficulty. The insurer later failed.[33] Members in *keiretsu* have actually begun to sell the crossholdings of shares that bind them together. The Industrial Bank of Japan bolstered its capital base not too long ago by selling 10 percent of its holdings of other firms. Many companies, in the words of Gillian Tett of *The Financial Times,* are "scrambling to unwind their huge cross holdings," often at the expense of their associates.[34] Most of the banks blame these sales on the government's failure to move ahead rapidly enough with financial reforms, but this is mere cover. They are selling their cross holdings to raise capital for their own needs, without regard to the effect on the other firms in the *keiretsu*. This behavior is hardly new to Americans and market participants in other Western nations, but it is revolutionary to the Japanese. Of course, since firms in these *keiretsu* built up tremendous cross holdings of stock during earlier years, they will remain a fact of Japanese business life for some time. According to Daiwa's Institute of Research, cross holdings still account for 47 percent of the ownership of all shares in Japan. But the direction of change is also clear. The recent figure is down considerably from the level of 55 percent in the early 1990s.[35]

In concert with this new sensitivity to profitability and efficiency, companies have begun to experiment with employee incentives to elicit greater efforts to increase corporate returns. The process has added to the other pressures that have begun to unravel both the lifetime employment system and the strict seniority approach to promotion and pay that have characterized corporate life in Japan since it emerged from the ashes of World War II. Some firms have also tried to increase their flexibility by turning to the use of temporary staff, which allows them to fill needs quickly when they arise, and then just as quickly shed staff when those needs dissipate.[36] Other firms have added incentives for productivity by tying bonuses to strict performance criteria. Still others have responded by simply promoting talent above those with seniority and rank.[37]

Moving clearly along these new lines, Nomura Securities, the giant broker/dealer, announced a management shakeup in 1997 that violated many of the old maxims of Japanese business. When Hideo Sakamaki resigned his presidency under a cloud of scandal, the firm reached down several levels in its hierarchy to find his replacement, Junichi Ujiie.[38] To some extent the scandal forced this atypical move. Nomura needed someone who had no connection to its old, corrupt power clique. But for strategic business reasons, the firm also wanted someone with the kind of Western experience Mr. Ujiie possessed and that his seniors at Nomura did not. The motivation for the move means less than Nomura's willingness to break with the formerly inviolable seniority system. The behavior of other Nomura Group firms has offered confirmation of a new thinking. The firm's asset management subsidiary, for example, chose as chief investment officer Takahide Mizuno, promoting him over several more senior (both in age and rank) employees. Further, when business results failed to meet expectations, the firm summarily relieved the asset management subsidiary's president, Tadashi Takubo, another act that would have been impossible only a few years ago.[39]

As part of this rather sudden new effort to reward merit and promote a concern for the bottom line over sheer size, companies have begun to experiment with stock option plans. Such plans had long been illegal in Japan, but the pressure to improve corporate responsiveness prompted a repeal of the law in 1997. Within two months of this change, 35 large companies leapt at the opportunity to provide incentive to their workers with these plans. Those doing so included such august names as Toyota Motors, the trading company Nichimen Corp., the video game maker Konami Co., and Daiwa Securities. Making clear the purpose of the stock option plans, or, as the Japanese legislation refers to them, *stokku opushan,* Toyota president, Hiroshi Okuda commented: "It's often been said that Japanese executives are not interested in the stockholders of their own company. We want our executives to be aware of and interested in the stock price, and to make efforts to get it to go up."[40] This effort to raise profitability by focusing executives on the stock's price might sound old hat to Westerners, but to Japanese it is radical.

Among the reforms that have facilitated this transformation of corporate practice and priorities, one of the most significant was the repeal of the law against holding companies that went into effect on February 25, 1997.[41] Holding companies were banned in Japan by the American occupation after World War II, because the large prewar *zaibatsu* conglomerates were blamed for Japanese militarism. Without the holding company structure, Japanese firms developed cumbersome corporate ownership arrangements, in which each division of the firm effectively owns pieces of other divisions. For instance, in the Nomura Group, when Nomura Asset Management was established, it was part owned by the Nomura Research Institute, part by Nomura Securities, part by Nomura's real estate arm, and so on. The list exceeded one hundred companies. The asset management firm, in turn, owned pieces in all these other entities. Such arrangements can make it impossible to determine where controlling interests lie, let alone the origins of revenues and costs. A holding company will make the accounting a lot clearer. Shareholders will have less difficulty knowing what they own. And, senior management will have less difficulty getting the information it needs (and was so long denied), to control the firm, set its priorities, determine which activities and strategies are most profitable, as well as which programs should get funding and which should not. The appeal is obvious. Just weeks after the government repealed the old law, corporate leaders, such as Nomura Securities, Mitsui Group, and the retailer Daichi, expressed an interest in restructuring as holding companies.[42]

Once this transition gains momentum and firms gain greater ability to sort out where their profits reside, they will begin to engage in the dramatic corporate restructurings that are commonplace in the West. Companies will spin off less profitable divisions, sell them to one another, merge, take one another over, and effectively engage in all the aggressive activities for which

American industry is famous—or infamous. Some of these deals will waste time and resources and, again following the American model, have structures designed only to enrich a few managers. Still, the practice of tearing down firms and reconstituting them will also provide a critically important means for large companies to adjust to changing environments by channelling resources to pursue the profitable products and services that the consumer prefers and the economy needs for the future. Contrary to commentary in the States and fears in Japan, such restructurings do not always aim simply to punish weak corporate sisters by getting rid of them. Frequently, spin-offs and sales of divisions hinge on the question of placing a group that no longer suits one corporation with a different company that can use it to more profitable advantage. Regardless of the good or evil of these practices, they undeniably will introduce a dynamism that Japan has lacked, a responsiveness to the signals of the global market, and, of course, moneymaking opportunities.

Beyond the holding company law, other aspects of the government's reform package will facilitate a heightened dynamism in Japanese practice by beginning to cut through the thicket of rules that govern Japanese business life. As described earlier, these regulations once might have served the interests of Japanese business, but now hamper its ability to deal with the changes facing the economy. Whether the old biases in these controls once helped or hurt industry, they certainly have not kept up with the changing times. As Japan faces more challenging changes in the future, it is unlikely that even the most effective and enlightened regulatory and tax authorities could keep its inducements and preferences in tune with the needs of the nation or of Japanese business. Deregulation has made a tentative start in correcting this. So have recent efforts to broaden the corporate tax base by simplifying the array of tax breaks and penalties that have distorted corporate spending for so long.[43] By beginning to dismantle this bureaucratic structure, reform has begun to give business more flexibility than it had to make decisions on allocations of funds without having to worry about adverse tax consequences. And that has begun to help management adjust more effectively to future demands.

At the same time, the beginnings of deregulation have begun—just barely—to reinforce the process by cleaning up Japan's real estate morass. Real estate losses and the inflexibility of the rules governing this market have contributed greatly to the bad loan problem at Japanese banks and the inefficient use of land.[44] By reducing taxes on the sale of land, deregulation will encourage people to buy and sell more often, freeing funds for sellers, who have better uses for assets, and putting the land into the hands of those who can develop it more effectively for their own enrichment and for that of the economy as well. New rules that loosen zoning restrictions and allow land to change hands before reporting the transaction to the authorities (instead of only afterwards), will have a similar effect by facilitating transactions and efficient use.[45] In time, these small changes—small at least next to the still formidable body of old rules constipating the real estate market—should lead to more effective and more profitable land use. Banks will shed bad loans and business will be able to develop parcels that had been left idle or had only marginal uses, such as for agriculture in the suburbs of Tokyo and other major cities. Generally, the change will allow Japanese business to allocate the resources at its disposal more efficiently than in the past, free creditors' balance sheets from the land holdings on which borrowers have defaulted (albeit at a loss), and perhaps ultimately allow developers to earn healthy returns as they begin to provide this crowded, underhoused nation a housing stock that is commensurate with its wealth.

Along with deregulation, recent reforms will encourage these critical changes in corporate practice by introducing greater competition into Japanese corporate life. This may not directly facilitate flexibility or the quest for greater profitability, but it will certainly spur management to make their operations as efficient and responsive to market signals and customer demands as they can. The new airline agreement with the United States denied the Americans the "open skies" approach that they sought, but it will nonetheless allow American carriers into many more Japanese markets than previously. Japanese carriers will need to improve customer service and probably cut ticket prices. To rally against the new American competition, they just might seek to expand their domestic routes or fly more varied overseas routes than before. In either case, they will have to serve their consumer and business markets better. Similarly, the new rules have opened the important and once static, rigidly regulated areas of information and telecommunications. Nippon Telephone and Telegraph (NTT), in return for permission to enter the fast-growing global market, has agreed to break into three companies, two regional and one long-distance carrier. KDD, the original Japanese international carrier, has received permission to enter the domestic market, to compensate for the new competition from NTT.[46] KDD has sought a partnership with Teleway Japan, a long-distance operation affiliated with Toyota, to help it prepare for its entry into the domestic market. New rules that relax strictures on the price of phone calls will allow a general lowering of phone rates as competition heats up. Further, they will liberalize the connections between domestic public lines, lease lines, and internet telephony.[47] This is considerably more competition than any Japanese telecommunications firm has faced or buyer enjoyed. Indeed, despite

American complaints to the contrary, Japan soon will have one of the most open telecommunications markets in the world, more so than that of the United States. Reduced telephone rates will raise the general levels of profitability of the rest of Japanese business. And by giving the Japanese many new options in this critically important area, the new, more competitive environment will add to the general flexibility of Japanese business in adjusting to the changing economic and demographic imperatives.

In addition to easing regulations, these business changes have been fueled by the sad series of scandals that have rocked Japan in recent years. The latest round began in 1991, when the press revealed that Nomura Securities and its fellow brokers in the "big four" at the time, Daiwa, Nikko, and the now defunct Yamaichi, were protecting valued clients from stock market losses by making special trades at prices other than those prevailing in the open market. Subsequent investigation revealed that the illegal practice had gone on for some time. This illegal practice would not have been necessary had Japan's economic machine not slowed, causing her stock market to fall significantly for the first time in years. In traditional fashion, resignations were offered and accepted. But growth remained slow, and other doubtful practices began to emerge. With each scandal, more questions arose about the way Japan was conducting its business. As the Japanese public and regulators became more suspicious, the reasons to investigate became stronger. By 1997, the Japanese public and the world discovered that major financial and industrial firms had for years been paying off gangsters, called *sokaiya,* who specialized in extorting money from corporate managements by threatening to disrupt shareholder meetings. People learned that for years companies had bribed civil service officials, with trips and other entertainment in order to secure information about bank examinations so that they could then hide the evidence of other corrupt practices. The public watched Tokyo's Public Prosecutor's Office raid the formerly untouchable Ministry of Finance. They read about several suicides of prominent civil servants in the MOF, the resignation of the Finance Minister, Hiroshi Mitsuzuka, and his deputy, the highest-ranking civil servant in the Ministry, Takeshi Komura. And the Japanese got a glimpse of similar problems at the Bank of Japan as well.[48]

Having lost confidence in the efficiency and the ethics of corporate Japan, as well as their civil service, the public, and especially investors, have begun to rely on more professional, specialized, and certainly more probing assessments of Japanese companies and how they are managed. Credit rating agencies in the United States and elsewhere have begun to take a harder look than they did in the days when it was natural to assume growth and bureau-

cratic support for Japanese companies. And investors in Japan have taken their
assessments more seriously than before. Downgrades in corporate credit ratings have shocked Japanese, especially those corporate managers whose downgraded companies have found it more difficult and expensive to obtain credit
and secure business relationships both inside and outside of Japan.[49] Perhaps
most telling of all, the scandals and poor profits have tried the once seemingly
endless patience of Japanese shareholders. Annual meetings, unlike the quick,
quiet, perfunctory affairs of the past, have heard some difficult questions. An
individual at Sumitomo Trust's shareholders meeting for 1996 actually
demanded the resignation of senior management for not having properly controlled the trading operation that lost a spectacular amount in copper futures
over a period of years.[50] Subsequently, shareholders sued Sumitomo Trust's
management team on this point. Such disruptions and suits are common
enough in America; in Japan they have great shock value and speak to a future
with very different relationships between shareholders and corporate management. The Sumitomo suit was settled in a way that released no details. The
retailer Takashimaya was not so shielded. In 1996, a group of its stockholders
won a suit against management for paying bribes. This was the first such successful suit in Japanese history. The court awarded shareholders damages
exactly equal to the ¥170 million ($1.35 million at the exchange rate of the
time) that the management had paid out in bribes, and, in a special motivation
for management to change its ways, the court held the company's directors
personally responsible, also for the first time in Japanese history. Following
this, shareholders at Nomura Securities brought suit against that firm's former
president, Hideo Sakamaki, for the bribes Nomura had paid out under his
administration.[51] At the time of this writing, that suit is still pending. Fear of
shareholder suits provided a critical motivation for Hitachi and Nissan Motors
when they refused to help their *keiretsu* partner, Nissan Insurance.[52] Adding
institutional weight to shareholder ire, the Pension Fund Association, which
represents the largest group of institutional investors in Japan, has begun to
insist loudly and publicly that corporate managers focus on profitability and
shareholder interests.[53] The group has even begun to grade companies according to its own "Corporate Governance Indicator."[54]

   While the scandals and suspicions have disrupted the day-to-day life of
the economy, they have done much to persuade companies, even those not
involved, to change their approach to business. More forcefully than any arguments from reformers, the scandals have shown that the cozy relationship
between business and the bureaucracy in the Iron Triangle is prone to abuse,
inefficiency, and financial profligacy, and, if left unchecked, will impede Japan's

progress into the globalized future. Because the scandals have dragged down corporate presidents and board members (whether or not they were directly involved), management has added self-defense to the more purely business reasons to embrace the principles of control and accountability. For all these very pointed reasons, corporate Japan has begun to jettison what one observer described as "the murky web of favors-for-favors relationships, in place since the days of the pre-war *zaibatsu* conglomerates."[55] Because each new scandal has brought penalties and made dealing overseas more difficult, they have redoubled the drive to strengthen management controls and systems to ensure internal accountability—an integral part of the effort to improve profitability. For Machiavellian reasons, if not moral purposes, in the late 1990s Japanese corporations have begun to embrace the ethics outlined in the 1990 "Charter for Good Corporate Behavior," put out by the Federation of Economic Organizations, or Keidanren, the country's premier business group.[56]

All these changes in Japan's way of conducting business will help meet her most fundamental needs for their future. The focus on profitability will smooth the transition from manufacturing and exports by making Japanese firms more sensitive to pricing, cost, and other market signals. That heightened sensitivity, more certainly than any bureaucratic direction, will alert them to the deteriorating suitability of the old standby of mass production for export, and the increasing potential in services, control, and finance activities. Further, this new emphasis on profitability and corporate flexibility will enable Japan to perform as a headquarters: to act less as a workshop than as a clearing house for information, to determine where and where not to apply resources, and to function as a coordination center for the disposition of both financial, labor, and other economic resources.

In assessing the means by which Japan will make this transformation, it is worth noting that none of these changes explicitly targets larger national needs, though all will help Japan adapt to the new future environment. Instead, this remarkable change has begun because individual economic units have strived to make the gains or avoid the costs implicit in the particular imperatives facing them. With hardly any top-down direction at all, they have moved the overall economy in the direction that it needs to go. Japanese business is changing its emphasis and orientation because each individual firm has become concerned over poor efficiency and low ROE, the repercussions of the corruption scandals, or has found some particular way to benefit from the unfolding environment. The rhetoric surrounding the new concentration on profitability, decisive management, and clear accountability does not include an acknowledgment of Japan's growing need to abandon her former dependence on manufacturing and exports in favor of management services, design, and finance. The practical world of day-to-day business is concentrating on its narrow concerns, not on sweeping national needs. Yet, as is so often the case, that concentration has begun to adjust to the new environment before its contours even become clear to the economy's managers.

In all this change, both Japanese and foreigners will find a plethora of moneymaking opportunities. It is impossible to list all the avenues open to exploitation. As in all economies, a thorough grasp of all the opportunities requires greater imagination than belongs to any one person or group of people. This is why bureaucracies fail to run economies successfully, whether in Washington or Tokyo, especially when the environment is the least bit dynamic. But even without an ability to itemize each new opportunity associated with this transformation, the nature of these new business opportunities does yield to some generalization: The chances for growth and profits will reside less in the fabrication and sale of products, and more in the transfer of management practices and policies that have succeeded in the West but are new to Japan. Therefore, opportunities will abound for Western consultants, systems experts, writers and implementers of software, experts in stockholder relations, and a whole array of business and accounting people familiar with the monitoring practices that make a management hierarchy work, give it control over the firm's divisions, assess accountability, and determine contributions to profits. Japan will also require the creation of firms that monitor those providing the systems and data to industry, and ensure the integrity and accuracy of these systems. The lack of trust that the Japanese have begun to feel toward their officials will only heighten the need for such monitoring services. This management services and assessment "industry," usually invisible except to those involved, is a major part of business management support in every developed economic power. It is frequently overlooked by the popular press and politicians (probably because it seldom is romanticized by labor leaders, writers, and artists). But this "industry" is critical to modern business, is poised for great growth in Japan, and will offer tremendous opportunity to those who have the imagination and the position to serve the needs of that growth.

Some companies have already begun to exploit these opportunities. Recently, the services of the American credit-rating agencies Moody's and Standard & Poor's have become much sought after in Japan, as have those of smaller, more specialized agencies. In time, full-fledged Japanese equivalents will develop to comparable size and stature. But things will go beyond straightforward credit analysis. Indeed, Japan already has had a taste. In mid-1997, the Maryland-based Institutional Shareholders Services Company gained prominence by advising Nomura Securities and the Dai-Ichi Kangyo Bank against rehiring the auditors who were in place when the firms were paying bribes. The American accounting and consulting firm Arthur Andersen has landed a contract, from the Japanese government no less, to audit the scandal-ridden Nuclear Power Reactor and Nuclear Fuel Development Corporation, called Donen, which, as mentioned earlier, has had two nuclear accidents and clumsily tried to conceal them from the public and the Diet.[57] These are remarkable examples of change, as well as signs of the opportunities it will bring. Not too long ago, the government would not even have considered an investigation, and if there was one, its own ministries would have conducted it. As all facets of the economy focus increasingly on accountability and where applicable, profitability, this kind of independent audit, rare in Japan even now, will be common, as will systems to guard against violations. In Japan, Price Waterhouse has begun to anticipate the need and increased its staff there by one thousand professionals just for the initial surge in demand.[58] Sumitomo Bank recently turned to Bankers Trust to help it build an internal system to control risk in its trading operations and determine accountability.[59] More such links will develop and contracts will be awarded, but the greatest immediate moneymaking opportunities stemming from changes in Japan's economy and business practices will emerge in the financial sphere.

THE FINANCIAL REVOLUTION

Since financial markets anticipate and frequently exaggerate change in the "real economy" (as financial people like to call the business of producing and selling goods and services), the developing new attitudes toward trade and ways of conducting business should reverberate more quickly and more clearly there than elsewhere in the economy. Financial reforms, though far from complete, will multiply the effect by allowing greater diversity and freedom of action, even as they root out some of the corruption and abuse common in the old, closed system. And as with other business responses, the practical, narrowly focused business adjustments in the financial markets will serve Japan's overall national needs for the future.

The prices of shares on the Tokyo Stock Exchange are probably the single most telling indication of these changes. To be sure, Japanese stocks have offered little reason for optimism in recent years. After selling off sharply in the early 1990s, stocks generally have fluctuated at relatively low levels ever since. At the time of this writing, they remain well down from their former highs in 1989. It is easy, of course, to predict a general market recovery as Japan's economic transformation unfolds and the economy recovers direction, but the relationship is much more complex than anticipating straightforward cyclical swings. Comparative price movements should trace the subtlety of the expected reorientation of Japan's economy, prompting a shift in the pricing of certain groups of stocks relative to one another and relative to corporate fundamentals such as stockholders' equity, earnings, and profitability.

These kinds of interrelationships were less relevant in Japan's period of great growth when all eyes were on the high-flying Nikkei stock market index. Then, the rising market affected almost all shares across the board. Investors acted as if every aspect of Japanese business and finance was bound to prosper. They believed that the guidance of Japan's civil service bureaucracy would forestall failure and eventually bring success to even the most doubtful enterprise. Japanese and foreigners could buy into almost any sector of the market, almost any stock, and ride the wave upward. Similarly, it mattered little how expensive a stock was relative to the company's business "fundamentals"—its earnings power, net worth, dividend payout, free cash flow—in short, all of the benchmarks of business success used by investors worldwide. Japan's fast-growth economy seemed to provide assurances that these "fundamentals" would catch up in short order. In the late 1980s, stock prices stood at sixty to seventy times current earnings and five or more times the stockholders' equity, what analysts call "book" value. Prices far outstripped comparable "valuation ratios" in the United States and Europe.[60] There was no way to explain the difference either, except in terms of the faith in Japanese growth. The Japanese stock market seemed to operate in a different universe from others.

Now, however, without growth or the assured protection of the bureaucracy, not only have stocks suffered generally but the market's uniformity and its uniquely high valuations have disappeared as well. Discrepancies in performance from sector to sector and stock to stock have widened, and, as in the West, investors have had to become much more selective about which industries and firms they buy in the stock market. Further, questions of valuation—e.g., prices relative to cash flows, present and prospective earnings, and debt ratios—which have long been issues in Western markets, have finally become critical for investors in Japan, as have questions about the quality of management and the mix of a firm's product lines.[61] The Japanese stock market has begun to price itself like other developed stock markets. Unlike in the past, when Japanese stocks bore no relation to those of other countries, there is now an analytical correspondence to explain differences.[62] Thus, profit returns relative to stockholders' equity recently ran at less than one-third the American rate, so Japanese stock prices stood lower by half relative to stockholders' equity or "book" than in the United States.[63] In a sense, this makes Japanese stocks look cheap next to the American counterparts, and consequently relatively attractive. Certainly at such valuation levels, there is great potential for a stock price surge, should Japanese companies succeed in their present quest to raise profitability—that is, their ROE—toward American levels. Indeed, by the time this book is published, the adjustment may already have begun. The critical difference from the past, however, is not an individual forecast but rather that such a comparison of value is possible at all.

Beyond these critical issues of selectivity and valuation, pricing in the Japanese market for some time to come will need to deal with the effects of the ongoing trend toward deregulation and increased competition. Although in the long run deregulation tends to help industries, initially it can hurt existing firms, because typically, regulation protects firms under its supervision. By keeping competition out, regulation can create an environment in which firms can charge higher prices than they otherwise might, and so fatten their profit margins. Even if the regulators forbid such monopolistic price gouging, then the protection that it gives from competition tempts firms to become inefficient and cost heavy. Either way, when deregulation brings new competition, it destroys the cozy situation by lowering sales prices or by demanding greater efficiency or both. This is what happened in the United States in the 1970s, when the government deregulated the airlines, or in the 1980s, when it opened up the utilities and telecommunications areas. But in Japan today, as in the United States previously, the excitement caused by the deregulatory change has prompted a confused response. Analysts claim that the deregulation of a market or sector will free an existing industry leader to use its size or financial strength to improve its position. They recommend the stock on this basis. Sometimes, this argument works, but more often than not, these "leaders" suffer from the loss of the regulatory protection before they can effectively meet the challenge of the new competition. Their stock prices reflect these circumstances first by losing value before they can rise with the ultimate adjustment. Facing a future of deregulation, this kind of risk seems now to loom especially over the Japanese market sectors of transportation, banking, brokerage, telecommunications, and retailing, to name a few. Buying opportunities will, of course, present themselves when waves of pessimism depress relative prices sufficiently to account for the effect of deregulation, what financial people call "discounting." But otherwise, the risks are clear. With this kind of pressure in mind, it has become popular from time to time to recommend investing, in the words of one pundit, in the "25 percent of the Japanese market that is globally competitive" and not protected by regulations.[64] But neither is necessarily safe. A general trend in this direction will tend to bid these stock prices up beyond what is justified, even by excellent business prospects, leaving the stocks vulnerable to a "correction," despite good returns in the company's line of business. Unlike Japan's past, a generalized group of winners will offer less and less reward. Successful strategies will need continual selectivity and careful attention to valuation.

As the Japanese stock market continues to adjust to the pressures and priorities of the new economic environment, the government's financial reform efforts will generally reinforce the trend. As described in previous chapters, the "big bang" financial reforms have the general objective of bringing Japanese financial markets up to the global standard, or, as the official pronouncements say, *"gurobaru standado."* While broad and diverse in the changes that they promote, of particular relevance in the present context is the abolition of fixed broker commissions. This invites greater competition and with it the search for more efficient techniques, as well as an effort to provide a wider range of services both to institutions and individuals. Similarly, greater competition and increased dynamism will stem from the abolition of the old limitations on currency transactions and rules that now permit pension funds more latitude in where they can invest around the world, and what financial instruments they can use to make those investments. The effects will multiply because the reforms also now permit foreign fund managers to solicit business from Japanese pension funds, and to sell mutual fund or unit trust type products to Japanese individuals and institutions. In this same vein, the new rules also begin to tear down walls between commercial banks, investment banks, and brokers, allowing each to compete in the others' markets. These liberalizations will broaden Japan's financial markets and further open a wide field of profitable endeavor by: easing procedures required for corporations to issue bonds, in the domestic market or abroad; abolishing the tax on securities transactions; permitting trading in a wide range of derivative instruments, such as futures on commodities, currencies, stock and bond indices as well as options on individual securities and options on futures; allowing the issuance of unit trusts to invest in real estate, which in the United States are called real estate investment trusts (REITS); and granting firms permission to "securitize," that is, issue bonds backed by portfolios of financial assets, such as mortgages, auto loans, even credit card receivables.[65]

As part of this quest to come up to the "global standard," the authorities have gone beyond liberalizations and the abolition of the old, constraining rules, and made efforts to eliminate the abuses of the once-cozy relationship of privilege and protection enjoyed by Japan's banks and brokers. In a stark reversal of practice, the Ministry of Finance and the Bank of Japan have stopped pampering Japanese financial institutions and ignoring their shady practices. Recently, financial regulators have called on the Ministry of Justice to help them prosecute the illegalities that they once ignored.

The year 1996 brought the first sign of this change, when prosecutors arrested the real estate developer Kichinosuke Sasaki. He was accused of trying to block the sale at auction of a piece of real estate that he had once owned but had defaulted on its mortgage.[66] Until that time, failed developers frequently blocked sales in an effort to gain time to seek a better price for their property. It was illegal, but the blocked lenders, on whom the developers had defaulted, seldom complained and prosecutors seldom pressed charges on their own. Mr. Sasaki's arrest signaled an end to such indulgent practices.

More signs of a new regime emerged in 1997, when the government pursued brokers and other businesses that had paid extortion to the *sokaiya* gangsters. When the Ministry of Finance suspended major securities dealers from trading in response to the scandal, it was something new. The withdrawal of brokering licenses from individuals involved was also a more severe penalty than those issued in the past.[67] If that was not clear enough, the Ministry drove the point home by arresting Nomura Securities' former president, Hideo Sakamaki, after he was forced to resign.[68] This was a far cry from the approach to scandal in 1991, when the Ministry allowed an earlier Nomura president, Setsuya Tabuchi, to resign and then return to the firm as a well-paid "consultant." At the time of the latest Nomura scandal, the press speculated that the broker's problems would impede reform.[69] It is now apparent that the government was able to use it to promote reform. The Ministry of Finance underscored the message months later when it forced Yamaichi Securities to close, even before the company was technically insolvent, because of its questionable practices in addition to the *sokaiya* payoffs.[70] Since then, the Ministry has extended its campaign against many of the long-standing financial abuses of the old system. In a recent round, it began to prosecute the common practice of manipulating stock prices through rumors. For years the MOF turned a blind eye to speculators who sell stocks short, that is, before they own them, and then start rumors to depress the price so that they can buy the stock cheaper when they have to make delivery on their sale. Now the Ministry has adopted the Western practice of vigorously policing this and other such price manipulations.[71]

The interaction of these financial reforms with the new valuation regime in the Japanese stock market and the reorientation of Japanese business will create a financial revolution across a broad front, accompanied by an attractive array of moneymaking opportunities. Some of the opportunities will develop from the almost sure surge of mergers, acquisitions, leveraged buyouts (LBOs), spin-offs, stock swaps for divisions of companies, and the like, that this interaction will create. The weakening of the cross holdings in the *keiretsu* families of firms, the quest to improve corporate profitability, the new holding company law, and the greater ease that the "big bang" and like reforms offer stock transactions all point decisively in this direction. Not only can spin-offs and acquisitions help firms reorganize and revamp themselves to raise profitability, but financial deregulation will also make it easier than it was to accomplish these changes in the open stock market.

Anticipation in the Japanese financial community is palpable. People with experience in mergers and acquisitions (M&As) have become highly valued and command commensurate salaries.[72] As a harbinger of more dramatic changes to come, Asahi Breweries, Citizen Watch, and even Toyota Motors have initiated programs to buy large blocks of their own shares on the stock exchange.[73] This kind of self-acquisition is common in the West but is very new to Japan. Typically, a management decision to buy back their own company's stock reflects a judgment of where corporate cash can best be used. Repurchasing shares, by pushing up the stock's price, also guards against other firms acquiring them, though the giant Toyota has little to fear in this respect. Whatever the specific motivations of each individual company, these purchases stand as an augury of the growth of still more un-Japanese financial practices. Certainly, in Japanese financial circles people see this phenomenon only as a modest beginning. "The story in Japan today is share buybacks," said Wakabo Komatsu, a market analyst with the Daiwa Institute of Research in Tokyo. "Next will be M&A and LBO's [leveraged buyouts]."[74]

The mergers and acquisition trend will create tremendous opportunities to make money in Japan. Openings for stock speculation that were not previously available will emerge for Japanese and foreign investors alike. But the largest potential lies on the investment banking side, where the structuring and underwriting of the deals should generate huge fees. Here, foreigners have an edge. They possess much wider experience and superior expertise than their Japanese counterparts. As already indicated, M&A people are hot. The Chase Bank, sensing the potential, has already set up a special mergers-and-acquisition team in Tokyo. Though the big deals have yet to emerge, that team has already arranged for the foreign purchase of several Japanese pharmaceutical businesses and for the sale of a group of Japanese-owned hotels. Chase's people have also arranged Eastman Kodak's $14.9 million purchase of a controlling stake in the Japanese camera-maker Chinon Industries.[75] The advantages of experienced foreigners in Japan's financial transformation do not stop with mergers and acquisitions. Westerners have a greater expertise with derivative instruments, such as futures, options, and securities, like callable bonds, that have options attached to them, or as bond people like to say "imbedded" in them. They should gain disproportionately from the growth of this market, at least initially, as Japan's needs impel her to develop still other financial instruments and practices. Indeed, the dominance of foreign expertise in these areas has Japanese executives speaking of a "Wimbledon Effect," drawing an analogy between their predicament and what happened in London after its "big bang," when the Americans leveraged their initial advantages to grab a lot of the new business. The British then lamented the temporary decline of their own position in their own market by pointing to their diminished stature in tennis. The world-class tennis tournament is British, they said, but all the players are foreign.

Foreigners should also have an edge in the potentially explosive growth of Japanese bond and money markets, especially in the area of "securitization." Developed in the United States, this practice allows financial institutions to bundle their loan portfolios or mortgages to back a new bond that they then sell to investors in the open market. The issuing financial institutions gain new capital from the action and relieve themselves of the risk of continuing to carry the loans on their books. The investors get a relatively high return on a portfolio of loans that, because it is well diversified, carries less risk than any single loan in the group that backs it. This market started by bundling mortgages into mortgage-backed securities (MBS) and has grown exponentially in the United States, encompassing other lending, mostly automobile loans and credit card debt. Over the years, the variety of legal arrangements surrounding these securities has multiplied, but the basic structure and purpose has remained unchanged. Now this practice looks especially well-suited to Japan's situation. The banks there have huge portfolios of questionable loans that they would like to get off their books, even at a loss. Securitization will enable these banks to bundle their loans and sell them away to others. Of course, to sell the risky bonds effectively, they would have to offer the buyers a discount from their stated or face value. But that is better than the alternative, for without the securitization option, the banks can choose either to hold on to the risky loans and hope that things get better, or to write them off entirely at a 100 percent loss. At least with securitization, the banks could get something for them in the present. And the whole financial system would thereby get a fresh financial flow for new lending, and thereby provide the desperately needed flow of funds to support economic growth. The securitization option, of course, was closed until the "big bang" financial reforms explicitly permitted it. And Japanese finance has welcomed the change. Sanwa Bank was the first to avail itself of the practice, selling about ten percent of its bad loans or ¥30 billion ($240 million at the average exchange rate of the day) in real estate-backed bonds in the domestic Japanese bond market.[76] Following that, Sumitomo Bank structured a comparable deal for the bundling and sale of ¥40 billion ($307 million) of its real estate loan portfolio.[77] In short order, "securitization" became the new financial buzzword in Tokyo's Nihonbashi financial district.

The potential market for this kind of debt in Japan is huge. If Japan were to securitize a portion of her mortgage loans comparable to that already securitized in the United States, it would produce a bond market approaching ¥13 trillion ($104 billion at the average exchange rate of the late 1990s), a growth rate of 2000 percent from its 1997 base of about ¥620 billion ($5.0 billion).[78] And these figures are only for mortgages. Once securitization gains popularity, as occurred in the United States, a market for bonds backed by other sorts of loans will increase the volume. The development of real estate investment trusts (REITS) will add still more to this growth. REITS, long used in the United States to create a kind of closed-end mutual fund for individuals and institutions to acquire an interest in a diversified real estate portfolio, ought to appeal to the Japanese market for many of the same reasons that the mortgage-backed bonds will. REITS and mortgage-backed bonds will also help create a more fluid, efficient, and useful real estate market than that of the past, when rigid strictures inhibited growth and limited the ability to adjust when things went wrong. These trusts, like other forms of securitization, are set to grow now that the financial reforms allow it.[79]

The returns for trading in such markets, not to mention the impressive underwriting fees to bring these bonds and trusts public, will create tremendous revenues for those involved. And Western expertise will bring much of the return to foreigners, especially in the beginning. The Japanese have little experience in structuring these complicated and sometimes risky deals. They have relied mostly on Americans to date. It was America's Goldman Sachs, not a Japanese investment bank, that brought Sumitomo's asset-backed issue to market and, of course, won the underwriting fees. When the Nippon Credit Bank decided to develop securitized products, it turned to America's Bankers Trust.[80] For its issue, Sokura Bank chose Merrill Lynch over the Japanese competition.[81] Bank of Tokyo-Mitsubishi Trust used Morgan Stanley to manage its ¥500 billion ($4 billion at the average exchange rate of the day) offering, and

Tokai Bank used Salomon Brothers for its ¥230 billion ($1.8 billion) deal.[82] Though less active than the Americans, the British also seem poised to edge out the Japanese competition. ING Barings and Barclay's Bank have revealed that they are close to securitization deals.[83]

The transformation of Japanese financial markets and the opportunities that will come with the change should extend well beyond the advent of securitization and REITS, significant as those events will be. The Japanese corporate bond market generally is poised for tremendous growth. During most of the postwar period, bonds played only a small role in Japanese finance. While the stock market was riding high, most corporations could easily supplement their bank borrowing by issuing stock at a handsome price. Banks dominated the market for borrowed capital. But with the setbacks of the 1990s, both these financing sources have dried up. The stock market remains depressed enough to discourage new issuing. Indeed, the shares have remained so cheap that firms are doing the reverse and buying them back. And the banks are so burdened with bad debt that they have had to curtail their lending severely, even to the best quality credits. In time, securitization will free the banks from the worst of this bind, but that will take time, and it is doubtful that they ever will recapture their former dominance. So companies will have to go to the bond market to raise needed funds. The "big bang" and other financial reforms will facilitate the process by easing the rules regarding such issues, both for Japanese issuing abroad and in their domestic market. The reforms, by breaking down the old barriers between commercial banks, investment banks, brokers, and dealers, will also help to enlarge the potential market and increase its liquidity.[84]

Already the response has been impressive. The value of bond issues recently has surged, at times by 50 percent from one month to the next.[85] Early in 1998, for example, Toyota Motor Corporation floated its first domestic Japanese bond issue since 1971, a ¥200 billion ($1.5 billion at the average exchange rate of the day) deal.[86] Tokyo Electric, with its top-grade, triple-A credit rating, has gravitated to the bond market, claiming that it can raise funds more cheaply, easily, and reliably there than from Japan's beleaguered banks. Nissho Iwai Corp. sold ¥80 billion ($640 million) recently because it needed "to raise funds as soon as possible." The company was so unsure of the banks' willingness or ability to meet its needs that it hardly investigated that alternative. After long years away from the market, other new issuers read like a who's who of Japanese industry: Japan Airlines, Nissan Motor Co., Kawasaki Steel Co., NEC Corp., and Nippon Yusan KK.[87]

The market is still small by European, and especially by American standards, but clearly the opportunities will multiply. Dealer operations will gain the greatest net benefit from underwriting, but also from the trading. Bond trading tends to yield higher returns to dealers than equity trading. In much of this straightforward bond issuing and dealing, Japanese and foreigners will gain equally. Neither has special advantages over the other. Most of the new issues will be what financial people call "straight bonds," which offer a strict maturity date and a simple coupon return. Japanese have as much experience and expertise with these as do their foreign competition. Toyota's bond deal, for instance, had no trouble sharing the underwriting leadership equally between Merrill Lynch and Nomura Securities. But not all the issues will be straightforward. Tokio Marine and Fire signaled the change recently, issuing what it called an "earthquake bond." With a ten-year maturity, it pays a premium yield to the buyer, about twice what he or she would get from a "straight" Tokio Marine and Fire bond. The catch is that the buyer forfeits all interest and principal if Tokyo suffers a significant earthquake.[88] It is an attractive and imaginative way for this property and casualty insurer to diversify some of its risk in Tokyo earthquake insurance. And it is indicative of the kind of diverse bond opportunities that will emerge for imaginative underwriters and alert investors as this market expands.

The changing environment in Japan should also produce a new flow of bond buyers to match the increases in issuing. Even at present levels, there are plenty of potential investors. Japanese pension assets are a huge ¥250 trillion ($2 trillion in the average exchange rate of the late 1990s), second in the world only to the United States, with close to $6 trillion in pension assets.[89] What is more, the pension funds are growing fast. They have recognized the coming demographic pressure, as described earlier, and are beefing up the asset base that they use to meet their pension liabilities. They will need new investment vehicles like these bonds for some of these new funds. The "big bang" and other reforms will reinforce the money flow, because they have opened up the range of instruments legally permissible for pension fund investing. Pension fund buyers might even welcome unusual bond structures, like Tokio Marine and Fire's "earthquake bonds," that promise the added return that these institutions need to meet the expanding demands of the growing population of pensioners. Even without this general need to beef up their asset base, financial reforms will free up buyers for these new bond markets, because they have expanded the range of firms permitted to advise pension funds. Previously, only insurance companies and trust banks could do this, and they were reluctant to invest aggressively. But the new range of investment advisors are not so timid, especially the foreigners. They are eager to deal in the new instruments and markets and to gain the higher returns available there.

In addition to supporting new bond markets, the liberalization in the field of funds management will immediately open more new business opportunities. Many funds managers—both the Japanese and the foreigners who have flocked to Japan—have already geared up for the coming bonanza. They have begun to cash in, not only on this opportunity among Japanese pension funds, but also on sales of mutual funds to Japanese individuals and institutions, now that financial reforms allow such transactions. Virtually every major fund manager in the United States, Great Britain, Germany, and Switzerland, and some minor ones, has opened offices in Tokyo or solicited Japanese pension funds from their home base.[90] Adding considerably to the trend, the largest American mutual fund manager, Fidelity, has recently entered Japan to get its share of what it has identified as Japan's ¥1.2 quadrillion ($9.6 trillion in the average exchange rate of the late 1990s) market in personal financial assets.[91] To sweeten the pot further, there is talk now about privatizing the management of part of the gigantic Japanese postal savings plan. That would provide an additional ¥250 trillion ($2 trillion) for managers to earn fees from investing and offering advice.[92] Beyond such practical moneymaking opportunities, the enlarging pool of investors should add to the dynamism and liquidity of Japan's financial markets generally.

All these potentials—for investment bankers, brokers, bond dealers, and funds mangers—offer such myriad new opportunities that Japanese financial firms are scrambling to gain expertise on a wide front, while foreigners search for a means to sell their expertise in the new marketplace. As a result, Tokyo recently has witnessed a remarkable spate of strategic alliances and outright acquisitions. Japan's Long-Term Credit Bank (LTCB) has linked with Swiss Bank to form the LTCB SBC Warburg Securities Co. that, according to its founders, will create a comprehensive alliance through three joint ventures: an investment bank, a new asset management firm, and Japan's first-ever private banking operation. With the Western expertise and the Long-Term Credit Bank's network, the new firm should become a formidable competitor. It will, in the words of LTCB's Katsunobu Onogi, "take Japan to the world and bring the world to Japan."[93] The rationale behind this union has even outlasted the firm's financial difficulties and the Japanese government's need to step in for a time to manage LTCB. In a parallel move, Nippon Credit Bank and Bankers Trust have also formed an alliance, though less extensive than the LTCB and the Swiss.[94] Other efforts are less comprehensive than these but nonetheless reflect the desire to leverage some of the new opportunities by bringing together the applicable domestic Japanese network and the financial expertise available abroad. Nippon Life, for instance, has joined with the huge American funds manager Putnam Investments to get a share of the new market for investing pension assets, selling mutual funds, and, in time perhaps, dealing with the postal savings plan.[95] Sumitomo Bank has turned to New York's Citigroup to develop an array of more attractive savings products for the retail market.[96] Even the Ministry of Post and Communications, which runs the postal savings network, has sought foreign expertise to better serve its now more dynamic market by engaging Citigroup to enlarge its network of automatic teller machines.[97] Merrill Lynch has found a link by buying the retail outlets of the failed Yamaichi Securities Co. and hiring back one-third of its former employees to cash in on these tremendous opportunities by forming a Japanese sales network for its wide variety of products.[98]

The rapid change in Japanese financial markets confirms the expectation that Japan's domestic economy and Japanese trade will continue to transform itself with increasing momentum in the future. Of course, as with much of the economic change elsewhere in Japan, this financial transformation is not driven by an explicit recognition of Japan's overarching longer-term fundamental needs. Nor is it a positioning for that long-term goal orchestrated by a central authority. On the contrary, like most effective economic adjustments, the transformation, and the array of investment and business opportunities that have come with it, have developed from the immediate needs of individual market participants, mostly generated from pressures on corporate and financing relationships. Even though the immediate motivation ignores longer-term fundamental national needs, these changes in the financial markets will support Japan's efforts to cope with them. The changes will broaden and deepen Japanese financial markets and make them more active. In this way, these straightforward moneymaking efforts will support Japan's increasing need to internationalize the yen and to position herself as headquarters nation in Asia. These expanded, more efficient and sophisticated financial markets will also help attract foreign capital, which Japan will need increasingly as her aging population depletes the strong domestic savings flow on which she has relied for years.

With continued reforms and innovations in the economy and the financial sector, the nation seems well positioned to create a smooth, if not painless, transition as she copes with her unavoidable economic and demographic pressures. Unfortunately, the kind of effective decentralized responses that will work so well to make the required economic transformation cannot serve Japan in her parallel need to assume a heightened diplomatic profile in Asia. As the final chapter of this book illustrates, that effort will present an array of difficulties for Japan, her allies, and neighboring states in Asia. Nonetheless, if these nations can cooperate in managing the diplomatic transition, it will allow Japan to gain control of her own national security, as well as contribute to the economic and political security of the region and the world.

TEN

JAPAN
AT THE
CROSSROADS

THE EXERCISE OF INTERNATIONAL LEADERSHIP will cause Japan the greatest difficulty in her transformation. It will also introduce the greatest uncertainty into Asian relations. Not only does the idea of Japanese prominence on the world stage run counter to her long-standing policy preferences of the last fifty years, but it also will disconcert, and perhaps frighten, other Asian states. Nonetheless, Japan's necessary responses to unavoidable economic and demographic pressures will force her hand. All the factors discussed here—moving industry overseas to secure cheap, plentiful labor resources; increasing imports to supplement constrained domestic production; expanding her reliance on foreign financial capital to supplement the savings depleted by her growing population of pensioners; reorienting her domestic economy from manufacturing and exports toward services and management functions—will expand the scope of her overseas interests and make her more dependent on them. In the face of such change, Japan will have to raise her diplomatic and military profiles, and exercise leadership among nations. Asia's recent economic and financial crisis has added an intense urgency to these demands. Increasingly, Japan will have to think and act, not in her customary national terms, but also in regional and global terms.

In taking these necessary steps, Japan and the region face two critical challenges. The most immediate is the financial and currency crisis that has beset all of Asia since 1997. The events surrounding this tremendous economic setback are clearly a test of Japan's ability to step forward into a position of leadership. They have also made crystal clear the weakness of Japan's old "way," and in so doing have reinforced all the other fundamental pressures on Japan to transform herself. In the longer run, beyond the immediate exigencies of the crisis, Japan's necessary transformation will create a second, more dangerous challenge by altering Asia's power balance. The shift will occur primarily from loosening the Japanese-American link, as Japan demands more independent political power in order to secure her new, expanded, and important interests overseas. Because the decreasing intensity of this relationship will deconstruct both a constant of more than fifty years, and a major stabilizing influence in Asia, all the nations involved in the region will need to seek new means of maintaining peace and security. Though many alternative stabilizing arrangements are feasible, the most promising approach to retaining all the elements offered by the old Japanese-American relationship would be to strengthen Asia's multilateral institutions, such as the ASEAN Regional Forum (ARF), which has added political and security issues to the economic agenda. Building on such new arrangements will not come easily; Asian nations have never embraced supranational institutions. Nonetheless, all interested powers, including China, Japan, and the United States, need to foster the strengthening and development of these sorts of institutions, for if each nation attempts to deal alone with the dangers, real or perceived, of a rising Japan, the risks from a misperception or mistake will rise geometrically.

AN IMMEDIATE CHALLENGE: ASIA'S CRISIS

Certainly, Asia's financial crisis, which began in the second half of 1997 and still affects the region, has heightened the urgency for Japan to assert economic and financial leadership there. By creating needs where once there was comparative prosperity, the sudden problems in the former wonder economies of Malaysia, South Korea, Singapore, Thailand, and especially Indonesia, have put Japanese economic and foreign policy into a pressure cooker. Suddenly, the world has begun to demand that Japan make many of the changes that she ultimately will have to make anyway in response to her own economic and demographic problems. While Japan began to open her economy to imports and broaden her financial markets cautiously and on her own typically measured schedule, her Asian neighbors suddenly became desperate for her to throw her doors open wide and take other measures to stimulate economic activity and the basic reform to keep it going. Similarly, her

Asian neighbors began to push Japan to accelerate the "internationalization" of the yen, as she will have to for her own fundamental reasons, into a base currency for trade and finance in the region. With this sudden urgency adding to Japan's already pressing fundamental issues, it has become harder for Japanese leadership to ignore the need for basic change in the nation's "way."

The Asian crisis broke into the headlines on June 25, 1997. On that day, Thanong Bidaya, Thailand's new finance minister, realized the perilous state of his country's foreign exchange reserve. With his country strapped for financial resources, he announced that the Thai Finance Ministry would no longer support Thai finance companies. It became clear that Thailand's situation was weaker than most had thought. Investors and speculators immediately began moving their assets out of the country. Seven days after Minister Bidaya's announcement, Thailand removed its currency, the baht, from its long-standing peg to the United States dollar.[1]

The financial turmoil in Thailand rocked all of East Asia. Panic spread, revealing weakness elsewhere, and creating it too. By year's end, the region's high-flying equity markets had crashed, and once rock-solid currencies had plunged. From late June, the baht declined 80 percent against the dollar in a period of just a few months. The Thai stock market, which had risen regularly for the previous five years, lost over half its value in less than six months. The Malaysian ringgit fell 60 percent against the dollar during that same time, while that country's stock market lost over one-third of its value. As the panic spread, traders, speculators, and investors awakened to financial flaws in economies and banking systems throughout the region. Suddenly the perennial good investments of many years looked weak and unstable. The Korean won waited to adjust until November of that year and then fell nearly 80 percent against the dollar in two months. The Korean stock market plunged by 40 percent during that same short time. The Philippine peso slid along with the baht and the ringgit. After holding a steady peg to the dollar through much of the 1990s, its dollar value fell 60 percent from early summer to year end. During that same short interval, the Philippine stock market lost a third of its value. Indonesia's rupiah followed the rest, falling over 80 percent in almost a straight line from 2,430 to the United States dollar in late June of 1997, to 12,700 in early January 1998. The Indonesian stock market sank with the currency, losing almost 60 percent of its value in those same six months. Other countries in the region fared comparatively better, but none did well. The Singapore dollar depreciated about 20 percent against its American equivalent. Mainland China held the line on its currency, the yuan or renminbi, as did Hong Kong its dollar, with Chinese backing. But Chinese stocks lost about 30 percent of their local value, as did those in Hong Kong.[2]

As the crisis gained momentum, the International Monetary Fund (IMF) became involved, governments were humiliated, scapegoats were found, ministers resigned, governments fell, credit ratings were downgraded, huge capital spending projects were canceled, and layoffs began. In Thailand, where the crisis emerged, the government called in the IMF less than a month after the baht began its fall, and agreed on a rescue plan by the end of August. By autumn, both Finance Minister Bidaya and Prime Minister Chavalit had resigned.[3] The international credit rating agencies classified the national debt as below "investment grade."[4] Before that first phase of the crisis was over, 56 of the country's 91 financial companies had closed their doors and thousands of workers had lost their jobs.[5] Korea at first denied the need for outside assistance, especially from the IMF, but as the losses mounted, it relented, and by early December 1997 agreed to IMF-dictated measures. Those involved the suspension of fourteen major financial institutions and cutbacks at many other banks and conglomerate families of firms, which the Koreans call *chaebols*.[6] Korea also lost the "investment grade" credit rating on its government debt.[7] Resignations were not required, because Korea had an election scheduled for mid-December 1997, which, understandably, resulted in a change of government and the election of a reform candidate as president, the former dissident Kim Dae-jung.[8] Indonesia initially negotiated hard with the IMF for its relief packages, largely because the reforms and closures, on which the IMF insisted, hit President Suharto's family and cronies. By December, credit agencies had downgraded Indonesia's government bond rating to "junk" status. Indonesia had to close sixteen troubled banks in order to get agreement on a relief package. Even then, the IMF complained of backsliding and began renegotiating its package before the year was out.[9] Within months, in early 1998, rioting had forced Suharto to resign.

Malaysia initially suffered less than many other of the former miracle economies, and that allowed its leadership to hide from the repercussions, at least for a while. As the ringgit and Malaysia's stock market headed down, Prime Minister Mahathir Mohamad began looking for scapegoats. While cutting back drastically on large public infrastructure projects, he first singled out American financier and currency speculator George Soros as the cause of his nation's problems. Instead of reviewing the nation's spending and regulatory regimes, he decided the problems were the fault of those, like Soros, who move funds around the world, searching for high returns and avoiding risk. He complained: "All these countries have spent 40 years trying to build up their economy and a moron like Soros comes along." He later demanded an end to Hong Kong currency trading because it facilitates these movements of funds. Soros retorted that Mahathir was a "menace to his country."[10] In time, Mahathir began to blame Asia's troubles on what he called an "international Jewish conspiracy." Throughout, he threatened to restrict trading in currencies and equities, and then reversed his decision when, after each threat, both the currency and stock markets fell. While the Prime Minister engaged in name calling and posturing, Malaysia's economy faced considerable strain. The government announced plans for an 18 percent cutback in spending right at the beginning of the crisis. On top of this, cutbacks in lending signaled slower growth and layoffs as well as bankruptcies. Despite Mahathir's antics, the situation held together well enough at first. The country retained its "investment grade" credit rating longer than most.[11] Eventually, however, the economic problems burdened the country, as it did the other Asian tigers. Foreign scapegoats became an insufficient shield. Prime Minister Mahathir turned on his former finance minister, Anwar Ibrahim, and slapped controls on credit and currency flows, in a dubious attempt to bring financial and economic stability, even as his political situation became shakier.

Although this shattering of the "Asian miracle" can trace causes to any number of issues, many of which paralleled Japanese problems, the immediate pressure grew most from relative currency shifts during the mid-1990s. It began in 1994 when China devalued its renmimbi by more than 50 percent, from 5.7 to the dollar to 8.7.[12] In that one move, the Chinese, whose exports were already beginning to challenge those of Southeast and Northeast Asia, undercut the major cost advantage that these other economies had previously enjoyed. Not only did Chinese products suddenly become cheaper on world markets, but, more important, China became a more attractive place for outside investors, including the Japanese. Compounding the problem for Korea and Southeast Asia, Japan's yen started to lose value against the United States dollar after 1995. Because most of these countries had pegged their currencies to the dollar in more or less formal ways, the dollar's rise against the yen ate away at their ability to undercut the prices of Japanese goods. Prior to this, the dollar's decline against the yen had given these countries a growing cost advantage. Between 1990 and the yen's point of greatest strength in 1995, the American dollar drew these other currencies down by over 40 percent against the yen. That currency shift effectively gave these emerging economies an ability to sell their exports much more cheaply than their Japanese competition, and to attract foreign investment, especially Japan's. But that advantage lost force after 1995 as the yen lost value. From the yen's strongest point at 84–85 to the dollar in April 1995 until mid-1997, just as the crisis began to erupt, the yen depreciated 36 percent against the dollar.[13] Since Malaysia, Indonesia, the Philippines, and these other states had already lost an export pricing edge to China's devaluation, the yen's drop created a double-barreled economic setback of substantial magnitude.

The currency impacts hit especially hard because these economies, accustomed to rapid growth over a long period, had fragile financial arrangements, as delicate as Japan's were when her financial bubble burst earlier in the 1990s. Just as in Japan, the extended period of growth in these other Asian tigers convinced investors and business managers that the rapid pace of expansion would go on indefinitely. That confidence tempted financial institutions, in some cases with government encouragement and pressure, to extend credit lavishly, with much less caution than they might have shown in a less expansive environment. Companies and government agencies spent exorbitantly for a future that they were certain would need much more factory space, more office space, better roads, and other huge infrastructure projects. Asset prices in financial and real estate markets rose to levels that could only be justified in the context of endless, rapid growth. Speculative financial capital flowed in from abroad and blew the bubble up even larger. But by late 1997, the currency shifts had so turned immediate export pricing advantages against these economies that the bubble burst. Indeed, early that year, *The China Analyst* magazine noted signs of the delicate situation, pointing to overcapacity in both property development and manufacturing. In June of 1997 the *Analyst*'s managing editor, Chen Zhao, worried that "somewhere down the road there is going to be a massive deflationary shock."[14] He and the world did not have to wait long. Less than two weeks after he wrote, the crisis erupted in Thailand.

All these Asian setbacks compounded Japan's problem in getting her own economy moving, as well as refurbishing and reshaping her own financial structure. Japanese banks and other financial institutions were big lenders in Asia, and Asia was a major market for Japanese products. But for Japan, the larger issue of the Asian crisis went beyond these straightforward, if unpleasant, economic and financial difficulties to strike at the heart of Japan's old "way" of social and economic organization. It added force to the questions raised by Japan's own problems about whether or not those policies can serve Japan's long-term fundamental needs as the premier economy in a suddenly troubled region of the world. As the crisis developed, it became increasingly clear that circumstances and attitudes had changed radically. Japan could no longer just mind her own business as she had in the past, often at the expense of her trading partners. Asia, the United States, the rest of the world, and even many leaders in Japanese business and financial circles expected Japan to think more broadly than she had before, to exercise responsible leadership for the relief of the immediate crisis, and to assist with the region's longer-term economic and financial recovery. Suddenly, it seemed, the old policies and the much preferred gradual approach to change were no longer options.

The pressure on Japan from the outside world became intense. The attitude was summed up by *The Financial Times:* "As the largest economy in Asia, [Japan] holds the key to economic revival."[15] Given the urgency of the situation, most of those looking to Japan for action expressed disappointment. The remarks by Robert G. Lees, Secretary General of the Pacific Basin Economic Council, a business group of over 1,000 firms operating in twenty countries in the Pacific were typical. "Despite its huge stake in the economic health of East Asia," he complained, "Tokyo's response has been surprisingly weak and limited."[16] United States Commerce Secretary William Daly protested that: "It is up to them [the Japanese] to lead Asia's recovery, not the United States."[17] United States Federal Reserve Board Chairman Alan Greenspan, in response to congressional questioning on whether Japan was doing "enough," flatly replied, "No, I think not."[18] That blunt reply from a man held in particularly high regard in international financial circles stung the Japanese. President Clinton added to the pressure, personally calling on Japan to take "bold" action and break through bureaucratic resistance. Even the Europeans joined in the criticism of Japan. Then German Economics Minister Günter Rexrodt wrote of Japan that she was not doing "enough…after the Asian crisis."[19] At an ASEAN summit in Kuala Lumpur late in 1997, representatives appealed to then Japanese Prime Minister Ryutaro Hashimoto to reverse his previous bias in favor of a restrictive Japanese fiscal policy. Indeed, the pressure was so great that he yielded, at least somewhat. "In Kuala Lumpur," he said, "I made the decision…our country must…prevent a world recession."[20]

Beyond all the urging and criticism, from within and without, the greatest persuader for Japan was the alacrity with which China stepped into the leadership role in her place. Competing directly with Japanese lending and aid in the region, China quickly and unilaterally offered a $1 billion aid package to Thailand, and followed up with over $1 billion more to South Korea, and an additional $200 million in export credit to Indonesia to help shore up that troubled economy. Especially early in the crisis, China made much of providing regional stability by holding the line on the renminbi, even as the yen fell (even though it was the renminbi's initial devaluation that did so much to precipitate the crisis in the first place).[21] At the height of the initial panic in October 1997, while meeting with President Clinton in Washington, Chinese President Jiang Zemin went out of his way (despite other Sino-American tensions), to offer a partnership with the United States to lead Asia out of its crisis. Presumably this Chinese partnership would replace America's usual partner, Japan. In early 1998, Chinese officials again asserted their quest for Asian leadership when they insisted on a series of special meetings with their American counterparts at the Vancouver meeting of the Asia-Pacific Economic Cooperation Forum (APEC).[22]

Japan has responded to all this pressure, and not just to please her allies or neighbors, or to prevent China from getting one up on her. Her policy makers have seen that easing Asia's economic and financial troubles will help protect Japan's own economy from additional recessionary forces. Some of these officials also realize that the demands of the moment are of a piece with Japan's ultimate need to address her longer-term pressures. But if the general direction is clear, the policy response has been somewhat muddled. Japan's political culture, as described earlier, includes strong interest groups that resist change, not only government bureaucrats, but also farmers, fishermen, construction workers, and the like, all of whom have benefited from the system's largesse over the years. So far, their efforts and arguments have confused and diverted Japan's effort to step up to regional leadership, even in the crisis. Resistance to a new Japan has come from outside the country as well. China sees Japan as competition, and so has no desire to see her fulfill any of the needs of Asian leadership, even if her failure will hold back Asia's recovery and strain China's economy. The Western nations, particularly the United States, have sent mixed signals. They are eager for Japanese reform and leadership to get Asia back on a secure growth track, but not at the expense of Western dominance. Westerners have welcomed Japanese contributions to funds administered largely by Western representatives at the IMF or the World Bank, for instance, and applauded Japan's willingness to advance loans to tide troubled economies over until international bodies can make more formal arrangements.[23] But these same Western powers quashed an independent Japanese proposal early in the crisis to establish a special yen fund to ease immediate financial strains in Asia.[24] The Westerners clearly feared a loss of influence.

Much of the immediate pressure on Japan has centered on fiscal policy. It seems that everyone wants the Japanese government to spend more and to cut taxes in order to stimulate the domestic Japanese economy. This push has built on pressures that predate the crisis. Even before Bill Clinton took office and made Japan-bashing fashionable, the United States ardently pressed Japan in

this direction.[25] Initially the United States hoped that greater Japanese consumer demand would increase the flow of imports, and so redress the chronic
trade deficit that America has with Japan. Asia's crisis stepped up the intensity
of the push by the United States and others, inside Asia and out. They have
argued that a stimulated Japanese economy would create demand for the products of these beleaguered Asian economies, thereby promoting the overall economic growth that they need to overcome their financial and currency problems. The demands for fiscal stimulus have come from all over, from
governments, supranational agencies like the G-7 and the IMF, even from
Japan's own leading business group, the Keidanren.[26] The chairman of Sony
Corporation, Norio Ohga, pressed the argument for fiscal stimulus in a particularly personal way. Reacting to government reluctance, he compared then
Prime Minister Ryutaro Hashimoto to the American President Herbert Hoover,
who presided over the beginnings of the great depression of the 1930s.[27] Naturally, Japanese officials have from time to time reacted testily to this pressure,
but Japan has tried a string of fiscal stimulus packages throughout this time, for
her own sake and for Asia's.[28] At the time of this writing, all had disappointed
by failing either to stimulate Japan's economy sufficiently or to convince those
pressuring her policy makers that they were sincere in the effort.

On a more fundamental level than the arguments for an immediate economic stimulus, this failure in the face of the crisis' urgency has added to the
general disenchantment with Japan's "way": her rigid controls, her emphasis
on exporting, and her reluctance to yield anything to the domestic Japanese
consumer. The crisis has served reform arguments, epecially in the current
debate, by focusing on the failure of the Japanese system's long-standing preference for public works spending over other stimulative fiscal measures, such
as tax cuts. True to the system that has dominated Japan since the close of the
Second World War, Japanese policy makers have long had this bias. There are
three reasons. First, government spending has left direction over money flows
and the economy in the hands of the bureaucrats, who administered the
spending programs. Second, public works spending allowed the Liberal
Democratic Party (LDP) to provide the firms and districts that support it with
the government largesse that formed the basis of its long-standing power.
Third, high statutory tax rates have made individuals and corporations desperate for the selective relief offered by tax loopholes, and thereby enhanced
the power of the bureaucrats who determine which economic activities warrant such tax breaks. The powerful Japanese civil service knows that by turning from the fiscal stimulus of public works spending to a general tax reduction, it will weaken these potent means of economic control. Despite their

resistance, the events of recent years have combined to change long-held opinion. Increasing numbers of Japanese have become convinced of the need to cut taxes in addition to or in place of public works spending initiatives. Circumstances have effectively set the direction for an inevitable shift in the emphasis of Japanese fiscal policy. Evidence of the change abounds. Bank of Japan Governor Masaru Hayami has supported the turn, saying in his first interview after his appointment: "I expect to see permanent tax cuts, and I hope to see corporate tax cuts."[29] When Prime Minister Hashimoto returned from the Kuala Lumpur summit determined that Japan should take leadership in resolving the crisis, he linked that effort to tax cuts (despite still strong resistance in his own party). It is apparent that the argument was strong, because to make it, Hashimoto had to admit a politically embarrassing reversal of his former policy of fiscal conservatism.[30, 31] After Hashimoto's resignation, the new Prime Minister, Keizo Obuchi, felt the same pressure and has pushed on with and enlarged these plans. As of early 1999, tax cut plans are still stymied in debate, but the tremendous power for this needed fundamental policy shift is apparent, especially in the face of Asia's crisis and its general demands for Japanese leadership.

Though this fiscal debate has grabbed the headlines, Asia's crisis has also produced demands for Japanese financial leadership. As with other areas of policy, the urgency of these demands has reinforced other, more fundamental pressures for change. It has also made the equation more complex. In many respects, the immediate arguments coming out of Asia fit well with the needs for Japan's financial transformation that stem directly from her own economic and demographic pressures. If Japan can make her financial markets more open and efficient, they will provide Asia with the needed additional flow of credit. Similarly, more open financial markets (in which institutions are transparent in their dealings), will increase world confidence in them and so increase the flow of financial capital into Japan and the region generally. But even as the crisis has pushed Japan to accelerate needed fundamental financial reforms, it has also pointed out the practical difficulties of asserting leadership. As a regional leader, Japan will need to present herself as something of a financial guarantor in the area, a "lender of last resort," as the United States Federal Reserve is sometimes called. Reforms that open her markets, like those of the "big bang" legislation, will of course promote this capability in the long run. But in the interim, they can detract from the ability to perform the role of guarantor by straining existing financial institutions, for increased competition will cause bankruptcies of weaker financial firms, public confusion, and even harmful panics. Together, these vaguely conflicting needs—of reform and openness on one side, and the appearance of stability and security on the other—have forced Japanese authorities into a rather delicate balancing act. On the one hand they have tried to shake out Japan's financial industry to improve its effectiveness and efficiency, and on the other hand, they have strived to protect it from the shocks that might cut off the flow of credit that is especially needed now in the face of Asia's crisis.

The upshot of this balancing act is that Japan has made substantive but halting progress in the area of financial reform. She has implemented the "big bang" and other measures that have shaped the beginnings of a revolution in Japanese finance and financial markets, broadening them and making them much more open than they were. She has made efforts to create a dynamic environment, leading the Japanese authorities to permit the bankruptcies of large but weak financial institutions. In 1997, the Ministry of Finance stood by while the Hokkaido Takushoku bank folded. The Ministry actually encouraged the closure of Sanyo Securities.[32] It did the same with Yamaichi Securities, which up until the day it closed was considered one of the "big four" among Japanese brokers. But balancing these reform efforts were those concerns that strains on the system could cause a "credit crunch."[33] Thus, Japanese authorities, while promoting financial reform, also have made proposals to establish funds that would support troubled banks. From early in 1998 onward, the government began to put amounts of public funds at the disposal of Japan's biggest banks in order to keep them lending, despite their constrained capital positions and their burden of bad loans.[34] Japan then also proposed to build a fund of subscriptions from banks operating in Japan, both domestic and foreign, to protect depositors and so also lessen the chance of panic.[35] Later in the year, further legislation passed, authorizing more money to support the banks.

Only time will tell whether Japan can succeed in this multifaceted attempt of simultaneously trying to proceed with financial reform, block panic, and keep credit flowing. Some will see the support as a legitimate palliative to the hardships of reform, while others will continue to see it as a means to retain her old system of control in the Iron Triangle. So far, market participants and editorial writers have been suspicious of this balance. They have fretted that any government assistance will weaken reform and reawaken the old government-run and government-supported approach to financial arrangements. Markets have retreated on the news of each support action, and editorial writers criticized both the principle of such support and the details of its implementation.[36, 37] By contrast, the Japanese stock market showed its approval of tough reforms by rallying after each bankruptcy, and each harsh measure dealt out in the name of reform.[38] Editorial writers, inside Japan and out, blessed these actions as well.[39] It is a difficult situation and clearly not all involved are aware of the complexity. Still, however worried market participants and journalists are about the balance of Japan's policy responses to date, it is plain that the Asian crisis has highlighted Japan's unequivocal need to provide the region with leadership by developing Tokyo into a leading financial center. The argument about change has ceased to be: "Should Japan do it?" and become one of: "How should Japan do it?" In promoting that shift, circumstances have helped put Japan on track for her ultimate need to cope with her basic economic and demographic pressures, in this case establishing efficient, dynamic, and well-informed financial markets suitable to the headquarters nation.

The Asia crisis in its particulars has also reinforced and highlighted other failures of Japan's old "way," such as the policy of pursuing a cheap yen simply to promote exports. The repercussions of Asia's troubles have shown both Japanese business leaders and policy makers that this basically beggar-thy-neighbor approach no longer works. At one time, undercutting the prices of competing national exporters propelled Japan's economy. That was when her competition came from the West and she was too small to have a major impact. But now that Asia has acquired an increased importance to Japan, that policy endangers her prosperity because a cheap yen drives down her neighbors' economies and destroys important markets for Japanese exports. Success now depends on a consideration of the economic, trade, and financial positions of those Asian neighbors, as well as her own. The Bank of Japan, at least, has awakened to the new environment and has begun to reverse its old, cheap yen policy. In the months following the crisis, it intervened heavily in currency markets to keep the yen's value up so that it would not offer competition to the other struggling Asian economies.[40] Explaining the policy and linking it explicitly with the lesson of the Asian crisis, Bank of Japan Governor Masaru Hayami said that it is inappropriate that "the yen should be so weak when Japan has about $10 billion in trade surplus each month."[41] The reasons to seek a strong yen differ slightly from those imposed by the fundamental needs implicit in Japanese demographic pressure, as well as economic maturation and globalization, but the direction of change is the same.

Recognizing the need for such fundamental change, Japan has begun to make institutional arrangements to protect against a recurrence of regionwide financial pressures, and that has redoubled all the other impulses pushing for the yen's "internationalization." As mentioned above, early in the crisis Japan advanced the idea of funding something akin to an "Asian Monetary Fund" to help alleviate the present strains and guard against future ones. When the

United States and other Western powers, protective of their influence, decried that move as competition to the IMF, Japan backed down, but then countered with the idea of a common currency system for Asia based on the yen. Effectively, this proposal recognized how the ASEAN link to the American dollar contributed to the crisis, and that as a consequence of the great growth of intra-Asian trade, a link to the yen, formal or otherwise, could have mitigated many of the problems. Joining with other regional officials in this recognition, Yuji Tsuhima, Chairman of the LDP's subcommittee on international economics and finance, described the proposed yen-based system as a means to "shield regional currencies from sharp dollar fluctuations."[42] A thorough internationalization for the currency in a yen-based system for Asian nations does indeed seem likely at some time in the future. It could acquire formal, multilateral aspects, like a regional IMF or a World Trade Organization (WTO), or it might take structure from a series of bilateral or even unilateral commitments. Whatever its contours, given the West's nearly unanimous objection to Japan's original proposal, the establishment of such a system is still a ways off. Doubtless, the Chinese would object too, but do not need to while the West is doing such an effective blocking job. Recognizing the hurdles involved, one anonymous Finance Ministry official allowed: "This is an idea of medium-term nature, and not an emerging policy move."[43] The exact timing or precise nature of such a yen-based system is, however, much less significant than Japan's clear willingness to reverse her old policy, and actively promote the yen as an international currency.

Even with the remarkable pressure of the Asian crisis and the positive signs to date, it is still far from clear whether Japan can and will take the necessary steps toward leadership, either for her own or for Asia's purposes. No doubt the future will see periods of progress toward the necessary changes and regressions away from it. Any number of incidents, especially those issuing from the Asian crisis, might overtake the situation and interrupt Japan's transformation or else propel her more quickly down the new path. Indonesia or Malaysia might fly apart politically as a consequence of the economic pressures now acting on them. China might assert itself even more aggressively than it has to date, or devalue the renminbi and compound all the pressures on Asia, including Japan. Chinese banks, already beleaguered in ways similar to those in Japan and the rest of Asia, might collapse and so compound all the financial troubles already so evident in the region. Doubts recently expressed in the West about how the IMF is handling the crisis might prompt an abrupt reversal of its policy and create a period of confusion. The introduction of Europe's unified currency, the euro, could stall, complicate, or accelerate the further internationalization of the yen, even within Asia. While the number of potential problems may seem infinite, the crisis has offered Japan something, by imposing demands for leadership that clearly push her in the same direction as her long-term fundamental needs.

A LONGER-TERM CHALLENGE: MINIMIZING THE SECURITY THREAT

Beyond the pressures and complications of the immediate crisis, the fundamental political and security implications of Japans' transformation will present ongoing diplomatic and security challenges for her and the region. As should be plain from earlier discussion, Japan's responses to her basic economic and demographic problems will impel her to become more active diplomatically than at any time since the end of the Second World War. The change surely will upset the already precarious balance of power in Asia's tense, post-Cold War environment. The "overlapping spheres of influence," to use the words of one renowned Asia hand, Harry Harding of the Elliott School of International Affairs at George Washington University, make the region particularly volatile when any new power relationship enters the matrix.[44] It is not exaggeration to suggest that a miscalculation in this setting could easily lead to armed conflict. The simultaneous rise of China seems ripe to recreate an old rivalry between the two nations that has led to war more than once in the past. While the China issue is the most dangerous, Japan's rise will also impinge on other Asian fault lines: (1) Chinese threats toward Taiwan; (2) the Koreas; (3) Russia's uncertain role in Asia and its uncertain relationship with Japan; (4) territorial disputes concerning ocean mineral rights and small, otherwise insignificant islands; and (5) suspicion among many ASEAN and other nations about either Chinese or Japanese desires for hegemony.

The tensions between China and Taiwan, and those surrounding Korea are the most obvious and the most immediately dangerous. China considers Taiwan a province, making the Taiwan Strait, in China's eyes, something of an inland waterway. In 1997 China made this clear by firing missiles into the strait to intimidate Taiwanese voting for more independently minded candidates in their presidential election. At the time, the situation became serious enough to prompt President Clinton to deploy the Pacific fleet to intimidate China in return. Japan took no part in the maneuvers. Nor does she have a vital interest in Taiwan itself or in the Taiwan Strait. Though the island was a Japanese colony until the end of the Second World War, modern Japan has shown no cultural or political affinity toward it. However, Japan's relative lack of interest does not mean that she would accept Beijing's dominance of the island. China is, after all, Japan's only potential economic rival in the region. An extension of Chinese hegemony over the island and Chinese control of Taiwan's remarkably prosperous economy would help tip the scale of relative economic power against Japan. To date, Japan has counted on the United States to secure Taiwan from Chinese dominance. But the rise of Japan's diplomatic and military profiles, and signs of wavering American commitment in Asia will impel Japan increasingly to develop an independent policy. Perhaps because of Taiwan's old colonial status, Japan might be tempted to go further than the United States has in the past, and do it faster in order to prevent the extension of Chinese power over the island. Certainly, Japan has made her interests clear. In 1997, when she left it ambiguous whether Japanese naval defenses would cover the Taiwan Strait in her new security arrangements with the United States, Japan simply refused to forswear interests in the island.[45] To make her position still more obvious, a Japanese government spokesman made a very public correction to those in the Diet who claimed that perhaps Taiwan and its Strait were off limits to Japan.[46] Some suggest that perhaps this public correction was staged to make a more blunt statement to China than straightforward diplomacy might allow. Staged or not, it succeeded in putting China on warning that the rise of Japan will complicate the Taiwan issue further, increasing the need to find a means of resolving conflict short of confrontation.

In Korea, the immediate threat stems from North Korean belligerence. That country's military government already has missiles in place that can reach western Japan and might have longer-range missiles that can effectively reach Tokyo. Evidence of nuclear capability point to still greater danger, as do reports from a high-level North Korean defector, Hwang Jang Yop, once the country's top ideologue, that the only way the North sees out of its impoverished economic state "is to use its formidable armed forces," presumably against South Korea but still a threat to Japan."[47,48] With these dangers clearly in mind, Japan became involved with American efforts to defuse the North's nuclear arms program and to give North Korea aid in order to reduce the desperation that could lead that volatile regime to war. But for Japan, the Korean situation is a lot more complicated than simply dissuading the North from fighting. Korea is an ex-colony. Both North and South hold considerable bitterness toward Japan, official and unofficial. That came through clearly not too long ago in a simple dispute between South Korea and Japan over some worthless islands in the Sea of Japan, called Takeshimas by the Japanese and Tokdos by the Koreans. Both Korean officials and the man on the street in Seoul made reference at the time to past Japanese abuses when Korea was her colony.[49] As of this

writing, South Korea still maintains a ban on importing Japanese films, entertainment, and Japanese popular culture in general.[50] Furthermore, Korea is a
direct economic competitor to Japan. More than any other Asian state, Korea's
economy produces the same kinds of products that Japan sells to the world, at
least for the time being. Steel, autos, heavy equipment, electronics, and computer memory are big parts of both economies.[51] Given the old bad feelings
and the natural economic rivalry, the tension between North and South Korea,
dangerous as it has been, has in some ways relieved Japan. While each of the
Koreas worried about the other, neither could focus on Japan. Thus while the
world and Japan look with hope at the tentative negotiations between North
and South that began in 1998, Japan cannot help but have some reservations.[52]
A unified, undistracted Korea could become a considerable economic rival and
diplomatic antagonist, if not military foe. Further, in Korean eyes, Japan's rising diplomatic and military stature could simply exchange the long-standing
tensions of a split Korea for new tensions across the Sea of Japan.

Smaller territorial disputes and Russia's role in Asia carry less urgency
than do the tensions surrounding Korea and Taiwan, but these are far from
insignificant and far from simple. Here, too, matters will become more complicated as Japan shoulders a more significant security role for herself. The collapse of Russian military power has eased fears in Japan, except to the extent
that a weakened Russia has freed China to pursue other interests. But at least
in this one respect, the rise of Japan's diplomatic profile and her power are not
particularly likely to cause trouble. Diplomatic relations between Tokyo and
Moscow have warmed. Russia wants Japanese investments, and Japan wants
access to Siberia's resources, particularly oil and natural gas.[53] Of course, the
two powers still have failed to sign a treaty of peace from World War II. The
sticking point is the disputed Kurile Islands north of Japan's Hokkaido Island.
And tensions sometimes still flare, such as in a 1997 incident when the Japanese police claimed to have captured a Russian "spy."[54] But generally, both sides
have made efforts to find an accommodation. Indeed, the quick and quiet resolution of the spy flap speaks to just such a commitment. Japanese strength is
not likely to change this either. Indeed, it might even support more warmth
from the Russians, who could welcome it as a counterbalance to China.

As far as disputes over islands and mineral rights are concerned, Japan
has already become involved in two: one, mentioned above, with South Korea,
and the other, mentioned earlier, with both China and Taiwan over small
islands in the East China Sea, called Senkakus by Japan and Daioyu by China.
In the latter, Japan actually sent a small naval flotilla to protect her interests.
At press time, both disputes remain unresolved, though tension is not ongo-

ing. While these are the only problems of this kind that concern Japan directly, there are others that Japan cannot ignore, especially as her interests in Southeast Asia grow. Most notable among these are those in the South China Sea, where China, the Philippines, Indonesia, Vietnam, and Brunei all have conflicting claims concerning potential oil reserves. The Spratly Islands in particular are significant. At a spot appropriately called Mischief Reef, China built a small structure, which some referred to as an "installation," on territory clearly claimed by the Philippines. In response to complaints, China effectively dared the Philippines to do something about it. The Philippines sent ships but effectively did nothing.[55] Despite Chinese highhandedness in this instance and others concerning oil drilling in areas claimed by Vietnam, so far these disputes have resulted in few serious security eruptions, primarily because these smaller Southeast Asian nations are intimidated. Nonetheless, the tension has the potential to escalate. Because of that, and because they reflect starkly on China's growing strength and assertiveness, these otherwise minor disputes are highly significant to Japan. As Japanese power becomes more evident and independent, the chance for escalation from such disputes will also grow.

Ultimately, the growing rivalry between a rising China and a rising Japan will create the greatest security risk in the region. Even if Japan were not embarking on the huge series of changes in the nature of her economy, her relationship with the rest of Asia, and in her diplomatic and military profile, a Sino-Japanese rivalry for regional leadership if not hegemony would be hard to avoid. Because of China's size and central position, throughout history those in the region have either accepted its dominance or challenged it directly. While global imperatives of the Cold War hid this pattern, it has become clearer now that the Cold War has ended. Japan will not have the option of sidestepping the natural rivalry, especially given her need for a looser bond with the United States.

Issues of power in Asia simply have to revolve around China. It is the "middle kingdom"—not just in the English translation of China's name for itself, but in Asian geography as well. In that sense, China has the same problem in Asia as Germany has in Europe. In the nineteenth century, the Western imperialist powers defeated China and subordinated it in order to complete their dominance of Asia. When Japan rose as a power late in that century, it had to confront China and first defeat it in order to establish Japanese primacy. She did so in the Sino-Japanese war of 1894–95.[56] (Later, in 1904, Japan turned to Russia, which at the time was the other major power in Asia that could challenge Japanese primacy.)[57] When Japan's ambition grew in the 1930s, she again turned on China, her inevitable rival in the region.[58]

China may not yet dominate Asia, as some observers have claimed, the way "the United States dominates its region," but it has the potential to do so, especially since the collapse of the Soviet Union has relieved it of one great challenge.[59] Certainly, China aspires to primacy in the region if not outright dominance. Chinese leadership and much of its population, which, as described earlier, is growing increasingly nationalistic, wants "to recapture the nation's historical place in East Asia," in the words of one long-term Asia watcher, Robert S. Ross of the John King Fairbank Center for East Asian Research at Harvard University.[60] Japan knows this and naturally wants to head off China's ambitions, for if they succeed, Japan would have to accept either outright dominance by China or isolation in a China-dominated Asia. At the same time, China sees Japan (with or without her American alliance) as the major impediment to its goal of primacy in the region.

The situation is not yet at a point of confrontation. Japan is still too close to the United States to make a direct diplomatic challenge to China or to present herself as a direct target of Chinese intimidation, much less aggression. Moreover, neither China's economy nor its armed forces yet has the strength to realize the nation's historic goal of regional leadership. But it is apparent that China is making efforts to close the gap between aspirations and abilities. Both the pace of economic growth and defense buildup speak to those efforts. Chinese planners have placed particular emphasis on maritime capability, spending dramatically on submarines, and investigating the possibility of adding aircraft carriers to their navy.[61] China has also completely revamped its land military doctrine, from utilizing overwhelming manpower to a high technology approach better suited to support action away from immediately adjacent areas.[62] And on an even more ominous note, China has revised its nuclear doctrine to give itself greater flexibility in the projection of power, shifting from a policy of "minimal deterrence," designed simply to ward off attack, to one of "limited deterrence," which Chinese military writing has described as "sufficient counter force…to deter the escalation of conventional or nuclear war."[63] That requires much greater capability than was originally assumed. Taking a long view to countering Japan's potential as a geopolitical power, China has even begun to search for potential allies by developing a loose anti-Japanese coalition in Northeast Asia. China has played on the apprehensions of both Koreas by referencing Japan's wartime abuses in the region. Editorials in China's *Xinhua* news service remind readers of the region's "lingering memory of Asia's bitter past" and the need for "vigilance" against the revival of Japanese military power.[64]

Whatever the Chinese have started in Korea, the incipient Sino-Japanese rivalry has found its main diplomatic battleground in the ASEAN nations of Southeast Asia. Japan and China have each tried to extend its influence in this grouping of states. For their part, these ASEAN states, desiring the hegemony of neither China nor Japan, have tried feebly to play each off against the other. The way in which China and Japan have proceeded in this competition speaks to their very different sources of strength. Japan has used the sheer size of her economy, plus aid, investment, and close trading relationships to woo the ASEAN nations into her embrace. China cannot proceed this way. Its economy falls far short of Japan's, even in these troubled times. The most recent official figures put China's overall GDP at less than one-fifth that of Japan's.[65] Neither does China trade as much with the ASEAN nations as Japan does.[66] In contrast to Japan's wooing style, the Chinese seem to have relied on a combination of military intimidation and conciliatory gestures. Previous discussions have touched on China's outright bullying of ASEAN members over disputed territories in the South China Sea.[67] China has even made public a map of the region that clearly claims for itself huge ocean tracts and islands. Many of these show promise for producing oil or gas, and are claimed variously by Malaysia, Brunei, the Philippines, Vietnam, and Taiwan. It was just such a revelation that prompted Indonesia to mount extensive naval and military maneuvers in 1996.[68] In this same spirit, China has pushed its oil exploration into waters that Vietnam claims as its own.[69] But at the same time as China has engaged in this military intimidation, the Chinese have spoken of "partnerships" in Asia that imply prospective, lucrative trade links and economic supports.[70] The effect has been to show the other nations of Asia, with both stick *and* carrot, the wisdom of playing with China.

Since Japan's inevitable rise as a geopolitical power will undoubtedly intensify this dangerous Sino-Japanese rivalry, as well as add to tensions in Korea and Asia's other tender spots, all the nations involved—including the United States—need to investigate means to disarm the situation at each step in Japan's transition. That effort must focus on the role played to date by the Japanese-American security arrangements. These arrangements have ensured an American presence in Asia, and in turn, have given the region stability and predictability on a number of levels. Whatever the diplomatic pose of other Asian nations—the ASEAN states, the Koreas, even China and Russia—they all have implicitly counted on this strong Japanese-American link as an anchor in Asian relations, and a welcome constant. Early on, the Japanese-American arrangements soothed Asia simply by making it impossible for any repeat of the Japanese military action that devastated the region during World War II. Later, as the immediate fears and memories of the war faded, the American presence offered assurance by checking Japanese economic hegemony, if not directly, then by providing a counterbalance. By imposing an overwhelming military superiority, the American presence in the Japanese relationship has defused or even forestalled potential tensions between Asian states for years. Since the end of the Cold War, the United States has played a particularly welcome role in buffering the natural Sino-Japanese rivalry. During the Cold War, of course, America was not able to do this, but while the world was divided effectively into two camps, regional rivalries were hidden anyway. Fortunately when these rivalries began to assert themselves after the Cold War, the United States could shed its strong ideological perspective and focus on stability, not just serve Cold War strategy selectively, but universally. Indeed, the United States has effectively positioned itself as a natural check on any ambitious Asian power. It must seem to other Asian states that by comparison to Japan and China, the United States, if not quite the "benign power" described by Donald S. Zagoria of Columbia University's East Asian Institute, is nonetheless a relatively evenhanded one.[71]

Unfortunately, that subtle arrangement will not suit Japan's future needs. The treaty simply does not give her the room that she needs to secure her growing overseas interests, especially in Asia. This includes her industry resident abroad, her need for imports and overseas financial capital, and her facility to develop her place as headquarters nation in Asia's division of labor. Ultimately, Japanese foreign policy will mirror, on at least a regional scale, what American foreign policy does for America's diverse interests in most regions of the world. These considerations naturally will complicate notions of national security beyond straightforward concerns for the integrity of Japan's borders, as they have for America. Since there is little in the present Japanese-American arrangement that can accommodate these needs, the United States, if it were to insist on this old bilateral alliance, would face increasing friction with Japan over time. Eventually, Japan would have to break away of her own volition, and act entirely on her own. She may even seek an affiliation with another power in the region. Even Russia or China are possibilities, as former United States Ambassador to Japan, Michael Armacost, has pointed out.[72] Since no nation in the region would benefit from such a unilateral break, better that the United States accommodate Japan's needs by making the security arrangement looser and more flexible, than by trying to hold old patterns and tempting its complete dissolution.

Since this loosening of the Japanese-American link is inevitable, Asian stability will require new arrangements to replace the salutary aspects of that old relationship. These must keep the United States as an active player in Asia, as the old treaty has. America is the only secure mediator, buffer, and intimidator of intimidators, because it is the only nation with sufficient power to make the outcome of conflict obvious. While this kind of power is present, neither Japan nor China can position itself too aggressively against each other or any other Asian state. As one respected writer on security issues, Richard K. Betts of Columbia University, points out, the risk of confrontation is least when there is parity or clear dominance, as there is now. But without the powerful American presence, the temptations for competition and conflict will grow. Since there is no way to compare the very different strengths of China and Japan, no one could know which would prevail in a confrontation.[73] They could convince themselves of the potential for dominance. The impulse toward an arms buildup, though already considerable, would become that much more intense. Smaller Asian states would feel vulnerable and begin the dangerous game of lining up behind one or the other of these powers. Even more dangerous, they could try to play off one against the other.[74]

There are, of course, no perfect substitutes for the role that the United States has played in the security treaty with Japan. Nonetheless, it would seem that strong multilateral and supranational structures would provide the best alternative for Asia. If the United States and other nations in the region can foster collective security arrangements, if not necessarily collective defense treaties, then they might establish a formal means to hold the stabilizing American presence in Asia and use it to back institutions that are capable of resolving disputes and helping to check aggressive national ambitions. The switch toward a more multilateral security arrangement need not happen suddenly. It is probably best that the change come gradually, introducing the multilateral arrangements only as the bilateral Japanese-American link loosens. Japan should not object, since her needs for increased room to maneuver will only come in stages. Meanwhile, the multilateral arrangement could provide the added immediate benefit of creating a forum to resolve minor disputes within its membership, even as it ensures the stabilizing effect of the American power available to forestall major rivalries, confrontations, and attempts at political hegemony.

The specific institutional structure of such a multilateral arrangement is, of course, problematic. It is pointless to guess at or try at this stage to characterize it in detail. However, there are general aspects that would be essential for success. Obviously, the arrangement will have to pin American power in Asia, as the treaty with Japan has for so long. Beyond this, the arrangements would need as much of an East Asian flavor as possible. The UN, for example, embraces too many diverse interests to fulfill this role, despite Japan's strong predilection for this world body. Similarly, the new multilateral arrangement could prove unwieldy if it included such nations as India or Bangladesh, which, though Asian, have concerns very different from those of East Asia. For the nations of East Asia, membership should be as broad as possible without inviting intransigent conflicts, which would render it useless. A Pacific version of NATO would have a great attraction, because it would involve the kind of cohesion that it would need to serve the complex needs of the region. That is impossible in the present political climate. But if the arrangement cannot mirror NATO, it still would require something more substantive than the loose character that presently typifies Asian associations.

Developing such a cohesive multilateral device in East Asia doubtless will face significant hurdles. Unlike Europe, Asia has never shown itself amenable to international arrangements. Interests in the region have been too fragmented to allow a coalition of any breadth. The region includes nations with huge populations of over 100 million, like Japan and Indonesia, and small sultanates like Brunei. Some nations are rich in national resources, like Malaysia, and others have huge landmasses, like Russia, and, of course, China. Others, like Japan and Singapore, are both land and resource poor.[75] There are, of course, defense arrangements in this part of the world. The United States has alliances with five countries in the region, three of which—Australia, Japan, and South Korea—provide significant military facilities. But these are all bilateral relationships.[76] There is life left in the old, post-colonial, multilateral five-nation defense group, which includes Australia, Britain, Malaysia, New Zealand, and Singapore. It displays an ability to cooperate on major security issues in a mixed Western and Asian group.[77] But generally, multilateral efforts, even when they have shied away from political matters and stuck to trade, have faltered under Asia's diverse interests. Japan's 1965 proposal of a Pacific Free Trade Area went nowhere. A joint Japanese-Australian 1979 proposal for an Organization of Pacific Trade and Development (OPTAD) met resistance from ASEAN, which suspected Japanese and American collusion to dominate and force a political agenda. The separate 1980 proposals of Australia and the Soviet Union to create a Conference on Security and Cooperation in Asia (CSCA) to parallel the Conference on Security and Cooperation in Europe (CSCE) did not get off the ground, because members suspected Soviet manipulation of the agenda to oppose American maritime interests. In 1993, the Canadians proposed a North Pacific Cooperative Security Dialogue (NPCSD) to exchange information, but it died, largely from neglect. Also in 1993, the research institutes from a broad number of Pacific powers proposed the Council for Security Cooperation in the Asia Pacific (CSCAP), but it failed because of China's objection to the inclusion of Taiwan.

Still, for all this history of jealousy and competing interests, there are recent, if tentative signs of greater multilateral cooperation. In 1984, ASEAN formalized meetings between ministers of the ASEAN nations, the United States, Japan, Canada, Australia, New Zealand, and the European Community. In time this group, referred to as the ASEAN Post-Ministerial Conference (ASEAN-PMC), also included South Korea. This arrangement strengthened in the 1990s, as the nations in the area began to feel the post-Cold War pressures and perhaps also the increased potential for a Sino-Japanese rivalry. It became the ASEAN Regional Forum (ARF). This group (though at present mostly a talking shop without much of a charter and too broad to handle the critical Asian security issues) might form the basis of a stabilizing influence after the Japanese-American relationship no longer can. Extending a small hope in this regard, Harry Harding of the Elliot School of International Affairs at George Washington University has described ARF as "evolving into a Conference on Security Cooperation in Asia."[78] That might overstate matters today, but it is indeed encouraging. Adding further encouragement, the Japanese Prime Minster's Council on Japan and the Asia-Pacific Region for the Twenty-first Century has pushed an Asian equivalent to Europe's Conference on Security Cooperation in Europe and has identified ASEAN and the ARF as a starting place.[79] With Japanese support, and especially if ARF can work with the Asia-Pacific Economic Cooperation (APEC) Forum, the organization's incipient strength offers hope for success in building this critical new arrangement. ASEAN's resilience in the face of the recent economic and financial turmoil offers additional reassurance on the future ability of multilateral arrangements in the region.

A FINAL WORD ON RISK

As always in looking to the future, there are few assurances. Asia simply could fail to develop such a multilateral body and disintegrate into an anarchy of mutual suspicion as the Japanese-American relationship fades. It is also quite possible that the United States and Japan will try to cling to their security arrangement long after it impedes Japanese interests and, by doing so, turn what once brought stability to the region into a source of tension and instability. There are other risks to a successful smooth transition as well. The turmoil in Indonesia and Malaysia caused by Asia's financial and economic trouble, or in China, as it adjusts to its own development problems, or on the Korean peninsula, could tear the region apart long before Japan, the United States, the ASEAN nations, or any other player can make the necessary adjustments or build the institutions to deal with the pressure.

Even beyond the particularly difficult spheres of diplomacy and security, Japan could fail at any stage in her anticipated economic and financial adjustments. Japanese politics is not well suited to making the difficult choices facing the country, or to the inevitable social and economic strains that those choices will bring. Political leaders will face the constant temptation to retreat from reform and fight the inevitable and necessary change. The wavering path of Japanese economic and financial reform so far gives reason for at least some Western skepticism about Japan's ability to stay the course. Even with good will, the best intentions, and strong, wise leadership, circumstances will create ample room for mistakes and miscalculations, some of which, in Japan's group-oriented culture, could snowball into ugly situations. The risks are profound, and it would be folly to ignore them.

But for all the uncertainties and potential conflicts, there are, in the unfolding environment in Japan, clear trends that are pushing Japan to change along definable lines, disrupting trends to be sure, but certain nonetheless. These form the backbone of this book, and, they, too, should not be ignored. They are definite signposts for the future. Whether Japan is willing to change or not, she nonetheless must respond to the inexorable pressures of globalization, a maturing economy, and an aging population. If she wants to protect her economic and national well-being, she will have to open her economy and her financial markets; cease her absorbing emphasis on exporting manufactures; decentralize her approach to economics; allow her industry more freedom to manage its own affairs, including to move abroad; and develop her domestic economy into a regional management and service center. And, for all the understandable doubt, there is much evidence that the Japanese, their business community, and their leadership are beginning to take the steps demanded by the situation. Even if Japan fails to make each step as neatly, quickly, and effectively as she and the world might hope, there is still reason to expect her to respond to the challenge, as she has successfully to other challenges in her past. Doing so will transform her from the failed economic machine that she seems to have become in the late 1990s into a major power in every sense of that phrase.

NOTES

CHAPTER TWO: DESCENT FROM HEAVEN

1. T. R. Reid, "Kobe Wakes to a Nightmare," *National Geographic,* July 1995.
2. E. Kuribayshi et al., "A Comparative Study on Typical Measure of Earthquake Preparedness in Local Government Between Japan and the USA: Lessons from the Disaster of Japan's Earthquake in Kobe on 17 January 1995," *The Kobe Earthquake: Geodynamical Aspects,* ed. C. A. Brebbia (Boston: Computational Mechanics Publications, 1996).
3. Reid, "Kobe Wakes."
4. S. Takada and J. Uno, "Damage and Restoration of Lifelines During the 1995 Great Hanshin Earthquake," *The Kobe Earthquake: Geodynamical Aspects,* ed. C. A. Brebbia (Boston: Computational Mechanics Publications, 1996).
5. Masaki Otani, Letter to the Editor, *Time,* February 20, 1995.
6. Joshua Ogawa, "Nonlife Firms Survive Kobe Quake: Life Insurers Suffer Record Losses." *Japan Economic Almanac,* The Nikkei Weekly, Nihon Keizai Shimbun, 1996.
7. Tashio Shinmura, "Slow Response to Damage Reveals Inadequate Preparedness," *Japan Economic Almanac,* The Nikkei Weekly, Nihon Keizai Shimbun, 1996.
8. Reid, "Kobe Wakes."
9. Shinmura, "Slow Response to Damage."
10. All figures from Takada and Uno, "Damage and Restoration of Lifelines," and also, Kuribayshi et al., "Measures of Earthquake Preparedness."
11. Hajime Takano, "An Elegy to Civilization: A Halfway Summary of the Great Hanshin Disaster," *Insider Magazine,* Internet edition, February 13, 1995.
12. Ibid.
13. Ibid.
14. Reid, "Kobe Wakes."
15. *The New York Times,* webpage summary, January 22, 1995.
16. David Van Biema, "When Kobe Died," *Time,* January 30, 1995.
17. Reid, "Kobe Wakes."
18. Takano, "An Elegy to Civilization."
19. The author heard this story separately in several private conversations with people in business, financial, and academic circles. Though its authenticity is unver-

ified, it is indicative nonetheless of the sudden contempt held for the once-revered civil servants.

20. Cable News Network broadcast of January 31, 1995.
21. Takano, "An Elegy to Civilization."
22. *The Yomiuri Shimbun,* Internet posting, January 26, 1995.
23. Cable News Network broadcast of January 31, 1995.
24. Takano, "An Elegy to Civilization."
25. Kuribayshi et al., "Measures of Earthquake Preparedness."
26. Reid, "Kobe Wakes."
27. Both quotes drawn from private e-mail correspondence.
28. All quotes from Takano, "An Elegy to Civilization."
29. Quoted from "The Decline of Faith and Discipline," *The Economist,* November 18, 1995.
30. All references from "Chronology 1995," *Japan Economic Almanac,* The Nikkei Weekly, Nihon Keizai Shimbun, 1996.
31. Sachiko Sakamaki, "The Fight to Know," *Far Eastern Economic Review,* April 10, 1997.
32. Gerald Baker, "Arrest Is Part of a Tale of the Japanese 'Bubble'," *The Financial Times,* December 7, 1995.
33. "Seven Arrests Made Over 'Jusen' Loans," *The Japan Times,* June 27, 1996.
34. Sheryl Wu Dunn, "Big New Loss Makes Japan Look Inward," *The New York Times,* June 17, 1996.
35. "Okamitsu Admits Taking Bribes," *The Japan Times,* March 17, 1997.
36. For just one contemporary reference on this, see Gillian Tett, "Japan Widens Probe Into Finance Ministry," *The Financial Times,* February 4, 1998.
37. See Gwen Robinson, "Staff at Japan N-Plant Played Golf During Fire," *The Financial Times,* March 20, 1997; and also, Robinson, "Japanese Nuclear Officials Lied About Accident," *The Financial Times,* April 10, 1997.
38. *The New York Times,* webpage summary, January 22, 1995.
39. These and other comments on these pages come from personal observations and conversations in which the author took part or overheard.
40. Tett, "Suicide Rate Up as Japanese Troubles Grow," *The Financial Times,* June 1, 1998.
41. "The Decline of Faith."
42. "Americans Feel More Satisfied than Do Japanese, Poll Shows," *The Nikkei Weekly,* April 24, 1995.
43. "The Decline of Faith."
44. These and other observations reported here were gleaned firsthand by the author.
45. Principle Shigeto Tsuru, *Japan's Capitalism: Creative Defeat and Beyond* (Cambridge: Cambridge University Press, 1993), 3.
46. "Americans Feel More Satisfied."
47. For readers who are interested in delving deeply into the system in which Japan has lived (and progressed) since the Second World War, Chalmers Johnson, *MITI and the Japanese Miracle: The Growth of Industrial Policy 1925–1975* (Stanford: Stanford University Press, 1982) is a classic discussion. Eamonn Fin-

gleton's, *Blindside: Why Japan Is Still on Track to Overtake the U.S. by the Year 2000* (Boston: Houghton-Mifflin, 1995) gives a thorough discussion of its nature and strengths. Karel van Wolferen, *The Enigma of Japanese Power* (New York: Alfred A. Knopf, 1989) takes a more critical and negative view of Japan's approach as do: Yukio Noguchi, *1940 Taisei (The 1940 System)* (Tokyo: Toyo Keizai, 1995); Ichiro Ozawa, *Nihon Kaizo Keikaku (Blueprint for a New Japan)* (Tokyo: Kodansha, Ltd., 1994); and Masao Miyamoto, *Oyakusho no Okite (Straitjacket Society)* (Tokyo: Kodansha Ltd., 1995). R. Taggert Murphy takes a narrower, financial focus but offers insight about Japan's approach in *The Weight of the Yen* (New York: W. W. Norton, 1996). For more technical, less editorialized discussions, see: Tsuru, *Japan's Capitalism*; Takafusa Nakamura, *Nihon Keizai: Sono Seicho to Kozo (The Post War Japanese Economy, Its Development and Structure, 1937–1994)* (Tokyo: University of Tokyo Press, 1995); *Japan: A New Kind of Superpower?* eds. Craig Garby and Mary Brown Bullock (Washington, DC: The Woodrow Wilson Center Press, 1994); and Tsuru Kotaro, *Nehon-teki Shijo-Keizai System (The Japanese Market Economy System)* (Tokyo: Kodansha Ltd., 1994).

48. This point of historical analysis was stressed at some length by Ichiro Ozawa, Diet member and head of Japan's main opposition New Frontier party, in a talk given at the Council on Foreign Relations in New York on April 28, 1997, even as he forcefully advocated a liberalization of Japan's strict regulations.

49. See Marius B. Jansen, "The Meiji Restoration," in Marius B. Jansen (ed.) *The Emergence of Meiji Japan* (Cambridge: Cambridge University Press, 1995).

50. From Shinji Yashino, *Nihon Kogyo Seisaku,* quoted in Fingleton, *Blindside,* 252.

51. Tsuru, *Japan's Capitalism,* 9.

52. This speech on the terms of the U.S.-Japan Mutual Security Treaty, 1951, was quoted in Brian Reading, *Japan: The Coming Collapse* (London: Orion Books, 1993), 1.

53. Quoted from Fingleton, *Blindside,* 108.

54. Tsuru, *Japan's Capitalism,* 91.

55. Quote of the Japanese journalist, Takao Kawakita, from Fingleton, *Blindside,* 147.

56. Noribumi Tsukado and Hiroshi Fukunaga, "In Japan the War Is Over, But the 1940 System Lives On," *Tokyo Business Today,* September 1995.

57. Gardner Ackley and Hiromitsu Ishi, "Fiscal, Monetary and Related Policies," in *Asia's New Giant—How the Japanese Economy Works,* eds. Hugh Patrick and Henry Rosovsky (Washington, DC: The Brookings Institution, 1976), 236–7.

58. See Fingleton, *Blindside,* 252–4.

59. Tsuru, *Japan's Capitalism,* 105.

60. Explained to the author during a private conversation with a N.Y.S. Liquor Authority agent in the Shanger-La Bar, Park Avenue, Long Beach, New York, June 1968.

61. Fingleton, *Blindside,* 161.

62. Tsuru, *Japan's Capitalism,* 100–1.

63. Ibid., 108–9.

64. Fingleton, *Blindside,* 154; 174.

65. For chilling examples of how the press is controlled and used to bring down

politicians, see Fingleton, *Blindside,* 180–6; and also, van Wolferen, *The Enigma of Japanese Power,* 93–100.

66. Quoted from Fingleton, *Blindside,* 182; and appearing originally in *Mainichi Daily News,* June 20, 1993.
67. For a detailed and insightful study of the lack of official accountability in Japan, see van Wolferen, *The Enigma of Japanese Power,* 25–43; 202–20; 340–7.
68. Tsuru, *Japan's Capitalism,* 116–17.
69. Quoted from Tsuru, *Japan's Capitalism,* 104.
70. *Hojin Kigyo no Jittai (Facts and Statistics on Corporate Enterprises),* Ministry of Finance, 1990; 1995.
71. Joel Kotkin and Yoriko Kishimoto, *The Third Century: America's Resurgence in the Asian Era* (New York: Crown, 1988), 110.
72. See *Mainichi Daily News,* December 4, 1989; and *Osaki Evening News,* December 5, 1989.
73. Fingleton, *Blindside,* 196.
74. Yumiko Ono, *Asian Wall Street Journal,* October 5, 1992.
75. Murphy, *The Weight of the Yen,* 91.
76. Tsukado and Fukunaga, "The 1940 System Lives On."
77. Reading, *Japan: The Coming Collapse,* 225.
78. Fingleton, *Blindside,* 198.
79. For a complete study of these differences see Kiyohiko G. Nishimura, "The Distribution Systems of Japan and the United States: A Comparative Study from the Viewpoint of Final-Goods Buyers," *Japan and the World Economy* (Amsterdam: North Holland Press, 1993).
80. All price comparisons are based on the author's personal observations.
81. An understanding of the limited financial options available in Japan has come to the author through personal conversations and a failed attempt to establish a catalogue shopping scheme.
82. Junesay Iddittic, *The Life of Marquis Shigenobu Okuna: A Biographic Study in the Rise of Democratic Japan* (Tokyo: Hokuseido, 1951), 169–170.
83. Robert Keatley, *America and the World 1982* (New York: Pergamon Press, 1983), 704.
84. *BusinessWeek,* December 13, 1993.

CHAPTER THREE: THE BREAKDOWN OF OLD WAYS

1. Nikkei 225 Index of Japanese stocks. (Bloomberg Data Base, January 1999).
2. Data from the Real Estate Economy Institute published in *Quarterly Economic Review,* Nomura Research Institute, 1992; 1997.
3. Japanese GDP in 1998 averaged just under ¥500 trillion. GDP data from Japan's Economic Planning Agency. (Bloomberg Data Base, March 1999).
4. Quoted from Jathon Sapsford, "Japan's Obuchi Faces Defiance on Banking Bills," *Wall Street Journal,* August 6, 1998.
5. Yukiko Ohara of UBS Securities Ltd. in Tokyo, estimated bad debt at banks to be ¥100 trillion and 20–30 percent more at other financial institutions.
6. Japan's Economic Planning Agency data. (Bloomberg Data Base, January 1999).

7. U.S. Department of Commerce data. (Bloomberg Data Base, January 1999).

8. Nikkei 225 Index of Japanese stocks. (Bloomberg Data Base, January 1999).

9. Quoted from a private conversation between the author and Setsuya Tabuchi in January 1990, and also a popular reference at the time, much quoted in the Japanese and U.S. financial press.

10. In the first half of 1989, the Nikkei 225 Index equaled seventy times the earnings of its constituent companies for the previous four quarters, which were the best quarters for them as a group, ever. (Bloomberg Data Base, January 1999).

11. In 1993, the level of the S&P 500 stock index stood at just under twenty-five times the earnings of its constituent companies. (Bloomberg Data Base, January 1999).

12. Data from Japan's Economic Planning Agency. (Bloomberg Data Base, January 1999).

13. According to U.S. Department of Commerce data posted on the Bloomberg Data Base, during the four full recessions in the United States since 1967, the average decline in real GDP equaled 2.25 percent. In the U.S. recession of 1990–92 real GDP fell by 2 percent.

14. Unemployment in the United States by 1998 had declined to about 4.5 percent of the labor force. In Europe, the rate was still above 7 percent. (Japanese Ministry of Labor Statistic; U.S. Department of Labor Statistics; OECD statistics; from the Bloomberg Data Base, January 1999).

15. Bank of Japan releases. (Bloomberg Data Base, January 1999).

16. For a detailed description of Japan's admirable response during that difficult time, see: Takafusa Nakamura, *The Post War Japanese Economy*; and also, Takafusa Nakamura, *Lectures on Modern Japanese Economic History* 1926–1994 (Tokyo: LTCB International Library Foundation, 1994), lecture #6, "Emergence as an Economic Power," 227–262; lecture #7, "Economic Globalization," 263–283.

17. See Fingleton, *Blindside,* p. 12.

18. *International Financial Statistics* (International Monetary Fund, 1996).

19. From the mid-1950s to 1970, Japanese exports grew by over 16 percent a year without one year of decline. *International Financial Statistics,* (International Monetary Fund, 1971).

20. Japan's Economic Planning Agency. (Bloomberg Data Base, January 1999).

21. *International Financial Statistics* (International Monetary Fund, historic database, January 1999).

22. Statistics quoted from James Shinn, "Japan as an 'Ordinary Country'," *Current History,* December 1996.

23. Statistics quoted from Peter Possell, "Economic Scene," *The New York Times,* July 11, 1996.

24. Johsen Takahashi and Noriko Hawa, "An Economic Metamorphosis for Japan?" *Japan Quarterly,* July–September 1990.

25. *Economic Report of the President* (Council of Economic Advisors, 1997).

26. Figures quoted from "Bricklayers' Blues," *The Economist,* July 5, 1997; Nomura Research Institute, *Quarterly Economic Review,* May 1997; and Michiyo Nakamoto, "Hashimoto Takes a Political Gamble with Income Tax Cuts," *The Financial Times,* April 11–12, 1998.

27. The size of the spending package is from Ministry of Finance data. The under-lying deficit estimate is from the Organization for Economic Cooperation and Development excluding the social security surplus, which is clearly earmarked. All data quoted from Baker, "Japan Ready to Put Financial House in Order," *The Financial Times,* July 16, 1996.

28. McGraw-Hill Data Resources Data Base, January 1999.

29. Tsuru, *Japan's Capitalism,* 188.

30. Statistics quoted from Takafusa Nakamura, *The Post War Japanese Economy,* 223.

31. Ibid., 91.

32. Nakamoto, "Bureaucrats Pull Japanese Airline Strings," *The Financial Times,* May 22, 1997.

33. Science and Technology Agency, *Kagaku Gijutsu Hakusho* (*White Paper on Sci-ence and Technology,* 1991); and also, Takafusa Nakamura, *The Post War Japan-ese Economy,* 274.

34. Quoted from William Dawkins, "Japan Goes Back to the Drawing Board," *The Financial Times,* September 16, 1996.

35. Data drawn from daily trades. (Bloomberg Data Base, January 1999).

36. Official Bank of Japan Discount Rate from Nomura Research Institute, *Quar-terly Economic Review,* November 1992.

37. From December 1987 to December 1989, the yen fell by 18.5 percent against the U.S. dollar. (Bloomberg Data Base, January 1999).

38. Story told in Murray Weidenbaum, *Neoisolationism and Global Relations* (St. Louis: Center for the Study of American Business, Policy Study 130, May 1996), 2.

39. Kenichi Ohmae, "Vox Populi," *Far Eastern Economic Review,* March 30, 1997.

40. "Taking Stock," *Far Eastern Economic Review,* May 15, 1997.

41. Marlyn Williams, "Japanese Firms Spending Up To 13 percent More on IT," *Newsbytes News Network,* May 10, 1996.

42. *International Financial Statistics.*

43. Statistics quoted from Takafusa Nakamura, *The Post War Japanese Economy,* 247.

44. Baker, "Japan Bank to Ease Ties with Large Corporations," *The Financial Times,* July 12, 1996.

45. "Japanese Electronics, Fade to Black," *The Economist,* September 30, 1995.

46. Peter Landers, "Sharing the Wealth," *Far Eastern Economic Review,* May 21, 1997.

47. Japanese Economic Planning Agency data. (Bloomberg Data Base, January 1999).

48. Calculation in an Internal Strategy Memo, Nomura Investment Management Co., March 1997.

49. Japanese Economic Planning Agency data. (Bloomberg Data Base, January 1999).

50. Harumi Yamamoto, "The Lifetime Employment System Unravels," *Japan Quar-terly,* October–December 1993.

51. Ibid.

52. "Salariless Man," *The Economist,* September 16, 1995.

53. WuDunn, "When Lifetime Jobs Die Prematurely," *The New York Times,* June 12, 1996.

54. Nomura Research Institute, *Quarterly Economic Review,* August 1997.

55. WuDunn, "When Lifetime Jobs Die."

56. Tett, "Japanese Postal Arm to Cut Jobs," *The Financial Times,* August 15, 1997.

57. Yamamoto, "Lifetime Employment Unravels."

58. "Salariless Man."

59. Yamamoto, "Lifetime Employment Unravels."

60. Nakamoto, "Pay Deals Show Talks Trend," *The Financial Times,* April 10, 1997.

61. This point was explained hurriedly to the author in Tokyo's denke district by a discount merchant—not in rice but in electronic appliances. Since the defiant discounting has taken hold, official import and price restrictions have given way too.

62. Observation made firsthand by the author in a supermarket near Kamakura.

63. Figures quoted from David P. Hamilton, "New Imports: One Tokyo Family Loves Its Italian Shoes and American Broccoli," *Wall Street Journal,* March 14, 1997.

64. Susan MacKnight, "Japan's Changing Distribution System: Will It Help U.S. Exporters?" *Japan Economic Institute* Publication No. 23A, June 17, 1994.

65. Sakamaki, "The Malling of Japan," *Far Eastern Economic Review,* August 8, 1996.

66. Nakamura, *The Post War Japanese Economy,* 202.

67. Ibid., 203.

68. Ibid.

69. Reading, *Japan: The Coming Collapse,* 141.

70. van Wolferen, *The Enigma of Japanese Power,* 229.

CHAPTER FOUR: THE WAR BETWEEN REFORMERS AND BUREAUCRATS

1. Quoted from Mike Millard, "Can Japan Reform Itself?" *Tokyo Business Today,* September 1995.

2. Quoted from Gerry Evans, "Can Japan Change?" *Euromoney,* February 1994.

3. Ozawa, *Blueprint,* 11.

4. Quoted from Millard, "Can Japan Reform Itself?"

5. Ibid.

6. Ozawa, *Blueprint,* 199.

7. Ibid.

8. Quoted from Guy de Jonquières, "Of Pork Merchants and Rice Inspectors," *The Financial Times,* January 4, 1996.

9. Miyamoto, *Straitjacket Society,* 14.

10. Paul Kennedy, *The Rise and Fall of Great Powers: Economic Change and Military Conflict from 1500 to 2000* (New York: Random House, 1987).

11. Hiroshi Fukunaga, "Reform is Possible," *Tokyo Business Today*, September 1995.

12. Millard, "Can Japan Reform Itself?"

13. Takao Kichiro in "View from the Top," *Euromoney,* February 1994.

14. Shoichiro Toyoda, "The Need for a Vigorous Society," *The Japan Times,* June 27, 1996.

15. Johsen Takahashi, "Short Fuse Makes 'Big Bang' Action Urgent," *The Nikkei Weekly,* March 17, 1997.

16. Robert Alan Feldman, "The Golden Goose and the Silver Fox," *Economic Outlook,* Salomon Brothers, June 12, 1996.

17. Quoted from Michael Gonzalez, "Japan's Mini-Revolution," *Asian Wall Street Journal,* October 22, 1996.

18. Quoted from Landers, "Turncoat Technocrat," *Far Eastern Economic Review,* April 30, 1998.
19. Ozawa, *Blueprint,* 12.
20. "Give State Tasks to Local Authorities: Panel," *The Japan Times,* December 21, 1996.
21. Hiroshi Kato, "Fiscal Crisis is on the Horizon," *Sankei Shimbun,* November 24, 1995.
22. Noguchi, *1940 Taisei.*
23. Quoted from Tsukado and Fukunaga, "1940 System Lives On."
24. Noguchi, *1940 Taisei,* 138.
25. Noguchi, *1940 Taisei,* 132.
26. Noguchi, *1940 Taisei,* 96.
27. Ozawa, *Blueprint,* 3.
28. Ozawa, "The Third Opening," *The Economist,* March 9, 1996.
29. Ozawa, *Blueprint,* 12.
30. Minoru Tada, "Reliable Opposition Needed," *The Japan Times,* March 29, 1996.
31. Ozawa, "The Third Opening."
32. Sakamaki, "The Fight to Know," *Far Eastern Economic Review,* April 10, 1997.
33. Ibid.
34. Ibid.
35. Ibid.
36. Fukunaga, "Reform is Possible."
37. Quoted from David Shirreff, "MOF Clings to the Same Old Levers," *Euromoney,* February 1994.
38. Quoted from Baker, "Japan's Way of Government Under Review," *The Financial Times,* February 9, 1996.
39. Quoted from Shirreff, "Bureaucrat Bites Back," *Euromoney,* February 1994.
40. Bunji Kure, "Orderly Liberalization of Financial Markets," *Economic Eye,* March 1984.
41. Toyoo Gyohten in "View from the Top," *Euromoney,* February 1994.
42. Quoted from Sakamaki, "Mr. Yen Moves Up," *Far Eastern Economic Review,* July 17, 1997.
43. Quoted from Shirreff, "MOF Clings."
44. Ibid.
45. Ibid.
46. Atsuo Hiraro in "View from the Top," *Euromoney,* February 1994.
47. Leon Hollerman, "The Headquarters Nation," *The National Interest,* Fall 1991.
48. Fingleton, "Japan's Invisible Leviathan," *Foreign Affairs,* March/April 1995.
49. van Wolferen, "No Brakes, No Compass," *The National Interest,* Fall 1991.
50. For seminal work on the first school of thought, see Johnson, *MITI and the Japanese Miracle.* For a more popular treatment of this view on the power of Japan's bureaucracy within her system, see James Fallows, *More Like Us* (Boston: Houghton-Mifflin, 1989). For other recent works along these lines, see Chalmers Johnson and Barry Keehn, "Rational Choice and Asian Studies," *The National Interest,* Summer 1994; Fingleton, *Blindside*; Johnson, *Japan: Who Governs? The Rise of the Developmental State* (New York: W. W. Norton, 1995); and

also, Fingleton, "Japan's Invisible Leviathan." For a particularly forceful expression of this kind of thinking, see Hollerman, "The Headquarters Nation." For the most comprehensive statement of the alternative thinking on Japanese bureaucracy, see van Wolferen, *The Enigma of Japanese Power*; van Wolferen, "No Brakes, No Compass"; and also, Murphy, *The Weight of the Yen.* For excellent balanced reviews of both schools of thought, see Ivan Hall, "Samurai Legacies, American Illusions," *The National Interest,* Summer 1992; and Murphy, "Making Sense of Japan," *The National Interest,* Spring 1996.

51. For an authoritative review of this and other scandals of the time, see Masumi Fukatsu, "Political Reform's Path of No Return," *Japan Quarterly,* July–September 1994.

52. See, for example, "Corruptions and Ambiguous Japan," *The Japan Times,* March 26, 1997.

53. For a detailed account of these events, see Fukatsu, "Political Reform's Path"; and also, Jacob M. Schlesinger, *Shadow Shoguns: The Rise and Fall of Japan's Post-War Political Machine* (New York: Simon and Schuster, 1997).

54. Fukatsu, "Political Reform's Path."

55. "A Reformer Falls in Japan," *The New York Times,* April 9, 1994.

56. "Reform Won't Change Japan After All," *The Economist,* July 13, 1996.

57. William Dawkins, Michiyo Nakamoto, and Gwen Robinson, "LDP Gains Fail to Seal Majority in Japanese Vote," *The Financial Times,* October 21, 1996.

58. Ryutaro Hashimoto, *A Vision of Japan: A Realistic Direction for the 21st Century* (Tokyo: Bestsellers, 1993).

59. "Hashimoto's Japan," *The Economist,* January 13, 1996.

60. Dawkins, "Japan's Old Guard Makes a Clean Sweep," *The Financial Times,* November 8, 1996.

61. See Dawkins, "Japan's Old Guard"; and also, Sebastian Moffett, "Creative Tensions," *Far Eastern Economic Review,* November 21, 1996.

62. Robinson, "Stir in Japan as Sato Gets Cabinet Post," *The Financial Times,* September 12, 1997.

63. Moffett, "Creative Tensions."

64. Moffett, "Back to the Future," *Far Eastern Economic Review,* October 31, 1996.

65. Quoted from Moffett, "Back to the Future."

66. Dawkins, "Tokyo Finance Ministry Under Threat," *The Financial Times,* February 8, 1996.

67. See Benjamin Fulford, "Proposals Likely to Trim, Not End, Bureaucratic Control of Fiscal Policy," *Japan Economic Almanac,* The Nikkei Weekly, Nihon Keizai Shimbun, 1997; and also, Sapsford, "Japan Leaders to Divide Finance Ministry," *Asian Wall Street Journal,* September 26, 1996.

68. Sapsford, "Japan Leaders to Divide Finance Ministry."

69. "Who's the Boss?" *The Financial Times,* January 27, 1998.

70. Bloomberg Newswire, Bloomberg Data Base, May 22, 1997.

71. William Dawkins and Richard Lambert, "Bank of Japan Set to Win Greater Self Rule," *The Financial Times,* February 6, 1997.

72. For a detailed analysis of all the proposals, see Jathon Sapsford and Bill Spindle, "Japan to Unveil Financial Market Reform," *Wall Street Journal,* June 12,

1997, and "FT Guide to: Japan's 'Big Bang'," *The Financial Times,* May 5, 1997.

73. Dawkins, "Deregulation Moves Approved," The Financial Times, March 29–30, 1997.

74. Tett, "Japanese Parliament Set To Legalize Stock Options," *The Financial Times,* May 8, 1997.

75. James Paradise, "Pressure for Change," *Far Eastern Economic Review,* July 25, 1996.

76. Dawkins, "Japan Weighs Plan to Lift Economic Controls," *The Financial Times,* July 13–14, 1996.

77. "Japan," *SBC Warberg,* November 14, 1996.

78. "Give State Tasks to Local Authorities: Panel," *The Japan Times,* December 21, 1996.

79. For a review of the initial phase of the "Program," see "Government Adopts Deregulation Steps," *The Japan Times,* March 30, 1996.

80. Dawkins, "Japan Weighs Plan."

81. "Unwinding Red Tape," *The Economist,* April 12, 1997.

82. Nakamoto, "Japanese Insurance Price Controls Axed," *The Financial Times,* February 25, 1997.

83. Sapsford, "Japan's Hashimoto Orders New Reforms to Bolster Sluggish Real Estate Market," *Wall Street Journal,* March 19, 1997.

84. Sapsford, "Japan's Measures on Fiscal Overhaul Have Lost Their Punch," *Wall Street Journal,* March 11, 1997.

85. "Japan," *SBC Warberg,* November 14, 1996.

86. Makoto Sato, "Diet Plan to Audit Bureaucracy Shelved," *The Nikkei Weekly,* March 17, 1997.

87. John Plender, "Fear of Collateral Damage," *The Financial Times,* April 1, 1997.

88. Ryu Kumite, *Asahi Shimbun,* December 19, 1996.

89. Robinson, "Hashimoto Loses First Round in Battle with the Bureaucracy," *The Financial Times,* August 23–24, 1997.

CHAPTER FIVE: GROWING OLD IN YOUTHFUL ASIA

1. Survey results drawn from Sakamaki, "No, Thanks," *Far Eastern Economic Review,* April 3, 1997 and "Births at Record Low," *Japan Economic Almanac,* 1997.

2. Statistics drawn from Douglas Ostrom, "Babies Grow Up: The Changing Demographics of the Japanese Labor Force," *Japan Economic Institute Report,* No. 32A, August 23, 1996.

3. N. Ogawa, "Impact of Change in Population and Household Structure Upon the Allocation of Medical Resources in Japan," in *Japan and the World Economy* (Amsterdam: North Holland Press, 1993), 139.

4. Ministry of Labor, Rodo Hakusho (*Labor White Paper*) (Tokyo: 1996), 53; 56.

5. Statistics drawn from Ostrom, "Babies Grow Up."

6. Ibid.

7. Ogawa, "Impact of Change in Population," 153.

8. Statistics drawn from Ostrom, "Babies Grow Up."

9. According to the Ministry of Labor figures, men constitute some 64 percent of the Japanese workforce and women 36 percent. The 10 percentage point increase required for Japanese women's participation to equal that of their

American counterparts, would therefore add about 7 percent to the total available Japanese labor force, thus increasing the workers per retiree by only one-tenth of a percent from 1.4 to 1.5.

10. Economic Planning Agency Economic Welfare Bureau edition, *Choju Sakai No Kozu, Jinsei 80-Nen Jidai No Keizai Shakai System Kochiko No Hoko* (*Plan for a Long-Life Society, Toward Building a Socio-Economic System Fit for the 80-Year Life*) (Tokyo: Government Printing Office, 1986).

11. Statistics drawn from James H. Schulz, Allan Borowski, and William H. Crown, *Economics of Population Aging* (New York: Auburn House, 1991), 128.

12. Ibid., 324.

13. Ibid., 146.

14. Naoki Tanaka, "Gendai No Shakai System A Jinsei 80 Nen Jidai Ni Miatte Iruka" (Is the Contemporary Social System Compatible with the 80-Year Life Era?), in Seimei Hoken Bunka Center (Life Insurance Culture Center) edition, *Choji Shakai A Sentaku No Jidai* (*The Long-Life Society Is the Time of Options*) (Seimei Hoken Bunka Center, 1988).

15. McGraw-Hill Data Resources Data Base, January 1999.

16. McGraw-Hill Data Resources Data Base, January 1999.

17. According to Japan's Economic Planing Agency, Japanese savings in 1997 equaled about 18 percent of GDP and exports equaled about 6 percent. Japan's overall GDP expanded by 4.6 percent per year during the second half of the 1980s, excluding the effects of inflation, and by 1.3 percent per year in the first seven years of the 1990s. A growth rate of 4.6 percent per year compounds to 17 percent in three years and nine months, while a growth rate of 1.3 percent per year compounds to 17 percent in thirteen years.

18. For an excellent detailed analysis and calculations of these potential shortfalls in Japan's standard of living, see Feldman, "The Golden Goose."

19. An alternate means for calculating the 8.1 percent decrease in the proportion of the working-aged population is to compare it to the overall proportion of the population in that age group only. The figure 8.1 as a percent of 62.7—the starting proportion of people available for work—comes to just under 13 percent.

20. Productivity growth at the 1990s rate of 0.6 percent per year compounds to 15 percent in about twenty-five years.

21. McGraw-Hill Data Resources Data Base, January 1999.

22. Kathy M. Matsui, "A Changing Playing Field for Pension Funding," *Barrons,* July 8, 1996.

23. "Japan's Debt-Ridden Future," *The Economist,* August 3, 1996.

24. Calculated from data from Russell Jones, "Japan's Pension Dilemma," *Japan Monetary Bulletin,* Lehman Brothers Global Economics, April 22, 1996; Japan's Economic Planning Agency figures on the Bloomberg Data Base, and (*Statistical Yearbook* Government of Japan, 1997).

25. "Effect of Aging Populations on Government Budgets," *Outlook,* Organization for Economic Cooperation on Development, June 1995.

26. Yoshiro Hayashi, "The Medical Care System in an Aging Society," in *Japan and the World Economy* (Amsterdam: North Holland Press, 1993), 175.

27. Ministry of Health and Welfare, *Kokumin Eisei no Doko* (*Health State of the*

Nation, Annual Report) (Kosei Tokei Kyokai, 1990).

28. Ogawa, "Impact of Changes in Population," 145.
29. Hayashi, "The Medical Care System," 177.
30. Yahuki Kobayashi and Michael R. Reich, "Health Care Financing for the Elderly in Japan," *Social Science Medicine* (London: Pergamon Press, 1993), 347.
31. Ibid., 344.
32. Both figures quoted from "Japan's Debt-Ridden Future"; and verified by telephone contact with the ministries.
33. Ministry of Finance figures from *Capital Market Trends* (Nomura Research Institute, March 1998).
34. "Effects of Aging Populations."
35. *Economic Report of the President, 1997.*
36. "Effects of Aging Populations."
37. Martin Wolf, "Japan Looks to Asia," *The Financial Times,* June 11, 1996.
38. "Asian Enterprises Looking Strong," *Japan Times,* June 27, 1996.
39. Berhard Eschwieler, "Japan's New Wave of Foreign Direct Investment," *Asian Financial Markets,* Morgan Guarantee Trust Company, October 18, 1996.
40. Quoted from "Indicators," *Far Eastern Economic Review,* August 1, 1996.
41. Survey, *World Money,* April 1996.
42. "The Discreet Charm of Provincial Asia," *The Economist,* April 27, 1996.
43. These deals and arrangements are catalogued in Sato, "Diversification Into Non-Japanese Deals Becoming Key to Profits, Survival," *Japan Economic Almanac,* The Nikkei Weekly, Nihon Keizai Shimbun, 1996.
44. Internal Memoranda, Sharp Corporation, Business Planning Area, Tokyo, 1996.
45. "Asian Enterprises Looking Strong."
46. *Japan Economic Almanac,* The Nikkei Weekly, Nihon Keizai Shimbun, 1996; 1997.
47. Sumic Kawakami, "Exporting a Surplus," *Far Eastern Economic Review,* July 4, 1996.
48. "The Discreet Charm of Provincial Asia," *The Economist,* April 27, 1996.
49. Kawakami, "Exporting a Surplus."
50. Edward J. Lincoln, *Japan's New Global Role* (Washington, DC: The Brookings Institution, 1993), 165.
51. Masato Ishizawa, "Industry Shifts More High-Tech R&D Overseas to Top Foreign Talent Pool," *Japan Economic Almanac,* The Nikkei Weekly, Nihon Keizai Shimbun, 1996.
52. Wolf, "Japan Looks to Asia."
53. Kawakami, "Exporting a Surplus."
54. Lincoln, *Japan's New Global Role,* 177.
55. Economic Planning Agency, *Ajia Taiheiyo Chi'iki* (Ministry of Finance Printing Office, 1989), 96.
56. Statistics quoted from James Harding, "Shanghai Finds Japanese Easy To Do Business With," *The Financial Times,* April 9, 1997.
57. Lincoln, *Japan's New Global Role,* 167.
58. Kawakami, "Exporting a Surplus."
59. *Survey,* Japanese External Trade Organization, June 21, 1996.
60. Ibid.

61. Dawkins, "Moving Abroad," *Financial Times,* December 5, 1996.
62. Lincoln, *Japan's New Global Role,* 165.
63. See Yoshiaki Nakamura and Minoru Shibuya, *The Hollowing Out Phenomenon in the Japanese Industry,* Studies in Trade and Industry No. 19 (Research Institute of Trade and Industry, Ministry of International Trade and Industry, 1995).

CHAPTER SIX: FINANCING CHANGE

1. Although I am told that, in Japan, this phrase has been in use since the 1930s, the first major use of it in modern Western discussion of Japan was in Hollerman, "The Headquarters Nation." I use it here in a more comprehensive way than Hollerman did in his essay.
2. See technical discussions of population projections in *Japan Statistical Yearbook* (Ministry of Health and Welfare, 1997); (*Current Population Reports* (Bureau of the Census, 1997); and *World Population Prospect* (United Nations, 1996).
3. Tsuru, *Japan's Capitalism,* 112–13.
4. *National Accounts* (Japan's Economic Planning Agency, 1997).
5. Referenced in "Current Ideas on Japan," *The Financial Times,* March 12, 1996.
6. MacKnight, "Japan's Changing Distribution System."
7. Quoted from "Current Ideas on Japan," *The Financial Times,* March 12, 1996.
8. Dawkins, "Foreign Groups Thrive in Japan," *The Financial Times,* January 19, 1996.
9. *Japan Statistical Yearbook* (Statistical Bureau of the Management Coordination Agency, 1997).
10. *National Accounts* (Japan's Economic Planning Agency, 1998).
11. *Survey of Current Business* (United States Bureau of Economic Analysis, April 1998).
12. "Manufacturing Could Fall," *The Nikkei Weekly,* October 18, 1995.
13. Reference from Hollerman, *Japan Disincorporated: The Economic Liberalization Process* (Stanford: Hoover Institution, 1988), 137.
14. Economic Planning Agency, *Ajia Taiheiyo Chi iki—Han ei no Tetsugaku: Sogo Kokuryoku no Kanten Kara Mita Nihon no Yakuwari* (*The Asia-Pacific Region—The Philosophy of Prosperity: Japan's Role Seen from the Viewpoint of Overall National Power*) (Tokyo: Ministry of Finance Printing Office, 1991).
15. Internal papers were described to the author during private meetings with Bank of Japan officials. See also Bank of Japan, *Annual Report 1995,* 28–65.
16. Quoted from Patrick Smith, Becoming Nihonjin (New York: Pantheon Books, 1997), 101.
17. "Back to Basics in Japan," *The Economist,* May 25, 1996; and also, Jon Choy, "Research and Development in Japan: Back to Basics," Japan Economic Institute Report, September 27, 1996.
18. Quoted from Patrick Smith, *Becoming Nihonjin,* 103.
19. Quoted from "The Struggle to Create Creativity," *The Economist,* June 28, 1997.
20. "Back to Basics in Japan."
21. Nakamoto, "Launching a Challenge," *The Financial Times,* December 5, 1996.
22. Choy, "Research and Development in Japan."
23. Fingleton, *Blindside,* 319.

24. Steve Glain, "Japan's Trading Giants Spark Venture-Capital Boom," *Wall Street Journal,* May 15, 1997.
25. Nakamoto, "Cable Operator Breaks into Japanese Telecoms," *The Financial Times,* October 1, 1996.
26. Nakamoto, "Toyota in Talks Over World Wide Telecoms Alliance," *The Financial Times,* January 15, 1997.
27. Dawkins, "Time to Pull Back the Screen," *The Financial Times,* November 18, 1996.
28. Quoted from Steve Glain, "Japan's Trading Giants."
29. Gonzalez, "Japanese Banks Get One Right," *Wall Street Journal,* January 5, 1996.
30. These references are all drawn from Landers, "Venture Vanguard," *Far Eastern Economic Review,* July 31, 1997.
31. Landers, "Opening Markets," *Far Eastern Economic Review,* July 24, 1997.
32. Fumio Sumiya, "Shift to Production Abroad Weakens Keiretsu Ties Among Parts Markets," *Japan Economic Almanac,* 1996.
33. "Fabulous and Fabless," *The Economist,* March 29, 1997.
34. "Shareholders' Benefit Takes Priority," *The Nikkei Weekly,* May 7, 1996.
35. Atsushi Yamakoshi, "Restructuring, Reengineering, and Japan's Management System," *Japan Economic Institute Report,* July 5, 1996.
36. Akio Mikuni, "A New Era for Japanese Finance," *Asian Wall Street Journal,* July 2–3, 1993.
37. Murphy, *The Weight of the Yen,* 176.
38. "Tokyo Summit no Goshen to Moon" (The Misreading and Burden of the Tokyo Summit), *Asahi Shimbun,* May 7, 1986.
39. "Shunju" Column, *Nihon Keizai Shimbun,* May 8, 1986.
40. Quoted from Murphy, *The Weight of the Yen,* 202.
41. Ibid., 185.
42. Fingleton, *Blindside,* 285.
43. Richard C. Koo, "Battling the Weak Yen Demon," *The International Economy,* July/August 1996.
44. Murphy, *The Weight of the Yen.*
45. This theme has formed the basis of numerous books and articles. In addition to Murphy's very readable work, a detailed and scholarly description of the Japanese policy and its interaction with American deficits can be found in Takafusa Nakamura, *Lectures on Modern Japanese Economic History,* 287–90.
46. George Melloan, "Is There a Cloud of Deflation Blowing Up from Asia?" *Wall Street Journal,* November 25, 1997.
47. *The World Economy and Financial Market in 1995: Japan's Role and Challenges* (Tokyo: Nomura Research Institute, 1996), 127.
48. Fingleton, *Blindside,* 285.
49. Ibid., 287.
50. Study quoted from Murphy, *The Weight of the Yen,* 153.
51. Toru Iwami, *Japan in the International Financial System* (New York: St. Martin's Press, 1995), 85.
52. This partial list is drawn from a complete discussion in: Dilipk Das, *The Yen Appreciation and the International Economy* (New York: Macmillan, 1993), 82–3,

and also, Masana Haegawa, "Reform of Financial and Capital Market System: Further Improvement of Market Mechanisms Takes on New Urgency," in *Capital Markets and Financial Services in Japan: Regulation and Practice* (Tokyo: Japan Securities Research Institute, 1995), 176–9.

53. "Hashimoto Wants Europeans to Have a 'Major Currency'," *The International Herald Tribune,* June 26, 1997.

54. See Tett, "Japan Says It Will Intervene to Back Baht," *The Financial Times,* July 19–20, 1997; and also, Sapsford, "Japan's Banks Will Keep Asian Spigot Flowing and Help Avoid Credit Crunch," *Wall Street Journal,* September 8, 1997.

55. See Lionel Barber, "Japan Pushes Regional Rescue Fund," *The Financial Times,* September 23, 1997; and also, "Japan to the Rescue," *The Economist,* October 11, 1997.

56. See Tett, "Japan Tries to Calm Fears Over Regional Fund," *The Financial Times,* September 25, 1997; and also, Gillian Tett, John Ridding, and Ted Bardacke, "Idea Whose Time Has Come," *The Financial Times,* October 9, 1997.

57. See Darren McDermott and Pierre Goad, "Asian Bailout-Fund Idea Sprouts Strings," *Asian Wall Street Journal,* September 24, 1997.

58. See Iwami, *Japan in the International Financial System,* 82.

59. For a thorough description of the policy shifts during this period, see: Iwami, *Japan in the International Financial System,* 82–4; and also, Masaru Tanaka, "Foreign Exchange Market: Deregulation and Development," in *Capital Markets and Financial Services in Japan: Regulation and Practice* (Tokyo: Japan Securities Research Institute, 1992).

CHAPTER SEVEN: DIPLOMACY, ARMS, AND ASIAN INVESTMENTS

1. For a complete review of Japan's diplomatic links in Asia or lack thereof during this time, see Takashi Inoguchi, "Distant Neighbors? Japan and Asia," *Current History,* November 1995.

2. See Michael Vatikiokis et al., "Fears of Influence," *Far Eastern Economic Review,* January 30, 1997.

3. While this is a very popular story in Japan, told frequently in business, financial, government, and academic circles, the author has never found a reliable source to verify its truth.

4. The Mahan quote and an excellent analysis of late nineteenth-century Japanese thinking are offered in Jansen, *The Emergence of Meiji Japan,* 272.

5. For a broad-based discussion of "comprehensive national security" in the context of Japan's strategic objectives, see Walter Hatch and Kozo Yamamura, *Asia in Japan's Embrace* (Cambridge: Cambridge University Press, 1996), 115–29. For a discussion of Japanese foreign aid, see Susan J. Pharr, "Japanese Aid in the New World Order"; and for more common notions of security, see Peter J. Katzenstein and Nobuo Okawara, "Japanese Security Issues," both in *Japan: A New Kind of Superpower?* eds. Garby and Brown Bullock, (Washington, DC: The Woodrow Wilson Center Press, 1994).

6. For a detailed description of this phase of Japan's foreign aid program, see Lincoln, *Japan's New Global Role,* 219–20.

7. Statistics for the Japanese Ministry of Foreign Affairs and the U.S. State Department, quoted from: Robinson, "Japan to Lose Top Donor Title," *The Financial Times,* April 9, 1997; Economist Intelligence Unit, "Japan: International Relations and Defense," in *EIU Country Profile 1996–1997* (London: Economic Intelligence Unit, 1996), 47; and also, Ministry of Foreign Affairs, *Japan's ODA Annual Report 1997.*

8. *Japan Times Weekly Overseas Edition,* April 15, 1989.

9. Quoted from Shinichi Kitaoka, "What Nonmilitary Assistance Can and Cannot Accomplish," *Economic Eye,* Summer 1991.

10. Statistic quoted from Mike M. Mochizuki, "Japan as an Asia-Pacific Power," in *East Asia in Transition,* ed. Robert S. Ross (Armonk, NY: M. E. Sharpe, 1995).

11. *Geographical Distribution of Financial Flows to Developing Countries 1987/90* (Paris: OECD, 1992).

12. Statistics quoted from Kitaoka, "What Nonmilitary Assistance Can and Cannot Accomplish."

13. Statistics quoted from Hatch and Yamamura, *Asia in Japan's Embrace,* 131.

14. James Sterngold, "Japan Builds East Asia Links, Gaining Labor and Markets," *The New York Times,* May 8, 1990.

15. Lincoln, *Japan's New Global Role,* 145.

16. *Development Cooperation,* 1992 Report (Paris: OECD, 1992), A72.

17. *Japan's Official Development Assistance ODA 1989 Annual Report,* Ministry of Foreign Affairs (Tokyo: Association for Promotion of International Cooperation, 1990), 111.

18. Alexander R. Lone, *Development Cooperation: Effects and Policies of the Members of the Development Assistance Committee, 1993 Report* (Paris: OECD, 1994), 119.

19. Mochizuki, "Japan as an Asia-Pacific Power."

20. Lone, *Development Cooperation,* 119.

21. Margee Ensign, *Doing Good or Doing Well? Japan's Foreign Aid Program* (New York: Columbia University Press, 1992), 59.

22. Observation made by Tan Siew Hoey of the quasi-government Institute of Strategic and International Studies in Kuala Lumpur, quoted from Hatch and Yamamura, *Asia in Japan's Embrace,* 141.

23. Hatch and Yamamura, *Asia in Japan's Embrace,* 130.

24. Ibid., 138.

25. Ibid., 123.

26. Ibid., 145.

27. Dan Biers, "A New Japanese Co-Prosperity Captures East Asia," *Seattle Post Intelligencer,* November 25, 1991.

28. Quoted from Hatch and Yamamura, *Asia in Japan's Embrace,* 40.

29. Bruce Gilley, "Polite But Firm," *Far Eastern Economic Review,* May 29, 1997.

30. Oda Toshino, "Practical Business Approach to Vietnam and the International Synergy," remarks on a discussion in Tokyo sponsored by the American Chamber of Commerce in Japan, November 15, 1993.

31. Quoted from Vatikiokis et al., "Fears of Influence."

32. Jeffrey Frankel, "Unblocking the Yen," *The Economist,* November 16, 1991.

33. For details, see Thomas U. Berger, "From Sword to Chrysanthemum," in *East Asian Security,* eds. Michael E. Brown, Sean M. Lynn-Jones, and Steven E. Miller (Cambridge, MA: MIT Press, 1996).

34. For details, see Mochizuki, "Japan as an Asia-Pacific Power."

35. Quoted from "The Growth Triangle," *Business Times* (Kuala Lumpur), April 15, 1992.

36. Rajan Menon, "The Once and Future Superpower," *The Bulletin of Atomic Scientists,* January/February 1997.

37. See Peter Landers, Susan Lawrence, and Julian Baum, "Hard Target," *Far Eastern Economic Review,* September 24, 1998.

38. Mochizuki, "Japan as an Asia-Pacific Power."

39. Economist Intelligence Unit, "Japan: International Relations and Defense," 10.

40. Figure quoted from Marcus W. Brauchli, "Polled American, Japanese Have China on Their Mind," *Wall Street Journal,* June 16, 1997.

41. This paper is described in detail in Economist Intelligence Unit, "Japan International Relations and Defense," 10.

42. Quoted from Michael Richardson, "Seapower: The New Lure for East Asia," *International Herald Tribune,* September 28, 1996.

43. Figures from paper quoted from Robinson, "Call to Revise Japan's Pacifist Constitution," *The Financial Times,* July 7, 1997.

44. Figures quoted from Neil Renwick, *Japan's Alliance, Politics, and Defense Production* (Oxford: Oxford University Press, 1995), 111–112; and also, Nigel Holloway and Charles Bickers, "Brothers in Arms," *Far Eastern Economic Review,* March 13, 1997.

45. Quoted from Nigel Holloway, "Touchy Issue," *Far Eastern Economic Review,* October 23, 1997.

46. Figures quoted from Charles Wolf, Jr, "Asia in 2015," *Wall Street Journal,* March 20, 1997. Mr. Wolf is dean of the Rand Graduate School of Policy Studies.

47. James Kynge, "Beijing to Embrace ASEAN in Pursuit of a New Order," *The Financial Times,* August 25, 1997.

48. For an excellent, quick survey of the nationalist trends in China and its literature, see Matt Forney, "Patriot Games," *Far Eastern Economic Review,* October 3, 1996.

49. Quoted from "Between the Dragon and the Deep Blue Sea," *The Economist,* July 13, 1996.

50. *Budget of the United States, FY1997* (Washington, DC: U.S. Government Printing Office, 1996).

51. Figures quoted from Satoshi Isaka, "Alliance with U.S. Remains Key to Maintaining East Asian Security," *Japan Economic Almanac,* 1996.

52. Robert Delfs and Michael Vatikiokis, "Low-Key Diplomacy," *Far Eastern Economic Review,* January 14, 1993.

53. Richard Halloran, "Military Trim," *Far Eastern Economic Review,* February 6, 1997.

54. Quoted from "Between the Dragon."

55. Quoted from Delfs and Vatikiokis, "Low-Key Diplomacy."

56. Figures quoted from Richard K. Betts, "Wealth, Power, and Conflict: East Asia After the Cold War," in *East Asia in Transition,* ed. Robert S. Ross (Armonk, NY: M. E. Sharpe, 1995).

57. Quoted from Charles Bickers, "Bear Market," *Far Eastern Economic Review,* September 4, 1997.
58. Figures quoted from Betts, "Wealth, Power and Conflict."
59. "Taiwan War Games Show Military Might," *The Japan Times,* June 24, 1997.
60. "Querying About S. Korean Missile Plans," *Xinhua News Service,* December 2, 1996.
61. Jeremy Grant, "Vietnam Briefs ASEAN on Row with Beijing," *The Financial Times,* March 21, 1997.
62. "Scraply Islands," *The Economist,* May 24, 1997.
63. Gordon Fairclough, "Floating Flashpoint," *Far Eastern Economic Review,* March 13, 1997.
64. For a quick review of this work, see David Harries, "Asia's New Arms Race," *Far Eastern Economic Review,* July 17, 1997.
65. Comment of an anonymous Indonesian official, quoted from John McBeth, "Exercising Sovereignty," *Far Eastern Economic Review,* September 19, 1996.
66. Figures quoted from James E. Auer, *The Postwar Rearmament of Japanese Maritime Forces, 1945–1971* (New York: Praeger, 1973), 64–6.
67. Moffett, "Back to the Barracks," *Far Eastern Economic Review,* September 19, 1996.
68. Johnson, *Japan In Search of a "Normal" Role,* University of California Policy Paper No. 3 (Institute on Global Conflict and Cooperation, July 1992), 24.
69. For a careful investigation of this line of thinking, see Tamotsu Aoki, *Nihon Bunka-ron no Henyo* (*Transformation of the Theory of Japanese Culture*) (Tokyo: Chuo Konon-sha, 1990), 7–16.
70. For a description of the circumstances surrounding the law enabling the SDF, see Peter J. Katzenstein, Cultural Norms and National Security (Ithaca, NY: Cornell University Press, 1996), 133.
71. Katzenstein, *Cultural Norms and National Security,* 146.
72. Katzenstein, *Cultural Norms and National Security*, 132.
73. Figures quoted from Berger, "From Sword to Chrysanthemum."
74. This sequence of changes is well covered in Katzenstein, *Cultural Norms and National Security,* 132–3.
75. Shuji Kurokowa, "Keidanren Boci Seisan Iinkini no Seiji Kodo" (*Political Behavior of Keidanren's Defense Production Committee*) in *Nihon-gata Seisaku Kettei no Henyo* (*Transformation of Japanese Style Policy Making*), ed. Minoru Nakano (Tokyo: Toyo Keizai Shimpo-sha, 1986), 216.
76. Figure quoted by Steven K. Vogel, *Japanese High Technology, Politics, and Power,* Berkeley Roundtable on the International Economy, Research Paper No. 2 (Berkeley, CA: University of California, March 1989), 66.
77. Katzenstein, *Cultural Norms and National Security,* 147.
78. Menon, "The Once and Future Superpower."
79. Katzenstein, *Cultural Norms and National Security,* 135.
80. Peter J. Katzenstein and Nobuo Okawara, "Japan's National Security," in *East Asian Security*; and also, Katzenstein and Nobuo Okawara, "Japanese Security Issues," in *Japan: A New Kind of Superpower?*
81. For a detailed description of all the ins and outs of Japanese relations with the West during the Gulf War see Yoshio Okawara, "Japan's Global Responsibili-

ties," in *Japan's Emerging Global Role,* eds. Danny Unger and Paul Blackburn (Boulder, CO: Lynne Rienner Publishers, 1993); Robert M. Immerman, "Japan in the United Nations," in *Japan: A New Kind of Superpower?*; and also, Lincoln, *Japan's New Global Role,* 119–21; 220–8; 230–5.

82. Quoted from Daniel Unger, "The Problem of Global Leadership: Waiting For Japan," in *Japan's Emerging Global Role.*

83. For a detailed description of the fate and nature of the PKO legislation, see Katzenstein and Nobuo Okawara, "Japan's National Security," in *East Asian Security*; Katzenstein and Nobuo Okawara, "Japanese Security Issues," in *Japan: A New Kind of Superpower?*; and also, Lincoln, *Japan's New Global Role,* 234–42.

84. Katzenstein and Nobuo Okawara, "Japanese Security Issues" in *Japan: A New Kind of Superpower?*

85. Immerman, "Japan in the United Nations," in *Japan: A New Kind of Superpower?*

86. Quoted from "Japan Pushes for Security Council Seat," *The Japan Times,* June 23, 1997.

87. Yoshio Okawara, "Japan's Global Responsibilities," in Japan's Emerging Global Role.

88. Quoted from Toshihiro Yamauchi, "Gunning for Japan's Peace Constitution," *Japan Quarterly,* April–June 1992.

89. Ozawa, Blueprint, 120–1.

90. *Asia Times,* June 13, 1997.

91. Quoted from Eiichi Furukawa, "Changes in Southeast Asian Views on Japan," *Japan Echo,* Autumn 1993.

92. For examples of such attitudes and protests, see Lee Poh-Ping, "Japan and the Asia-Pacific Region: A Southeast Asian Perspective," in *Japan: A New Kind of Superpower?*

93. "Under the Sun," *American Legion Magazine,* April 1997.

94. Both quoted from Poh-Ping, "Japan and the Asia-Pacific Region."

95. From a talk he gave in Kyoto, Japan on February 13, 1992, quoted from Poh-Ping, "Japan and the Asia-Pacific Region."

96. Robinson, "Singapore's 'Outspoke' PM Appeals to Japan Over China," *The Financial Times,* August 30–31, 1997.

97. Mochizuki, "Japan as an Asia-Pacific Power."

98. Katzenstein, *Cultural Norms and National Security,* 133.

99. Tada, "A Blow to the Constitution," *The Japan Times,* September 26, 1997.

100. Frank McNeil, "Apathy or Change in Japan?" *Current History,* November 1995.

101. For a detailed and technical discussion of the changes in Japan's armed forces, armament, and defense posture, see Katzenstein, *Cultural Norms and National Security,* 134–137.

102. For a complete list of the new treaty's provisions, see "Tokyo, Washington Issue new Guidelines on Defense," *The Japan Times,* September 24, 1997.

103. Quoted from Tetsuchi Kajimoto, "SDF Faces Tough Battle in Meeting New Demands," *The Japan Times,* September 24, 1997.

104. Ibid.

105. "Hashimoto Attempts to Defuse China's Fears over Guidelines," *The Japan Times,* September 25, 1997.

106. "Asia-Pacific Opinions Mixed on New Defense Guide," *The Japan Times,* September 25, 1997.
107. Patrick E. Tyler, "China Counters U.S. and Japan on Security Pact," *The New York Times,* April 19, 1996.
108. "Japan's War with China Revisited," *The Economist,* September 6, 1997.
109. "China Warns Japan Against Widening Defense Cooperation," *The Japan Times,* September 26, 1997.
110. Quoted from Landers, "Yes Men," *Far Eastern Economic Review,* September 25, 1997.
111. For the reaction when the Council was established, see Delfs and Michael Vatikiokis, "Low-Key Diplomacy."
112. Furukawa, "Changes in Southeast Asian Views."
113. Hatch and Yamamura, *Asia in Japan's Embrace,* 201.
114. Robinson, "Drive in Japan for a Greater Security Role," *The Financial Times,* May 27, 1997.
115. "Regional Briefing," *Far Eastern Economic Review,* July 24, 1997.
116. Vatikiokis et al., "Fears of Influence."
117. Bruce Clark, "Japan Keen for Bigger Part on World Stage," *The Financial Times,* May 1, 1996.
118. "Regional Briefing."
119. Quoted from Frank Ching, "New World Order Emerging," *Far Eastern Economic Review,* December 4, 1997.
120. "Japan, Russia Plan Forum to Draw Up Peace Treaty," *The Japan Times,* November 10, 1997.
121. "Head of Japanese Military Department Visits Russia for the First Time Ever," *The Current Digest of the Post Soviet Press,* 48 (17): 1996.
122. Quoted from Dawkins, "Japan and Russia Agree to Cooperate on Defense." *The Financial Times,* May 1, 1996.
123. Chrystia Freeland, "Russia and Japan in Peace Pledge," *The Financial Times,* November 3, 1997.
124. Ching, "Russo-Japanese Ties Inch Forward," *Far Eastern Economic Review,* December 5, 1996.
125. For a chronicle of the events surrounding the withdrawal and resumption of Japanese grant aid to China, see Dawkins, "Japan Resumes Official Grant Aid to China," *The Financial Times,* March 29–30, 1997.
126. de Jonquières, "Japan Relaxes Conditions for Chinese Entry into WTO," *The Financial Times,* September 15, 1997; and also, Robinson, "Japan Denies EU Claims on China Talks," *The Financial Times,* September 17, 1997.
127. Dawkins, "LDP Defense Team to Beijing," *The Financial Times,* June 4, 1997.
128. Gilley, "Polite But Firm."
129. Dawkins, "Japan Agonizes Over Hong Kong Boycott," *The Financial Times,* June 13, 1997.
130. For more details on the incident, see Peter K. P. Tsang, "Island Fever," *Far Eastern Economic Review,* November 21, 1996; and also, Dawkins, "Japan Tries to Calm Dispute Over East China Sea Islands," *The Financial Times,* October 5–6, 1996.
131. *World Military Expenditures and Arms Transfers 1995–1996,* U.S. Arms Control and

Disarmament Agency (Washington, DC: U.S. Government Printing Office, 1997).

132. Comparisons drawn from Richardson, "Seapower: The New Lure for East Asia."

133. Figures from U.S. Arms Control and Disarmament Agency, quoted from Betts, "Wealth, Power, and Conflict."

134. Statistics drawn from Economist Intelligence Unit, "Japan International Relations and Defense."

135. Quoted from Richardson, "Seapower: The New Lure for East Asia."

136. Figures from Japan's Defense Agency and China's Ministry of Defense, quoted from Menon, "The Once and Future Superpower."

137. Moffett, "Back to the Barracks."

138. Robinson, "Japan Close to Joining U.S. Defense Scheme," *The Financial Times,* October 30, 1996.

139. Moffett, "Coming In from the Cold," *Far Eastern Economic Review,* June 6, 1996.

140. Eiichiro Sekigawa, "Japan Ponders Building Military Recon Network," *Aviation Week & Space Technology,* June 10, 1996.

141. Michael H. Armacost, *Friends or Rivals* (New York: Columbia University Press, 1996), 212–3.

CHAPTER EIGHT: RISK IN THE TRANSITION TO A MORE POWERFUL JAPAN

1. Armacost, *Friends or Rivals,* 217.

2. Statistic quoted from Berger, "From Sword to Chrysanthemum," in *East Asian Security.*

3. To further investigate this line of thinking, see Kenneth N. Waltze, "The Spread of Nuclear Weapons: More Might Be Better," *International Institute for Strategic Students,* Autumn 1981.

4. For a review of these powerful protests, see Matake Kamiya, "Japan and the Bomb," *Look Japan,* June 1996.

5. See, Shintaro Ishihara, *The Japan That Can Say No* (New York: Simon and Schuster, 1991), 55–6; and also, Shintaro Ishihara and Jun Eto, *Dank "No" to Ieru Nihon* (*The Japan That Can Say a Firm No*) (Tokyo: Kodansha, 1991), 170–83.

6. Bill Clifford, "Japan Presses World Banks on Lending," Nikkei Weekly, March 21, 1992.

7. "'Tenanmon Jiken' Igo no Chugo ku to Nihon" (China and Japan after the Tiananmen Incident), *Gaiko Foramu,* September 1989.

8. Clark, "Japan Keen for Bigger Part on World Stage."

9. For a description of several Japanese actions at the United Nations that were contrary to the United States, see, Lincoln, *Japan's New Global Role.*

10. For a thorough discussion of the ins and outs of these trade negotiations, see Mochizuki, "Japan as an Asia-Pacific Power." For details on Japan's final rejection of the position of the United States, see Michiyo Nakamoto and Neil Buckley, "U.S. and Japan Seek 11th Hour Deal on Semiconductor Trade," *The Financial Times,* July 31, 1996; and also, "Chips on America's Shoulder," *Far Eastern Economic Review,* May 30, 1996.

11. Masato Ishizawa, "Relationship Mellows with Accords Inked on Semiconductors, Insurance," *Japan Economic Almanac,* 1997.

12. *The Japan Times,* August 6, 1997.
13. See Nakamoto, "Agreement on Japanese Port Practices," *The Financial Times,* November 1–2, 1997; and also, Bob Davis and Norihiko Shirouzu, "Shipping Fight Shows Change in Trade Policy," *Wall Street Journal,* October 20, 1997.
14. See, Asra Q. Nomani and Douglas A. Blockman, "U.S., Japan Near Accord to Open Skies," *Wall Street Journal,* September 19, 1997; and also, Michael Skapinker, "Japan Resists U.S. Open Skies Drive," *The Financial Times,* September 9, 1997.
15. For an excellent review of the market drop and the associated panic, see Dawkins, "Japan Flexes Its Financial Muscle," *The Financial Times,* June 25, 1997.
16. For a detailed study of the *kokusanka* approach, see Michael J. Green, *Arming Japan* (New York: Columbia University Press, 1995).
17. Kent E. Calder, *Asia's Deadly Triangle* (London: Nicholas Brady Publishing, 1996), 87.
18. For a particularly forceful example, see Tada, "A Blow to the Constitution."
19. "Revisionism Revived," *The Economist,* May 3, 1997.
20. For one review of his position, see Takeshi Sato, "Next Cabinet to Face Major Defense Debate," *The Japan Times,* September 26, 1996.
21. Reviewed in "The Decline of Faith and Discipline," *The Economist,* November 18, 1995; and also, Moffett, "Past Perfect," *Far Eastern Economic Review,* November 21, 1995.
22. Robert S. Ozaki, *The Japanese: A Cultural Portrait* (Tokyo: Charles E. Tuttle Company, 1978), 193.
23. For an exacting and complete description of traditional Japanese notions of debt and many implications for that culture, see Ruth Benedict, *The Chrysanthemum and the Sword.* This classic work, first published in 1946, has been reprinted dozens of times. References here are from the New American Library edition (New York: 1974).
24. Quoted from Benedict, *The Chrysanthemum and the Sword,* 141.
25. For illustrations of this remarkable tradeoff and other examples of how the power of this debt burden motivates the Japanese, see Benedict, *The Chrysanthemum and the Sword,* 141.
26. Benedict, *The Chrysanthemum and the Sword,* 141.
27. Quoted from Benedict, *The Chrysanthemum and the Sword,* 222.
28. Ozaki, *The Japanese: A Cultural Portrait,* 182.
29. Ibid., 184–5.
30. See van Wolferen, *The Enigma of Japanese Power*; and also, Miyamoto, *Straightjacket Society.*
31. For a summary, see Shuichi Kato, "Japan's Empty Core," an interview with NPQ magazine, July 1987.
32. For a recent example in English, see Nicholas D. Kristof, "Real Capitalism Breaks Japan's Old Rules of Market Civility and Loyalty," *The New York Times,* July 15, 1997.
33. See van Wolferen, *The Enigma of Japanese Power,* 291.
34. Yasuhiro Nakasome, quoted from van Wolferen, *The Enigma of Japanese Power,* 264.

35. van Wolferen, *The Enigma of Japanese Power,* 270.

36. Robinson, "'Karashi' Award May Not Spell Death to Overwork," *The Financial Times,* October 10, 1997.

37. The author was told this story by several different Japanese colleagues at various times. Although unable to find supportive evidence, the story's wide acceptance nonetheless speaks to the role of the group in Japanese society.

38. Quoted from Benedict, *The Chrysanthemum and the Sword,* 216.

39. Quoted from Benedict, *The Chrysanthemum and the Sword,* 217. See also, van Wolferen, *The Enigma of Japanese Power,* 252.

40. For a complete discussion of this aspect of Japanese corporate life, see van Wolferen, *The Enigma of Japanese Power,* 167–8.

41. For illustrations from Japanese literature, see Benedict, *The Chrysanthemum and the Sword,* 165–73.

42. For excellent analyses of Japan during this time, see Jansen, "The Meiji Restoration," and Iriye Akira, "Japan's Drive to Great Power Status," both in *The Emergence of Meiji Japan*; W. G. Beasley, *The Rise of Modern Japan* (Tokyo: Charles E. Tuttle Company, 1990), 38–69; and also, John Whitney Hall, *Japan From Prehistory to Modern Times* (Tokyo: Charles E. Tuttle Company, 1992), 253–84.

43. Quoted from Benedict, *The Chrysanthemum and the Sword,* 169, italics added.

44. See Benedict, *The Chrysanthemum and the Sword,* 171.

45. For a small sampling of this work, see Johnson, *MITI and the Japanese Miracle; Tsuru, Japan's Capitalism*; Takafusa Nakamura, *The Post War Japanese Economy*; Takafusa Nakamura, *Lectures on Modern Japanese Economic History*; and also, Reading, *Japan the Coming Collapse.*

46. This expression was first used in this context by Benedict, *The Chrysanthemum and the Sword,* 169.

47. Beasley, *The Rise of Modern Japan,* 179.

48. Ibid., 172.

49. For a detailed analysis of this difficult transitional period, see Beasley, *The Rise of Modern Japan,* 164–80.

50. Michio Katsumata, "Japan in the Year the Goalposts Moved," *Japan Economic Almanac,* 1996.

51. Yamakoshi, "Restructuring, Reengineering and Japan's Management System."

52. Ryu Murakami, *Coin Locker Babies* (Tokyo: Kodansha, 1997).

53. Moffett, "The Right and Its Wrongs," *Far Eastern Economic Review,* November 21, 1996.

54. Both incidents reported in Moffett, "Past Perfect."

55. See "The Man Japan Wants to Forget," *The Economist,* November 11, 1995.

CHAPTER NINE: GAINING PRACTICAL ADVANTAGE

1. Kazunori Iizuka, "Doing Business in a Changing Japan: Deregulation and Liberalization Provide Opportunities for American Business," *Issues and Trends,* Spring 1997. Mr. Iizuka is president of the Japan External Trade Organization in New York.

2. Iizuka, "Doing Business in a Changing Japan."

3. For a review of the initial reform measures, see "Government Adopts Deregu-

lation Steps," *The Japan Times,* March 30, 1996. For reviews of subsequent actions, see Dawkins, "Deregulation Moves Approved"; Tett, "Japanese Parliament Yet To Legalize Stock Options"; Paradise, "Pressure For Change"; Dawkins, "Japan Weighs Plan to Lift Economic Controls"; Give State Tasks to Local Authorities"; "Unwinding Red Tape"; Nakamoto, "Japanese Insurance Price Controls Axed"; Sapsford, "Japan's Hashimoto Orders New Reforms."

4. MacKnight, "Big Could Be Bigger," *Japan Economic Institute Report,* (28A), July 26, 1996.

5. Iizuka, "Doing Business in a Changing Japan."

6. *Japan Exports and Imports: Commodity by Country,* Ministry of Agriculture, Forestry, and Fisheries and Japan Tariff Association (Tokyo: Japanese Government Printing Office, 1997).

7. *Foreign Agricultural Trade of the United States,* U.S. Department of Agriculture (Washington, DC: U.S. Government Printing Office, 1997).

8. Iizuka, "Doing Business in a Changing Japan."

9. Ibid.

10. Michiyo Nakamoto and Jonathan Annells, "Neon Offer Highlights U.S. Troubles," *The Financial Times,* March 16, 1997.

11. "Business Briefing," *Far Eastern Economic Review,* September 25, 1997.

12. Dawkins, "Barriers Fall to Import Invaders," *The Financial Times,* March 19, 1996.

13. Iizuka, "Doing Business in a Changing Japan."

14. Ibid.

15. "Structural Shifts Favor Rising Imports," *Focus Japan,* October 1996.

16. Quentin Hardy, "Motorola Expected to Win Japan Cellular-Phone Deal," *Asian Wall Street Journal,* March 26, 1997.

17. Tim Burt and Michiyo Nakamoto, "Ericsson to Join Global Multimedia Research," *The Financial Times,* October 9, 1997.

18. John Boyd, "Compaq Struggles in Japan," *The Japan Times,* March 27, 1997.

19. James Kynge and Sheila McNulty, "ASEAN Pledges to Speed Up Tariff Cuts," *The Financial Times,* December 16, 1997.

20. William Dawkins and Laura Tyson, "China, Japan Straighten Trade Ties," *The Financial Times,* September 18, 1996.

21. For details on these moves, see "Local Base Key to Success For Regional Corporations," *The Nikkei Weekly,* March 17, 1997.

22. "Fussy Consumers Underpin Samsung Sales Strategy," *The Nikkei Weekly,* March 17, 1997.

23. "Kia Motors Readies for Drive with Research Spending," *The Nikkei Weekly,* March 17, 1997.

24. "Mailorder Sales Turn Clubs into Hit of Golf Outfit," *The Nikkei Weekly,* March 17, 1997.

25. Statistics quoted from Neil Weinberg, "Buy Japan Now!" *Forbes,* September 8, 1997.

26. Statistics quoted from "In Japan Banks Set to Cut Costs," *International Herald Tribune,* July 23, 1997.

27. Gillian Tett and Richard Waters, "Nomura Plans to Shed 2,000 Jobs," *The Financial Times,* October 23, 1998.

28. Sachiko Hirao, "Correct Wrongs from Within," *The Japan Times,* June 26, 1997.
29. Landers, "American Accents," *Far Eastern Economic Review*, July 31, 1997.
30. "In Japan Banks Set to Cut Costs."
31. Quoted from Stefan Wagsty, "Risks as well as Rewards," *The Financial Times,* December 16, 1997.
32. Nakamoto, "Drive for Home Market," *The Financial Times,* November 15, 1996.
33. Landers, "Sharing the Wealth," *Far Eastern Economic Review,* May 29, 1997.
34. Tett, "Japanese Banks in Losses Warnings," *The Financial Times,* November 21, 1997.
35. Statistic quoted from Sapsford, "Japan Girds for Change on Lending," *Wall Street Journal,* October 14, 1997.
36. See "Agencies Get ISO Certificate"; and "Temporary Staff Boosts Flexibility," both in *The Japan Times,* September 24, 1997.
37. The author has discussed such plans with several Japanese management committees and exchanged information on the same subject with other firms.
38. "Mr. Clean," *The Economist,* April 26, 1997.
39. The author was present at the firm when these decisions were made and knows firsthand the difficulty top management and all involved had in breaking with precedent.
40. Spindle, "Corporate Japan Embraces Stock Options," *Wall Street Journal,* July 30, 1997.
41. Chris Gay, "To Have and To Hold," *Far Eastern Economic Review,* March 13, 1997.
42. Ibid.
43. For an exact review of corporate tax revisions, see "Japan's LDP Proposes Huge Tax Cuts," *Reuters Wire,* December 16, 1997.
44. Paul Abrahams, "Disappointment at Japan's Tax Plans," *The Financial Times,* December 17, 1997.
45. Nakamoto, "Japan Plans to Sort Out Its Property Mess," *The Financial Times,* October 17, 1997.
46. Hamilton, "Nippon Telegraph Has Agreed to Split into Three Firms," *Wall Street Journal,* December 6, 1996.
47. Nakamoto, "The Competition Hot-Line" *The Financial Times,* December 16, 1997.
48. A list of references on the details of these scandals would fill a second volume. For material on the scandals themselves, the following articles provide a good review: Robert Steiner, "Nomura Remains Tainted by Scandal," *Wall Street Journal,* April 16, 1997; Nihon Keizai Shimbun, August 6, 1997; Dawkins, "Japanese Brokers Probed in Wake of Nomura Scandal," *The Financial Times,* June 5, 1997; Tett, "Japanese Broker's License Suspended," *The Financial Times,* July 26–27, 1997; Nakamoto, "Japanese Car Group Hit by Scandal," *The Financial Times,* October 24, 1997; and also, David P. Hamilton and Bill Spindle, "Yamaichi Folds in Japan's Biggest-Ever Failure, *Wall Street Journal,* November 24, 1997. For a review of the dramatic "raid" at the Ministry of Finance, see the coverage provided by *The Financial Times,* especially: Gillian Tett and Paul Abrahams, "Japan Finance Minister Quits in Wake of Arrests," *The Financial Times,* January 28, 1998; Tett, "Japan's Mighty Minister Tumbles," *The Financial Times,* January 27, 1998; Tett, "Ministry Suicides Raise Tension as Japan Probes Corruption," *The*

Financial Times, January 30, 1998; and also, Tett, "Japan Widens Probe into Finance Ministry," *The Financial Times,* February 4, 1998.

49. Spindle, "Japan's Rude Awakening: The Ratings Game," *Wall Street Journal,* November 26, 1997.

50. WuDunn, "Prying Open the Japanese Shareholders Meeting," *The New York Times,* June 28, 1996.

51. Both cases described in Tett, "Nomura Shareholders Sue Former Executive," *The Financial Times,* May 3–4, 1997.

52. Landers, "Sharing the Wealth," *Far Eastern Economic Review,* May 29, 1997.

53. Spindle, "Policy Wonk Rails Japan's Pension Funds," *Wall Street Journal,* August 15, 1997.

54. *Nihon Keizai Shimbun,* July 21, 1997.

55. Robinson, "Japanese Companies Admit Bad Behavior," *The Financial Times,* April 4, 1997.

56. Sayuri Daimon, "Ethics Charter in Just a Start," *The Japan Times,* June 25, 1997.

57. Robinson, "U.S. Team to Probe Japanese N-Group," *The Financial Times,* October 17, 1997.

58. Sandra Sugawara, "Foreigners See Opportunities as Japan Deregulates," *International Herald Tribune,* July 26–27, 1997.

59. Sapsford, "Japan Bank Taps BT to Develop Risk Gauge," *Wall Street Journal,* October 7, 1997.

60. Data from Nikkei 225 Index in Japan and the S&P 500 index in the United States. (Bloomberg Data Base, January 1999).

61. This selectivity theme has appeared in broker reports on the Japanese market and in the financial press. For recent examples in publicly available documents, see: Sapsford, "Gap Grows Between Japan's Strong, Weak Banks," *Wall Street Journal,* December 10, 1997; Henny Sender, "Beware the Sun," *Far Eastern Economic Review,* April 24, 1997; John Plender, "Japan's Fistful of Nettles," *The Financial Times,* January 13, 1997; and Baker, "On a Collision Course," *The Financial Times,* January 18, 1996.

62. For a detailed study of the old differences between market valuation ratios and responses, see M. Bloch et al., "A Comparison of Some Aspects of the U.S. and Japanese Equity Markets," in *Japan and the World Economy* (Amsterdam: North Holland Press, 1993).

63. Calculation based on Nikkei 225 price-to-book ratio of 2 and S&P 500 price-to-book ratio of 3.9. (Bloomberg Data Base, January 1999).

64. Quoted from Sender, "Beware the Sun."

65. For a detailed review of the provisions of other "big bang" financial reforms and some follow-up measures, see: Baker, "The Doors Are Open," *The Financial Times,* April 2, 1996; "Government Adopts Deregulation Steps," *The Japan Times,* March 30, 1996; "Japan's LDP Proposes Huge Tax Cuts"; Smith, "Where Does the Japanese Securities Industry Go from Here?" *Institutional Investor,* December 1995; and also, Abrahams, "Disappointment at Japan's Tax Plans."

66. WuDunn, "Big Japan Developer Seized for Blocking Land Auction," *The New York Times,* May 28, 1996.

67. Robinson, "Tokyo Plans Securities Crackdown," *The Financial Times,* April 15, 1997.
68. Tett, "Tokyo Sends Signal with Nomura Arrest," *The Financial Times,* May 31–June 1, 1997.
69. WuDunn, "Nomura Scandal in Japan Hurts Plans for Reform," *The New York Times,* March 22, 1997.
70. See Hamilton and Spindle, "Yamaichi Folds in Japan's Biggest-Ever Failure."
71. Tett, "Japan Cracks Down on Stock Market Abuses," *The Financial Times,* January 7, 1998. Beginning in late 1998, the MOF and the Bank of Japan began to lose some moral authority in busting old abuses. Bureaucrats at both institutions have come under investigation for just the kind of corruption that the Ministry is trying to root out. The scandals surrounding the policing bureaucrats have, of course, embarrassed reformers and raised questions about the durability of efforts to change Japan's system. But such concerns are surely exaggerated. The arrests and resignations have rid the Ministries only of those who would resist the new efforts to stamp out the old cozy relationships. Certainly, the knowledge of such corruption at high levels in the ministry has heightened the zeal of those who want to change the system. No doubt the revelations of more scandal among the bureaucrats as well as the business leaders in the Iron Triangle have also won new reform converts as well.
72. Landers, "American Accents."
73. Neil Weinberg, "Buy Japan Now!" *Forbes,* September 8, 1998.
74. Quoted from Weinberg, "A Japanese Michael Milken?" *Forbes,* September 8, 1997.
75. Steiner, "Tokyo Regains Its Place as a Financial Hub," *Wall Street Journal,* May 29, 1997.
76. Tett, "Japanese Bank Sells ¥30 Billion of Bad Property Loans," *The Financial Times,* May 9, 1997.
77. Tett, "Securitization is the New Buzzword," *The Financial Times,* October 17, 1997.
78. Figures quoted from Nakamoto, "Japan Plans to Sort Out Its Property Mess," *The Financial Times,* October 17, 1997.
79. Sapsford, "Japan Panel Backs Creation of Real Estate Investment Trusts," *Wall Street Journal,* April 1, 1997.
80. Tett, "Japanese Bank Sells ¥30 Billion."
81. Sapsford, "Bankers Trust Plans Broad Link with Nippon Credit Bank of Japan," *Wall Street Journal,* April 10, 1997.
82. Steiner, "Tokyo Regains its Place."
83. Sapsford, "Japan's Asset-Backed Securities Market May Benefit Foreign Investment Banks," *Wall Street Journal,* July 17, 1997.
84. Sapsford, "New Rules Roil Japan Bond Underwriting," *Wall Street Journal,* June 11, 1997.
85. Figures quoted from Sapsford, "Japan's Bond Market Takes Off as Banks Scale Back Lending," *Wall Street Journal,* January 21, 1998.
86. Lisa Shuchman, "Toyota to Offer First Bond Issue in Japan Since '71," *Wall Street Journal,* February 5, 1998.
87. All these examples drawn from Sapsford, "New Rules Roil."
88. "An Earthquake in Insurance," *The Economist,* February 28, 1998.

89. Statistics quoted and updated from Weinberg, "Shortchanged Investors," *Forbes,* July 15, 1996.

90. See "Asset Managers Merge Before 'Big Bang'," *The Nikkei Weekly*, March 17, 1997.

91. "Fidelity to Offer Funds Directly to Individuals," *The Japan Times,* March 27, 1998.

92. For details about the initial proposals on the postal savings system see: Stephanie Strom, "Crusader Takes on the Postal Piggy Bank," *The New York Times,* November 18, 1997; and also, "Return to Sender," *The Economist,* October 18, 1997.

93. Quoted from Gillian Tett, and John Gapper, "SBC Looks to Japan Tie-Up," *The Financial Times,* July 16, 1997. Other details of the deal draw from Sapsford, "Swiss, Japan Banks Tie Up for 'Big Bang'," *Wall Street Journal,* July 16, 1997.

94. Sapsford, "Bankers Trust Plans Broad Link."

95. Gwen Robinson and John Authers, "Nippon Life Links with Putnam," *The Financial Times,* June 6, 1997.

96. Sapsford, "Japan Bank Taps BT."

97. "Citibank Tying Into Japan's Postal Savings ATM System," *Bloomberg News Wire,* October 30, 1996.

98. "Enter Merrill," *The Economist,* January 3, 1998.

CHAPTER TEN: JAPAN AT THE CROSSROADS

1. "The Day the Miracle Came to an End," *The Financial Times,* January 12, 1998.

2. All currency statistics compiled from trading reports on the Bloomberg Data Base, January 1999. All equity statistics are quoted from local currencies and are drawn from the International Finance Corporation (IFC) Investible Emerging Markets indices posted on the Bloomberg Data Base, except the returns for Singapore and Hong Kong, which came from Morgan Stanley Capital International (MSCI) indices on the Bloomberg Data Base, January 1999.

3. "Asian Markets and the Domino Effects," *The Financial Times,* January 12, 1998.

4. SBC Warburg Dillon Reed, *The Credit Advisor,* February 1998.

5. Nayan Chanda, "Blown Away," *Far Eastern Economic Review,* December 25, 1997; January 1, 1998.

6. Ibid.

7. SBC Warburg Dillon Reed, *The Credit Advisor,* February 1998.

8. "Asian Markets and the Domino Effect."

9. Ibid.

10. Quoted from "Asian Markets and the Domino Effect."

11. SBC Warburg Dillon Reed, *The Credit Advisor,* February 1998.

12. Statistics compiled from trading reports on the Bloomberg Data Base.

13. Ibid.

14. Quoted from Peter Montagnon, "Over-Capacity Stalks the Economies of Asian Tigers," *The Financial Times,* June 17, 1997.

15. "Lex," *The Financial Times,* February 21–22, 1998.

16. Robert G. Lees, "If Japan Won't Help Rescue Asia, China Might," *The International Herald Tribune,* February 21–22, 1998.

17. Quoted from Tom Buerkle, "U.S. Assails Japan Over Reforms," *The Interna-*

tional Herald Tribune, February 21–22, 1998.

18. Quoted from Schlesinger, "Fed Chief Joins a Chorus of Critics and Stresses Fix for Banking Crisis," *Wall Street Journal,* February 26, 1998.

19. Tett, "Japan's Bank Chief Adds Voice to Call for Action on Crisis," *The Financial Times,* April 6, 1998.

20. Quoted from Nakamoto, "Hashimoto's Conversion Came at Summit," *The Financial Times,* December 18, 1997.

21. See Robinson, "Beijing Offers Jakarta $200 Million Aid," *The Financial Times,* April 14, 1998.

22. See Lees, "If Japan Won't Help Rescue Asia."

23. For examples of Japanese assistance to international bodies and the praise given by Westerners, see John Burton and Gillian Tett, "Japan Aid for Seoul 'To Come After IMF Deal'," *The Financial Times,* November 21, 1997; and also, Sander Thoenes and Gillian Tett, "Japan and IMF to Act on Indonesia Crisis," *The Financial Times,* January 26, 1998. For examples of reactions to short-term relief provided by Japan, see Sapsford, "Japan Makes Big Bridge Loan to South Korea," *Wall Street Journal,* December 19, 1997.

24. This incident was reviewed in chapter 6. For other details, see Lionel Barber, "Japan Pushes Regional Rescue Fund," *The Financial Times,* September 23, 1997; "Japan to the Rescue," *The Economist,* October 11, 1997; and also, Nakamoto and Tett, "Japan May Urge Common Currency System for Asia," *The Financial Times,* February 21–22, 1998.

25. For a thorough review of the trade and macroeconomic pressures placed by the United States on Japan over the years, see Mochizuki, "Japan as an Asia-Pacific Power," in *East Asia in Transition.*

26. For examples of some of these pressures, see Francis Williams, "Japan Urged to Step Up Economic Reforms," *The Financial Times,* January 29, 1998; Schlesinger, "Greenspan to Tokyo: Act on Economy," *Wall Street Journal,* February 26, 1998; and also, "Japan's Struggle," *The Financial Times,* April 9, 1998.

27. Willis Witter, "Japanese Seek Relief via Reagan," *The Washington Times,* April 7, 1998.

28. For examples of official Japanese resistance, see Hamilton, "Japan Slams U.S. Economic Exhortations," *Wall Street Journal,*" March 23, 1998; and also, Tett, "Japan's Bank Chief Adds Voice to Calls for Action on Crisis," *The Financial Times,* April 6, 1998.

29. Quoted from Tett, "Japan's Bank Chief Adds Voice."

30. Nakamoto, "Hashimoto's Conversion Came at Summit."

31. Nakamoto, "Hashimoto Takes a Political Gamble."

32. For details on these events and "big bang" reforms, see chapters 6 and 9, as well as Stephanie Strom, "In Tokyo, Taking a Collapse in Stride"; and also, Sharon R. King, "Watchful Waiting on Japan," both in *The New York Times,* November 26, 1997. Also see, Peter Landers and Dan Biers, "This Will Hurt," *Far Eastern Economic Review,* December 4, 1997.

33. For an illustration of public and private concerns in this regard, see Tett, "Japan Braces for Credit Crunch as Banks Look Hard at Lending Plans," *The Financial Times,* December 20–21, 1997; and Norhiko Shirouzu and Jathon Sapsford,

"Japan's Banking Woes Beget a Credit Crunch," *Wall Street Journal,* December 22, 1997.

34. Sapsford, "Japanese Banks Get Some Breathing Room," *Wall Street Journal,* March 18, 1998; and also, Abrahams, "Japan Pumps $14 Billion into Bigger Banks, *The Financial Times,* March 14–15, 1998.

35. See Tett, "Japan Plans Fund to Protect Depositors," *The Financial Times,* March 5, 1998; and also, Sapsford, "Japan's Bailout Fund Won't Squeeze Banks," *Wall Street Journal,* February 27, 1998.

36. On the day after the $14 billion fund was announced, the Nikkei Index lost almost 1½ percent. (Bloomberg Data Base, January 1999).

37. For illustrations of such adverse reactions, see Landers, "Same Old Story," *Far Eastern Economic Review,* January 8, 1998; "Reality Hits Japan"; "Japan's Banks"; and also, Desai, "A New Miracle Needed."

38. For example, the Nikkei rose by more than 10 percent in the first two business days following the Yamaichi closure. Statistics from Bloomberg Data Base, January 1999.

39. For example, see "Reality Hits Japan," *The Economist,* November 29, 1997; "Japan's Banks," *The Financial Times,* March 16, 1997; and also, V. V. Desai, "A New Miracle Needed," *Far Eastern Economic Review,* December 25, 1997; January 1, 1998.

40. For an example of one instance of such intervention, see Tett, Nakamoto, and Baker, "Tokyo Props Up Yen By Heavy Dollar Sales," *The Financial Times,* April 11–12, 1998; and also, Sapsford, "Japan's New Central Banker Pursues Firm Yen," *Wall Street Journal,* April 13, 1998.

41. Quoted from Chikako Mogi and Takeshi Takeuchi, "Bank of Japan Chief Touts Independence," *Asian Wall Street Journal,* March 25, 1998.

42. Quoted from Nakamoto and Tett, "Japan May Urge Common Currency System for Asia," *The Financial Times,* February 21–22, 1998.

43. Ibid.

44. Harding, "International Order and Organization in the Asia-Pacific Region," in *East Asia in Transition.*

45. Robinson, "Japan Snubs China on Taiwan Defense," *The Financial Times,* August 21, 1997.

46. "Kajiyama Upsets China," *Far Eastern Economic Review,* September 4, 1997.

47. "N. Korea 'Able to Hit Japan'," *The Financial Times,* April 15, 1997.

48. Andrew Pollack, "Defector Says North Korea Seems Intent on a War," *The New York Times,* April 21, 1997.

49. "Wanted: A Quiet Japanese," *Far Eastern Economic Review,* December 5, 1996.

50. Allan Y. Song, "Diplomacy and Yakuza Films," *Far Eastern Economic Review,* June 12, 1997.

51. For a quick comparison, see SBC Warburg Dillon Reed, *The Asian Advisor,* April 1998.

52. See Mary Jordan, "North Korea Offers Thaw in Relations with South," *International Herald Tribune,* February 20, 1998; Michael Schuman, "North Korea's 'Wartime Mobilization' Belies Hope of a Thaw Before Peace Talks," *Wall Street Journal,* March 16, 1998; "It's Good for the Koreas to Talk," *The Economist,*

April 18, 1998.

53. For recent details, see Peter Landers and Sergei Blagov, "Warmth in Siberia," *Far Eastern Economic Review,* October 30, 1997.

54. Robinson, "Spy Saga Revives Worries About Russians," *The Financial Times,* August 9–10, 1997.

55. For a description of the incident, see "Scraply Islands."

56. For a review of the Sino-Japanese conflict in the nineteenth century, see Beasley, *The Rise of Modern Japan,* 110–11, 145–7; Hall, *Japan from Prehistory to Modern Times,* 303–7.

57. For a review of the Russo-Japanese conflict at the turn of the nineteenth century, see Beasley, *The Rise of Modern Japan,* 151–2; Hall, *Japan from Prehistory to Modern Times,* 304–7.

58. For a review of Japan's invasion and subjugation of China in the 1930s, see Beasley, *The Rise of Modern Japan,* 174–208; Hall, *Japan from Prehistory to Modern Times,* 338–46.

59. See Gerald Segal, "'Asianism' and Asian Security," in *Politics and Security of East Asia,* A Foreign Affairs Custom Anthology prepared for Professor Victor Cha of Georgetown University (New York: W. W. Norton and Co., 1997).

60. Robert S. Ross, "China and the Stability of East Asia," in *East Asia in Transition.*

61. For more details on the Chinese military, see the review of the joint Japanese-American assessment in Robinson, "Call to Revise Japan's Pacifist Constitution"; and for still more details, see Neil Renwick, *Japan's Alliance, Politics, and Defense Production* (Oxford: Oxford University Press, 1995), 111–12.

62. Nigel Holloway, "Revolutionary Defense," *Far Eastern Economic Review,* July 24, 1997.

63. Alastair Iain Johnston, "China's New 'Old Thinking'," in *East Asian Security.*

64. *Xinhua,* January 18, 1993, quoted from Robert S. Ross, "China and the Stability of East Asia," in *East Asia in Transition.*

65. GDP figures for 1997 from the International Monetary Fund, telephone inquiry.

66. Robert S. Ross, "China and the Stability of East Asia."

67. Ibid.

68. John McBeth, "Exercising Sovereignty," *Far Eastern Economic Review,* September 19, 1996.

69. See Vatikiokis et al., "Drawn to the Fray," *Far Eastern Economic Review,* April 3, 1997; and also, Tony Walker and Jeremy Grant, "China Denies Exploring for Oil in Vietnamese Waters," *The Financial Times,* March 18, 1997.

70. For an illustration of the conciliatory aspects of Chinese policy, see Kynge, "Beijing to Embrace ASEAN in Pursuit of a New Order."

71. Donald S. Zagoria, "The United States and the Asia-Pacific Region in the Post-Cold War Era," in *East Asia in Transition.*

72. Armacost, *Friends or Rivals,* 216.

73. Betts, "Wealth, Power, and Conflict," in *East Asia in Transition.*

74. For an illustration of this luxury afforded smaller Asian states, approaching China, by relying on American security support, see Vatikiokis, "Friends and Fears."

75. For a complete discussion of such differences, see Gerald Segal, "East Asia and the 'Constrainment' of China," in *East Asian Security.*

76. Joseph S. Nye, Jr, "The Case for Deep Engagement," *Foreign Affairs,* July/ August 1995.
77. In 1997, this group engaged in its largest naval maneuvers in the South China Sea. See Charles Bickers, "Frolics at Sea," *Far Eastern Economic Review,* May 15, 1997.
78. All this history is discussed in much greater detail in Harding, "International Order and Organization in the Asia-Pacific Region," in *East Asia in Transition.*
79. Furukawa, "Changes in Southeast Asian Views."

ACKNOWLEDGMENTS

THIS BOOK BEGAN WITH AN ARTICLE I wrote in 1995, entitled "Losing the Thread in Japan." It was my extreme good fortune that this piece caught the attention of Joseph Epstein, editor of *The American Scholar* at the time, who coached me, encouraged me to persevere in this first effort, and then gave my work a place of prominence in his publication. It was there that Henning Gutmann, formerly of Addison-Wesley, noticed it. The book was his idea. My good luck held, for when Henning realized what a neophyte I was, he put me in touch with a fine literary agent, Joseph Spieler, whose formidable talents and patience helped bring the project to fruition.

The production of the manuscript brought out great kindness and welcome assistance from so many people. Jon Beckmann's editing improved the book chapter by chapter through the fifteen-month ordeal of its writing. Once the manuscript reached Perseus Books, Christopher Carduff and then Julie Stillman applied their impressive skills to refine the prose, clarify the argument, and pace the presentation. Nick Philipson ably saw the book through publication.

Susan Ezrati patiently read several drafts, offering many suggestions for improvement and calling my attention to serious substantive issues that deserved treatment in the discussion. Equally important from my standpoint, she offered dollops of encouragement at crucial points in the effort. My daughter, Isabel, to whom the book is dedicated in part, graciously offered her support, too, characterizing the project as "cool."

Richard Ting and Nina Young provided diligent and imaginative research assistance. Their work was especially impressive considering the vague instructions that I provided them. Kyoko Okabe, Junko Negishi, and Mitsutoyo Kohno helped with the translation to and from Japanese. Cathy Mannarino patiently typed endless drafts with only a hint of the exasperation that must have welled up inside her—that would have in me, were I sitting at her keyboard.

279

Friends and professional associates at Nomura Asset Management and elsewhere enhanced the quality of this presentation either by providing general insight into Japan's circumstances and potentials or by kindly reading chapters in draft form. Though I am hesitant to mention any names for fear I might leave someone out, some individuals were particularly noteworthy in providing me help: Nobumitsu Kagami, Susumu Ishii, Yoshimitsu Matsuki, Takahide Mizuno, Shigeki Sakaki, and Harmo Sawada.

Good and respected friends, Richard Miller and James Gibbons, read vast portions of the manuscript and made corrections and suggestions for which I am grateful. Holly Miller also read portions of the manuscript, making helpful suggestions on both style and substance. She also offered welcome encouragement and consistently expressed confidence when my own lagged.

The contributions of all these people have made this book clearer, better written, and more accurate than it would otherwise have been. Any remaining mistakes are, of course, mine entirely.

INDEX